Uneasy Alliance

Twentieth-Century
American Literature,
Culture and Biography

COSTURES NEW SERIES 150

Series Editors:
C.C. Barfoot, Theo D'haen
and Erik Kooper

Uneasy Alliance

Twentieth-Century
American Literature,
Culture and Biography

Edited by
Hans Bak

 Amsterdam-New York, NY 2004

The paper on which this book is printed meets the requirements of "ISO 9706:1994, Information and documentation - Paper for documents - Requirements for permanence".

ISBN: 90-420-1611-6
©Editions Rodopi B.V., Amsterdam - New York, NY 2004
Printed in the Netherlands

For

G.A.M. Janssens

Teacher, mentor, friend

CONTENTS

PREFACE

Writing in 1961, in opposition to the formalist excesses of the New Criticism, critic Malcolm Cowley observed:

> Literature is not a pure art like music, or a relatively pure art like painting and sculpture. Its medium is not abstract like tones and colors, not inorganic like metal and stone. Instead it uses language which is a social creation, changing over the years with the society that created it. The study of any author's language carries us straight into history, institutions, moral questions, personal stratagems, and all the other aesthetic impurities which the New Critics are trying to expunge.[1]

Cowley evinced a complex understanding of the paradoxical relationship between personal morality and aesthetics, writer and public, literary merit and cultural context. At the time, he was writing against the grain of a dominant mode of text-oriented literary criticism, strongly ensconced in the Cold War-governed U.S. academe of the late 1940s and 1950s. His pluralistic and open approach to writing would gain wider currency after the aesthetic principles and underlying assumptions of the New Criticism had come to be discredited in the debunking and demythologizing 1960s and 1970s, and the canon of established American writers had been opened up to allow for inclusion of new voices formerly not represented or heard. This recanonization of American literature – perhaps the most striking development in American writing of the 1980s and 1990s – was predicated on a redefinition of the role and function of literary criticism, a revaluation of ideology and cultural politics, and (a hallmark of what was sometimes referred to as "the postmodernist breakthrough") a blurring of boundaries: between high and low forms of art, between center and margin, between literature and other disciplines. In the process, the approach to literature as an art (easily associated with a presumably exclusionist formalist approach) was

---

[1] Malcolm Cowley, "Criticism: A Many-Windowed House," in *A Many-Windowed House: Collected Essays on American Writers and American Writing*, ed. Henry Dan Piper (Carbondale and Edwardsville: Southern Illinois University Press, 1970), 246.

often made subservient to political, ideological and cultural concerns. In such a politicized cultural climate the aesthetic, as the German Americanist Heinz Ickstadt has argued, had "fallen into disrepute" and a concern with form and literary quality – what distinguishes a literary text from other texts – was easily dismissed as "suspiciously reactionary," a mode of cultural and political elitism, or, worse, "a questionable return" to an "ancient" New Critical approach. Recently, we have been witnessing a search for a new interface between textual and contextual readings, between a literary and a cultural approach, in the awareness that a literary (as opposed to a non-literary) text "has the power to even subvert its own ideological complicity" and that "the aesthetic does not deny the political, ethical, or historical dimensions of literary texts but engages them and mediates between them."[2] Thus, a cultural reading need not exclude a literary one; attention for the cultural function or cultural work of a text does not preclude attention to its literary distinctiveness. Rather, the search makes for an uneasy alliance between disciplines and dimensions and may yet open up opportunities for enriching interactions and new insights.

The essays gathered in the present volume exemplify this awareness of the paradoxical nature of literary texts both as works of literary art and as documents embedded in and functioning within a culture. They recognize the internal complexities of literary texts, but also consider the complex interrelations between author, text, reader and culture: thus, criticism may bring into play the literary sensibility of the critic but also the biography of the author; the social, political, economic, institutional, historical and cultural context; questions of race, ethnicity, class and gender; the implicit moral meaning of a work; the developments within an oeuvre; the mechanics of literary reputations; the circumstances of literary production; and the sort of reading public envisioned by the author. Conjointly, the essays offer fresh and often interdisciplinary perspectives on twentieth-century American writers of more or less established status (such as Henry James, Edna St. Vincent Millay, E.E. Cummings, Vladimir Nabokov, Flannery O'Connor, Saul Bellow, Michael Ondaatje, Toni Morrison

---

[2]   For a revaluation of aesthetics and the aesthetic in recent literary and cultural studies, see *Aesthetics in a Multicultural Age*, eds Emory Elliott, Louis Freitas Caton and Jeffrey Rhyne (New York: Oxford University Press, 2002), in particular Heinz Ickstadt's "Toward a Pluralist Aesthetics" (263-78). The passages quoted above appear on pages 263-65.

or Sandra Cisneros) as well as on those who, for reasons of fashion, politics, ideology, or gender, have been unduly neglected (such as Booth Tarkington, Julia Peterkin, Robert Coates, Martha Gellhorn, Isabella Gardner, Karl Shapiro, the young Jewish-American writers, Julia Alvarez, and writers of popular crime and detective fiction).

Though the essays have been arranged chronologically by subject matter – starting with an analysis of the 1908 New York edition of James' *Portrait of a Lady* and concluding with a series of considerations of the new multicultural writers from the 1990s – a number of subsidiary motifs and concerns bring the essays in dialogue with each other across the lines of time. They might, as a result, have been grouped differently, by theme or approach. Thus, the essays by Gert Buelens (on Henry James), Peter Rietbergen (on Booth Tarkington), C.C. Barfoot (on the sonnets of Edna St. Vincent Millay) and Susan Castillo (on Flannery O'Connor) offer close critical re-readings from a literary or literary-cultural perspective. Gonny van Beek-van Overbeek (on Julia Peterkin), Richard Kennedy (on E.E. Cummings) and Inez Hollander-Lake (on Martha Gellhorn) offer biographical reconsiderations and discuss the interrelations between a writer's biography (including the dynamics of love) and the makings of a literary career. The essays by Edward Margolies (on the writers of New York), Mathilde Roza (on Robert Coates) and Hans Bak (on Bharati Mukherjee, Michael Ondaatje and Sherman Alexie) discuss the complex ways in which twentieth-century American (and Canadian) writers have explored the impact of urban life, in particular its mass cultural and multicultural manifestations. Diederik Oostdijk (on Karl Shapiro as editor of *Poetry*), Marian Janssen (on Isabella Gardner's role as "postillion for Pegasus") and Jaap van der Bent (on Vladimir Nabokov and the controversial Paris publishing house Olympia Press) focus on circumstances of literary production and examine the role and function of editors and publishers in the making and unmaking of literary reputations (an aspect also touched upon in Gonny van Beek-van Overbeek's consideration of the career of Julia Peterkin). René Verwaaijen (on Alfred Kazin's reasons for admiring Lincoln), Jan Bakker (on Saul Bellow) and Derek Rubin (on the younger "post-acculturated" Jewish-American writers) offer revaluations of the Jewish-American imagination across the generations. Kathleen Ashley (on Toni Morrison's tricksters), Mary McCay (on Sandra Cisneros) and Loes Nas (on Julia Alvarez) provide critical examinations of important representatives of African-

American and Latina writing. Theo D'haen and Hans Bertens, finally, offer serious considerations of forms of popular crime and detective fiction. Conjointly, the essays explore the fruitful interactions and uneasy alliance between literature and ethics, film, biography, gender studies, popular culture, avant-garde art, urban studies, anthropology and multicultural studies.

The essays in this volume have been written in tribute to G.A.M. Janssens, who for over thirty years taught American literature at the University of Nijmegen, the Netherlands, where he was the first Dutch professor to hold a chair in the field. His teachings, writings, research interests and scholarly initiatives have inspired many of his students (some represented here) to commit themselves to a career in American literary scholarship. His many professional friends and acquaintance, in the Netherlands and beyond, in Europe as well as the U.S., have come to respect his wide-ranging erudition and his knowledgeable and sophisticated readings of American writers. As is testified by his writings on contemporary American literature (most signally his 1976 monograph *De Amerikaanse roman, 1950-1975*), G.A.M. Janssens – "Gerry" to his friends and colleagues – was above all a *reader* of literature, possessed of an exquisitely refined sensibility and a subtle sense of what John Updike called "the aesthetic niceties of novel writing," for whom literature was always more complex and paradoxical than any theory, ideology or current intellectual or political fashion might want to make it. His approach to literature was marked by what he himself defined as "an intelligent, undogmatic appreciation of the broad range of forms of expression between tradition and experiment."[3] Open to the pluriformity of poetry and fiction, he was convinced that a literary reading, and literary criticism in general, would be more convincing as "the critic allows his feeling for order to be disturbed by the imagination of the writer."[4] Criticism thus became, at heart, an art of approximation, of exploring the possibilities of form, and reading became a perpetual source of delight and discovery. It is this sense of the pleasure of reading which Janssens has passed on to countless generations of students, colleagues, friends and readers of his writings.

---

[3]   G.A.M. Janssens, *De Amerikaanse roman, 1950-1975* (Amsterdam: Polak and Van Gennep, 1976), 7. Translation mine.
[4]   *Ibid.*, 9.

But Janssens was equally sensitive to the literary, cultural, biographical and historical factors at play in the literary situation. An avid reader of biographies, he had a sharp intuition for the role and function of editors, publishers, critics and men of letters in the shaping of writers' careers, and a strong interest in the influence, on individual writers as well as on the larger cultural scene, exerted by literary periodicals. His path-breaking study *The American Literary Review: A Critical History, 1920-1950* (The Hague: Mouton, 1968) revealed the complex interactions between literature, politics and culture in the interbellum era. For many years he himself helped edit *The Dutch Quarterly Review of Anglo-American Letters* (published by Rodopi, Amsterdam), perhaps the single most important effort to launch a periodical devoted to English and American literary criticism in the Netherlands. Viewing literature in its broader social, cultural and institutional context, he was the natural person to initiate the founding of an American Studies program at Nijmegen University.

His two major books, on the contemporary American novel and on the American literary review, have set the direction for a large number of sequel research projects, many of which have resulted in book publication in the U.S.: on American men of letters (Malcolm Cowley, Alfred Kazin), on American literary periodicals (*The Kenyon Review*, *Poetry Magazine*), on twentieth-century American novelists who had not yet received the scholarly attention they deserved (Louis Auchincloss, Hamilton Basso, John Clellon Holmes). The current Nijmegen research program in American Studies on "Magazines and Periodicals as Instruments of Twentieth-Century American Culture" (launched in collaboration with the Roosevelt Study Center in Middelburg, the Netherlands, and involving projects on *The Reporter*, *The Paris Review*, *Commentary*, and *Evergreen Review*) is in an important sense a continuation and expansion of Janssens' research initiatives in the area.

The essays in this volume have been written in the spirit of the writings, teachings, and research interests of G.A.M. Janssens. Together they testify to the ongoing pertinence of an approach to literature that is open, undogmatic, sensitive and sophisticated and that seeks to do justice to the complex interaction and uneasy alliance of literature, culture and biography in twentieth-century American writing.

Hans Bak

METAPHOR, METONYMY, AND ETHICS
IN *THE PORTRAIT OF A LADY*

GERT BUELENS

Enter ethics, whose specialty is articulating the relation between freedom and necessity, desire and the law.

In this essay I want to use the above definition of ethics, taken from Geoffrey Galt Harpham,[1] one of the leading writers on the subject of literature and ethics, as a springboard for a reading of Henry James' *The Portrait of a Lady* (1881; New York Edition, 1908). Yet, though I find Harpham's definition useful, believing both that it sheds light on important aspects of ethics and that it is relevant for James' novel, I do not wholly share his view that the relation between his key terms is best articulated by noting that "the stark *ought* of ethics [proclaims] the law to a creature who is presumed to be free to follow it or not. If human beings were not free, there would be no need for urging, but if they were not in fact bound by the law, there would be nothing to urge" (395). I want to complicate this picture by bringing in another pair of terms – metaphor and metonymy – that have the added virtue of belonging to the field of rhetoric and are thus arguably more properly literary than Harpham's keywords. My intention is not to align either of these figures with one of the poles in Harpham's definition. Rather, I aim to show how paying due attention to the complex operation of these tropes in *The Portrait of a Lady* enables us to see that freedom and necessity, desire and the law, are not the neatly opposed poles that they might appear to be. Indeed, the most intensely charged ethical moments in this novel occur when the fraught interpenetration of these realms is at its most pronounced.

Since the time when Roman Jakobson offered powerful evidence for the deep structural distinction between metaphor and metonymy

---

[1] Geoffrey Galt Harpham, "Ethics," in *Critical Terms for Literary Study*, eds Frank Lentricchia and Thomas McLaughlin (Chicago: University of Chicago Press, 1995), 404.

(now half a century ago), most students of rhetoric have agreed that these two tropes together form a basic skeleton, to which all other figures may be related.[2] When one takes this perspective, then one is of course using metaphor and metonymy as what Hans Kellner calls "'inflatable tropes' that can be understood as 'figures of words', 'figures of thought', 'figures of comprehension', and 'figures of discourse'," referring respectively to the paradigmatic and the syntagmatic.[3] For Jakobson, too, metaphor and metonymy are shorthand terms for what he calls the "two different semantic lines" along which a stretch of discourse may develop: "one topic," he writes, "may lead to another either through their similarity [belonging to the same paradigm] or their contiguity [belonging to the same syntagm]. The metaphorical way would be the more appropriate term for the first case and the metonymic for the second, since they find their most condensed expression in metaphor and metonymy respectively."[4]

"Similarity" is the key feature of metaphor, yet this statement needs to be importantly modified. In the classic textbook example of metaphor – "he was a lion in the fight" – it is clear that the subject of the sentence displayed a similarity to a lion, yet it is equally clear that this subject was not, in actual fact, a lion. Metaphor, David Lodge comments, "creates a relationship of similarity between dissimilars."[5] Metaphor, to quote another rhetorical definition, "creates the relation between its objects," a relationship that consists in the essential quality that the objects are thought to share, no matter how unrelated they are in actual fact.[6] Metonymy for its part deals in items that are intimately linked to one another in real, syntagmatic contexts, without anyone claiming that they share a paradigmatic quality – not even temporarily, not even for the duration of the figure of speech. When

---

[2]   On this point, see also Beverley Haviland, "The Sin of Synecdoche: Hawthorne's Allegory against Symbolism in 'Rappaccini's Daughter,'" *Texas Studies in Literature and Language*, 29 (1987), 294-95. I have greatly benefited from Haviland's overall remarks on metaphor and metonymy.

[3]   Hans Kellner, "The Inflatable Trope as Narrative Theory: Structure or Allegory?" *Diacritics*, 11 (1984), 14-28.

[4]   Roman Jakobson, "Two Aspects of Language and Two Types of Aphasic Disturbances," *Word and Language*, vol. 2 of *Selected Writings* (The Hague: Mouton, 1971), 63.

[5]   David Lodge, *The Modes of Modern Writing: Metaphor, Metonymy, and the Typology of Modern Literature* (1979; London: Arnold, 1983), 112.

[6]   Hugh Bredin, "Metonymy," *Poetics Today*, 5 (1984), 52.

you say "Sorry, that's what the White House has decided," the White House is a metonymy for the American President, not because that mansion would somehow (magically) enjoy the same power as this political leader, but because the White House happens to be the executive residence of the President of the United States. The link between that building and political power is "habitually and conventionally known and accepted .... We must already know that the [two things] are related, if the metonymy is to be ... understood."[7]

Delightfully unconventional creature that she is, the heroine of *The Portrait of a Lady* is, of course, drawn more to strikingly metaphorical ways of thinking about her own character than to socially sanctioned metonymical ones. In a famous passage early in the novel, the narrator thus recounts of Isabel Archer that "Her nature had, in her conceit, a certain garden-like quality, a suggestion of perfume and murmuring boughs, of shady bowers and lengthening vistas, which made her feel that introspection was, after all, an exercise in the open air, and that a visit to the recesses of one's spirit was harmless when one returned from it with a lapful of roses."[8] There is, for Isabel, a likeness between her nature and richly appointed gardens that is hardly merely conventional; rather: it is the essential quality of her own self as opposed to other people's that can thus be captured. "But she was often reminded that there were other gardens in the world than those of her remarkable soul, and that there were moreover a great many places which were not gardens at all – only dusky pestiferous tracts, planted thick with ugliness and misery" (56).

Isabel's attitude is contrasted to that of Madame Merle, for whom context is of central importance. The point in one of their early conversations when, as the narrator informs us, Madame Merle becomes "very metaphysical" is worth quoting at some length:

> When you've lived as long as I you'll see that every human being has his shell and that you must take the shell into account. By the shell I mean the whole envelope of circumstances. There's no such thing as an isolated man or woman; we're each of us made up of some cluster of appurtenances. What shall we call our 'self'? Where does it begin? where does it end? It overflows into everything that belongs to us –

---

[7] Bredin, "Metonymy," 57.
[8] Henry James, *The Portrait of a Lady* (1908), Norton Critical Edition, ed. Robert D. Bamberg, 2nd edn (New York: Norton, 1995), 56. Subsequent references are to this edition and will be given parenthetically in the text.

> and then it flows back again. I know a large part of myself is in the clothes I choose to wear. I've a great respect for *things*! One's self – for other people – is one's expression of one's self; and one's house, one's furniture, one's garments, the books one reads, the company one keeps – these things are all expressive. (175)

In this little speech, Madame Merle not merely points to the crucial role played by a person's context – one's "shell," "circumstances," "appurtenances" – ; she goes quite a bit further in identifying such an "envelope," such a "cluster," as "expressive" of "one's self." The self for one thing cannot be restricted to some essential core that belongs solely to "an isolated man or woman"; rather, it "overflows" into the syntagmatic realm that envelops it. For another, the self is determined just as much by this context ("and then it flows back again"; "we're … made up of some cluster of appurtenances"). As a whole, the speech gives voice to the metonymical idea that the context of a thing or person may stand in for the latter.

Isabel strenuously denies the truth of her friend's claims for the metonymical. She thinks

> just the other way. I don't know whether I succeed in expressing myself, but I know that nothing else expresses me. Nothing that belongs to me is any measure of me; everything's on the contrary a limit, a barrier, and a perfectly arbitrary one. Certainly the clothes which, as you say, I choose to wear, don't express me; … it's not my own choice that I wear them; they're imposed upon me by society. (175)

For Isabel, the things that Madame Merle rhapsodizes are more handicaps than assets. Far from being able to act as representative of the essential self, one's context is a social imposition that stands in the way of true self-realization. This is one of the reasons, perhaps the key one, why Isabel Archer is unwilling to marry a suitor for her hand that would have struck many of her contemporaries as too good a catch to be true:

> Lord Warburton loomed up before her, largely and brightly, as a collection of attributes and powers which were not to be measured by [any] simple rule …. What she felt was that a territorial, a political, a social magnate had conceived the design of drawing her into the system in which he rather invidiously lived and moved. (95)

To marry Lord Warburton would be to embrace all the extensions and limitations that, to reactivate Madame Merle's phrase, a large "cluster of appurtenances" brings with it. "She couldn't marry Lord Warburton; the idea failed to support any enlightened prejudice in favour of the free exploration of life that she had hitherto entertained or was now capable of entertaining" (101).

Isabel is eager for the freedom to discover not just life in general, but her own life in particular: "you could have made her colour, any day in the year, by calling her a rank egoist. She was always planning out her development, desiring her perfection, observing her progress" (56). The "introspection" that she regularly indulges in is motivated by a desire to know what she is really like – how she may be paradigmatically understood. Her imagination is oriented towards the discovery of her true nature, and examines the latter by means of the metaphorical avenue that was illustrated earlier by the extended garden simile. Isabel Archer is bent on testing the limits of her world and is therefore grateful to her aunt for taking her from the provincial American town in which only books can feed her imagination to the European theater that provides a more appropriate stage for someone who wishes to develop her essential nature, perfect it, witness its progress. The portrait of a lady of the novel's title may thus be thought of to some extent as reflecting Isabel Archer's tendency to idealize her own person.

Even more than his aunt, Ralph Touchett enters into the spirit of Isabel's enterprise. Plagued by the weakness of his lungs, he cannot himself live up to the ambitions that he might have cherished. His desire to "put a little wind in [Isabel's] sails," to enable her "to meet the requirements of [her] imagination," can be seen as an attempt to live vicariously through the young woman. When Ralph completes the statement I have just quoted by observing that "Isabel has a great deal of imagination," his father's retort, "So have you, my son," makes explicit the paradigmatic link that exists between Isabel's character and Ralph's own (160). Pushing the point, we could say that Ralph treats Isabel metaphorically, in this sense that he recognizes a fundamental similarity between their natures, and wishes to see her act out the Ralph, as it were, that he cannot be due to the limitations that his health has placed on him.[9] He wishes to see Isabel behave as the

---

[9]   Notice in this connection that, in his first extended sketch of Ralph and his illness, the narrator attributes to him a doubling whereby the need to take care of himself is translated into the task of "taking care of [not himself in the least], but an

enterprising explorer that he believes himself essentially to be; he wishes to see her flourish freely in the active worlds that have been closed to him by his handicap.

Yet is such a metaphorical account of Ralph's relation to Isabel the only one possible? Could we not say with equal justification that the life Isabel leads as a rich woman is actually metonymically indebted to Ralph? After all, it is really, unbeknownst to her, Ralph's fortune that has transformed Isabel's identity from a young lady with a great deal of imagination into one who commands the wherewithal to enact her imaginings. Regarded from Ralph's perspective, his secret endowment of Isabel with half his fortune turns his cousin into a syntagmatic extension of his own self. Here is someone who will for the rest of her life be indelibly linked to him no matter what she does – no matter how different she may in the end prove to be from himself – merely by virtue of the fact that he has split "the whole envelope of his circumstances" (to quote another of Madame Merle's phrases) neatly into two financially equal halves and ensured that she possess one.

The rhetorical complexity that marks Ralph's philosophy and conduct is quite absent from Isabel's course of action for most of the book. If her early exchanges with Madame Merle give voice to her preference for the metaphorical, Isabel's conscious decision to marry Osmond is entirely based on this predilection too. Defending her choice to a skeptical Ralph Touchett in Chapter 34 of the novel, Isabel singles out the fact that Osmond is "so independent, so individual" (290). When Ralph points to Osmond's lack of importance in the world, Isabel counters by saying that she is "far more struck with what he has and what he represents than with what he may lack" (291). It is clear that "what [Osmond] represents" is not to be taken metonymically, as it was in the case of a Warburton, but metaphorically, like Isabel's view of herself. Indeed, the portrait that this lady paints of herself is matched by the idealized portrait she creates of this "gentleman" who she believes "knows everything, ... understands everything, ... has the kindest, gentlest, highest spirit." Osmond to Isabel embodies the supreme realization of the very values that she had detected in her own beautiful nature. They thus belong to the same paradigm, and it is this fact that dominates the conclusion of

---

uninteresting and uninterested person with whom he had nothing in common. This person, however, improved upon acquaintance ... " (45).

her clash with Ralph over her imminent marriage, culminating in a comparison of Osmond to Lord Warburton, whom her aunt had wanted her to marry. Osmond "has none of [Warburton's] great advantages – no property, no title, no honours, no houses, nor lands, nor position, nor reputation, nor brilliant belongings of any sort." But for Isabel, "It's the total absence of all these things that pleases me" (293). Forgetting at this point how much Osmond can be thought of in terms of the objects he has collected, Isabel presents her future husband as totally devoid of syntagmatic accoutrements.

Isabel's ethical life at this stage centers on a re-articulation of the concept of freedom, which now manifests itself in her strong-headed determination to marry a man who stands firm in his pursuit of non-material values, in his "wilful renunciation" of the "grubbing and grabbing" that goes on in the world (227, 296). Osmond, to Isabel, is a highly moral creature – a very honest man." She tells Ralph how immensely grateful she is to his father for having "put it into my power to marry a poor man – a man who has borne his poverty with such dignity, with such indifference. Mr. Osmond has never scrambled nor struggled – he has cared for no worldly prize." (293) As Ralph reflects at the end of their conversation, Isabel has "invented a fine theory about Gilbert Osmond," and she is determined to stick to it in the face of the strongest opposition (294). The fortune she has inherited initially enabled Isabel to enjoy the freedom to roam the world. It now affords her the opportunity to use that freedom to moral effect, following a moral principle (a law) that those like her aunt and Ralph fail to acknowledge when they talk of one's husband's putative importance in the eyes of the world.

There is an ironical contrast, of course, between the emphasis Isabel is constantly placing on her freedom, as well as the fondness she shows for a metaphorical understanding of the nature of the self, and the reality that she is the object of all sorts of manipulations that prove beyond the shadow of a doubt that her position in the world is heavily determined by metonymical processes. In addition to Ralph's role in making her rich (and Ralph's ensuring that Isabel should be prevented from realizing his agency by metonymically substituting his father's "will" for what was in fact his own), there is Madame Merle's scheming so as to "put" Isabel in Osmond's "way" (207), and her arranging their first meeting so that it takes place at Osmond's house, since she knows that "As cicerone of your museum you appear to particular advantage" (209). Serena Merle never wavers in her faith in the power of the metonymical – her belief that persons' surroundings may perfectly stand in for them and show them in a much better light than anything they do or say. Indeed, as I have argued in greater detail elsewhere, Pansy Osmond plays a crucial part in securing Isabel for her father.[10] Not only is she prominently present at the initial meeting, forming the subject on which the husband-and-wife-to-be conclude their first private conversation,[11] it is also during a private visit to Pansy that Isabel seems to decide to marry the girl's father.

Isabel's acceptance of Osmond, incidentally, is not explicitly covered in the text of the novel; neither is his proposal of marriage. What we get instead is the following sequence of events. During a visit to Rome, Osmond declares his love, a declaration which Isabel rejects "with an intensity that expressed the dread of having, in this case too, to choose and decide" (263). Isabel announces that she will travel the world for a year or so. Osmond asks Isabel to go and see his "little daughter" before she leaves Italy and to tell her that "she must love her father very much" (265). We get an account of that visit, and learn in the next chapter that Isabel is waiting for Goodwood, who has crossed the Atlantic to see for himself whether it is true that Isabel has taken her momentous decision to marry Osmond. Only later on in this chapter does the novel recount to us, in one of its few flashback interruptions to chronology,[12] that Isabel and Madame Merle have indeed spent the better part of a year making a "pilgrimage to the East" (274). That James decides to juxtapose the scene with Pansy (before the pilgrimage) and the one with Goodwood (after it) cannot be satisfactorily explained otherwise than by assigning to the conversation with Osmond's daughter a great deal of significance in Isabel's actual decision to marry the man. What is more, that Isabel has this conversation with Pansy is due entirely to Osmond's request to this effect, a request that he formulated within minutes of Isabel's defensive response to his declaration of love. There is no coincidence about that juxtaposition either.

It is not just what Pansy says, on which more in a moment, but the

---

[10]   See my "Metonymy and Mimesis in *The Portrait of a Lady*," *Q/W/E/R/T/Y: Arts, Littératures et Civilisations du Monde Anglophone*, 8 (1998), 153-57, from which a few passages have here been summarized.
[11]   "She's such a dear little girl," Isabel remarks. "Ah," Osmond responds, "she's a little saint of heaven! She is my great happiness." (228; end of Chapter 24)
[12]   Cf. M.E. Grenander, B.J. Rahn and Francine Valvo, "The Time-Scheme in *The Portrait of a Lady*," *American Literature*, 32 (1960), 127-35.

very aspect that she presents to the observer that may already play the trick. "How well the child had been taught, said our admiring young woman; how prettily she had been directed and fashioned; and yet how simple, how natural, how innocent she had been kept!" (267) It is as though Osmond, sensing that he is not making much headway in his direct wooing of Isabel, decides to withdraw into the background himself (where he remains for something like ten months), but not without first having ensured that he would in the meantime be indirectly represented to Isabel by the young girl that he has taken such pains to shape into a pleasing little thing – simple, natural, innocent. Osmond's strategy in securing Isabel's hand in marriage is in this sense metonymical that he sets up a process of signification in which what seems logically most dispensable to the activity of wooing – a daughter, more often regarded as an inconvenience than an asset to the man who would win over a young woman – is retained, while what seems logically essential – the man himself – is temporarily deleted.

But what Pansy says to Isabel is also important, underlining how she truly represents Osmond's interests – however unconsciously. When Isabel communicates Osmond's message to his daughter in a slightly modified form, "'Be very good … give pleasure to your father'" (269), Pansy responds in a fashion that seems to trigger Isabel's "passionate" feelings for Osmond:

> "I think that's what I live for … He has not much pleasure; he's rather a sad man."
> Isabel listened to this assertion with an interest which she felt it almost a torment to be obliged to conceal. It was her pride that obliged her, and a certain sense of decency; there were still other things in her head which she felt a strong impulse, instantly checked, to say to Pansy about her father; there were things it would have given her pleasure to hear the child, to make the child, say …. She was obliged to confess it to herself – she would have taken a passionate pleasure in talking of Gilbert Osmond to this innocent, diminutive creature who was so near him …. (269)

Crucially, it is only now, at the end of the conversation, that the reader is for the first time offered revealing remarks on Isabel's emotions with regard to Osmond. It seems that her decision to accept him is taken at this very moment. Nowhere before has the text used such heavily charged wording to characterize Isabel's sentiments towards

Osmond as here ("torment ... to conceal," "strong impulse," "passionate pleasure"), nor does it reactivate such a register at any point before it is clear that Isabel's acceptance has been made public. Osmond has cunningly put into practice Madame Merle's insight that context may act more powerfully for a person than anything they themselves might undertake. Pansy, as a metonymical substitute for her father, has won Isabel for him.

How can the framework I have been sketching help us make sense of the concluding scenes of *The Portrait of a Lady*? One fundamental point is that Isabel has come to recognize that the choices she believed she had made freely, independently, in this manner confirming her own paradigmatic essence, were in fact orchestrated by those around her. She has been caught in a web that was spun not just by the "evil"-intentioned Serena Merle and Gilbert Osmond but also, unintentionally, by the more happily inspired Ralph Touchett. The latter fact in particular makes it clear that life in society involves one in all sorts of contiguities, no matter how much one may be inclined to introspection and the cultivation of metaphors of the free and independent self. When Caspar Goodwood offers Isabel a chance to escape from what she has meanwhile come to regard as the misery of her marriage, his words are seductive indeed. They appeal forcefully to that side of Isabel that would still be swayed by the romance of freedom: "We can do absolutely as we please; to whom under the sun do we owe anything? ... The world's all before us – and the world's very big" (489). Goodwood's understanding of the independent self is very much like Isabel's in the earlier parts of the novel: "It would be an insult to you to assume that you care for the look of the thing, for what people will say, for the bottomless idiocy of the world. We've nothing to do with all that; we're quite out of it; we look at things as they are" (488). A firmer rejection of Madame Merle's strong emphasis on "the company one keeps" as an expression of the self is hard to imagine (175).

It is not just Goodwood's words that are seductive; so is his manner. Especially in the version James revised for the New York Edition, the final scene of the novel is as erotically charged as one is likely to find anywhere in James.[13] The imagery is of "float[ing] in fathomless waters," and undergoing "a rushing torrent." Even before

---

[13]   Bonnie L. Heron, "Substantive Sexuality: Henry James Constructs Isabel Archer as a Complete Woman in His Revised Version of *The Portrait of a Lady*," *The Henry James Review*, 16 (1995), 131-41.

Goodwood acts, Isabel is thinking that "she had never been loved before. She had believed it, but this was different; this was the hot wind of the desert, at the approach of which the others dropped dead, like mere sweet airs of the garden" (488). Isabel believes that "to let him take her in his arms would be the next best thing to dying," a belief that is "a kind of rapture, in which she felt herself sink and sink." These descriptions indicate a vividly aroused desire, to be sure, and when Isabel finally "felt his arms about her and his lips on her own lips," the sensation is not an unpleasant one that she tries to get rid of immediately. Rather, "His kiss was like white lightning, a flash that spread, and spread again, and stayed." What is more, the narrator notes that "while she took [the kiss]" – note the active involvement that the verb "to take" implies – "it was extraordinarily as if ... she felt each thing in his hard manhood that had least pleased her, each aggressive fact of his face, his figure, his presence, justified of its intense identity and made one with this act of possession." What is so extraordinary is that what Isabel had disliked from a distance, now becomes "justified" in the close proximity of the kiss, in her submission to "this act of possession" that is so much in line with the "intense identity" of these traits of Goodwood's "hard manhood."

But the upshot of this emotional experience is not, as one might have thought, that Isabel accepts the sensuous side of her character, acknowledging that, for the sake of desire, she has to allow herself to be thus possessed by a man. In fact, the reverse may be said to happen. The imagery of the scene is sensuous, yet it also clearly brings out the bound and unfree condition that giving in to such sensuality involves, a condition that is like being drowned, exposed to lightning and submitted to possession. There is, in other words, a sharp contrast between Goodwood's talk of freedom and independence and the force with which he imposes his sexual power on Isabel, appealing directly to what she has called early in the book "the deepest thing" within her soul: the "belief that if a certain light should dawn she could give herself completely" (56). It is such a complete surrender of the self that Caspar Goodwood is really demanding of Isabel, and on which depends the sexual fulfillment that he holds out.

It is worth recalling here Harpham's description of ethics as an articulation of "the relation between freedom and necessity, desire and the law." What is so crucial about the long scene with Goodwood, it seems to me, is that it helps Isabel to realize that the opposition between "freedom and necessity, desire and the law" can be a fatuous one. Implying as it does that freedom and desire belong together, just as do necessity and the law, Harpham's formulation cannot do justice to the final scene of *The Portrait of a Lady*, and the ethical decision in which it culminates: Isabel's choice of the "very straight path" that leads back to Rome. As we have just seen, Goodwood's "act of possession" makes it clear that desire can be the opposite of freedom. Sexual fulfillment may depend on a complete relinquishing of a person's freedom and independence. The choice that Isabel faces at the end of the story is between a bound condition that masks itself in metaphors of freedom while exacting a surrender of the essential self (Goodwood) and a bound condition that is situated at the more superficial level of "the observance of a magnificent form" that Osmond expects of her (446). Osmond's "wish to preserve appearances," we could say, amounts to a metonymical bondage only: it requires Isabel to live by Madame Merle's rule that "One's self – for other people – is one's expression of one's self; ... one's house, one's furniture, one's garments, ..., the company one keeps" (175). It does not draw on her fund of "passion," guarded "within herself, deep down," hoarded "like a large sum stored in a bank – which there was a terror in having to begin to spend" (263). Paradoxically, there is likely to be more freedom for Isabel at Palazzo Roccanera – Osmond's "house of darkness" (360) – than in the "very big" world Goodwood proposes to explore with her, causing her to respond "as if he were pressing something that hurt her," and sealing their putative compact with a kiss that is "like white lightning" (489).

We should not be misled by James' imagery of light and dark here. The white lightning that Goodwood produces may be erotically pleasurable. "But when darkness returned she was free" (489). Adrian Poole cogently argues that the privileged term in *The Portrait of a Lady* is "dusk," rather than light.[14] It would seem that the overabundance of white light that Goodwood produces (recall also that "if a certain *light* should dawn she could give herself completely" – a prospect that Isabel has consistently dreaded [56]) needs to be first offset by complete darkness before a measure of freedom can be recovered. The location that then allows the heroine to come to a final decision about the direction of her life is the highly liminal one of the

---

[14]   Adrian Poole, "Dying Before the End: The Reader in *The Portrait of a Lady*," *Yearbook of English Studies*, 26 (1996), 150-51.

Gardencourt doorsill. She is attracted to the house on her flight from Caspar by the "lights in the windows," yet is never shown to enter its brightness, instead pausing with "her hand on the latch," in the dusk of that threshold (489-90). It is here that Isabel sees "a very straight path."

Thus, desire and freedom are surprisingly at odds in the denouement of James' novel. But so, it could be argued, are necessity and the law, to turn to the two remaining terms from Harpham's schema. If Isabel, in the early parts of the novel, tries to base her decisions on moral principles (which Harpham would dub "laws") that Ralph thinks of disparagingly as "fine theor[ies]" with little relation to reality (294), joined in this sentiment by Isabel herself in the fireside chapter,[15] this tendency is much reduced by the end. Though Harpham is not talking about James in his observations on the ethics of literature, his other key-term, necessity, may be usefully invoked not as the near-synonym of "law" that he intends it to be, but as a shorthand phrase for another type of ethical imperative, that I have elsewhere summarized as "the ethics of metonymy."[16] Reaching the insight that a bound condition is unavoidable in social life, Isabel Archer is well on her way towards embracing an ethical attitude that will become much more pronounced in later Jamesian works, such as *The Ambassadors* and *The Wings of the Dove*. This attitude places less emphasis on abstract laws and general principles – on the need to find a "good ... formula" to account for one's actions, as Isabel puts it to herself in Chapter 55 (481) – and more on the need to react to the demands of a situation in which one finds oneself. These two alternatives may be termed metaphorical and metonymical in character respectively, the basic *modus operandi* of metaphor as a figure of thought applying to the former in that a paradigmatic connection is perceived between discrete ethical decisions that share their rootedness in a certain law or principle; that of metonymy to the latter because a syntagmatic connection is seen to exist between a moral agent and the situation that calls for an ethical decision. Like the rhetorical figures of metaphor and metonymy, neither of these ethical alternatives should be thought of as superior to the other;

---

[15] "Isabel's cheek burned when she asked herself whether she had really married on a factitious theory, in order to do something finely appreciable with her money" (358).
[16] See my "The Ethics of Metonymy," lecture at the Second Ghent Conference on Literary Theory, December 1999, and "The Ethics of Metonymy in James' 'The Real Thing,'" paper at the 117th Annual MLA Conference, New Orleans, December 2001.

rather, they are complementary. If I here tend to privilege the metonymical it is because it has received scanter attention than the metaphorical, even though its relevance to many of the ethical problems posed in modern literature is high.

In the closing scenes of *The Portrait of a Lady*, Isabel Archer's recognition of the decisive role played by metonymy in her life also results in her tentative embrace of an ethics of metonymy. When she arrives in London, *en route* for Gardencourt to be with the dying Ralph, Isabel already indicates to Henrietta Stackpole her intention to return to Rome, explaining that this is the promise she made to Pansy Osmond. When Henrietta questions the rationale for this undertaking, Isabel agrees:

> "I'm not sure I myself see now," Isabel replied. "But I did then."
> "If you've forgotten your reason perhaps you won't return."
> Isabel waited a moment. "Perhaps I shall find another."
> "You'll certainly never find a good one."
> "In default of a better my having promised will do," Isabel suggested. (469)

The fact that Isabel is "not sure ... now" but was "then" can be explained in respect of the type of ethical attitude that I have briefly sketched: an ethics in which the demands of a particular situation at a particular time prompt one to take up a responsibility that one cannot easily explain with reference to any clear law; rather, one undertakes to fulfill the obligation simply because one is there. Isabel has "forgotten [her] reason" because there never was "a good one" – there never was a readily identifiable ground on which to commit herself to the daughter of her tyrannical husband and his deceptive one-time lover. The Isabel who strongly disagreed with Madame Merle over the nature of the self – insisting on its supreme sovereignty over against her friend's assertion that we are intimately tied up with what happens to be our context – that Isabel seems to have changed considerably when she is prepared to return to a husband (who she knows will make her "a scene of the rest of my life" [469]) for no other reason than that she made a promise not to abandon this man's daughter.

It is also this altered Isabel who ultimately proves resistant to Goodwood's siren song of absolute freedom. In fact, as we saw, it may well be in the dissonant clash between the metaphors of the sovereign self that he spouts and the imprisonment of a sexual bondage that he really exacts that Isabel finds that "better" reason for returning to her husband that she is looking for upon her arrival in England (469). Thus Isabel's adoption of the "very straight path" back to the Osmonds must be regarded as a high-level ethical negotiation of the relation between freedom and necessity, desire and the law. Recognizing that her earlier pursuit of lofty principles could not protect her from the mundane manipulations of down-to-earth reality, and that the hot breath of desire extinguishes any measure of freedom, Isabel willingly submits to the necessity that the situation in which she finds herself presents. The "abrupt and unsatisfactory" ending that many readers have noted reflects the tentative nature of the ethical resolution that James here develops.[17] It will only be in later works that he arrives at a more fully elaborated ethics of metonymy that can stand the test of further plotting.

---

[17] John Updike, "Introduction," *The Portrait of a Lady*, by Henry James, World's Classics (Oxford: Oxford University Press, 1999). Rptd *Compass*, 4 (September 1999), 16.

A VARIETY OF AMBERSONS: RE-READING BOOTH TARKINGTON'S AND ORSON WELLES' *THE MAGNIFICENT AMBERSONS*

PETER RIETBERGEN

> *Peter Bogdanovich: "Francois Truffaut once said that, if Flaubert reread Quixote every year, why can't we see Ambersons whenever possible? Did you ever hear that quote?"*
> *Orson Welles: "No. Thank you for passing it along."*[1]

"Have you read the book?" "No, but I've seen the movie!" It is a conversational exchange that one may hear at many a party. To many critics of contemporary civilization, it signals the deplorable disappearance of a reading culture, perhaps even of literacy from the lives of the young. Nor is it a tendency which is likely to reverse itself in decades to come. By way of introduction to an essay on the topic of "fiction into film," a comparison between the written and the visual rendering of the same theme, it is tempting to speculate briefly on the consequences of this change from a written to a visual culture.

How many people will know of Jane Austen's exquisite novels, all of them major or at least minor literary classics, only through the various movies and, of course, the television series made after them? How many people nowadays will actually have read Margaret Mitchell's novel *Gone with the Wind*, which was highly popular in its time but never was considered a literary masterpiece, while they probably have seen the 1939 movie, which to many has become part of the filmgoers' canon and which, to equally many, conveys the essence of what they believe Margaret Mitchell wanted to say?

From the beginning the movies ransacked the literary heritage of the western world, to provide cinematic drama if not with the texts at least with the plots that a voracious industry needed to feed an equally

---

[1] Orson Welles and Peter Bogdanovich, *This is Orson Welles*, ed. Jonathan Rosenbaum (New York: HarperCollins, 1993), 98.

voracious audience. Sometimes, movie makers were genuinely touched by the books they had read, and felt compelled to convey their emotions to a public that otherwise might not have the benefit of ever knowing what masterworks their culture had produced. Perhaps rather more often, the works, whether major or minor, that constituted the literary canon simply were used to give status and thus credibility to the new medium. Even before movies became talkies, literary luster was thought to have a beneficial effect on a film: as early as 1914, when Giovanni Pastrone conceived his *Cabiria*, one of the earliest triumphs of Italian cinema and, incidentally, a major influence on the work of D.W. Griffith and other American film makers, he asked the acclaimed poet Gabriele D'Annunzio to provide the intertexts.

From the first there have been critics who lament not only the increasing tendency to substitute the filmed image for the written word but the very process itself. They hold to the belief that a work that has been granted the status of literature cannot possibly be turned into a film that even remotely does justice to the complexity and intensity of the original. Moreover, they are convinced that if someone were to see the film version of a novel first, he will be unable to appreciate the original text, because his mind will be saturated with the filmic images.

There are many reasons why such a stance seems to me untenable. First of all, the criteria used to qualify a text as a literary one seem to be unstable, fraught with problems of definition and, therefore, lacking in the precision required to sustain a profitable discussion of the wider issues involved. Then, the argument seems based on a misunderstanding of the reading process itself, which, if anything, remakes a given "public" text into as many meaningful personal ones as there are readers. For this reason alone, the discussion seems, indeed, a futile one.

There are at least three additional elements to be considered that bear upon the issue, albeit side-wise. The generations born after the 1950s have been educated in a visual rather than an oral/written culture. They have been raised on images produced by the cinema, by television, by the video clip, by the illustrated press and, more recently, by computerized mass media with, among others, their cache of interactive stories. Moreover, they have traveled, either in body or in mind, and they have seen places and people their parents had only read and fantasized about. Thus, when they read, their minds cannot help evoking a visual background to many if not all aspects of the texts; they take their references from a gigantic encyclopedia of images that have attached themselves to the written word and interpret it, to a degree unparalleled since man started reading.

My second observation may seem to contradict this first one, yet it has a distinct bearing on my general argument. In particular since the late 1970s or early 1980s, many movies, especially successful television ones, have produced their own texts, as a surprising spin-off. Series like *Star Trek* or *The X-Files* are now followed by "Star Trek–the Book", or some such novelistic enterprise, mostly not written by the person who conceived the original idea, or even the person who wrote the script for the movie, but by independent authors; regardless of whether they are employed by the media moguls who produced the film version, they cash in on its success. Also, we find that literature itself has been increasingly influenced by the languages of other media, with texts being structured as if they were a newsreel, a movie script, etcetera – John Dos Passos' 1930s trilogy *USA* perhaps being the first of its kind. While such texts may have been written with an ulterior filmability, and the subsequent monetary success in mind, their authors also may have realized their readers were part of a changing culture. This situation poses at least two questions which lie outside the scope of the present essay: first, whether we are going to judge these texts on their literary merits as well, and second, what the phenomenon in itself tells us about the reading habits and needs of a largely visually-oriented public.

Returning to the examples I used above, it seems to me that Jane Austen's novels are to a significant degree about the uses and abuses of social conventions, what we today would term structures of psychological internalizations, and that Margaret Mitchell's novel is about the vanishing sense of honor of the Ashleys and Melanies, and the zest for life of the Rhetts and the Scarlets. If these assumptions are true, it may well be that most modern readers fail to really understand the issues and dilemmas that created these novels in the first place. And, if this is so, should not we then not conclude that it is not only the movies which fail to dramatize these central elements of many a literary work, but that most readers – in increasing numbers – have difficulty grasping these elements, as such themes are becoming alien to their culture? Education, then, seems necessary, both in the field of film and of literature.

Starting from the idea that "a film can only compete with literature if it understands the powers it has that are denied to the page,"[2] I should like to propose that an intelligent, culture-conscious reading of a text, whether that text is a novel, a film, a painting or building, may help reveal part of its significance, not *sub specie aeternitatis* but for the reader's own time, and that it may prompt him to interrogate products of past culture by posing questions that are meaningful precisely because they are related to the present.

The novel

Booth Tarkington (1869-1946) can hardly be said to be among the pre-war novelists who still are devoured by the contemporary public. Yet, in the 1920s and 1930s his reputation and even more the fortune he made from it were solid indeed. Twice the winner of the much-coveted Pulitzer Prize, Tarkington was considered the talented, eminently readable, somewhat wistful chronicler of the changing world of small-town life in the American Midwest. He largely took his inspiration and his themes from his own experiences in Indiana, where he grew up in comfortable middle-class circumstances and which he even served as a member of the House of Representatives.[3]

His first novel set the tone for his subsequent oeuvre: *The Gentlemen From Indiana* (1899) painted a picture of the life and culture of Tarkington's Midwestern world that, even then, he saw vanishing, slowly but inexorably. He went on to write over forty novels, nearly all of them works of gently-voiced social and, indeed, cultural criticism. Yet, he was no reactionary. He showed himself fully aware of the forces that worked to change society – his 1928 volume of reminiscences was titled *The World Does Move* – but nevertheless deplored the loss of certain values in the process. Both as to style and content, Tarkington's works show the influence of William Dean Howells, whose *The Rise of Silas Lapham* obviously had an impact on his views of the changes in society and the way they affect people. Theodore Dreiser seems another

---

[2] This is one of the few illuminating ideas in an otherwise flawed biography of Welles by David Thomson, *Rosebud: The Story of Orson Welles* (New York: Knopf, 1996), 224-25. In the absence of any system of notes its many potentially valuable statements cannot be checked. Moreover, as if in a cinematic voice-over, it has fictionalized dialogues between the book's author and an unnamed "other" that comment on the story as told in the biography.

[3] I am aware of only two biographies: James L. Woodress, *Booth Tarkington: Gentleman from Indiana* (1955; rptd Greenwood Press, 1969), and Keith J. Fennimore, *Booth Tarkington* (New York: Twayne, 1974).

influence, though Tarkington is less harsh in his criticism of society and his characters move in different social circles.

The Magnificent Ambersons – which won him his first Pulitzer Prize in 1918, and which he later combined with *The Turmoil* (1915) and *The Midlander* (1924) into a trilogy significantly entitled *Growth* – contains most of Tarkington's favorite themes. The novel tells its story in thirty-five chapters. The first one sets the scene, sometime in the last years of the nineteenth century.[4] In a small Midland town – supposedly Tarkington's Indianapolis – inhabited by the descendants of settlers who still adhere to their thrifty ways, where carriages in summer and sleighs in winter are the means of transportation for the well-to-do, while a horse-drawn tram conveys the ordinary people to their various businesses at a leisurely pace, life is tranquil, well-ordered. Everyone knows his place in society, as denoted by the clothes they wear and even by the neighborhood they live in. Thus, most of the more prominent citizens live in "Amberson's Addition," a wide-laned, tree-shaded quarter where each house has a very spacious garden and where the intersections of the roads are adorned with the cast-iron statuary of classically-draped females, a personal preference of the scheme's inventor and owner, Major Amberson, the wealthiest man in town, who made his fortune in 1873, after the Civil War.

The Major, who lives in a palatial house that is the pride of the town, has two sons and a daughter, Isabel. The latter, a beautiful girl, falls in love with a dashing young man, Eugene Morgan. However, during one of the parties that are the sparkle in the life of the town's gilded youth, Eugene makes a fool of himself (by stumbling over the violoncello he used to serenade his beloved) and, therefore, of her – or so Isabel feels. She decides not to marry him, instead choosing an utterly respectable, but also very dull youngster. It is unclear whether, at this stage, the reader is to infer that already Isabel is bowing to the restrictive social code of the town she is born in, even though her family actually rules it.

From her marriage to this Wilbur Minafer a son is born, George Amberson Minafer, who is the book's tragic hero. As predicted by the town's doyenne – "She couldn't love Wilbur, could she? ... Well, it will all go to her children, and she'll ruin 'em!" – he grows up his mother's and his grandfather's darling, coddled, petted and, in the end, utterly

---

[4] Not, I think, in 1873, as Carringer, in his reconstruction of Welles' movie, wrongly assumes (Robert L. Carringer, *The Magnificent Ambersons: A Reconstruction* [Berkeley: University of California Press, 1993], 19-21). It seems likely he confuses Welles' script with the novel's text.

spoilt.[5] His world is one in which Ambersons rule, and mankind obeys. No wonder that all through the book people positively long to have him finally get his "come-uppance" (29).

The plot starts thickening when young George returns from school, and, at a ball given in his honor, meets Eugene Morgan, who also has returned to his home town, not the social and financial failure people had expected him to become but a successful inventor-businessman, experimenting with the new medium of transportation, the gasoline-driven car, or 'automobile'. Moreover, Morgan has a beautiful daughter, Lucy, with whom George soon finds himself in love. But though they delight in each other's company, it is quite clear from the beginning that Lucy has problems with George's overbearing ways, though she pretends only to lightly mock them. George, on the other hand, constantly fails to understand Lucy's more cultured and, indeed, more principled as well as practical way of thinking – or so Tarkington implies. All the time, George does not really warm to Morgan, whose cars he considers symbols of a change that in other ways, too, is affecting the town; yet, he cannot help being fascinated by their speed.

A first real shock comes to George when he finds out that Mr. Morgan is, actually, his mother's first love. His uneasiness intensifies when George realizes that, especially after his father dies, his mother's feelings for Eugene resurge. When he discovers that "the town talks," he is utterly enraged and, moreover, emotionally perturbed. He uses his emotions as well as his mother's love for him to force her to give up her chance of happiness with Morgan; he accepts, too, that it will mean breaking with Lucy. The son and his mother go abroad. When, after a number of years, they finally return, Isabel is dying. Yet her son dominates her even then, denying her her last wish, to once more see Eugene. It is only after her death and that of his grandfather, which follows shortly after, that he realizes what he has done.

Meanwhile, it has become obvious not only that George's own father has left his wife and son little or no money, but also that his grandfather Amberson, whose wealth was not only the symbol of the town and of a certain age but also the basis of the family's position and power, has suffered severe losses. At old Amberson's death, George and his aunt Fanny, his father's only sister, are left penniless: he because, as Tarkington seems to imply, the old money simply has vanished over

---

[5]   Booth Tarkington, *The Magnificent Ambersons* (Paris: Louis Conard, Paris, 1920), 21. Subsequent page references are given parenthetically in the text.

time, and she because she has ventured her entire capital backing an inventor who had promised her a fortune when his new electric light for automobiles would conquer the world – Tarkington's implication being that new money, too, will be the sand on which people's dreams are built.

In Chapters 30 and 31, which are among the novel's longest, the real impact of what he has done dawns on George. He tries to defend himself to his aunt Fanny, invoking his youth and inexperience:

> You were older than I, and if you were so sure you were *wiser* than I, why did you just stand around ... and let me go ahead? You could have stopped it if it was wrong, couldn't you? (285-86)

His aunt shakes her head:

> No George ... nobody could have stopped you. You were too strong, and – and she loved you – too well. (286)

To enable his aunt, his one remaining relative, to end her life in tolerable gentility, George takes a dangerous job with a factory producing nitroglycerine. Ironically, he is run over by a small car on one of his Sunday walks that take him on rather distracted amblings through the town he no longer recognizes as his own. Eugene and Lucy both read of his accident in the newspaper, assuming it has marred "his tall and graceful figure" – clearly the symbol of this last and most magnificent Amberson. It makes them think of his mother, who loved him so much, as if Tarkington wants us to understand that it is really Isabel's love – the mother's love, that is the essence of one's youthful life - that for long constituted George's being. They both come to the hospital, where George asks Eugene's forgiveness. Eugene realizes that, in doing so, he is "true at last to his true love."

Meanwhile, from Chapter 27 we have come to understand that Lucy never has stopped loving George, though she knew she could not marry him: "It was absurd," she had told him at their last meeting: " ... it couldn't help but be ..., the way I am and the way you are, it couldn't have been anything else" (256). It is essential for a deeper understanding of the novel to see that what Lucy found lacking in George was, indeed, a spirit of enterprise:

"You haven't settled on anything to do .... What *are* you going to do George?" she'd once asked him. "I expect to live an honourable life," he said. "I expect to contribute my share to charities, and to take part in – in movements." "What kind?" "Whatever appeals to me," he said. (174-75)

The conversation could have occurred thirty years after the novel's period, in Tarkington's own days or, indeed, in our own times, as other American youth of gilded attraction contemplate their future.

With the hospital scene, the novel closes. Contrary to what some readers have remarked, to me it seems an open ending. We do not know what is going to happen, emotionally, between the protagonists, nor do we know if George will regain the strength of his legs and resume his job as part of America's working force.

Throughout the novel, Tarkington seems to hint at a psychological problem that is never really made explicit. Even before he becomes aware of who Eugene Morgan is, at the big ball at the Amberson Mansion described in Chapter IV, we find George, who is unconsciously experiencing his own sexual awakening, ruminating on the femininity and the sexual allure of his mother; however, he rejects both when he realizes that they imply that she might ever belong to a man – excluding, of course, his father from this picture, for we do not consciously think of our parents as sexual beings. It seems as if the author shrinks from this almost Freudian element, and yet cannot withstand its possibilities, even finds them essential to the development of his plot: indeed, after George has told his mother that she cannot marry Eugene and has to stop seeing him altogether, Tarkington observes: "not less like Hamlet did he feel and look" (249).

I find this interpretation, which has been advanced before,[6] convincing since Tarkington was too good a novelist to convince either himself or his readers that a credible plot could be built on George's wounded sense of social status and family pride alone; notwithstanding the fact that such feelings played a not unimportant role in the life of small communities like the one the author knew and wanted to sketch. Nevertheless, it is also evident that Tarkington, even if he may subconsciously have been casting George into a Freudian, oedipal relationship with his mother, did not intend this to be the novel's main theme. Admittedly, there are powerful traces of such a relationship, like the recurring hysteria with which George rejects any idea of Isabel ever

---

[6]   Among others by Carringer, 21, who entitled the first chapter of his study "Oedipus in Indianapolis."

loving another man and like her own letter, in which, after she has called him the sacred gift God gave her, she remarks:

> Good night, my darling, my beloved, my beloved! You mustn't be troubled. I think I shouldn't mind anything very much as long as I have you "all to myself" – as people say – to make up for your long years away from me at college. (251)[7]

Their departure on a trip that forces them to live together for a number of years – a honeymoon, a marriage? – might be interpreted as hinting at a more than normally strong bond as well. But then, so might Eugene's happiness in the face of his daughter's decision not to marry after she has broken with George (referred to in Chapter 34) and, indeed, Lucy's own admission: "I don't want anything but you." If one decides to hold to the oedipal interpretation of Tarkington's novel, one must accept that the two situations mirror one another.[8]

Yet, to find out what the novel really is about, it is necessary to have a closer look at its structure, in particular at the way in which the novel intertwines two major themes and develops them through a number of metaphors.

In Chapter 18, significantly half-way through the text, the town is serenely sketched as evening falls, with moonlight shining on the trees, the patter of carriage horses plodding along the roads, and the almost silent sounds of bicycles swishing by, carrying singing, guitar-playing youngsters to their parties. The atmosphere is idyllic. But it is the eventide of a vanishing society, for the quiet is broken by the "horrid sounds" of a "frantic devil", the car: "there are a great many more than there used to be," someone says. Tarkington follows this up with a few, cleverly ambiguous words: "there, in the highway, the evening life of the Midland city had begun" (178-79).

Equally significantly, in Chapter 15 George and Lucy quarrel: a man grounded in tradition, *his* supreme wish is to be "a gentleman" – "don't you think that being things is rather better than doing things?" a friend of his had once asked Lucy (154-55) – while *she*, the daughter of a modern automobile maker, finds that his ideas do not seem like ideas to her at all; after all, she was, as Tarkington remarks elsewhere, "an independent,

---

[7] Carringer, 24, quotes this passage too, but by changing some of the words and the original punctuation he makes the quote suit his own interpretation rather more than is warranted.

[8] I owe this suggestion to my colleague, Dr. Jolanda Jansen.

masterful, self-reliant little American" (253). Once more, two cultures clash. Once more, an idyll ends.

In the next chapter, George, to his entire family's dismay, brusquely attacks Eugene as the maker of a monster, the automobile. From then on, his dislike of his mother's suitor grows to ever greater intensity. When, in Chapter 25, George, unknown to Isabel, has told Eugene not to see her again, and awaits his mother's reaction on the big staircase, Tarkington describes the large stained-glass panels that light the landing: they show the figures of "Love and Purity and Beauty", but "the colours were growing dull; evening was coming on" (238). People, through their own actions – but also through the process of time? – are losing the things that seem most valuable.

While, through his decision regarding his mother's future, George consciously also gives up his chance of happiness with Lucy, denying, in a way, his love for her, the larger scene of the town must lose its happy innocence as well. In Chapter 28, Tarkington concisely and visually describes the fundamental change from a rural to an industrial society, with all its social and cultural implications. By now, the town "befouled itself and darkened its sky .... Gasoline and electricity were performing the miracles Eugene had predicted" (263-64).

But the novel is not an exposition of simple and simplified opposites. Tarkington has made clear already that Eugene is far from being a crass modernist. Responding to George's vehement rejection of automobiles at the dinner party given by old Major Amberson, he said:

> I'm not sure he's wrong about automobiles .... With all their speed forward they may be a step backward in civilization – that is, in spiritual civilization. It may be that they will not add to the beauty of the world, nor to the life of men's souls. (Chapter 19, 188-89)

Unlike George, who is still young, Eugene accepts the inevitability of change while at the same time deploring its consequences. So does Tarkington, who in that same Chapter, goes on to describe the new society, for "the great change was in the citizenry itself." The town was increasingly populated by people who had not been born there:

> There was a German quarter; there was a Jewish quarter; there was a negro quarter – square miles of it – called "Bucktown"; there were many Irish neigbourhoods; and there were large settlements of Italians, and of Hungarians, and of Rumanians, and of Serbians and other Balkan peoples. But not the emigrants, themselves, were the almost dominant

type on the streets downtown. That type was the emigrant's prosperous offspring .... A new Midlander – in fact, a new American – was beginning dimly to emerge. (264-65)

Clearly, Tarkington is not entirely happy with this new 'type'. It is idealistic, and optimistic, yes, but it believes "in hustling and honesty because both paid." It sees "the perfect beauty and happiness of cities and of human life" in the building of ever more factories, as these bring "Prosperity." But this prosperity amounts to nothing more than credit at the bank that, in its essence, brings them "nothing that was not dirty, and, therefore, to a sane mind, valueless" (265-66). To introduce the metaphor dear to him, Tarkington has Lucy, who on first coming to the town had decorated her drawing room in white, decide to "put everything into dull grey and brown," knowing that it could not drive away the encroaching soot. We realize that she is willfully deceiving herself because in doing so "it no longer looked so dirty as it was" (267). She is losing some of her innocence; we feel she is growing up.

A definite clue to Tarkington's intentions comes in Chapter 35, when the tale nears its end. To me it seems that Tarkington wants his readers to see George's decision – the cruelty of which he admits to himself only after his mother has died, feeling "sorrow for what sacrifices his pride and youth had demanded of others" (Chapter 32, 307) – as part of a process. It is the process of personal growth that by the very loss of youth entails the awareness of the inadvertent cruelty of youth that thinks its own values and interpretations of life and the world absolute. Yet I feel that, at the same time, this very process is the novel's emotional, personal counterpoint to a far more encompassing socio-cultural one, viz. that of the coming of age of America itself, which was losing its innocence as well:

> ... the new great people who had taken their places – the Morgans and Akerses and Sheridans – they would go, too. George saw that. They would pass, as the Ambersons had passed .... Nothing stays or holds or keeps where there is growth, he somehow perceived vaguely but truly. (Chapter 35, 338)

This hints at acceptance, both on George's and on Tarkington's part; elsewhere George realizes "he had too emphatically supported the ideal of being rather than doing" – which, surely, is another of youth's characteristics. Yet we are also made to realize that becoming an adult, losing one's innocence, is painful, and that something irretrievable has been lost in the process: purity. That, indeed, seems one of the novel's main themes, metaphorically and at the same time realistically rendered by the recurring reference to the soot that comes to cover everything: the town, the houses, the people living there, and even their souls – "all people were soiled," it is said in Chapter 31.

Though, on a first reading, George may not appear to be the most appealing of characters, his personal development is indeed the necessary counterpoint to the larger process. He articulates his rejection of the "new age" represented by the motor car – though it is partly inspired by his very personal, emotional rejection of his mother's suitor, who every way looked the part of the man of "the new era" – and yet in the end he has to become part of that process, working in a gunpowder plant, with the machines he loathes. For not only has he grown up, he has also personally grown, and logically so, Tarkington implies, for, as George's uncle had told him at their final parting in Chapter 31: "the stuff of the old stock is in you. It'll come out and do something" (294). And when, in Chapter 32, George applies for his job, his new boss tells him: "You certainly are the most practical young man I ever met" (317).

Like his town, then, George, too, becomes part of the new era, and inevitably grows up, as part of a historical process. The ending might thus be seen to reflect the essentially optimistic view that Tarkington had of his country and its people, however much he might deplore the passing of certain of its old ways. After all, as Eugene had remarked in Chapter 6: "There aren't any times but new times" (69).

In the end, Booth Tarkington's *The Magnificent Ambersons* seems to be about youth and adulthood, about safety and growing up, about the loss of old, unquestioned ideals and certainties, and the painful acceptance of change, of uncertainties, of new responsibilities.

The film
Orson Welles started his career as the boy wonder and ended it as the scapegoat of America's new communications' industries, first of radio and then of film. Moreover, he became a myth and an icon of film as art, despite the fact that he only made two really great films.

From Welles' early years onwards, "high" literature, often theatrically re-worked, constituted his fare. Trained as a classical actor, starring in Shakespeare, he held the stage in one of Roosevelt's New Deal initiatives, the *Federal Theatre*, and, from 1937 onwards, in the *Mercury,* which he had founded with a few like-minded spirits. From 1934 onwards, he also was eagerly exploring the possibilities of the new medium of radio, adapting the literary texts that inspired him for the CBS-series *The School of the Air for the Americas*,[9] and, later, *The March of Time*. Broadcast pieces were directed and often acted by him, based on texts ranging from Charlotte Brontë's *Jane Eyre* to H.G. Wells' novels, but it was his adaptation of the latter's *War of the Worlds* that brought him fame and notoriety; indeed, its rendering of an extraterrestrial invasion that drove thousands of Americans out of their homes was so life-like that it caused many listeners to think another hoax was played on them when, three years later, the Japanese attack on Pearl Harbor was announced by radio as well.

In the meantime, Welles also made his first film, *The Hearts of Age*, a five-minute piece showing the influence of, among others, expressionist European film makers like Friedrich Murnau.[10] Significantly, he himself took the role of Death just as, in his famous 1937 adaptation of Shakespeare's *Julius Caesar*, he had portrayed the Roman dictator as a fascist leader, dispensing death as well.[11] In 1939, Welles was called to Hollywood by RKO Pictures and given an unprecedented free hand in the making of his films, and an extremely lucrative contract to boot. Nevertheless, his first effort at a major film ended in failure, as so many of his future projects were to. Having himself adapted Joseph Conrad's *Heart of Darkness* into a film script, and planning to make the protagonist's eye coincide with that of the camera, a procedure known as "the subjective camera," he was not able to finish it, probably because RKO felt that such new-fangled ideas would not please the public. He tried to use the stratagem again in *The Magnificent Ambersons*, but decided it did not work well there.[12]

The film that, after a number of other false starts, was to be his first, was not based on a literary text. Indeed, so much did people see its resemblance to contemporary reality, more precisely to the tabloid-stuff vicissitudes of media magnate William Randolph Hearst, that the movie, *Citizen Kane*, though since included in many a person's list of "hundred best films ever made," was controversial, to say the least, the more so as,

---

[9] *This is Orson Welles*, 331. The appendix to the paperback edition of the tapes of the Bogdanovich-Welles conversations contains a chronological survey of everything produced by Welles, and provides an excellent survey of the range of Welles' reading.
[10] C.M. Valentinetti, *Orson Welles* (Milan, 1993), 23.
[11] Cf. Laura Mulvey, *Citizen Kane* (London: BFI Publishing, 1992), 37.
[12] *This is Orson Welles*, 31, 504.

at the same time, Welles was publicly suspected of leftist sympathies and kept under surveillance by J. Edgar Hoover's FBI.[13]

For his second film, Welles turned to literature again. He had already transformed Booth Tarkington's novel into a successful radio drama,[14] in which, significantly   for those critics who hold to a Freudian interpretation of Welles' effort, he himself took the role of young George. Now he proposed to film it. However, having nearly finished it, he was – or pretended to be – called on to go to Brazil, to help make a series of government-sponsored films that would be part of the American war propaganda, among them *It's All True*.

After Welles had left, and contrary to what had been agreed between him and his collaborators, the latter decided to shoot an inordinate footage of new scenes, as well as redoing a number that had been finished already. Also, they reduced the film to half the projected total playing time. All this, apparently, was caused mainly by RKO's misgivings about the audience's negative appraisal of Welles' second cinematographic effort, which became apparent during the film's previews in the studio – though scrutiny of the answer slips shows that there were as many positive reactions as negative ones.[15] However, the personal vanities of the men involved in the production process played a part as well, as did the very problematic communications between Welles in Rio and the studio at Hollywood: it was not only that creative cutting by telephone simply was impossible; also, Welles' own tendency to self-destructive behavior, so marked in later years, manifested itself already in his haughty indifference to keeping reasonable appointments.[16]

However, a recent author, Robert L. Carringer, has explained what happened on the basis of his interpretation of the man Welles himself. In Carringer's reading, Welles' oedipal, Hamletian relationship with his mother as well as his ambivalence towards his father bothered him so much that he could not provide a satisfactory script dealing with such

---

[13] Welles, though gaining his reputation through *Citizen Kane*, has been denied the authorship of the script by some critics like Pauline Kael, who maintained that Henry Mankiewicz should be given all the credit, instead of sharing it with Welles. See Pauline Kael, "Raising Kane," in *The Citizen Kane Book*, with "The Shooting Script" by Herman J. Mankiewicz and Orson Welles (Boston: Little, Brown, 1971).

[14] It had been broadcast on October 29, 1939: *This is Orson Welles*, 354.

[15] These have been edited in *This is Orson Welles*, 116 ff.

[16] The sequence of events is outlined, with new documentary evidence, in *This is Orson Welles*, 115 ff, which is clearly pro-Welles. Cf. also: Thomson, *Rosebud*, 208-17, who rightly points out the possibility of another interpretation.

problems as presented in Tarkington's novel; this marred the entire
making of the film from the start, and, so Carringer says, proved its
undoing because it provided the persons involved in the film with the
pretexts for recutting it.[17] Though, as my reading of the novel
demonstrates, psychological elements should be properly considered, I
do not find all that many traces of such problems in the original script
and, therefore, cannot accept this psychological interpretation.[18] Nor do I
find that Welles' portrayal of young George is all that unsympathetic, as
if, as both Carringer and Bogdanovich suggest, he wanted to punish
himself for his own secret feelings. Rather I would argue that, by
choosing an actor like Tim Holt – who, if anything, looked a bit like him
though he lacked his tallness – Welles did identify in a rather more
positive way with the George-persona. Indeed, Welles told Bogdanovich
that George was the "tragic hero" of the film.[19]

Luckily, the original script has been preserved, as has a large amount
of the discarded footage. The text has been published, not once but
twice, albeit with diverging interpretations by the two scholars
concerned.[20] As far as the remaining footage permitted, the film itself
has been reproduced in its reconstructed original version. Thus, it is
possible to analyze the ways in which Welles followed the book and,
perhaps, find out if, to what extent and why he chose to depart from it.[21]

On March 28, 1942, the actor Joseph Cotton, who took the part of
Eugene Morgan in *Ambersons,* wrote a highly emotional letter to Orson
Welles, then filming in Rio de Janeiro, explaining what had gone on and
was going wrong both in the making and the finishing of the film. He
said:

---

[17] Carringer, 27-29.
[18] Cf. *Ibid.*, 21-23. It seems that Rosenbaum, who rejects the Hamletian interpretation in
his preface to the edition of Welles script, has not read Tarkington either, or he would at
least have seen that there was nothing "secret" – *pace* Carringer – about a Hamletian
source for the film.
[19] *This is Orson Welles*, 99.
[20] In *This is Orson Welles*, 456-90, Rosenbaum has edited Bogdanovich's
reconstruction of Welles' original script. The other reconstruction has been presented by
Carringer, 44-277.
[21] The two earlier essays devoted to this question were hardly based themselves on a
thorough reading of Tarkington's novel: Joy G. Boyum, *"The Magnificent Ambersons*:
Reversing the Bias," in *Double Exposure: Fiction into Film* (New York: Dutton/Plume,
1985), 230-42, and S. Wigod, "Three Faces of *The Magnificent Ambersons*," in
Transformations: From Literature to Film, ed. Douglas Radcliff-Umstead (Kent: Kent
State University Press, 1987), 84-90.

You have written doubtless the most faithful adaptation any book has ever had, and when I had finished reading it I had the same feeling I had when I read the book. When you read it, I had that same reaction only stronger. The picture on the screen seems to mean something else. It is filled with some deep though vague psychological significance that I think you never meant it to have .... The emotional impact in the script seems to have lost itself somewhere in the cold visual beauty before us and at the end there is definitely a feeling of dissatisfaction ... chiefly, I believe, because we have seen something that should have been no less than great. And it can be great, I'm sure of that.[22]

Cotton's letter is one of the many documentary pieces which make Jonathan Rosenbaum's edition of Welles' long conversations with Peter Bogdanovich – one of many film makers who clearly stated his debt to the genius of the maker of *Citizen Kane* – such a valuable source. Through these talks, we have been able to greatly increase our understanding of at least Welles' own – not always objective – views of his films and their history. The taped and published interviews include many bits of previously unknown interesting information about the making of *Ambersons*. Reading them, however, I was struck by the fact – possibly indicative of a film maker's professionally distorted view – that Bogdanovich never seems to realize that the characters in the film have their definite basis in a novel, always treating them as if they were Welles' rather than Tarkington's inventions; David Thomson, Welles' most recent biographer, shows the same tendency.[23] This is the more remarkable because Welles himself has reminded us that his father, who was something of an inventor himself and, moreover, dabbled in car construction like Eugene Morgan, knew Tarkington long before he wrote the novel; Welles even suggested there was a lot of his father in the character of Morgan.[24] Thus, when Bogdanovich states that "what Welles was saying in the lost original version of *The Magnificent Ambersons* about technology's destruction of the environment and the quality of life had become all too real," he seems totally oblivious that Welles owes this insight to Tarkington's text.[25] The same occurs when he states that the script of the film is one of the tightest ever written and

---

[22]   *This is Orson Welles*, 121-22.
[23]   Cf. Thomson, 201, 204, 206 for several examples.
[24]   Thomson, 199, in a rather strange way, implies that this may not be true, but does not actually say it is one of Welles' many life-aggrandizing fabrications.
[25]   *This is Orson Welles*, xxxi, 103.

that the prologue establishes all the characters in three or four situations – which, actually, it does not, but insofar as Welles was able to introduce his protagonists in a compact way, it was Tarkington who enabled him to do so.

Welles himself was as enthusiastic about the novel in the late 1960s, when these conversations were taped, as when he first read it in the 1930s. He praised its "grace" and ascribed the qualities of the film to the novel, adding that the parts he put in himself, for which Tarkington's text did not provide the basis, were "a careful imitation of his style." He even maintained that though a writer like Mark Twain produced some masterpieces, he wrote trash as well, whereas Tarkington's oeuvre was readable throughout, with the exception of his outdated children's stories. His film after the book, Welles said, would have been the best one he had made, better indeed than *Citizen Kane*, had it not been for the mutilations it had suffered.[26]

However this may be, Welles wrote the script, sometime in 1940/1941, all by himself – there is no doubt about it in this case, as there is with *Citizen Kane* – and then went on to rehearse it with the cast, a relatively small group whom he took through the text for as long as five weeks before any part of the movie was actually shot on the set. As for getting the feel of the period, he thought that, it being his parents' past-presence, he would not have had to study it, though in fact he did.[27] It resulted in beautiful, though very costly sets that in no mean way contribute to the film's impact.

From an analysis of the original script it becomes clear that Welles, at least in the movie's first part, besides presenting the development of the novel's characters, tried to translate Tarkington's verbal images into pictorial and, indeed, aural equivalents; what remains of the original music composed by old *Kane*-hand Bernard Herrmann – much of it was discarded in the revised edition as being too somber and replaced by more conventional violin throbbing – is memorable and entirely suited to the mood Welles sought to convey.[28] Thus, the opening scenes magnificently blend Tarkington's tale of the town's changing social and cultural life – shown in a sequence presenting the changing fashions in clothing and customs – with the unfolding of the Ambersons' and Morgans' personal drama in Chapter 2, using the text both for the film's

---

[26] *Ibid.*, 96, 149.
[27] *Ibid.*, 104.
[28] An analysis of the music is given by K. Kalinak, "The Text of Music: A Study of *The Magnificent Ambersons*," *Cinema Journal*, 27/4 (1988), 45-63.

off screen narrator – always Welles – and for the novelistic characters who start appearing shortly after.

Yet, there is a rather significant change when Welles has Eugene Morgan introduce himself to young George at the ball as follows: "George, you never saw me before in your life. But from now on you're going to see a lot of me." This strikes a threatening note that is absent in the text, and somewhat uncharacteristic of Eugene's character.[29] On the other hand, the novel's suggestion of George's uneasy awareness of his mother as a sexual being, so important to the oedipal interpreters of the movie, is lacking in the script, possibly because it is an interior monologue in the novel and thus rather difficult to render visually. Yet, some of the lines from Chapter 11 indicating that George's father had no qualms about the renewed acquaintanceship between his wife and her former friend, are included in the ball scene, as if to balance the psychological picture. Also, the role of the automobile as a metaphor for the change that the arrival of the Morgans brings and on which George is going to concentrate his hatred of Eugene, is referred to.

Chapters 7 and 8, in which George's rejection of Eugene is becoming more manifest, are aptly summarized in the next shots, while all the emotional essentials of Chapters 9 to 13 are compressed into the filmishly famous sleigh-ride scene – of George and Lucy – occurring in Chapter 7. If it had not been cut – as, incomprehensibly, it was – it would have given the audience some of the most important clues to the novel's meaning: the images of the gold-dusted, music-filled past of a small town are remembered by both Isabel and Eugene, riding by in their motor car, as being the essence of their youth, but they are slowly driven away by the smoke- and soot-covered present. Significantly, Welles has retained Lucy's saying that she, really, is always thinking about what will happen when she grows older, rather than about the past. Tarkington clearly presents her as the image of modern America, a strong dose of common sense mixed with emotion, and Welles follows this interpretation, thus, with Tarkington, adhering to the rather conventional American view of womanhood as the guardian of the nation. Another though different bow to conventionality is the kiss which Welles lets George give Lucy when their carriage overturns during the snow ride:[30] it is a strange choice, as there is not the faintest hint of it in Tarkington's text.

[29] Thomson's idea (200) that Eugene is the film's "romantic hero" strikes me as utterly unconvincing.
[30] It is indicated in the script: Carringer, 125.

Chapter 14, in which Wilbur Minafer dies, is summarized in a few shots showing the Amberson family plot-and-tomb, and the mourners at home. Because a small but essential insert has been eliminated in the revised version, the action then proceeds rather jumpily to Chapter 16, in which George has returned home after having graduated from college. He perceives the changes that even affect the once-magnificent Amberson grounds: the foundations for apartment houses which are now rising from them exemplify both a changed culture and the old Major's reduced circumstances. The audience's comprehension of the effects of change is enhanced as, unlike in the novel, in the movie the next scene is set in Eugene's car factory, which turns out "a car and a quarter a day." As in the novel, Isabel is seen and heard glorying in her friend's success.

From here on, as if to accentuate the inevitability of the changes, throughout the film the day and night scenes – skillfully chosen to give the movie a structure of visual alternation – are accompanied by images and sounds of automobiles, showing that Welles wanted to underline their growing presence in society.

The shots that depict the gist of Chapter 17 are important because they bring out the differences between the ideals held by George and those that have been instilled into Lucy by her father, and which George increasingly perceives as such: "I dare say I don't care any more for your father's ideals than he does for mine."

Unless it was part of a cut sequence of which no description remains,[31] the elegiac mood that I find characteristic and essential in Chapter 18 – "the evening life of the Midland city had begun" – , and which makes it into one of the novel's crucial chapters, is not captured in the shots that follow, though the text of the script retains a few important sentences: "Summer's dying. How quickly it goes, once it begins to die," Isabel says. Admittedly, it is disturbing – as Welles' followers have repeatedly argued – that the men who did the recutting of the movie chose to eliminate this entire scene; but at least the story-line still can be followed without them. It is Welles' decision not to somehow capture the atmosphere of this chapter that I find more difficult to understand.

Strangely, too, Welles himself seems to have introduced the short scene in which Eugene asks Isabel to tell her son of their love. It is one of the novel's strengths that it has no such scene; rather, in Chapter 20 Isabel tries to find out what it is in Eugene that irks George, resulting in

---

[31] In *This is Orson Welles*, 468, Bogdanovich/Rosenbaum note that a 6.5-minute-long series of shots was eliminated; but it does not occur in the reconstruction. See Carringer, 163.

his promise not to be uncivil anymore, but to avoid both contact and conflict.

On the other hand, Welles has chosen to incorporate the essence of Chapter 19 in his script as here the emotional and the larger societal views that are at the back of Tarkington's text are displayed in the dinner table conversation between George and Eugene on the future role of cars. It cleverly and dramatically continues into the scene in which Aunt Fanny discloses something of the town's talk about the relationship between Isabel and Eugene, which is the gist of Chapter 21. This is immediately followed by the scene in which George confronts Mrs. Johnson, the town's biggest gossip, to find out the truth of these rumors – the novel's twenty-second chapter – and proceeds to the conversation (in Chapter 23) between George and his uncle, which runs to the heights of hysteria, with George declaring that any marriage of his mother would be unspeakable, monstrous, horrible. The scenes containing these lines were later eliminated, partly with Welles' consent.[32] Whether or not they made the audience uncomfortable is unclear; but the very fact that they were included in Welles' original script suggests that he does not appear to have had any problems with the Hamletian and oedipal connotations that, I would argue, are present precisely in these lines.

Chapter 24 is rendered dramatically in the following scenes, which show George denying his mother's suitor access to their house, and thus to her.[33] The shots eliminated from this part of the film, though faithfully adhering to some of the lines of this Chapter's text, to my view do not constitute a significant loss.

It does not seem that the prophetic scene in Chapter 25 – in which George awaits his mother's reaction while standing under the big stained-glass window on the landing – was ever included in the script, although the windows do figure in some of the movie's shots. The letter sent by Eugene to Isabel, in which he explains to her the dilemma from which she has to extract herself, and the one sent by Isabel to George, in which she gives up her love for Eugene to retain George's love for her, are read by the senders, showing the recipients only to the accompaniment of appropriate music; though somewhat tampered with in the revised version, the original novel's feeling is not entirely absent.

---

[32] In *This is Orson Welles*, 471, the Bogdanovich/Rosenbaum synopsis of the cuttings is inaccurate. Compare the reconstruction of the script in Carringer, 189, 190.

[33] Carringer,197, wrongly interprets the script's reference to one Aggie bringing George something to eat: a precise reading of the novel indicates that the Aggie/Maggie referred to is not Agnes/Aggie Moorehead, who plays Fanny, but just a maid called in by Isabel.

The subsequent Chapter 26 is faithfully rendered, too, except for the choice that George puts before his mother which was not included in Welles' script, though it is dramatically very apposite: "Do you think if you did what he wants you to do I could bear to stay another day in this town, mother? Do you think I could ever bear even to see you again if you married him? I'd want to, but you surely know I just – couldn't!" (247-48).

The original version of the scene in which Isabel writes to George, and George's answer to it, has been eliminated in the revised version, and replaced by a totally inept one combining the two moments without even a single reference to the original text.[34]

The next scene – in which George, saying goodbye to Lucy, slowly comes to realize that he, too, is losing something essential in having asked his mother to renounce Eugene, while Lucy, who seemingly makes light of it, faints in a drugstore after George has left – continues the story much as does the novel's twenty-seventh chapter, though part of the short dialogue seems to stress Lucy's unfeelingness beyond what Tarkington writes and implies.

Not surprisingly, the changes taking place in the protagonists' emotions as well as in the town – the loss of love, the loss of innocence and beauty – that are vital to Chapter 28, are absent from Welles' script, as they are largely descriptive in Tarkington's text. Yet, some visualization might have helped to tie the emotional story to its larger background, without, I think, sounding a lecturing note that would have patronized the audience, which Welles said he always was afraid of doing when making a movie.[35] It is rather strange to find that in Welles' own ideas for a revised version, at least some of Tarkington's text and of the appropriate visualization would have been included after all; it shows that, in a way, even at this stage (which, if reactions had been otherwise, would never have been reached) Welles had not yet fully digested his own ideas about the script and its relationship to the novel.[36]

The next scene, discarded in the revised version, shows Aunt Fanny and the old Major musing about their dwindling fortunes and the ways to recoup them through investing in the new industries; as in the novel, it points towards the inevitability of change, of the need to adapt to a new world. The elimination of that part of the conversation which turns to the role of cars in the process is deplorable, because it refers to the novel's

---

[34]   Cf. Carringer, 207-12.
[35]   *This is Orson Welles*, 98.
[36]   Cf. Welles' notes for the revisions as published in Carringer, 295.

central theme, which Welles wanted to stress.[37] So does the following scene, based on the very significant passage in the novel describing the visit Uncle George – Jack in the film, probably to avoid confusion in the audience – pays to the new Morgan Mansion. Aptly taking a few lines from the dialogue – "I wonder, Lucy, if history's going forever repeating itself" – Welles managed to retain Tarkington's unwritten conclusion and moral: new money builds new houses, away from the ever-spreading soot of the town, but, in the end, it will be superseded by the money of yet other people who will have to venture out even farther to find sootless fresh air, and, by implication, innocence. The cutters who produced the revised version showed their lack of understanding of the script by changing the few lines of this text into an entirely senseless exchange of words.[38]

Inevitably, the rather moving parts of the dialogue between George and his dying mother that make Chapter 29 a memorable and even terrifying one, are part of Welles' script. It also contains the lines in which George tells his Aunt Fanny he definitely does not want Eugene admitted to the sickroom. In the revision, part of the scene was cut, this time, I would say, without major loss to the sequence of the action. But significantly, the revised version tries to make the entire Amberson family responsible for this decision, instead of only George, as if to make him a less unsympathetic character.[39]

Welles' version of Chapter 30 inexplicably leaves out George's growing awareness of the awful thing he has done. Instead of the long and very convincing dialogue with his aunt that we find in the novel, the script summarizes a lot of descriptive material about the Ambersons' financial downfall and the old Major's death. Part of this was eliminated in the revised version, which must have left the audience with a rather strange feeling, as it makes the next scene, in which George and his uncle part, after they have been left virtually penniless, almost incomprehensible.

It is at this point in the movie – the famous or infamous reel 14 – that the biggest changes occurred, both in Welles' treatment of Tarkington's text, and in the way his cutters dealt with the material he had shot.

Welles wanted to show George "walking homeward slowly through what seemed to be the strange streets of a strange city ... for the town

---

[37] Cf. the revised scene in: *This is Orson Welles*, 478.
[38] Cf. the passages in the two versions of the script in Carringer, 221. Also the description of the new scene in: *This is Orson Welles*, 467-77.
[39] Cf. the sequences as presented in Carringer, 223-34.

was growing ...," while his own voice provided the narration.[40] Visually, this was to have been a very impressive sequence, but part of it was eliminated by his collaborators. Then comes the scene of George's last night in the old Amberson Mansion, during which he asks his mother, and God, to forgive him, and which ends with the narrator telling the audience that, finally, George Amberson Minafer had got his come-uppance, lines actually taken from Chapter 33.

Chapter 32, which renders George's decision to agree to his aunt Fanny's scheme that they set up house together, and for himself to find a well-paid job, is faithfully reproduced in the script, but the real reason for George's decision – "I might be a little decent to somebody else, perhaps" (cf. 315-16) – is not used. Instead, to the long conversation between Lucy and her father, in which she tells of her feelings for George and of her inability to marry him because of his overbearing attitude, Welles added a line that is not in the book: in the script Eugene expresses the hope that Lucy will "forget", whereas in the novel Lucy herself implies that she does not want to remember. This may seem a small nuance only, but it considerably alters the perspective and apparently was inserted to prepare for Welles' sentimental version of the movie's end.

This is followed by the scene showing George's accident, to which Welles visually added material totally absent from the novel both in actual content and in spirit: two cuttings from newspaper articles accusing the automobile of taking too many lives. The added material tells us more about Welles' view of the reality of the 1940s, than about the world of the early twentieth century as Tarkington wrote and thought about it. There is one rather enigmatic remark Welles made when talking to Bogdanovich: "What was all my own was a third act which took the story into a darker, harder dimension."[41] As there are no "acts" in the film, it is difficult to guess what Welles really meant, but he might have been referring to this one scene. But then again, the remainder of Welles's treatment of the third "act" – if indeed he meant the movie's end – is precisely rather less somber than Tarkington's text.

The following scenes, which should have captured the spirit of the novel's final pages, are strangely conceived, for, unlike the reader of the novel, the viewer of the film does not see George anymore. Eugene's visit to a New York medium through which he hopes to get into contact

---

[40]   The scene is in the reconstructed script: see Carringer, 242 ff.
[41]   *This is Orson Welles*, 96.

with his lost love, Isabel, and which results in her admonition that he should be "kind" (and go and visit her son in hospital), never even occurs in Welles' script. Instead, we see Eugene visiting Aunt Fanny in her genteel boarding house, and telling her of his visit to George in the hospital. Eugene, in Welles' words, describes what happened. In the script, we learn that George had said:

> You must have known my mother wanted you to come here today so that I could ask you to forgive me.

The novel, however, has it differently:

> You must have thought my mother wanted you to come, so that I could ask you to – to forgive me. (351)

Moreover, Eugene admits that it seemed to him "as if someone else was there" in that hospital room. Thus, in the end, Welles does introduce the supernatural after all, not once but twice, albeit in a way totally contrary to the novel's meaning.

Welles' setting this scene in the boarding house could be explained from his wish to create a situation which could show the emotional tensions that bound Fanny to Eugene whom, after all, she had loved from the start. Yet, in doing so at this point, he really messed up the structure of a script that had shown many strengths, precisely by creatively condensing – and then visually rendering and indeed magnifying – the essence of a long but powerful novel. If Welles thought he was faithfully following Tarkington's style and intentions, here he clearly was mistaken.[42]

Indeed, I cannot agree with Carringer that it was "wise" for Welles to dispense with the medium – and, moreover, with the hospital scene in its original form – as, admittedly, he had done already in the radio version.[43] Perhaps he thought listeners and viewers of the 1940s might think this reference to the supernatural less than credible even if it was entirely part of the cultural make-up of the period described by the novel and, indeed, of Tarkington's own times.

---

[42] *Ibid.*, 98.
[43] Carringer, 25, in his introduction to the reconstruction of the script. Rather gratuitously he adds that the use of the medium is "not one of Tarkington's finer displays of creative imagination"; such remarks show he knows little about the times the novel was set in.

Carringer's interpretation of Welles' decision serves his idea that Welles was unhappy with the character of George for the deeper psychological reasons mentioned above, and hence in the film not only vilified him but in the end did away with him altogether.[44] This, I would argue, is highly debatable, if only because it does not fit in with the final happiness that George is supposed to find, which, if anything, was invented by Welles himself. For that, indeed, is the most blatant alteration he made in Tarkington's open-ended text, and another, even stranger bow to Hollywood's increasing tendency to insist on happy endings.[45] It occurs in the very same scene at the boarding house when, during his conversation with Fanny, Eugene admits that, like her, he thinks Lucy and George will marry after all. RKO's revised version, while being cloyingly sentimental in its own way, at least avoids this pitfall and ends with Tarkington's far more memorable original text, in which Eugene realizes that in forgiving George he has been true to his true love, Isabel.

Moreover, confronted with the studio's wish to alter this scene, on April 2, 1942, Welles came up with a revised version of his own that departs even more drastically from the novel, and would have created a happy end that, surely, could not have satisfied anyone but the staunchest champions of such endings.[46] Finally, in the 1960s, Welles considered reshooting the end all by himself; alas, he has not told anyone what kind of ending that would have been.[47]

As a novel, *The Magnificent Ambersons* may still be read for its well-crafted style and its careful, sensitive yet balanced analysis of the ways in which modern culture, symbolized by the car, changed American society. The emotional dimension of the plot – centering around George's decision about his mother's relation with Eugene and, therefore, about his own future with Lucy – may fail to completely convince a present-day reader unless one takes into account its function as counterpoint to the larger theme, and reads it as a metaphor for the process in which youth (with its ideals of stability and its cruelties in the judgment of others) gives way to adulthood (with its acceptance of

---

[44] Carringer, 25-26.
[45] Thomson writes that Welles "added a lengthy final sequence that is not in Tarkington's novel" (201). Actually Welles discarded Tarkington's end and replaced it with his own.
[46] *This is Orson Welles*, 123.
[47] *Ibid.*, 114.

change and the awareness that one must, perhaps, not judge precisely so harshly).

The film Welles made, while adhering to the book's essentials, as he said himself, mainly tried to dramatize the second, more personal element. Yet, given his otherwise faithful rendering of that part of the text, it is precisely here that Welles departs from the original in a number of sometimes strange ways, as we have seen above. Indeed, the process of George's growth is stressed rather less than in the novel, which to me seems a pity; the same holds for Welles' choice of the film's end, which I find far from satisfactory. In this connection it must be remarked that nobody seems to have noticed that Welles, when trying to save his own version of the film, in his many suggestions for alterations and even entirely new shots and scenes, stayed considerably closer to the book than was the case in his original script. Indeed, if his ideas in the Spring of 1942 had been realized, his own revised version would have been considerably more faithful to Tarkington's work than either his own film or the one finally released.

Seeking to introduce the primary theme – the changes occurring in the microcosm of American society that is the town in which occur the Ambersons' rise and decline, but surely not their fall, if my interpretation is correct – Welles effectively used the aural and visual possibilities of a film, as well as selectively presenting this theme through the emotions involved in the dialogue. This aspect of the film is realized without cinematographic preaching and thus communicates that part of Tarkington's message rather well. Welles shows himself mildly critical of the dying plutocracy represented by the Ambersons while, at the same time, displaying feelings of nostalgia for the age of innocence they lived in. This innocence, in a way, haunted *Citizen Kane* as well. Yet it must not be understood as Welles' personal interpretation of Tarkington's text because it is precisely the rather elegiac mood that gives the novel its charm and, indeed, meaning. Welles, in using as a vehicle the eloquence with which the novelist verbally conveyed his nostalgia, created a series of images that, in their eloquence, can still convince a public.

In this connection we must consider a remark made by Welles to Peter Bogdanovich; he then "remembered" that *The Magnificent Ambersons* was about grace and gallantry, or at least about the idea of such virtues that, while out of date and irrelevant, still had a definite appeal to him in the early 1940s.[48] Yet one may wonder if here, as is so

---

[48]   *Ibid*, 96.

often the case in recollections, Welles really remembered what led him to adapt the book in the first place; the movie as envisaged by him, and as finally made, does not seem to stress these values, precisely, I would argue, because they are not central to the novel. Yet, in another of his conversations with Bogdanovich, Welles indicated that the entire film really was about the automobile wrecking a golden world.[49] While this may be true of the first part of Welles' original script, its second part certainly does not bear out this interpretation. In short, we must be wary of Welles' own memories in judging his work.

Finally, I would like to return to a remark made by Bogdanovich to Welles, namely that he did not see the film's "social points" until the fourth or fifth time he watched it. This seems to indicate that Bogdanovich had not read the novel before seeing the film, which I think not at all unlikely, as in his conversations with Welles he appears to have no idea that the setting for the long sequence depicting the ball is the Amberson Mansion's top floor, a point very explicitly made by Tarkington's description: that third floor ballroom precisely was what made the mansion the city's landmark.[50] Admittedly, I find such a lack of informedness – which we also find in Thomson's recent biography of Welles – highly strange in those who seek to understand the nature and effect of Welles' filmic adaptation of novels.

But does Bogdanovich's comment also mean that if one has not read the novel, the social commentary is, indeed, all too cleverly hidden in the film? If that were true, and assuming that not many viewers will take the trouble of watching *The Magnificent Ambersons* all that many times, one should have to conclude that Welles failed to live up to his own ambition to make a film that precisely could convey this social aspect, in analyzing the elements that converted an Eden into a modern society. I find it difficult to judge Bogdanovich's remark as I, for one, had read the novel before seeing the film. Yet I think that for all his qualities he was, perhaps, not the film's best viewer. Even nowadays, an audience watching *The Magnificent Ambersons* will be struck by the beauty of the film's composition and of its individual shots. Insofar as Welles used his medium to enhance the essence of the novel by a visually conceived tale of the characters' development, an audience will understand at least some of the important points which Booth Tarkington tried to make, even if it may never have read the original text. However, if only

---

[49] *Ibid.*, 114.
[50] *Ibid.*, 113.

because Welles' version of the changes in American culture was decidedly more somber than Tarkington's – as Joseph Cotton and other early viewers have rightly seen – we would be well-advised to return to the novel.

STEPPING THROUGH A LOOKING-GLASS:
THE WORLDS OF JULIA PETERKIN (1880-1961)

GONNY VAN BEEK-VAN OVERBEEK

While the Harlem Renaissance was gathering momentum in NewYork and other Northern cities in the early 1920s, in Fort Motte, South Carolina, a white Southern woman named Julia Mood Peterkin was thinking of ways to increase the family income. As mistress of Lang Syne, she was living with her husband and son on a plantation which still housed many descendants of the former Gullah slave population. She was, therefore, in an excellent position to observe the daily lives of her closest neighbors, who were all black. Considering the growing interest in African Americans and especially in the more colorful aspects of their daily lives Peterkin must have thought that she could tell their particular stories as well as, or even better than, any black person. That she was justified to think so became apparent upon the publication of her short stories and novels, when even prominent black leaders complimented her on depicting the black farming people with such reality and sympathy. One newspaper critic even complained that he was unable to decide on the merits of her novel *Green Thursday* (1924) because he did not know her "racial identity."[1] By contrast, the dramatic stories she told were considered by others to border on the sordid and were thought to be at the very least wildly exaggerated.

All in all Julia Mood Peterkin presents a fascinating picture: a beautiful, even flamboyant white woman, the mistress of an old plantation in the South, and the author of gruesome stories about black plantation life in which hardly any whites play a part, who could boast a personal history that would make an interesting novel in itself. In her excellent biography of this fascinating person, Susan Millar Williams clearly describes the different worlds Julia Peterkin managed to combine so well: her life as the mistress of Lang Syne, as the mother of Bill, the wife of William, and a prominent figure in South Carolina

---

[1] Susan Millar Williams, *A Devil and a Good Woman, Too: The Lives of Julia Peterkin* (Athens: University of Georgia Press, 1997), 82.

society. Her longtime affair with Irving Fineman is described candidly and given its proper place, while her relationship with D.L. Chambers, her liaison at her publishing firm Bobbs-Merrill, gets proper attention. Because of her close contacts with the Peterkin family Williams had access to much intimate information and could present an excellent and nearly exhaustive overall view. Yet Peterkin's correspondence with her editor D.L. Chambers and her lover Irving Fineman reveals that important nuances need to be made.

In particular if we take a closer look at the things Peterkin did, the decisions she took, it may become clear that she did not live different lives so much as create different worlds for herself. All of her life she struggled to get what she wanted most of all: attention, first from her grandfather who raised her after her mother's death, then from her father who upon his remarriage developed other interests. In particular once her husband had forfeited her faith in him by having her sterilized without her consent (about which more later), she tried to create her own world, one inhabited solely by black people living on the plantation. At the time there were about four hundred black people and five white people living there in what she described as "splendid isolation." When she started writing about the harsh world that also was or rather had been Lang Syne, she managed to upset a great many people, white as well as black, but never once did she seriously consider leaving the life she was used to for another one full of uncertainties, even after she became a well-known author and could have afforded to be independent. Although she had a long-time affair with Irving Fineman and could have lived with him, she stuck to her life in South Carolina. Her "world" might temporarily focus on different persons and provide a different perspective, but her "life" consisted of her family, the plantation and South Carolina. Without her proper place in these three orbs she would have been lost. I believe it is necessary to emphasize how much she was master of her own life and decided for various reasons, not the least important those pertaining to economic and social stability, that her life was in South Carolina, as mistress of Lang Syne and as a member of the Peterkin family. Still, this did not prevent her from creating her own worlds, imaginary and real, which sometimes took her out of South Carolina for longer periods at a time.

In an interview with the *New York World* of July 10, 1927, Peterkin announced: "I've only just begun writing. It's a new thing. My life has sort of crystallized into a certain mould and my writing is an incident in a pretty full life."[2] This "pretty full life" took place on Lang Syne plantation near Fort Motte, South Carolina, where Peterkin was mistress over five white people and several hundred black plantation workers. She had to take care of all their needs, listen to their problems and intervene in conflicts. Moreover, she frequently had an abundance of guests, some of whom stayed for a considerable length of time, as, for example, did Belle, a niece of Peterkin's husband, who just came riding up one day and announced that she had come to stay. As hospitality has always been an integral part of Southern living no one expressed surprise about this. Southern ways also encompassed strict rules of behavior, especially for white women of the higher classes who were regarded as embellishing fixtures for their husbands. This implied that they should never attract undue attention. To be mentioned by name in any newspaper, except at birth, marriage and death, was, as Peterkin's grandmother repeatedly told her, simply not done. After her marriage into the Peterkin family, Julia fitted in very nicely and willingly. But the trauma caused by the birth of her son William would induce her to start trying to escape from this old-fashioned restrictive plantation world.

William's birth had been heavy and prolonged. Peterkin took a very long time to recover both from the delivery and from a severe depression. The latter had also been brought on because her father, who was an M.D., and her husband had decided that she could never face such an ordeal again and had sterilized her without her consent, even without her knowing about it. Although Peterkin started recreating the history of her own life almost as soon as she started writing seriously, this is a part she withheld, except to those emotionally closest to her. The episode bred an anger in her that she could hardly face herself and which found its way indirectly into her novels, where she could hide behind the mask of black characters. In this way she managed to take some sort of revenge, as she knew that her family hated her writing almost exclusively about black people. Her novel *Scarlet Sister Mary* (1928) was shocking enough to them without the knowledge that she had voiced her own anger in it. In the family's opinion there were enough other interesting, even romantic aspects in her life which she could use in her stories as well as in her

---

2   Bobbs-Merrill papers, Lilly Library, Indiana University, Bloomington.

autobiography: there was no need to refer so blatantly to the sexual, and to them sordid, aspects of black plantation life.

Peterkin seems to have felt that she needed to embellish every aspect of her life. Thus she tells how she lost her mother when she was only three months old owing to complications following her birth, while actually her mother had died months later as the result of tuberculosis. Peterkin was then sent to live with her paternal grandparents and at the age of fourteen she was sent to Columbia College (Columbia, S.C.) together with her elder sister. One of her earliest remaining notes refers to the eve of her departure. In the note she describes how she is sitting and looking at a small picture of her mother, thinking over her life as it has been and what she would like it to be in the future. And she decides that her life will not be like that of the rest of the family: getting married and having babies, but that she "would live her own life. She would keep herself footloose – make her own pattern."[3]

Peterkin would use the theme of the poor motherless baby repeatedly in her short stories as well as in her novels. In *Green Thursday* Missie is the poor motherless child who has been sent to Kildee and Rose Pinesett to help with the children. She gains the love of Kildee, her substitute father, but his love goes beyond that of a father-daughter relationship. In *Black April* (1927) Breeze is sent off by his mother to live near his natural father April and so becomes a spectator of his father's downfall. In *Scarlet Sister Mary* it is Mary who is the poor motherless child who, to spite men, gives birth to numerous "fatherless" babies, implying that children could easily do without a father if they did have the love of a mother, a hint Peterkin's father could not have missed.

After her long illness (she refused to leave her bed for two years), Peterkin was nursed back to health by Lavinia Berry, a Gullah woman, who introduced her to the folklore and beliefs of the people living on the plantation. During her period of recovery Julia had become deeply impressed by the black people, who just like any white person could put on a mask to hide their true feelings, but were willing to drop it whenever emotions ran high, and who had the stamina to overcome burdens where white people bottled up and just lay down. She started making notes about the people and the events that took

---

[3]   File 28-613-3, Julia Peterkin papers, South Carolina Historical Society, Charleston, South Carolina.

place on the plantation and jotted down some of the remarks and sayings the black people made, trying to transcribe the dialect they used.

When her son went off to boarding school and she was looking about for a hobby to fill up the void his absence had created, at first she decided to go back to playing the piano. Before she had married William Peterkin she had been rather good at it and had even entertained ideas of becoming a concert pianist. She now sought to take lessons from Henry Bellamann, the Dean of the School of Fine Arts at Chicora College in Columbia. When during her first lesson it turned out she was far less accomplished than she had imagined, she started telling her instructor about her world at Lang Syne to distract him. Bellamann encouraged her to write down the stories she had told him. Later, in Peterkin's version, he brought Carl Sandburg over and insisted that she show him the stories. Sandburg suggested that she sent them to a publisher, and when Peterkin objected that he was only being polite, he mentioned H.L. Mencken as the severest critic in the country. She sent off her stories and Mencken recommended some of them to Alfred A. Knopf for publication. The actual story, it turns out, is more prosaic. After the first enthusiasm of Henry Bellamann she took a writing-course and at the same time sent an invitation to Carl Sandburg to visit the plantation, hoping he would write about the inhabitants. When he did not respond immediately she wrote him a note saying that nothing but "sudden death" would prevent a gentleman from accepting an invitation.

For all Peterkin's tendency to dramatize, the way she introduced her readers to her world at Lang Syne in the opening lines of *Green Thursday* cannot be easily improved on:[4]

> An old plantation with smooth-planted fields and rich woodlands and pastures, where little shaded streams run, lies right at the edge of a low wide swamp. Steep red hills, rising sheer above the slimy mud, lift it out of the reach of two yellow-brown rivers that sprawl drowsily along before they come together to form one stream. The rivers are hidden by huge trees garlanded with tangled vines, and the swamp seems a soft, undulating, colourful surface that fades into a low line of faint blue hills far away on the other side.[4]

---

[4]   Julia Peterkin, *The Collected Short Stories of Julia Peterkin,* edited with an Introduction by Frank Durham (Columbia, South Carolina: University of South Carolina Press, 1970), 143.

This was the setting of Peterkin's literary world which she peopled with persons intimately known and dear to her. To describe it she only had to look outside and walk in the immediate surroundings of her home. Yet even at the time the world she painted in her short stories and novels was rapidly vanishing. More and more of the plantation Negroes were moving to the big cities in search of a better, richer life. And Lang Syne itself would be drastically changed in appearance during her lifetime. A highway was to be built right in front of the plantation house and where once all that could be heard had been the sounds of animals and people living there, after the construction of the highway the noise of cars and of curious sightseers became much louder than the laughter of the Negroes.

The characters in Peterkin's fictional world strongly resembled some of the people actually living at Lang Syne. Thus, the foreman who plays a role in many of her short stories and who is the main character in her novel *Black April* was the actual foreman of the plantation, Frank Hart. The story of the loss of his toes was one of the first she told to Henry Bellamann. As Peterkin later said in an interview, they lived ten miles from everywhere: from a school, a church and a doctor. So when the foreman complained that he had no feelings in his toes, Peterkin was called upon to administer sympathy and if possible some sort of medication. She told him to bathe his feet in a tub of warm water and poured some disinfectant into the water. When she looked down a little later, to her great horror she saw his toes floating on top. The only way to save his life was to amputate his legs. As it turned out this could not stop the gangrene and Hart died anyway. Peterkin, though, immortalized him in the closing lines of *Black April*: "Bury me in a man-size box – You un'erstan'? – A man – size – box – I – been – six – feet—fo'—Uncle – Six feet—fo'!"[5]

Many of Peterkin's earlier stories dealt with the sometimes gruesome consequences of living in this "splendid isolation." Thus, there is the story of the baby that is born without a mouth and has to be cut a mouth by one of the old women living on the plantation, as it would certainly die otherwise. Another story tells of a baby that loses one of its eyes because a curious and hungry cock pecks at it when there is no one around to look after the baby. One of the most perfect short stories in Peterkin's oeuvre, "Over The River," tells of a deaf

---

[5]   Julia Peterkin, *Black April* (Indianapolis: Bobbs-Merrill, 1927), 316.

girl who is expecting a baby and walks miles to the main land to find the father of her child. When she encounters him in a group of fellow-laborers he pretends he does not know her. Overcome with grief at his denial she starves her baby to death pretending not to hear it cry for hunger, buries it, and walks all the way back to her village.

By far the majority of her stories are concerned only with black people. Whenever she tried to include white people in her stories they did not come near the standard of her "black" stories. In her short stories that contain a white character – like "The Merry-Go-Round" and the opening story in *Green Thursday*, "Ashes" – she cannot make the white characters come alive. While in "Ashes" old Maum Hannah, the black main character, is a person that you can picture to yourself, with her natural goodness, her simplicity, her anxiety about being displaced, and the trick she uses to save her own house, the white persons, such as the sheriff and the owners of the land, are flat and uninteresting rascals or do-gooders. In the unpublished novel in which she had intended to describe her own life, "On a Plantation," she could not make any of the characters come to life either. The novel, not surprisingly, was rejected by Knopf. Though Peterkin rewrote it and then subjected it to Mencken's scrutiny, he, too, advised her to forget about it and stick to her black plantation stories. This she did. She took out all the white characters, focused on the black ones, and turned a failure into a great success: *Black April.*

The original story described Helen West, a plantation mistress like herself. Her husband is up north most of the time. He is an unfeeling selfish person anyway, who is of no comfort to his wife. Their son is away at school. That leaves Helen the company of the plantation Negroes whose stories she puts down on paper. The whole story is a thinly disguised description of how Peterkin saw her life at that time. The narrator, an unnamed cousin, makes a pass at Helen and begs her to come away with him. She does not believe in divorce but is willing to commit a mortal sin for him. Just as Peterkin played with Irving Fineman, her lover, in real life, so in the novel Helen plays with her cousin, attracting him and then keeping him at a distance, using all the female wiles she is capable of. Peterkin decided to turn the story into a mystery script but when she sent this to Knopf it was turned down again, which gave her a legitimate excuse to change publishers. Several years later she managed to get most of her feelings about life and men into another black novel, *Scarlet Sister Mary.*

When Julia Peterkin's *Scarlet Sister Mary* was awarded the Pulitzer Prize in 1929 this came as a surprise to both author and publisher. Although the book had been nominated, inside information had been conveyed that the novel did not stand a chance, especially since it did not conform to the requirement that the prize-winning novel had to represent "the wholesome atmosphere of American life, and the highest standard of American manners and manhood." In a letter to D.L. Chambers, her editor at Bobbs-Merrill, Peterkin wrote that she was not surprised by this state of affairs: "Some years ago when I had not yet written a book, Mr. Burton [one of the judges awarding the prize] was my guest, and something occurred which made him seem ridiculous. I was not to blame but he has always felt I was."[6] But when Mr. Burton prematurely sang the praises of one of the other nominated novels, John Oliver's *Victim and Victor*, the jury felt obliged to reconsider. As Peterkin's first novel, *Green Thursday*, had not even been listed, the award for *Scarlet Sister Mary* was a great surprise, indeed.

Two years earlier Peterkin had taken the drastic step, unusual for a beginning author, of leaving her publisher Alfred A. Knopf for Bobbs-Merrill, a much less renowned firm. Knopf had not satisfied her need for publicity and circulation, and she blamed Knopf for the meager sales of *Green Thursday*. The contacts between Knopf and Peterkin had always been formal and utterly business-like. The firm gave her the impression that she should be grateful for the publication of her book by such a distinguished house. By contract Knopf had reserved the rights for her next two novels but when they refused her autobiographical novel "On a Plantation," she let herself be persuaded to join Bobbs-Merrill, much to the chagrin of H.L. Mencken, who had introduced her to Knopf in the first place. For a long time, as punishment for her unpardonable behavior, he would thwart her in every possible way. His wrath was so great that when he was asked to write a recommendation for Peterkin to be admitted to MacDowell's writing colony, he wrote back: "Unluckily, I cannot decipher Mrs MacDowell's letter,"[7] to avoid having to cooperate. Of course, Julia Peterkin was hurt.

---

[6]   Julia Peterkin to D.L. Chambers, March 30,1929, Bobbs-Merrill papers.
[7]   Undated letter to D.L. Chambers [before April 1, 1927] in which Julia Peterkin quotes from a letter Mrs. MacDowell wrote her about a recommendation for the MacDowell writers' colony, Bobbs-Merrill papers.

After the rather niggardly treatment by Alfred A. Knopf, the attention and warm appreciation of her new publishers came as a pleasant surprise to Peterkin. Often several letters a day passed between Indiana and South Carolina expressing a warm interest in the life and people on Lang Syne plantation from the side of D.L. Chambers. He would urge her in the most gentle terms to write another novel. Though from the very beginning Peterkin cautioned him not to expect too much from her, the support and enthusiasm she received at Bobbs-Merrill was truly bracing to her.

Whereas Knopf, as we saw, had been business-like and convinced of their own superiority, Bobbs-Merrill, represented by D.L. Chambers and Anne Johnson, were genuinely interested in her and the people she wrote about. All along she had been convinced that Knopf did not do enough to push her book. They had indicated that advertising would be a foolish waste of money and that her stories would be hard to sell. Although Peterkin pretended not to have any business sense and certainly not to understand anything of the publishing business, she kept a close eye on where her books were advertised, aware as she was of the economic consequences this might have.

After the publication of *Black April* in February 1927, review copies were sent out to all those who might be interested and willing to give favorable reviews. Many obliged, as did Robert Nathan, Henry Bellamann, Herschel Brickel, Lawrence Stallings, Walter White, and Morris Markey, to name a few. Most admitted to being skeptical at first: "I confess I approached it with the worst fore-bodings for I am heartily sick of the pseudo-negro literary fare which has been offered me up to date."[8] But very often praise followed: "it is the first real picture that I have seen of Negro life."[9] Keith Preston even wrote in the *Chicago Daily News* of March 24, 1927: "With such a book as *Black April* the south comes into its own in American literature."[10] Some remained deafeningly silent, as did H.L. Mencken, and as did *The State*, South Carolina's leading newspaper. Some requests for copies were surprising, as when The Pullman Porter Association asked for one. Sometimes the attention the book commanded took an awkward form, as when it was banned in Boston, Massachusetts. Members of the Boston Banned Book Club avoided this by simply

---

[8]   Ida A.R. Wylie to Mr. Coward, March 9, 1927, Bobbs-Merrill papers.

[9]   Howard W. Odum to D.L. Chambers, March 8, 1927, Bobbs-Merrill papers.

[10] Susan Millar Williams, *A Devil and a Good Woman, Too,* 113.

taking a list of all the banned books into a bookshop and ordering them all. Converse College, her Alma-Mater, even conferred the honor "Doctor of Letters" on her.

Still Peterkin was anxious that her works might not reach a wide enough audience. She suggested that Bobbs-Merrill include *The American Mercury, The New Masses, The New Republic* and *The Nation* in their publicity campaign instead of *The Daily New York World* only. Some of these she considered to be sophisticated and radical and to cater to a public that would be more willing to take notice of her books than the conservative ladies in South Carolina. D.L. Chambers replied that they were, of course, willing to work on the magazine advertising as she had suggested, even though he thought that the audience at which these magazines aimed had already been reached: "it is certainly worth trying, and all the more so because you feel that way about it."[11] Whether or not enough advertising was being done, by April 20, 1927 *Black April* was on the Bowker list of the twenty-five best selling novels throughout the country.

As Julia Peterkin did not always date her letters they have often had to be dated in relation to the answering letters. It is therefore not always certain when she wrote her letters, but during 1927 and 1928 letters between Fort Motte and Indianapolis were often sent several times a week. In October 1927 Peterkin announced that life was treating her hard, but that she had planned the "core" of a new novel. In the same month the book got a working title – "Scarlet Mary" – and she wrote that doing it was a hard job. D.L. Chambers answered: "If it's a hard job, so much the better – leave the easy little ones to writers of smaller caliber. You shall carve marble while they fiddle around with clay." And he continued:

> I do not wish to urge you on too swiftly. I know very well that you must write when and as you can; still I have hoped and shall continue desperately to hope that we may have the manuscript before long – in time to publish in the spring, when people are still thinking and talking of *Black April*. Then one book will sell the other.[12]

Throughout November 1927 letters were regularly sent encouraging Peterkin to keep on writing, urging her to finish the book

---

[11]   D.L. Chambers to Julia Peterkin, September 14, 1927, Bobbs-Merrill papers.
[12]   *Ibid.*, October 31, 1927, Bobbs-Merrill papers.

in time for the spring list. At the end of November Peterkin answered
to their supplications:

> You must not think about *Scarlet Sister Mary* for a *long* time. It is to
> be my last piece of writing and since I'm doing it for my own
> satisfaction I want to take my own time, write on it when I like and
> leave it alone when I like.[13]

Hastily D.L. Chambers retreated:

> Of course you must and shall do just as you like with Scarlet Sister
> Mary, and while we wait for her we shall try to content ourselves with
> her brother, *Black April*. I didn't mean to try to hustle you – never
> that. But I don't want you to forget how eagerly and hopefully we all
> look to you for the books that can come from no one else. You chill
> my blood when you speak of anything being your "last piece of
> writing."[14]

Having taken her stance Peterkin was prepared to be gracious and she
wrote back: "You are right to prod me about my Mary, for I am
indolent about writing. There is so much else to do, see, hear."[15] Once
again she applied her talents to attract men and keep them at her heel.
And Chambers was only too willing to play along and assure her that
Bobbs-Merrill was perfectly happy in their relationship with her. If
only she would finish her novel for them.

Shortly before February 11, 1928 Peterkin wrote to Anne Johnson:
"Have been working on my Scarlet Mary, but she develops slowly.
She must be right for she is *positively* my last. Writing wearies me to
death."[16] But finally towards April 1928 she let it filter through that
Scarlet Sister Mary might be ready for the fall list. Of course she
almost immediately withdrew her tentative promise in a letter of
before April 26 in which she announced that she had had so many
guests that she had not been able to work as planned, softening the
blow by mentioning that the story might be better for waiting. Here
she quoted Mencken who had written to her for the first time since
they had fallen out over her change of publishers. Although Chambers

---

[13]   Julia Peterkin to D.L. Chambers, before November 30, 1927, Bobbs-Merrill
papers.
[14]   D.L. Chambers to Julia Peterkin, November 30, 1927, Bobbs-Merrill papers.
[15]   Julia Peterkin to D.L. Chambers, before December 5, 1927, Bobbs-Merrill papers.
[16]   Bobbs-Merrill papers.

tried to be gracious about it, he was, understandingly, disappointed. Cautiously he tried to convince her that she should speed up:

> And isn't there such a thing as too much deliberation? You especially, I should trust with rightness and brilliance of attack. You know your people, your places, so completely that you can't go wrong. And you have thought so much about them that the emotional atmosphere must have matured to perfection. Isn't it possible that too much waiting and working over might smooth down power and poignancy.[17]

But Peterkin was not to be budged. She took every excuse to put off finishing the book and sending it off for publication. Although she said she would use a stenographer, none was up to par. Next she found fault with the proposed title. Henry Bellamann was used as excuse here. He did not like the title, and thought the book should be called "Scarlet Zeda," as the public already knew who Zeda was. All help was recruited to convince Peterkin that "Scarlet Sister Mary" was the perfect title for the new novel. At the publishing office they asked everyone working there or walking in what they thought of it. On the other end Peterkin sounded out all her acquaintances who were willing to listen as to what they thought of it, and then proposed "Pure Scarlet." Mr. Gittman, a friend who owned a bookshop, agreed. Finally, towards the middle of July, the jacket for the book was made and sent to Peterkin. She was enthusiastic and this was considered tacit approval of the title. *Scarlet Sister Mary* it was to be. In a letter dated "after June 1" she announced that the manuscript would soon be finished.

> Of course, it may not be right and it must not go into print until the last word is chosen properly. You and Anna and everybody must help me there. We must not let this be less good than what has gone before it.[18]

George Shiveley, the Bobbs-Merrill editor based in New York, immediately called her on hearing from Indianapolis that *Scarlet Sister Mary* was almost finished and arranged to go down to Fort Motte.

---

[17]   D.L. Chambers to Julia Peterkin, April 26, 1928, Bobbs-Merrill papers.
[18]   Bobbs-Merrill papers.

Although Peterkin claimed to be weary to death, she also announced she was thinking about doing a children's book for another publisher. When the Bobbs-Merrill firm was less than enthusiastic about this, she felt it was not being very generous. Wisely the firm decided to let it be until this could be discussed during the meeting between Peterkin and Shiveley. When the manuscript did finally come they were bowled over with joy and could not praise her enough. During George Shiveley's visit an idea for a new novel had apparently come up and already in the very next letter (June 13, 1928) Chambers started gently prodding her to start thinking seriously about this new idea. Meanwhile Peterkin seemed rather satisfied with the novel herself and decided to dedicate it to her husband, adding "He has been patient with much bad housekeeping these last months while I wrote. In fact he's been patient for years."[19] It was one of the rare times that she admitted that she might be quite a handful to put up with.

While Peterkin recovered from the exertion of writing a book, Chambers was busily planning his publishing program in which she was to play a major role. Peterkin, however, still had the children's book on her mind. Meanwhile a rumor was flying about that she was thinking of leaving Bobbs-Merrill for another publishing house run by their former employees Coward and McCann. Even before *Scarlet Sister Mary* was published in the fall of 1928, Peterkin had come up with an idea for a new book. It was to describe the life of one of Mary's daughters in Harlem. As Harlem was the focus of the art scene at the time, this seemed like an excellent idea, both from a cultural and from a commercial point of view, and Bobbs-Merrill encouraged her from the very start. There was one slight problem. The girl the story was to be based on was half-white. She was the daughter of one of Peterkin's friends, already deceased at the time, and had been a great embarrassment to him. According to Peterkin the girl had the best of two races, of two cultures in her: "She's lovely to look at with not only the best white South Carolina blood, but also the best black blood. She has the best traits of them both."[20] Bobbs-Merrill, in the person of D.L. Chambers, immediately reacted enthusiastically. He urged her to use her tremendous creative effort and offered to sit down with her and talk things over.

[19]   Julia Peterkin to D.L. Chambers, before June 28, 1928, Bobbs-Merrill papers.
[20]   *Ibid.*, before June 21, 1928, Bobbs-Merrill papers.

So far, they had progressed from purely business correspondence to letters addressed to "dear Julia Peterkin," letters of warm encouragement and admiration as well as letters containing chatter about all that was going at Lang Syne plantation. But during July and August of 1928 letters were frostily addressed again to "Mrs. Peterkin" and the relationship with Bobbs-Merrill seemed at a very low point. A letter of July 30, 1928 started out kindly enough saying that if she had really set her heart on doing the children's book for Coward and McCann and really thought Bobbs-Merrill were "greedy and dog-in-the-manger" for not allowing her to do it, they, of course, would not be such spoil-sports. Then it went on to point out that such a publication would really hamper their promotion of *Scarlet Sister Mary*, especially as rumors were flying about that she was about to leave Bobbs-Merrill for their former employees. The letter moved on to play on her sentiments by referring to opinions held by them all – George, Anne, the others and Chambers, himself. He pointed out that he and his company had only her best interest at heart and that it would be to her advantage to have at least three novels to her name so that she was firmly established in the literary world. Of course, she could always do a children's book later on. The fact was mentioned that Bobbs-Merrilll had spent almost 25% of the sales of *Black April* on advertising and promotion as well as the fact that this was done with a view to future publications. And Chambers did not forget to flatter her while pointing this all out to her:

> As we worked on *Black April* we looked forward to *Scarlet Sister Mary*. And as we work on *Scarlet Sister Mary* we want to have in view the novel about Mary's daughter (a whale of a book that would be!) and so on in a continuity of writing achievement and publishing service.[21]

He then went on to propose a deal. If she were to go on to write the book for Coward and McCann, she should try to do a novel for them at the same time. He was willing to grant her a waiver on the second book they contracted her for at the publication of *Black April*, thereby counting *Scarlet Sister Mary* as the first. Chambers closed by stressing that they wanted to continue their pleasant relations and had no wish to make her feel miserable. A long letter, in which Chambers explained why not only the firm Bobbs-Merrill but he, personally,

---

[21]   D.L. Chambers to Julia Peterkin, July 30, 1928, Bobbs-Merrill papers.

were against her going to another publishers, even if only for one book in a totally different genre, was sent on July 30, 1928.

By the middle of August Julia Peterkin had decided that her future lay with Bobbs-Merrill, and more in particular with D.L. Chambers, and promised: "I expect to give Bobbs-Merrill not only my next three novels but also *all* I ever write, provided you are managing the affairs of the firm."[22] All this strain on top of a summer spent in writing and revising became too much for Peterkin and she collapsed. She lost fifteen ponds and contracted tonsilitis.

Even before the official publication of *Scarlet Sister Mary* The National Book League of America, in the person of Walter White, made an offer to publish it. Although this was a great honor, it was considered to be economically unsound as the date of publication would have to be postponed to November 15. Moreover the Book League would pay $2500 – but would not absolutely guarantee publication. This move was not necessary as from the very start *Scarlet Sister Mary* was a resounding success.

In *Scarlet Sister Mary,* her prize-winning novel, Peterkin draws a picture of a young girl, Mary, who is deeply in love with her fiancé, July Pinesett. He is a very handsome rascal who persuades her to sleep with him before the wedding. It is the first of many sins for which she will be punished later in life. July tempts her to lead a life of sin, of dancing and singing worldly tunes. She is expelled from her church and then July leaves her for another woman. Mary is not to be comforted and decides that from now on she will not trust men but only use them. She will use the men to amuse herself and to give her children, who will give her all the love she needs. We do not need a whole lot of imagination, once we know the story of Peterkin's life, to read behind the lines and to discover the rage Julia herself must have felt after she discovered that she had been sterilized with the consent of her husband. In one of her letters to Irving Fineman, her longtime lover, she writes that "the bitterest experience a woman ever feels is the certainty that she has placed faith, hope in a man who proves unworthy."[23] One might have expected her to be equally angry with

---

[22]   Julia Peterkin to D.L. Chambers, August 18, 1928, Bobbs-Merrill papers.

[23]   Julia Peterkin to Irving Fineman, no date, 1932, Irving Fineman papers, Department of Special Collections, Syracuse University Library, Syracuse, New York.

her father who had, after all, initiated and performed the operation. Yet, throughout her life she continued to crave his approval. She dedicated *Black April* to him and could not rest easy until he had read it and spoken his approval. The dedication of the book served more than one purpose. On the one hand, it was meant to make her father react and give his approval of the stories she had written and which were being neglected in the South, so far. At the same time, the book served as a mirror to confront him with his failure as a father just as Breeze's father Black April fails to live up to his role as the biggest and strongest man on the plantation.

It is clear that Peterkin's two worlds, her literary world and the one she lived in from day to day, not only have common boundaries but overlap numerous times. She situated her stories on a plantation that was an amalgam of Lang Syne, which lay inland, and Brookgreen, a place the Peterkins owned on the coast, where they could escape from the oppressive summer heat. From the time she started considering publishing her stories she also started creating a public life for herself. While doing so, she kept on embellishing the line that her writing was an "incident in a pretty full life." Repeatedly, indeed, she observed that she was leading a full and rewarding life as a plantation mistress. She was a wife and mother first. Writing did not come to her naturally, but was hard work. The white world Peterkin lived in was that of the well-to-do South Carolinians. She filled her days with visiting and receiving visitors, with playing cards (she was a hot contract-player, as she told D.L. Chambers) and drinking bootleg, often to excess.

To outsiders she liked to portray her husband William as an almost chronic invalid who left her to run most of the plantation. From other sources (accounts of neighbors, friends and business acquaintances) it would appear he was a very good plantation manager, kind to the people who worked for him and a very likeable person although not very talkative. In her letters to her publishers she painted a picture of herself as the perpetually busy housewife who not only managed the house and its servants, but did the preserving, canning and baking herself. She also supervised the fieldworkers whenever necessary, which was very often according to her, and decided on, or at the very least had a decisive voice in, what to plant and other plantation policy. In claiming to have such an influence on plantation life Peterkin reverted to the tales about the original inhabitants of Lang Syne, an old Indian tribe supposedly led by a woman. It was said that the only women who could survive on the plantation were those who could "dominize" it.

In addition to all the work she claimed to be responsible for in the house and on the plantation she took part in several plays which were staged in Columbia and even played the leading role in *Hedda Gabler*, to the admiration of many full houses. She also served as a historian for the United Daughters of the Confederacy and she entertained numerous relatives every Sunday evening. In between all these necessary pastimes she had to find time for her writing and pretended that she thought it fun only if she could be "doing it at odd times when it was neither too hot nor too cold and nothing more amusing offered."[24] Yet in a letter to D.L. Chambers of January 18, 1932, written after she had finished *Bright Skin*, she complains "what shall I do next. Hours here are long and empty."[25]

Writing, in reality, was an arduous task that demanded long and dedicated hours. As she wrote to her lover Irving Fineman on September 10, 1928:

> Have just struggled through a novel Scarlet Sister Mary (I dislike the title) and it will appear October 26. I ached to do the woman. I know her well but the wretched drudgery of writing what I knew quite well was exhausting.[26]

The question arises why she would go to the trouble of writing at all when she really had such a rich and full life? In effect, by 1932 many things had changed. First the Peterkins had invested heavily in a project their brother-in-law had recommended. When a few months later the local economy went into recession they lost thousands of dollars.[27] When this was followed by the crash of 1929 and the prices of cotton dropped, notwithstanding an abundant crop, financial circumstances were less than satisfying. On a less mundane level Peterkin had been growing used to admiration and attention. She enjoyed being the focus of attention, even though she proclaimed to abhor public notice. She had also discovered that she could use the obligations of her different worlds to escape from the ones she found less attractive at that particular moment. While writing *Scarlet Sister*

---

[24]   Julia Peterkin to George Shively, October 1931, Bobbs-Merrill papers.
[25]   Bobbs-Merrill papers.
[26]   Julia Peterkin to Irving Fineman, September 10, 1928, Irving Fineman papers.
[27]   Susan Millar Williams, *A Devil and a Good Woman, Too*, 145-46.

Mary she had discovered how to hold her editor in thrall and she knew that her lover was fascinated by her complaints about her arduous job as a writer next to the demanding job of being a plantation mistress.

The void that was left after she had finished *Scarlet Sister Mary* may have been filled in part by the fact that she was leading yet another life, creating for herself yet another world, during some of the most productive years of her literary career: that of ardent lover and long-time mistress to Irving Fineman, a Jewish American and an instructor of mechanical drawing at the University of Illinois, she had met on the way home from France where they both had spent the summer of 1925. When they finally struck up a conversation Peterkin discovered that he had just sold an article to the *Menorah Journal* and had aspirations to become a writer. Peterkin had gone to France with her friend Blanche Kaminer and Blanche's daughter Binkie. She had decided to go to Europe to make up for what she felt was a lack in her education – and to spite William Peterkin, who was having an affair with Elizabeth Darby, the postman's wife.

It would be more than four years before she herself was to have an affair with Fineman. This would be largely an epistolary affair, although they managed to meet, if not on a regular basis, still more often than one might have expected, mostly in New York. Julia manipulated Irving as she did the other men in her life. She started out by writing coy flirtatious letters, praising his genius and emphasizing her own helplessness. After the meeting that would turn them into lovers, on November 30, 1929, they settled into a long-distance relationship. Every time Irving seemed to tire of that – he was after all a bachelor and of more than marrying age – Peterkin kept him on his toes with vague allusions to a brighter future and protestations that it was Fate, not she who kept them apart. "Physically I am fine. Otherwise – well, I try to remember that I've done nothing to deserve that rare thing called happiness."[28] And: "as long as I live, I shall be trying to swatch glimpses of you, exchange words with you. As for deserting you, that's not possible."[29]

Time and again she stressed the fact that she was not a free agent, not in her relationship towards him nor in the rest of her life. She not only referred to the laws concerning divorce in South Carolina but

---

[28] Julia Peterkin to Irving Fineman, April 3, 1930, Irving Fineman papers.
[29] *Ibid.*, May 27, 1930, Irving Fineman papers.

also to the fact that she considered their love not an act of volition but of fate:

> I know there is no such thing as freedom. Certainly there is no freedom where love is. Love that is free is not love at all, for love lays bonds upon us. Not the person who gives me love binds me; but the person whom I love does – and I see now, does permanently, for to him I have given something of myself and to him I must return or else be forever incomplete.[30]

Sometimes she played the totally dependent female, deeply grateful for every word of praise:

> What you write me about myself makes me feel so humble. I want you to think everything good of me and at the same time know that I'm none of it. This is also true: that I shall strive all the harder because of you to be the best thing I can manage to be. For to me you've a great precious soul, and I prize every minute I've ever spent with you. Every one, with no one else on earth am I so happy, so at peace and also, so peaceless. In you I find all experience, from keenest joy to deep searing misery. I am helpless about it all, I accept.[31]

Repeatedly she used the words from Micah to describe how wretched and imprisoned she was feeling in her other lives: "Therefore I will wail and howl; I will go stripped and naked; I will make a wailing like the dragons and mourning as the owls."[32]

All these letters might have made a great epistolary novel about her life. But whenever she tried writing about herself it turned out to be an utter disaster. At the time the relationship between Irving Fineman and Peterkin developed it would have been very well possible for Julia to live independently. She had an income from her books and short stories. She could have left William Peterkin and lived with Irving Fineman. As she told Fineman more than once, her marriage was a disaster. Hardly anywhere in her letters, either to Irving Fineman or to her publisher, is there any mention of her husband. Whenever she does mention him, it is to complain that he is ill again. Only rarely does she admit that he took charge of things or was in any way of assistance to her. She always implies that it was she who virtually ran

---

[30] *Ibid.*, undated, 1930, Irving Fineman papers.
[31] *Ibid.*, Summer, 1930, Irving Fineman papers.
[32] *Ibid.*, September 20, 1930, Irving Fineman papers.

the plantation. Still, by all accounts their marriage did not seem to be a very unhappy alliance to those witnessing it. In her letters to Fineman she frequently shifted moods, swinging from one extreme to the other. This she seemed to recognize herself, as she writes in a letter dated March 7, 1932: "I've an undisciplined, unreasonable thing inside me and it forever needs calming, soothing, comforting, and I resort to all sorts of trickery to keep it docile as possible, for it suffers horribly at times." And in the same letter:

> I'm more than two people perhaps. Here I think so. I wear a number of masks. I sometimes think you alone see me without any one of them. That's because you forgive my being what I really am.[33]

On top of all the different masks there was always one more layer: the veneer of her public life. Although at first she flaunted her newfound self, the author, in the face of those living close to her, when the South Carolina public and press continued to ignore her after the publication of her first short stories in the *Reviewer* she decided to keep a low profile for a while. She soon discovered that this had its advantages, too. Whenever she mentioned being ignored or even being told to quit writing by her family and by her fellow South Carolinians she was sure she would receive praise and encouragement from H.L. Mencken and Carl Sandburg. After she began her affair with Fineman her fame definitely became a handicap. Her abundance of red hair and regal stature made her more than noticeable. And although she was prepared to commit "mortal sin" for him, she did not want to be known as a licentious woman.

In her later years she repudiated all she had admired in "her" people. Early in her career she had said about herself, in *The New York World*: "My writing is less a creative thing than an attempt to record people I admire. The Negroes are not beasts; they're human beings." And in the same article she had remarked: "They meet life with courage and a grace that few people achieve. I like them; they've been my friend; I've learned so much from them."[34] In her old age she seemed to deny this admiration whenever racial integration became a topic of conversation. The mere idea that her grandchildren might go to school with blacks made her cringe.[35] The world of Lang Syne she

---

[33] *Ibid.*, March 7, 1932, Irving Fineman papers.
[34] *New York World*, July 10, 1927, clipping, Bobbs-Merrill papers.
[35] Susan Millar Williams, *A Devil and a Good Woman, Too*, 255.

had written about with so much warmth and admiration had vanished. Somewhere along the way she had lost interest in the black people on her plantation as persons. They were either dying (the older ones) or leaving for more profitable circumstances (the younger ones) at a time when she was dealing with all of her different worlds. Once her ideal plantation world had largely vanished, Peterkin no longer believed in the unique personality of her workers. They had become just people, although far less sophisticated than her white neighbors. And if after the publication of her first stories Negroes had doubted whether she was white or black and on finding out that she was a white plantation owner had exclaimed that she might be white but certainly had a black soul, after 1933 there could be no doubt anymore: she was white unto the bottom of her soul.

In December 1935 D.L. Chambers became president of Bobbs-Merrill after a long internal struggle for power. He kept writing her occasionally, urging her to finish the book she was apparently working on at that time. Times were hard for publishers and Bobbs-Merrill also had a financial interest in her because the advance of $15,000 she had received for *Bright Skin* in January 1932 still had not been earned back in June of 1935. Of course this was partly due to the Depression, as people had other things than buying books to worry about. But Peterkin hardly helped things along by refusing to appear at book fairs and other occasions that could have stimulated publicity.

Meanwhile she once again hid behind the facade of being the busy planter's wife. As late as April 1939 she wrote D.L. Chambers:

> Lord, I'm busy. What with planting, planning, farm book-keeping, days fly. Soon, asparagus shipping will be over and I'll have more time. Maybe then I'll start pushing a pencil.[36]

The correspondence between Bobbs-Merrill and Julia Peterkin had again become largely business-like, announcing republications of *Scarlet Sister Mary* in a cheap edition or the royalties for the condensation in "The World's Greatest Books."[37] Every now and then a line would be added expressing the hope that one of these days a book would be coming. But except for a lecture now and then, or a class she taught, Julia Peterkin disappeared from public life. And after the suicide of her daughter-in-law she turned inward, to the family that

---

[36] Julia Peterkin to D.L. Chambers, before April 24, 1939, Bobbs-Merrill papers.
[37] Letters of January 12 and February 1, 1940, Bobbs-Merrill papers.

was left, and did not even bother about keeping up the pretense of a social life, or the existence of worlds other than the one at Lang Syne, any more.

After the deaths of her father, her husband, and her daughter-in-law Peterkin no longer seemed to have the energy to balance all of her different worlds and she retreated into what had always been the core of her existence: her family life. She concentrated on raising her grandson and became more and more isolated, only rarely going back into one of her other worlds to give a lecture or an interview. On August 10, 1961 she died, more lonely than she had ever been before.

Works by Julia Mood Peterkin

"A Baby's Mouth," *Reviewer*, 3 (May 1922), 437-42.
"Over the River," *Reviewer*, 4 (January 1924), 84-96.
Green Thursday, New York: Knopf, 1924.
Black April, Indianapolis: Bobbs-Merrill, 1927.
Scarlet Sister Mary, Indianapolis: Bobbs-Merrill, 1928.
Bright Skin, Indianapolis: Bobbs-Merrill, 1932.
Roll, Jordan, Roll, New York: Robert O. Ballou, 1933.
The Collected Short Stories of Julia Peterkin, edited with an Introduction by Frank Durham, Columbia, South Carolina: University of South Carolina Press, 1970.

EDNA ST. VINCENT MILLAY'S SONNETS: PUTTING "CHAOS INTO FOURTEEN LINES"

C.C. BARFOOT

Though it was reared To Beauty, it was wrought
From what I had to build with: honest bone
Is there, and anguish; pride; and burning thought;
And lust is there, and nights not spent alone.[1]

The recent revival of interest in literary biography is one of the banes, and certainly not the "honest bone," of modern literary studies. Too often the biographer, however accomplished, threatens to swamp literary texts and the art of reading with intrusive probes into the private lives of great writers, a prurience which occasionally may descend into such tawdry bioflicks as *Iris* or *Sylvia*. A corpus of significant texts should be enough to satisfy our proper desire to extend our own imaginations into the created worlds of other minds. Those texts and those imagined worlds we may properly associate with the cultural territory, including the social and political territory, of other writers and artists, both contemporary and in the past and in the future, but we should be wary of prying into the personal relationships, however "authorized," of the men and women whose minds are responsible for the verbal artefacts they have bequeathed us. The good reader "reads between the lines" by reading the lines.

If some critics feel lost without their essential biographical tent poles, other academics can hardly move a step without taking with them a whole caravan of theoretical jargon, and they would feel naked and exposed without their terminological wrappings to wave in the air while their fingers wriggle quotation marks. To all of these positions, especially where they involve young colleagues striving to establish their research credentials with poststructuralist, postmodernist, postcolonialist, post-secular, post-literary masters, one may be more

---

[1]   From Sonnet cxxiv in Edna St. Vincent Millay, *Collected Poems*, ed. Norma Millay (New York and London: Harper and Row, 1956), 688 (first published in *Huntsman, What Quarry?*, 1939).

or less sympathetic. Nevertheless, the clutter of biographical and theoretical knowledge too often distracts attention from what really matters – the text, whether it is of a novel or of a play or of a poem. When it comes to poetry, how often one wishes one knew nothing about the author or the period, and that the words alone, the rhythms, the rhymes, the similes and the metaphors, the appositions, the assonances, the whole aesthetic assembly of language and speech could be left alone for the reader to participate in, meditate on, be moved by, mentally and emotionally thrilled and entertained by, without needing to worry about how it relates to the author's life and times, and what its bearing might be on all the philosophical skeletons rattling in the academic cupboard. Of no writer and of no corpus of work is this more true than that of Edna St. Vincent Millay. In this essay I will attempt to deliberately refrain from referring to any knowledge I may or may not have about her life, her life-style, her reception and reputation, her literary career, although I realize there is a mass of such information out there on the shelves and waiting to be retrieved from cyberspace. Indeed, a brief excursion onto the Internet revealed the offer of innumerable free essays about her life and work that I might have purloined, and a recent biography of the poet by Nancy Milford[2] that would have told me more than I would ever need to know. I resisted all offers on the principle that the less I know about an author's life, the more concentrated effort I will put into understanding the work, and that, on the whole, biographies of authors' lives are evasions of the work and distractions of the imagination. This is a credo all the more difficult to live with when reading and writing about Edna St. Vincent Millay's sonnets, and in particular one of her most overtly biographically tantalizing sequences, *The Fatal Interview*, first published in 1931.

Anyone reading Millay's *Collected Poems* through is bound to conclude that she is probably the most fluent poet in English – fluent almost in a literal sense, since from first to last her poetry flows expressively, frequently with exceedingly long lines of twenty or more syllables. Indeed, it soon becomes evident that despite the eloquent appeal of her poetry – and one is truly carried along by the swirl and eddy of her lines and gripped on those occasions when she reverts to

[2]   Nancy Milford, *Savage Beauty: The Life of Edna St. Vincent Millay* (New York: Random House, 2001).

tighter lyrical meters and more ballad-like quatrains – she is certainly too eloquent for her own good: so loquacious that earnest readers will find it difficult to take her seriously. Popular she may have been, and appealing she may still be, but too easily might she be dismissed as passé, a representative of a time when forward women set out to shock with their readiness to be as brazen as men, if not more so, and establish feminism as an audaciously outspoken sexual combat zone in which men could not compete without seeming witless and brusque:

> I, being born a woman and distressed
> By all the needs and notions of my kind,
> Am urged by your propinquity to find
> Your person fair, and feel a certain zest
> To bear your body's weight upon my breast:
> So subtly is the fume of life designed,
> To clarify the pulse and cloud the mind,
> And leave me once again undone, possessed.
> Think not for this, however, the poor treason
> Of my stout blood against my staggering brain,
> I shall remember you with love, or season
> My scorn with pity, – let me make it plain:
> I find this frenzy insufficient reason
> For conversation when we meet again.

In this well-known early sonnet of Millay, we recognize at once the particular value of the sonnet form for her art. The tradition of the form encourages her self-possession – the fourteen lines and their variety of rhyme schemes is a challenge to the poet to demonstrate restrained virtuosity, and wit and disdain are combined with hints of vulnerability and lurking anguish. Millay's usual confident flow, her willing expression of intimacy, her carefully cultivated and frequently extended parade of manners and mannerisms are here all decorously closeted (one might even say, corseted) within the conventional expectations of rhyme and rhythm of the sonnet form. This is a tightly controlled, allusive and risky game of bluff and counter bluff that nevertheless appeals to the reader immediately as a truthful revelation of a life relished for its drama and the expression of that drama. She knows that we know that the Petrarchan lady is bound neither to speak nor to be touched, and if this poem without shame divulges how far this particular woman has strayed from the Petrarchan model, nevertheless when it suits her to do so she will resort once more to the silence of the pedestal. At this stage in Millay's poetic career it is as if, after four centuries, she is determined to give that silent goddess a voice and by so doing muzzle the griping parade of generations of tediously repetitive male sonneteers:

> Loving you less than life, a little less
> Than bitter-sweet upon a broken wall
> Or brush-wood smoke in autumn, I confess
> I cannot swear I love you not at all.
> For there is that about you in this light –
> A yellow darkness, sinister of rain –
> Which sturdily recalls my stubborn sight
> To dwell on you, and dwell on you again.
> And I am made aware of many a week
> I shall consume, remembering in what way
> Your brown hair grows about your brow and cheek
> And what divine absurdities you say:
> Till all the world, and I, and surely you,
> Will know I love you, whether or not I do.

If in some respects she wants us to know that in no way is she a reticent lady, neither in terms of self-expression nor in erotic experience, and is even boastful to an extent and in a manner that risks her being dismissed as a tart, she also frequently reminds us that there is a melancholy, even a sorrowful, undertow to her permissiveness, an awareness that she has to pay a painful price for her determination to be the one who initiates and registers the delights of physical love-making rather than being the tranquil recipient of the swagger and adoring vows of a multiplicity of gentlemen:

> What lips my lips have kissed, and where, and why,
> I have forgotten, and what arms have lain
> Under my head till morning; but the rain
> Is full of ghosts tonight, that tap and sigh
> Upon the glass and listen for reply,
> And in my heart there stirs a quiet pain
> For unremembered lads that not again
> Will turn to me at midnight with a cry.
> Thus in the winter stands the lonely tree,
> Nor knows what birds have vanished one by one,
> Yet knows its boughs more silent than before:

I cannot say what loves have come and gone,
I only know that summer sang in me
A little while, that in me sings no more.[3]

Most of Edna St. Vincent Millay's sonnets in her first four books –
Renascance (1917), *A Few Figs from Thistles* (1920), *Second April*
(1921) and *The Harp-Weaver* (1923), all published between the ages
of twenty-five and thirty-one, an indication of her prolific fluency –
fluctuate between the pain of remembered loss, expressed with
graceful precision ("And entering with relief some quiet place / Where
never fell his foot or shone his face / I say, 'There is no memory of
him here!' / And so stand stricken, so remembering him"), and a
carefully nurtured but nonchalant determination not to be hurt again:

Oh, think not I am faithful to a vow!
Faithless am I save to love's self alone.
Were you not lovely I would leave you now:
After the feet of beauty fly my own.
Were you not still my hunger's rarest food,
And water ever to my wildest thirst,
I would desert you – think not but I would! –
And seek another as I sought you first.
But you are mobile as the veering air,
And all your charms more changeful than the tide,
Wherefore to be inconstant is no care:
I have but to continue at your side.
So wanton, light and false, my love, are you,
I am most faithless when I most am true.

The cultivated tone of indifference is belied by the fine craft of
the sonnet in Millay's hands, and the reader senses this is a carefully
wrought defensive strategy developed as a recognition that if the lady
cares to come down from the pedestal and play with the boys, she has
to be armed and armored, ready and prepared to shrug off the
inevitable injuries of the love game:

Only until this cigarette is ended,
A little moment at the end of all,
While on the floor the quiet ashes fall,

---

[3]   Sonnets xli, xl and xlii (*Collected Poems*, 600-602; first published in *The Harp-Weaver and Other Poems*, 1923).

And in the firelight to a lance extended,
Bizarrely with the jazzing music blended,
The broken shadow dances on the wall,
I will permit my memory to recall
The vision of you, by all my dream attended.
And then adieu, – farewell! – the dream is done.
Yours is a face of which I can forget
The colour and the features, everyone,
The words not ever, and the smiles not yet;
But in your day this moment is the sun
Upon a hill, after the sun has set.[4]

By the end of her poetic career, in the sonnets published in her posthumous volume, *Mine the Harvest* (1954), this guarded disdain had become an unwilling surrender, a recognition of lost energy, and a painful coming to terms with the prospect of death, paradoxically often couched in terms of a resigned and wistful combativeness as she ruminates on the course of her career, particular in its later more socially and politically engaged phase:

To hold secure the province of Pure Art, –
What if the crude and weighty task were mine? –
For him who runs, cutting the pen less fine
Than formerly, and in the indignant heart
Dipping it straight? (to issue thence a dart,
And shine no more except as weapons shine)
The deeply-loved, the laboured, polished line
Eschew for ever? – this to be my part?
Attacked that Temple is which must not fall –
Under whose ancient shade Calliope,
Thalia, Euterpe, the nine Muses all
Went once about their happy business free:
Could I but write the Writing on the Wall! –
What matter, if one poet cease to be.

She is old enough now to be realistic about the fragility of any poet's claim on fame, but equally determined to voice her political and cultural discomfort with the world about her, a world in which

---

[4]   Sonnets ii, x and xv (*Collected Poems*, 562, 570, 575; originally published in *Renascence, A Few Figs from Thistles* and *Second April*).

It is the fashion now to wave aside
As tedious, obvious, vacuous, trivial, trite,
All things which do not tickle, tease, excite
To some subversion, or in verbiage hide
Intent, or mock, or with hot sauce provide
A dish to prick the thickened appetite ....[5]

To paraphrase an earlier sonnet writer, "Millay! thou shouldst be living at this hour."

This partisanship is a stance, a style, a tone, an attitude that Edna St. Vincent Millay had been developing from the early 1930s, which first appears overtly in "Two Sonnets in Memory" of Sacco and Vanzetti, two Italian American anarchists executed on possibly false charges in 1927.[6] During the decade before the Second World War and during the war itself, Millay published many sonnets (and other poems too) deploring the state of the world both within and outside the United States and the initial reluctance of the American government to become involved. This culminated in a volume, *Make Bright the Arrows*, first published in London in 1941, most of the contents of which, for reasons partly political, partly a question of quality and present relevance, failed to find a place in the *Collected Poems*, compiled after her death by her sister.[7]

---

[5] Sonnet clxiii and the opening lines of Sonnet clxv (*Collected Poems*, 723 and 725).

[6] Sonnets cxxii and cxxiii (*Collected Poems*, 682-83; first published in *Wine from These Grapes*, 1934).

[7] From the original volume, described as "A 1940 Notebook," of the two dozen poems, including a fine epigraph and nine sonnets, only two poems ("To the Maid of Orleans" and "Memory of England [October 1940])" and two sonnets ("I must not die of pity; I must live" and "How innocent of me and my dark pain") made it to the *Collected Poems*. The sonnets excluded were "Peace was my earliest love ... ," "Gentlemen Cry, Peace!," "While London, while Berlin – two cities dear/To those who live in them – burn to the ground,/ Our statesmen fiddle on ... ," "Only the ruthless, now, .../Have courage and risk all," "You find 'outrageous' this? – these outraged hearts? – /Homes, griefs invaded?," "The Old Men of Vichy," "Where does he walk or sit and stir his tea,/ ... who will give,/When the day comes, England to Germany?" One appreciates that many of these sonnets, and other poems in volume too, were intended as propaganda as well as a means of the well traveled Millay venting her anger at the isolationism of her countrymen as well as the perfidy of many right-wing sympathizers in Europe, nevertheless it is regrettable that they were not allowed to bear witness to her understandable political outrage in the *Collected Poems*. It may be that with the onset of McCarthyism in the early 1950s either Norma

Of the 178 sonnets in Millay's *Collected Poems*,[8] there are three sequences: "Sonnets from an Ungrafted Tree" from *The Harp-Weaver* in 1923, "Epitaph for the Race of Man" that first appeared in *Wine from These Grapes* in 1934, and *Fatal Interview* that was published as a volume in 1931. In the first of the sequences, Millay uses the sonnet form as a means of constructing an impressionistic fiction of the memories, experiences and reflections of a woman, of uncertain age but presumably much older than the poet, who was then in her early thirties, busying herself with her everyday chores when she was not watching at the bedside of her dying husband. The setting appears to be a small farm, presumably in New England where it rains and it snows, and where not only the weather is bleak but the whole personal circumstances and mental framework of the protagonist. In "Sonnets from an Ungrafted Tree" the easy-going modish young poet, used to living in a risky ambience of erotic diversion, has deliberately chosen to empathize with a dreary and drab alternative world, entirely without glamour or adventure, full of dejection and desolation, with very occasional flashes of more colorful recollections of flowers and birds, and even of a time when she could think of "her body sluggish with desire." But unlike Millay's usual environment this is a world where expectations of personal happiness or achievement are low:

> Not over-kind nor over-quick in study
> Nor skilled in sports nor beautiful was he,
> Who had come into her life when anybody
> Would have been welcome, so in need was she.
> They had become acquainted in this way:
> He flashed a mirror in her eyes at school;
> By which he was distinguished; from that day
> They went about together, as a rule.
> She told, in secret and with whispering,
> How he had flashed a mirror in her eyes;
> And as she told, it struck her with surprise

Millay or the publishers thought it would not be politically expedient to republish most of these particular poems.

[8]   Apart from these numbered sonnets that appear together as a separate section in the last part of the *Collected Poems* (561-738), there are another four sonnets in the earlier part of the volume (291, 365, 371-72). There is another poem of fourteen lines on page 364 that might also be regarded as a slightly unorthodox sonnet. With the seven discarded sonnets from *Make Bright the Arrows*, this brings Millay's total number of published sonnets to about 190, which must make her one of the most prolific writers of sonnets in the history of the form.

That this was not so wonderful a thing.
But what's the odds? – It's pretty nice to know
You've got a friend to keep you company everywhere you go.[9]

Yes, "It's pretty nice to know/You've got a friend to keep you company everywhere you go." But not exactly exciting. Each of the sonnets in this sequence has a dragging final line, with seven instead of five stresses, which helps to emphasize the depression of minimal expectation:

Who planted seeds, musing ahead to their far blossoming.

Upon this roof the rain would drum as it was drumming now.

So stood, with listening eyes upon the empty doughnut jar.

But the oak tree's shadow was deep and black and secret as a well.

That here was spring, and the whole year to be lived through
    once more.

She had kept that kettle boiling all night long, for company.

That things in death were neither clocks nor people, but only dead.

"I don't know what you do exactly when a person dies."[10]

Personally Millay lived in a world of finely cultivated grafted trees with a classical provenance, but the success of this sequence suggests that she welcomed the opportunity to shift the focus of her poetic ordering of the Chaos of self, or any of her imagined selves, to someone totally different from herself, to examine and give voice to the Chaos of other selves. In one of her last sonnets in her posthumous volume, she expresses what amounts to her personal poetic credo:

I will put Chaos into fourteen lines
And keep him there; and let him thence escape
If he be lucky; let him twist, and ape

---

[9]   Sonnet liv (*Collected Poems*, 614; "Sonnets from an Ungrafted Tree," IX).
[10]   The final lines of Sonnets xlvi-xlvii, l, lv-lvi, lix-lxi (*Collected Poems*, 606-607, 610, 615-16, 619-21; "Sonnets from an Ungrafted Tree," I-II, V, X-XI, XIV-XVI).

> Flood, fire, and demon – his adroit designs
> Will strain to nothing in the strict confines
> Of this sweet Order, where, in pious rape,
> I hold his essence and amorphous shape,
> Till he with Order mingles and combines.
> Past are the hours, the years, of our duress,
> His arrogance, our awful servitude:
> I have him. He is nothing more nor less
> Than something simple not yet understood;
> I shall not even force him to confess;
> Or answer. I will only make him good.[11]

This clearly illuminates what the sonnet as a form meant for Edna St. Vincent Millay, why it appealed to her so strongly and why she was such a master-mistress of its form – all the Chaos that she was engaged with and intent on expressing and probing in her own life, her "anguish; pride; and burning thought / And lust," and the confusion, the misplaced energies, and continual threats of disaster she observed about her, for which she could not find solutions. She could neither change herself nor the world, but she could strive with her superb art to ensure that the Chaos both without and within "mingles and combines" with Order. Through the controlled confines of her art at least, she could take comfort in the belief that "she had him" (inevitably, Chaos is perceived by the poet as masculine):

> He is nothing more nor less
> Than something simple not yet understood;
> I shall not even force him to confess;
> Or answer. I will only make him good.

Edna St. Vincent Millay had wrestled with her desire to come to terms with the irresolvable predicament of human life in her 1934 sequence "Epitaph for the Race of Man," which is also presided over by the Chaos out of which life arose and to which it will return:

> Before this cooling planet shall be cold,
> Long, long before the music of the Lyre,
> Like the faint roar of distant breakers rolled
> On reefs unseen, when wind and flood conspire
> To drive the ship inshore – long, long, I say,

---

[11] Sonnet clxviii (*Collected Poems*, 728).

Before this ominous humming hits the ear,
Earth will have come upon a stiller day,
Man and his engines be no longer here.
High on his naked rock the mountain sheep
Will stand alone against the final sky,
Drinking a wind of danger new and deep,
Staring on Vega with a piercing eye,
And gather up his slender hooves and leap
From crag to crag down Chaos, and so go by.

Succinctly, in her "sweet Order," Millay traces the evolution of life on earth past the dinosaur, whose "veined and fertile eggs are long since cold" and the rise of later species of animal (birds, sharks, pythons). She seeks to be "scribe and ... confessor" to the "unhappy planet born to die," recording the wonders Earth would be able to relate "of Man, who when his destiny was high / Strode like the sun into a middle sky / And shone an hour," but realizes that this is a strictly human point of view, since as far as the planet is concerned

Man, with his singular laughter, his droll tears,
His engines and his conscience and his art,
Made but a simple sound upon your ears:
The patient beating of the animal heart.[12]

"Heart" and "art" are apt rhymes, since Millay goes on to remind us that it is only by his creative invention that man has a sense of having risen above all other creatures with a comparable pulsing organ.

Although in the face of millennia of physical and material challenges and disasters, both natural and man-made, human creativity will enable the species to survive – after the volcano erupts building "again / his paper house upon oblivion's brim", and after the flood "mak[ing] for shore, / With twisted face and pocket full of seeds"[13] – in the end humanity will obliterate itself, "for Man was weak / Before the unkindness in his brother's eyes":

O race of Adam, blench not lest you find
In the sun's bubbling bowl anonymous death,

---

[12] Sonnets cxli-cxliv (*Collected Poems*, 701-704; "Epitaph for the Race of Man," I-IV).
[13] Sonnets cxlviii and cl (*Collected Poems*, 708 and 710; "Epitaph for the Race of Man," VIII and X).

Or lost in whistling space without a mind
To monstrous Nothing yield your little breath:
You shall achieve destruction where you stand,
In intimate conflict, at your brother's hand.[14]

For mankind was flawed from the start, carrying that Chaos within, that "wild disorder never to be stayed," which Millay herself is so conscious of, and consequently doomed to extinction:

Alas for Man, so stealthily betrayed,
Bearing the bad cell in him from the start,
Pumping and feeding from his healthy heart
That wild disorder never to be stayed
When once established, destined to invade
With angry hordes the true and proper part,
Till Reason joggles in the headsman's cart,
And Mania spits from every balustrade.
Would he had searched his closet for his bane,
Where lurked the trusted ancient of his soul,
Obsequious Greed, and seen that visage plain;
Would he had whittled treason from his side
In his stout youth and bled his body whole,
Then had he died a king, or never died.[15]

At first sight "Epitaph for the Race of Man" is the most surprising of Edna St. Vincent Millay's works. In the *Collected Poems* it is placed out of chronological order and immediately before the sonnets from her posthumous collection. But this seems particularly appropriate, linking her more politically and socially troubled sonnets of the 1930s and 1940s, with her last poems where amongst other concerns she reflects on the part she may have played in making the world a less troubled place. She is clearly concerned that her poetry may be forgotten, but consoled by the expectation that the causes she embraced have not been lost:

And if I die, because that part of me
Which part alone of me had chance to live,
Chose to be honour's threshing-floor, a sieve

---

[14]   Sonnets cliv and clv (*Collected Poems*, 714-15; "Epitaph for the Race of Man," XIV and XV).
[15]   Sonnet clvi (*Collected Poems*, 716; "Epitaph for the Race of Man," XVI).

Where right through wrong might make its way, and be;
If from all taint of indignation, free
Must be my art, and thereby fugitive
From all that threatens it – why – let me give
To moles my dubious immortality.
For, should I cancel by one passionate screed
All that in chaste reflection I have writ,
So that again not ever in bright need
A man shall want my verse and reach for it,
I and my verses will be dead indeed, –
That which we died to champion, hurt no whit.[16]

If one is mainly familiar with Millay's early poems, such sequences as "Epitaph for the Race of Man" may come as a surprise or even as a shock. It clearly associates her with other writers of the 1930s holding dystopian views, such as Aldous Huxley (in *Brave New World*, 1932) and H.G. Wells (*The Shape of Things to Come*, 1933), in her dwelling on the destined fate of mankind. More curiously her meditations on the origins, evolution and destruction of the human species anticipate certain features of another sonnet sequence that was to appear at the end of the decade, W.H. Auden's "In Time of War" (1939).[17]

Finally, we come to Edna St. Vincent Millay's greatest sequence, *Fatal Interview*, written between "Sonnets from an Ungrafted Tree" and "Epitaph for the Race of Man" and apparently returning us to the familiar territory of lust and anguish, "and nights not spent alone," or if spent alone, then with tearful recrimination. However, this sequence, which may well be Millay's greatest achievement, and at the time of publication was certainly one of her most popular, may not be quite what it seems to be. Whether it is based on an actual love affair is irrelevant (I suppose it was) and instead of rushing to the latest biography to find out, the reader had better try to get hold of a copy of the work as it originally appeared. For no particularly defensible reason as far as I can see, in the *Collected Poems*, Norma Millay dropped the epigraph to the sequence –

---

[16] Sonnet clxiv (*Collected Poems*, 724).
[17] Auden's more overtly political sequence comes at the end of the book, *Journey to a War*, which he and Christopher Isherwood published as a result of their visit to China during the Sino-Japanese War in the first part of 1938.

By our first strange and fatall interview,
By all desires which thereof did ensue

Not only do these opening lines from John Donne's "Elegie XVI: On His Mistris" give the unsuspecting reader the source of the title, but it also suggests a great deal about Millay's tactics and strategy in this sequence. For a start, we may or we may not wish to speculate about the connection of Donne's poem with any real or imagined mistress that the poet may have had, or to be drawn to speculate that Donne is actually creating his vivid monologue in the context of his troubled courtship of the woman he was eventually to marry. All such conjectures may or may not be confirmed by our consulting biographies of the poet; in Donne's case enough is known about his life to support the biographer's ambition but not enough always to be certain about the occasion for his poems. Hence, we would be better served by concentrating on the wonderfully forceful poem in front of us. After the lines used by Millay as her epigraph, Donne's poem continues:

By our long starving hopes, by that remorse
Which my words masculine perswasive force
Begot in thee, and by the memory
Of hurts, which spies and rivals threatned me,
I calmly beg ...[18]

These lines equally well apply to Millay's sequence, with its peculiar feminine "perswasive force." Poetry of the power and passion found in *Fatal Interview* does not need to be locked into any other reality than its own. But Millay's link with Donne suggests something else – Millay seems to be deliberately breaking the silence of Donne's mistress, and after three centuries enabling her to speak. This is the woman's voice, the mistress's voice.

The drama of these fifty-two sonnets (one for every week of the year?) is not cast exactly in an antique voice, and we have no difficulty in understanding that it is written by a late modern rather than an early modern woman, but there are occasional anachronisms in the vocabulary and syntax ("leman," "were builded" and, above all,

---

[18]   John Donne, "Elegie XVI: On His Mistris," in *Complete Poetry and Selected Prose*, ed. John Hayward (London: The Nonesuch Library, 1955), 89.

"liefer")[19] that suggests that this is the voice of immutable woman bound to no place or time, using a form and a style of controlling the Chaos of love and lust that stretches across three centuries at least, and further back and further forward than that, demonstrated as clearly as anywhere in the fourth sonnet of the sequence:

> Nay, learnèd doctor, these fine leeches fresh
> From the pond's edge my cause cannot remove:
> Alas, the sick disorder in my flesh
> Is deeper than your skill, is very love.
> And you, good friar, far liefer would I think
> Upon my dear, and dream him in your place,
> Than heed your *ben'cites* and heavenward sink
> With empty heart and noddle full of grace.
> Breathes but one mortal on the teeming globe
> Could minister to my soul's or body's needs –
> Physician minus physic, minus robe;
> Confessor minus Latin, minus beads.
> Yet should you bid me name him, I am dumb;
> For though you summon him, he would not come.[20]

In most respects this is already an extreme example, as if to warn the reader early on that it is possibly not the world of cigarettes and cocktails we may have been expecting from our experience of Millay's earlier sonnets, but a culture of wisdom and know-how to be associated with robes and long beards (although she deliberately betrays her wry contemporary slant by the use of the word "noddle"). We read it as a metaphor of all the help that may be resorted to in states of emotional bondage, but it is also a reminder that this is a state of being encountered by innumerable beings in many different times and places. The agonies of the protagonist in this implied tale of

---

[19] These examples come respectively from Sonnets ciii, cvi, and lxxii, lxxiii, xcii (*Fatal Interview*, XXXIV, XXXVII, and III, IV, XXIII). However, "liefer" occurs in other of Millay's poems, and may be regarded as a feature of New England speech, but this is probably not the case with "bereaven" in Sonnet cliv ("Epitaph for the Race of Man," XIV) or "hight" ("called") in Sonnet clxxvi (all these examples from *Collected Poems*, 663, 666, 632, 633, 652, 714 and 736). Only "hight" and "bereaven" occur at the end of lines, so there is no sense in which Millay might be said to have resorted to anachronistic forms of the language in order to find a rhyme. It should also be noted that Millay usually uses standard British spellings for such words as "colour," "favour", "honour," "labour" and even "doughnut."

[20] Sonnet lxxiii (*Collected Poems*, 633; *Fatal Interview*, IV).

unhappy love are not just personal, but, like Donne's plea to his mistress that she should stay at home and not risk traveling with him and the expression of the anxiety and distress such a separation will create for both of them (also found in other poems of Donne's), the dramatization both of an individual case and of a universal experience – as is death, which haunts Millay not only in this sonnet sequence:

> Yet in an hour to come, disdainful dust,
> You shall be bowed and brought to bed with me.
> While the blood roars, or when the blood is rust
> About a broken engine, this shall be.
> If not today, then later; if not here
> On the green grass, with sighing and delight,
> Then under it, all in good time, my dear,
> We shall be laid together in the night.
> And ruder and more violent, be assured,
> Than the desirous body's heat and sweat
> That shameful kiss by more than night obscured
> Wherewith at length the scornfullest mouth is met.
> Life has no friend; her converts late or soon
> Slide back to feed the dragon with the moon.[21]

The protagonist of the sequence (and I insist on calling her "protagonist" rather than "Millay," whose authorial voice has disappeared in this complex poetic fantasy) is aware of all the cultural and poetic antecedents of her woes – the Olympian gods, the shape-shifter Jove and his multiple conquests, Endymion and Selene, the princes and princesses of folk-tale and legend[22] – and this vindicates her predicament and the means by which she finds a voice to express and explore the reckless manner in which the heart fails to have any "pity on this house of bone."[23] But her identifying with the "lively chronicles of the past," the fates of Isolde and of Helen of Troy, leads her to assert

> here and there,
> Hunting the amorous line, skimming the rest,

---

[21]   Sonnet lxxvii (*Collected Poems*, 637; *Fatal Interview*, VIII).

[22]   See, for instance, Sonnets lxxxi, lxxxv, lxxxvii, xcvi and cxxiv (*Collected Poems*, 641, 645, 647, 656 and 681; *Fatal Interview*, XII, XVI, XVIII, XXVII and LII).

[23]   See Sonnet xcviii (*Collected Poems*, 658; *Fatal Interview*, XXIX).

> I find some woman bearing as I bear
> Love like a burning city in the breast.
> I think however that of all alive
> I only in such utter, ancient way
> Do suffer love; in me alone survive
> The unregenerate passions of a day
> When treacherous queens, with death upon the tread,
> Heedless and wilful, took their knights to bed.[24]

But like tales of such lovers in the past, otherwise we would fail to remember them, we know it is bound to end badly. In *Fateful Interview*, the lovers have a moment of orgasmic bliss in a sonnet which concludes with another echo of Donne:

> O sweet, O heavy-lidded, O my love,
> When morning strikes her spear upon the land,
> And we must rise and arm us and reprove
> The insolent daylight with a steady hand,
> Be not discountenanced if the knowing know
> We rose from rapture but an hour ago.[25]

The happiness lasts for another sonnet or two, as the protagonist contemplates "the mute grave of two / Who lived and died believing love was true," but soon she is pursued by "Desolate dreams": "Weeping I wake; waking, I weep, I weep."[26]

After the break, Millay's protagonist, marvelously assisted as she is by the poet's ability to compel the arrogance and the domineering tyranny of chaotic passion to be channeled into the order the sonnet commands, makes a movingly stoic declaration (that nevertheless manages to join "gods" with "all the children getting dressed for school"):

> You loved me not at all, but let it go;
> I loved you more than life, but let it be.
> As the more injured party, this being so,
> The hour's amenities are all to me –
> The choice of weapons; and I gravely choose

---

[24]   Sonnet xcv (*Collected Poems*, 655; *Fatal Interview*, XXVI).
[25]   Sestet of Sonnet xxxvii (*Collected Poems*, 657; *Fatal Interview*, XXVIII).
[26]   See Sonnets c and cii (*Collected Poems*, 660 and 662; *Fatal Interview*, XXXI and XXXIII).

> To let the weapons tarnish where they lie;
> And spend the night in eloquent abuse
> Of senators and popes and such small fry
> And meet the morning standing, and at odds
> With heaven and earth and hell and any fool
> Who calls his soul his own, and all the gods,
> And all the children getting dressed for school ...
> And you will leave me, and I shall entomb
> What's cold by then in an adjoining room.

We may or may not wish to identify the poet with the speaker in these poems, ultimately it does not matter as long as we pay due regard to the poetic speech itself. As long as the poetry sustains the passion and resolve that it expresses we do not need to seek its grounds or its cause in biography. This is confessional poetry avant-le-mot and as the mode had been traditionally practiced in generations of sonnets; but then the very form and style of the sonnet protects it from being treated with the condescension of someone listening to a disconcertingly personal disclosure. Perhaps this is one of the reasons why since the revival of the sonnet as a popular poetic form at the end of the eighteenth century (to a large extent through the influence of another woman poet, Charlotte Smith, whose *Elegiac Sonnets* first appeared in 1784) women – such as Mary Robinson, Elizabeth Barrett Browning and Christina Rossetti[27] – have been the most graphic, dramatic and candid practitioners of the art. So near the end of *Fatal Interview*, Millay's protagonist can openly admit without cringing:

> I know my mind and I have made my choice;
> Not from your temper does my doom depend;
> Love me or love me not, you have no voice
> In this, which is my portion to the end.
> Your presence and your favours, the full part
> That you could give, you now can take away:
> What lies between your beauty and my heart
> Not even you can trouble or betray.
> Mistake me not – unto my inmost core
> I do desire your kiss upon my mouth;
> They have not craved a cup of water more

---

[27] As in Mary Robinson's *Sappho and Phaon* (1796) – a pair of legendary antique lovers Millay also celebrates ("Sappho Crosses the Dark River into Hades" in *Collected Poems*, 293-94) – Elizabeth Barrett Browning (*Sonnets from the Portuguese*, 1847) and Christina Rossetti ("Monna Innominata," 1881).

That bleach upon the deserts of the south;
Here might you bless me; what you cannot do
Is bow me down, who have been loved by you.

In the penultimate sonnet she can even celebrate her awareness of who has lost the most by the breakup of the relationship. As someone who has control of her inner and outer worlds, however chaotic either may be, by means of an esteemed poetic form, which is perhaps after all to be reverenced more greatly than any mortal being, she and her protagonist have an indisputable memorial, even a monument, to their experience whereas the lover may no longer have anything to regard with pride apart from his memory of a love-affair he was unable to sustain:

> If in the years to come you should recall,
> When faint at heart or fallen on hungry days,
> Or full of griefs and little if at all
> From them distracted by delights or praise;
> When failing powers or good opinion lost
> Have bowed your neck, should you recall to mind
> How of all men I honoured you the most,
> Holding you noblest among mortal-kind:
> Might not my love – although the curving blade
> From whose wide mowing none may hope to hide,
> Me long ago below the frosts had laid –
> Restore you somewhat to your former pride?
> Indeed I think this memory, even then,
> Must raise you high among the run of men.[28]

In the end the sonnet triumphs over all pain and disappointment, certainly in the hands of such a practitioner as Edna St. Vincent Millay. Elsewhere in this volume one of the contributors refers to Dylan Thomas as a masculine Edna St. Vincent Millay. This is not a comparison that I would support for a moment. However, before I came across this particular judgment, another comparison had occurred to me: in no biographical sense and on quite untheoretical grounds, it is clear that Edna St. Vincent Millay is the female Other, the feminine anti-self not only to Petrarch and all his love-lorn club mates, but also in distinctive ways to those two matching New

---

[28] Sonnets cix, cxiv and cxx (*Collected Poems*, 669, 674 and 680; *Fatal Interview*, XL, XLV and LI).

England Roberts, Lowell and Frost. No one who knows her work would ever commit the transgression she most feared:

> Let you not say of me when I am old,
> In pretty worship of my withered hands
> Forgetting who I am, and how the sands
> Of such a life as mine run red and gold
> Even to the ultimate sifting dust, "Behold,
> Here walketh passionless age!"[29]

---

[29] The opening lines of Sonnet xx (*Collected Poems*, 580).

PORTRAITS OF GOTHAM:
TWENTIETH-CENTURY AMERICAN CULTURE
AND THE WRITERS OF NEW YORK CITY

EDWARD MARGOLIES

Everyone came there – authors as far back as Washington Irving at the birth of the Republic, carrying on to the present day. To name only a few: Edgar Allan Poe, Walt Whitman, Herman Melville, Willa Cather, F. Scott Fitzgerald, Saul Bellow, Thomas Wolfe, Richard Wright, William Faulkner. Some loved the City's vitality, some feared the anomie; many had mixed feelings and moved away. Each felt intensely. Nor were they so different from the Spanish poet Lorca or the Swiss-French artist Mondrian. One felt the City's menace, the other projected bright happy complex patterns he called "Broadway Boogie Woogie."

When in 1889 the magisterial editor-author William Dean Howells gave up his longtime Boston residence to live in New York (having recently assumed the editorship of the relatively upstart *Harper's Magazine*), many among America's elite regarded the move as a distressing shift in cultural geography. Was Brahmin Boston, the cultural capital, losing out to the powerful financial attractions of polyglot New York? Until now the gothic popular fiction of nineteenth-century authors – George Lippard or George Thompson, as examples – painted the City in lurid tones of vice and crime. Even Matthew Hale Smith's celebrated studies of contemporary New York (*Sunshine and Shadow in New York*, 1868) depicted more shadow than sunlight. Among major writers, only Whitman imagined democratic possibilities – though even he expressed reservations in post-war years. Herman Melville meanwhile envisioned the City's inhabitants as trapped or imprisoned.

Thus what Howells' arrival portended, among other things, was a New York that would come under renewed scrutiny from American artists and authors. An "Ashcan" school of painting examining the City's street life would spring up at the end of the century, but several years earlier Howells would portray the City as almost a character in itself. Others followed suit – the City acting as a something more than passive setting that alters or defines one's writing and, in some instances, alters or defines the character of the author. Of course, an author's responses to his life *in* the City may be projected onto how he *sees* the City. And beyond: by portraying New York to accord with his experiences, the author may alter or redefine the image of the City. The way the world looks at the City, the way the City looks at itself. Processes of imagination produce endless consequences.

Mainly our writers were outsiders whose expectations were swallowed up in a mix of experiences they had not anticipated. Here at last among the myriad of identities the City proffered, they would discover their own. Alternatively, native New Yorkers, born and bred, who in time departed, seldom escaped their City consciousness and again and again imaginatively reentered the streets and neighborhoods of their childhood. What follows is by no means intended as comprehensive literary history, but rather to suggest varieties of transference between mind and City, City and mind.

To be sure, such exchanges do not occur in a cultural vacuum, and American perceptions of cities are fraught with ambiguities, as are their converse – small communities and Nature herself. Although New York City most flagrantly flaunts its dangers and attractions, one must ask why Americans so often look at cities with anxiety – an anxiety deeply embedded in the national psyche. Thomas Jefferson, for instance, feared for the character of city dwellers. They would, he said, depend for their survival on bankers, merchants, and manufacturers – and dependence on the uncertainties of urban capitalism breeds a vulnerability to demagogues. He would have preferred a nation of self-sufficient farmers, closer to Nature, to assure an enlightened democratic citizenry. Nature (domesticated), he believed, acted as an inherent good. Responses to cities today are not unlike Jefferson's. Civic unrest, immorality, and the artificiality of man-made environments are frequently cited as city problems, as if much the same could not be said of smaller communities. Yet when the social ills of small communities are conceded, Americans tend to blame cities for their baleful influence. Do cities, in some peculiar fashion, infect the otherwise pure-of-heart? The constant consciousness of cities, even among those who utterly disdain their presence, is an admission of their determinative historic role.

Concomitant with negative perceptions of the city is a consensual view that America's institutional development – at least until the present century – was determined by the accessibility, conquest and settlement of relatively unclaimed (by whites) western lands. Might that not be putting the cart before the horse? That is to say, might the conquest and settlement of the West represent a flight from the city, or more properly what the city seemed to symbolize, since in actuality most western expansion was undertaken by immigrants, farmers or other persons living outside cities. And what the city symbolized, beyond its presumed negative associations, was authority. For were not cities, both European and American, centers of concentrated governmental, financial and religious power? Escape west implied escape from the overarching authority of city institutions – an authority that restrained, taxed, and defined individuals according to social class.

The first West for Europeans was the east coast of the North American continent. But, in general, as the nation expanded westward to the Pacific, American cities to the east appeared to appropriate the mantle of authority European capitals once knew. By contrast, the aura of "West" would from time to time assume trans-geographical meanings; that is to say, areas apart and away from cities – perhaps, strangely, even east of cities, upstate, downstate, frontier, forests, small towns, villages. By distancing themselves from cities, Americans liked to imagine themselves distanced from authority, awakening to a new sense of independence. Surprisingly, some among the authority figures they fled, applauded. At the nation's start, for example, Presidents Washington, Adams, Jefferson, and Madison knew well the history of worker-peasant uprisings in European cities, and with the specter of violence and egalitarianism of the more recent French Revolution fresh in their minds, they welcomed an open, unclaimed West as a means of class tensions in overcrowded cities. (Which is not to say they could have been altogether easy about western farmers who twice in the late eighteenth century rebelled openly against paying government excise taxes and debts to eastern bank creditors.) Still, however varied their reasons, the rulers and the ruled, the governing class and the governed, more often than not at cross-purposes, were usually at one about the desirability of the West as opposed to the perils of the city. But as wilderness and frontier receded toward the end of the nineteenth century, cities and the West began to assume additional symbolic baggage. Professor Frederic Jackson Turner, in a widely publicized 1893 address, declared western frontier settlements the historic guarantor of democratic institutions, his implication being that the closing of the frontier bode ill for the republic.

Meanwhile nostalgic cultural references in the popular press portrayed the West as exemplifying the moral vigor and masculine energy of a younger American republic, now sadly dissipated by the presence of cities whose inhabitants lived lives of sybaritic decadence and/or proletarian barbarism. Pejorative allusions to cities were not, however, without their ironies when settlements in the West began producing the very phenomena for which the West was presumably intended as an anodyne. Indeed the very successes of western settlement caused western cities to spring up whose governing institutions were in large part modeled on those of eastern cities – which in turn catalyzed further waves of western emigration until at last it appeared there would be no more West to settle.

Despite such ironies, the rise of new cities was not always seen as a necessary evil. However much Americans claimed they detested cities, they also served paradoxically as a source of pride. Financial, cultural, and religious institutions were, after all, signs that high levels of civilization had been achieved. Fragmented visions of cities prevail to this day, but what makes the ambiguity especially odd is that in addition to their usual mixed images, cities have lately begun to assume the positive mythology of the West. Beginning in the 1890s (at about the time the census bureau announced officially there no longer existed a western frontier) southern and eastern European immigrants began seeking in cities dreams long associated with the West: independence, personal freedoms, economic opportunity. They were joined too by vast numbers of rural Americans, white and black, displaced from their homes by technological advances, agricultural depression, and racial persecution. Although none would claim these groups got along famously with each other or with longer-established city dwellers, they are now frequently perceived (often sentimentalized) as heroic just as were earlier generations of western emigrants. Just as early westerners had to subdue amoral untrammeled Nature and "lawless" Indians, so must city newcomers deal with indifferent or hostile slums, lumpen gangs, and cruel or exploitative bosses. In the popular literature, lone rangers with John Wayne-like integrity, no longer able to find respite or to repurify themselves in open country, revert to cities as Philip Marlowe-like private eyes fighting crime and corruption. Moreover, the ordinarily exalted West may now on occasion be depicted as mean, bleak, narrow and provincial. One need only think as far back as Mark Twain or to contemporary writers like Raymond Carver or Wallace Stegner, or to present-day films and documentaries revealing the ecological damage done to western lands and wildlife, and the "genocidal" treatment of Indians. Finally the peculiar reversal of East-West perceptions extends to individual freedoms. Whereas the West inevitably tested an individual's resources for survival, a corrupted West may now compel him to conform to hypocritical standards.

The city serves as a countercultural vision – not despite, but because of its seeming indifference to personal behavior, not despite, but because of its seeming anarchy – allowing the individual psychological space to attain his possibilities without fear of societal disapproval. The very "formlessness" of cities may be viewed as a challenge to create structure, neighborhoods, or political, ethnic, social communities, nor unlike pioneers who dominate Nature to create property and communities. If an open West once looked to beckon persons who might otherwise crowd into cities, the cities may now relieve the distressed countryside of their dispossessed. But unlike previous settler generations, the new city dweller cannot hope for self-sufficiency in a corporate environment. Perhaps Jefferson's dream of an agrarian nation (impervious to the wiles of demagogues) never really had much of a chance in a nation determined from the start on becoming rich.

Few would dispute that New York's early history diverges considerably from that of other Atlantic coast cities. And yet in a curious way, New York history anticipates much of what concerns Americans today. Like other East coast cities, New York was, as we have seen, the West for seventeenth-century Europeans departing their countries. But unlike other cities, New Amsterdam (as it was first called) could not very securely establish itself as a community ruled over and populated by a single ethnic or national or religious group. Try as they might, the city's first Dutch governors were unable to persuade their Netherlands stockholder-employers to limit settlement to persons of Dutch origin and preferably to members of the Dutch Reformed Church. As a consequence, when in 1664 the British took possession, the population of renamed New York consisted of sizable numbers of native Indians, Walloons, Finns, Swedes, Dutch, Irish, Jews, Huguenots, and Africans, along with others. It is said furthermore that one could hear spoken on the streets eighteen different languages.

British rule produced no less a diversity, and by the time New York was absorbed into the new American nation, immigrants from all parts continued to pour in. Meanwhile persons of black African ancestry – consisting perhaps of twenty or thirty percent of the population in the eighteenth century – increased in number over the next two centuries, especially after World War I with large infusions from the American South and the Caribbean. The City's ethnic proportions change constantly but never its heterogeneity. Which is not to suggest New York is or ever was a melting pot. Not quite. Still in its fashion the City always was and remains a concentrated image of the country's population diversity. The writer who writes of a particular ethnic group senses constantly the hovering presence of others.

Obviously a city with its plethora of subcultures is not always a happy microcosm of the nation at large. From the start, New York has had its share of lawlessness, poverty, civic corruption, racial and social tensions. What makes the city work – when it does – are the truces, the small compromises different groups make among themselves and one another. In their fashion interfusions of these sorts produce a kind of peculiar New York culture – and within the fluctuating culture, the writer discovers the ever-American struggle of the individual to realize himself in an ever-shifting community that makes demands on his freedom. The problem for the New York writer, often enough, is where to begin.

Complicating problem is that the city looks to be without tradition. Rather, in fact, the city appears forever to be rebuilding itself, reinventing itself, reconstituting its image. Perhaps *this* is the tradition. To be sure New York was not founded on ideological or religious or political grounds, and thus in later years has never had to bury or live up to romantic cachets associated with its birth. New York, pure and simple, was established to make money for its Dutch stockholders and its moneymaking proclivities remain a constant lure. Newcomers arrive for mainly economic opportunities (though often these are illusory) and shifts in population are generally determined by the flow of money in and out of the city. Freed of illusion and sentimentalities, while at the same time recognizing economic needs as essential for survival, New Yorkers have built a complex culture intended to slake the spiritual and aesthetic needs of its diverse, often restive communities. No other city has produced so rich a culture because, paradoxically, the main business of the city is not culture. And yet in no other city does there linger so strong a cultural consciousness of the mother countries of immigrants, not to mention the Southern cultures of migrating blacks. As a result along about the time of the "death" of America's Old West, epiphanies of New York as a kind of hybrid cosmopolitan frontier town begin to emerge. By 1917, with America's entry into World War I, very nearly all New York narratives embrace thematic elements often associated with the American West. Inadvertently wartime New York had become (and remains) an enigmatic national symbol.

Accordingly the reader who looks beyond the visuals of skyscrapers and tenements, subways and congested streets may find an odd amalgam of Western individualism, frontier violence, innocence and optimism joined with presumed New York materialism, worldly skepticism and institutional restraints. Added to this mix, often enough, are "scientific" determinist perceptions – a heritage perhaps of nineteenth-century Calvinist thought patterns regarding America's God-ordained western conquests. Fashionable new beliefs now however suggest that Nature, money, class or the mysteries of the libido predict human destiny. Inevitably then, the City's ever-shifting physical landscape will mirror the cultural predispositions of the artists. In its guises – and more likely in its disguises – the City expresses the contradictions and complexities of the American character.

One thinks in this regard of the conclusion of Ralph Ellison's *Invisible Man* where the African-American protagonist hides out in a Harlem basement seeking respite from the roiling conflicts in his head as much as from those on the street above him. At first glance his image does not suggest that of an American Everyman. And yet he asks: "Who knows but that, on lower frequencies, I speak for you?"[1] Perhaps in its own way the New York novel speaks for the larger America. New York as a metaphor, the nation as an oxymoron. The wonder of it is the business of the writer.

---

[1] Ralph Ellison, *Invisible Man* (New York: Random House, 1952), 439.

AMERICAN LITERARY MODERNISM, POPULAR CULTURE AND METROPOLITAN MASS LIFE: THE EARLY FICTION OF ROBERT M. COATES

MATHILDE ROZA

The exceptional Robert Myron Coates (1897-1973), a lesser-known writer of the "lost generation," produced some sadly neglected fiction. The author of five novels, three collections of short stories, and several volumes of nonfiction, Coates was primarily known during his lifetime as the author of *Wisteria Cottage* (1948), a widely-read terrifying novel about a psychopathological adolescent, and for his association, from 1927 to 1967, with *The New Yorker*, first as a writer of various non-fictional sections, including the famous "Talk of the Town" column, then as a book reviewer (from 1930 to 1933), and later as art critic (from 1937 to 1967). Between 1930 and 1967, *The New Yorker* published over a hundred of his short stories, many of which were reissued in three collections, *All the Year Round* (1943), *The Hour After Westerly* (1957) and *The Man Just Ahead of You* (1964). Accomplished though these be, Coates' true literary identity shines out in his first three novels, *The Eater of Darkness* (1926), *Yesterday's Burdens* (1933) and *The Bitter Season* (1946). In these authentically Coatesian works, the writer comes across as an idiosyncratic experimentalist who touted literary innovation and placed great value on the novel as art. A highly innovative yet careful composer, he was likened by lost generation spokesman and personal friend Malcolm Cowley to his father, a successful mechanical engineer who derived great pleasure from working as a part-time inventor: "I think of [Robert Coates] as a craftsman, an inspired mechanic working with words as his father had worked with pieces of metal, choosing and calibrating, fitting together, then grinding and polishing in the hope of achieving some ultimate invention."[1]

---

[1] Malcolm Cowley, "Reconsideration," *The New Republic*, 171 (November 30, 1974), 40. See also Cowley's "Afterword" to Robert M. Coates, *Yesterday's Burdens* (Southern Illinois University Press, Lost American Fiction Series, 1975), 157-73, and his essay "Figure in a Crowd," in – *And I Worked at the Writer's Trade: Chapters of Literary History: 1918-1978* (New York: Viking Press, 1978), 82-94.

The present essay discusses some of the author's original formal and stylistic experiments as conducted in his first two novels, and explores the unique way in which Coates, working against the cultural background of the 1920s and 1930s, mediated elements of avant-gardist literary modernism and American popular culture in his attempt to find new ways of rendering the disturbing human and social realities of metropolitan mass life in the interbellum era.

The Eater of Darkness: Coates and the 1920s

Coates became convinced of the necessity – and the possibilities – of innovative fiction during his first stay in Paris in the early 1920s, then the site of "nothing less than a vast, radical international flowering of every one of the modern arts."[2] Like the many American artists and writers who flocked to Paris after the war, he was thrilled by the stimulating artistic climate and immersed himself in the bohemian expatriate scene, striking up friendships with, among others, Ernest Hemingway, Arthur Moss, Malcolm Cowley, Matthew Josephson, Harold Loeb, Ford Madox Ford, Peggy Guggenheim and Gertrude Stein. With great enthusiasm the young writer tried his hand at a variety of modernisms – Cubism, Futurism, Expressionism, Dadaism and Surrealism, as well as unprincipled combinations of these – and published several extravagant short stories in the American expatriate little magazines *Gargoyle*, *Broom* and *Secession*.

Having acquainted himself with the entire range of modernist forces in Paris during his first expatriate period (1921-1923), Coates withdrew from the French capital in his second stay abroad (1924-1926) and lived in Giverny, the artist village in Normandy, some fifty miles from Paris. There he wrote his first heavily experimental novel, *The Eater of Darkness* (published in Paris by Robert McAlmon's Contact Publishing Company[3] in the fall of 1926), in which he recreated the heady confusion that to him had characterized the Parisian literary scene:

---

[2] Malcolm Bradbury, *Dangerous Pilgrimages: Transatlantic Mythologies and the Novel* (New York: Viking, 1996), 339.

[3] Robert McAlmon's publishing company was devoted to bringing out "books by various writers who seem not likely to be published by other publishers for commercial or legislative reasons" (McAlmon, quoted in Robert E. Knoll, *McAlmon: Expatriate Writer and Publisher* [Lincoln: University of Nebraska Studies, 1957], 184-85). By 1926, McAlmon had published works by Ernest Hemingway, Marsden Hartley, William Carlos Williams, Ford Madox Ford, Ezra Pound, Mary Butts, H.D., and Gertrude Stein. For a complete list of Contact publications, see Robert E. Knoll (1957), 81-84.

In the twenties, a cheerful combativeness was the rule, and the rows over matters of the minutest dogma reached fantastic proportions. There were schools within schools, and factions within factions ... all splitting up, warring briefly, and uniting again with such furious rapidity that it was advisable for the outsider (and the American, to a certain extent, was inevitably an outsider; we just didn't have the Frenchman's capacity for exuberant contentiousness) to keep a constant check on the disposition of forces, a sort of daily war map, if he wanted to make his way through the melee without embarrassment.[4]

As this retrospective description suggests, Coates took a spectatorial distance from the various schools and movements that he encountered in Paris. This enabled him to compose what he himself described as "a satiric symposium of the various modern influences" containing "burlesques of, variously, Dreiser, Sinclair Lewis, the Da-Das, Waldo Frank, modern advertising, the Imagists, etc."[5]

In *The Eater of Darkness* Coates employs incongruous combinations of literary styles and tones of voice.[6] Thus, he uses surreal imagery in an ostensibly realistic piece of writing; parodies Herman Melville in an "official" Scotland Yard Docket; employs high-flown religious rhetoric in a prayer to the "all-succoring and all-powerful Potato"; uses advertising slogans in ordinary dialogue and transforms stereotypical characters and situations common in popular entertainment. Throughout, Coates mocks the detective or mystery genre, either by listing non-interpretable details, or by being over-accurate. As a result, the reader of *The Eater of Darkness*, much like Oedipa Maas in Thomas Pynchon's *The Crying of Lot 49* (1966) is confronted with a host of supposedly significant but

---

[4]   Robert M. Coates, "The Art Galleries: 'Transition,'" *The New Yorker* (November 12, 1955), 195.
[5]   Robert M. Coates, Application for a Guggenheim Scholarship in 1928 (John Simon Guggenheim Memorial Foundation, New York City). In a review of *The Eater of Darkness* for the *Paris Tribune*, Elliot Paul recognized stylistic parodies of James Joyce, Waldo Frank, E.E. Cummings, Sherwood Anderson, Jean Toomer, Max Bodenheim, Frank Harris and Ben Hecht. See Hugh Ford, *Published in Paris: American and British Writers, Printers, and Publishers in Paris, 1920-1939* (New York: MacMillan, 1975), 75. The French surrealists were a target as well, especially Louis Aragon's novel *Le Paysan de Paris*.
[6]   See also Constance Pierce, "Language Silence Laughter: The Silent Film and the 'Eccentric' Modernist Writer," *Sub-Stance*, 52 (1987), 59-75; and Robert Sage, "Melodramadness," *transition*, 4 (July 1927), 155-59.

clearly nonsensical clues. He finds himself pondering the meaning of the password "Eggs are indeterminate but fowls are firm" or the significance of passages like the following:

> At 3:36, Mr. Randolph Flock, living at 842 East 75 St., coined the phrase: "You may have a barrel of money, but you look like a hogshead to me," which later won the $10,000 Slanguage Prize offered by the Daily News.[7]

Coates had no ulterior critical motive in his satirical renderings and pastiches of the various developments in European and American modern writing, nor did he intend any structured ad-hominem attacks, as Hemingway had done in his parody of Sherwood Anderson in *The Torrents of Spring*. Above all, Coates' stylistic spiritedness is a cheerful celebration of the creative process and the possibilities for literary experimentation.

Far from immature, *The Eater of Darkness* is yet essentially playful in spirit, a feature which disturbed and puzzled some early critics. While the novel met with high praise from some quarters (*The New York Herald Tribune*, for instance, considered it an "extraordinarily diverting book, compact with astonishing devices, unusual tricks with syntax, satire, mirth, and madness,"[8] while *The New York Evening Post* referred to it as "unique" and called it "one of the cleverest tours de force ever contrived by the pen of a wit"[9]), several other American critics resented the book's vaudevillian characteristics. Thus, the exasperated critic of the *Saturday Review of Literature* complained that Coates "continually jests at himself, giggles when he might to his advantage be straightfaced, and plays the slapstick clown with unpleasant monotony,"[10] while *The New Republic* wondered with equal irritation "what this clever young man would achieve if he were to take his tongue out of his cheek."[11] To the writer, however, this *jeu d'esprit* was an essential part of the times and hence of his report on the decade. Although he later suffered from feelings of guilt over having contributed to the anti-social, anti-political frivolousness that the

---

[7]   Robert M. Coates, *The Eater of Darkness* (New York: G.P. Putnam's Sons, 1959), 85.

[8]   Herbert Gorman, *New York Herald Tribune* (August 3, 1929), 2.

[9]   E.M. Benson, *New York Evening Post* (July 27, 1929), 6.

[10]   Anonymous reviewer, *Saturday Review of Literature* (November 23, 1929), 6: 460.

[11]   B.D., *The New Republic* 60 (September 18, 1929), 133.

decade came to be associated with,[12] he always felt that the innocence and integrity of the 1920s were the period's saving grace, and made up for whatever shortcomings the era might have had:

> It was a crazy time, and in many ways, too, an incredibly innocent one, but, for all that, productive. Perhaps the best thing to say is that it was truly a period of experimentation. There was indeed a ferment in all the arts … and if the headiness of all this made us sometimes a little punch-drunk or just plain silly, it must, I think, be conceded that we were honestly so.[13]

Robert Sage, who reviewed the novel for Eugene Jolas's *transition*, believed that *The Eater of Darkness* was so apposite of its time that it would have an early death: "In ten years time, no reader will remember that such a book as *The Eater of Darkness* ever existed."[14] Fortunately, the novel had more staying-power than Sage had granted it, and the book was reprinted twice in the United States, in 1929 by Macaulay's Publishing Company and in 1959 by Capricorn Press. In addition, interest was expressed in a radio- and a motion picture production of the work.[15] Up to this moment, however, the complex book with its stylistic hurly-burly has been able to resist this type of commodification. Aware that his book did not sell, Coates once mockingly prophesied that his work would "probably be the sensation of the second-hand dealers."[16] In a sense, time proved him right. Today, the original edition is for sale for prices up to $1500.

---

[12] See, for instance, Henry F. May, "Shifting Perspectives on the 1920's," *Mississippi Valley Historical Review*, 43 (1956), 405-27.

[13] Robert M. Coates, *The View From Here* (New York: Harcourt, Brace, 1960), 211.

[14] Robert Sage, "Melodramadness," *transition*, 4 (July 1927), 155.

[15] Pacifica Radio, a listener-supported radio station in Berkeley, asked permission to read *The Eater of Darkness* serially, in its entirety, in August 1971. Coates felt flattered and gladly gave permission for the production. California showed enthusiasm for a second time when, a few months later, a producing firm called Scriptorium Productions expressed interest in purchasing the motion picture rights to Coates' first novel. Coates was game, but his agent, Harold Ober, could not agree on a price with Scriptorium. After a prolonged correspondence and to the regrets of all parties, the project was abandoned. (Records of Harold Ober Associates, Princeton University Libraries, Manuscript Division, Princeton.)

[16] Robert M. Coates, letter [1929] written on the occasion of the tenth anniversary of the Yale class of 1919, published in *The History of the Class of 1919* (New Haven: Yale University Press, 1929), 171.

On closer scrutiny, the novel is much more than a satirical reflection of the decade's aesthetic turmoil. The book is very much an exploration of newly available artistic possiblities for the creation of an indigenous American art – a concern that Coates shared with writers like Hart Crane, William Carlos Williams, E.E. Cummings and the individuals associated with the nationalist literary magazines *The Soil, Contact, Broom* and *Secession*. When Coates was at work on his novel, America and its distinctive culture were very much in the limelight. Not only was Paris "awash with Americans and a hotbed of enthusiasm for things American,"[17] the revolutionary avant-garde too, especially the Futurists and Dadaists, celebrated America as "a vanguard artifact in its own right."[18] To them, America's energy, speed, modernity and general aliveness seemed an attractive alternative to old, war-devastated Europe. Coates observed the situation from close quarters:

> One of the minor ironies of the postwar-period is the fact that, while Americans were going to Europe to seek culture and freedom, Europe was filled with young artists looking longingly westward and itching to come over here. The cult of the machine, of speed and adventurousness, which dominated their work made them think of America as a land of promise.[19]

Prominent among those "young artists looking longingly westward" were the Parisian Dadaists, a group of exuberant and provocative artists which included Louis Aragon, André Breton, Paul Elouard, Philippe Soupault, and Tristan Tzara, who gave voice to their disgust at the dead sterility of traditional academic art and the mouldy

---

[17] Ann Douglas, *Terrible Honesty: Mongrel Manhattan in the 1920s* (New York: Farrar, Straus and Giroux, 1995), 108.

[18] Mathew Roberts, "Bonfire of the Avant-Garde: Cultural Rage and Readerly Complicity in *The Day of the Locust*," *Modern Fiction Studies*, 42/1 (1996), footnote 18. For a very illuminating article on the attraction of America to European "proto-Dadaist" artists like Marcel Duchamp, Francis Picabia, and Jean Crotti, see [Anon.] "French Artists Spur on an American Art," *New York Tribune*, Sunday, October 24, 1915, 2-3. Reprinted in Rudolf E. Kuenzli, "Articles on New York Dada from New York Newspapers," *Dada/Surrealism*, 14 (1985), 128-35. With regard to the situation in France in the 1920s, see Matthew Josephson, *Life Among the Surrealists: A Memoir* (New York: Holt, Rinehart and Winston, 1962), 125, and Philippe Soupault, *The American Influence in France* (Seattle: University of Washington Book Store, 1930).

[19] Robert M. Coates, "Modern," a Profile on William Lescaze, *The New Yorker*, 12 (December 12, 1936), 29.

and moribund culture whose principles art had enshrined. Coates was much interested in the movement, not in the least because it seemed to provide important clues to some of his own artistic problems. As a student at Yale University, the young writer had already developed a sharp distrust of the genteel avidity for high culture that had characterized Victorian America, and had become interested in popular culture, especially silent movies. His work for *The Yale Literary Magazine* displayed a Frank Norris-like interest in violence, a distaste for cerebration and a strong desire to write fiction attuned to "life." With these aesthetic preferences, he was understandably much interested in an art movement that offered suggestions as to how to appropriate "life itself" in art, and that delivered "if not the first, then certainly the most crucial blow at those distinctions once possible between fine art and popular art."[20] For Coates, embracing Dada was like killing two birds with one stone, while the adoption of Dada's formal properties – especially the use of non-literary material and the technique of literary collage – satisfied the writer's great interest in formal innovation.

What was perhaps most attractive to Coates and other young American writers was that the Dadaist revolt seemed to offer suggestions for the creation of an American indigenuous art that would address the then crucial question of the American artist's relation to mass or popular culture which, at that time, was increasingly coming to define America's cultural climate. The Dadaists' celebration of such manifestations of American popular culture as silent movies, Nick Carter novels, Krazy Kat cartoons, jazz, skyscrapers, advertising – everything that partook of America's speed, life and spontaneity[21] – as well as their embrace of the new world's

---

[20] Dickran Tashjian, *Skyscraper Primitives: Dada and the American Avant-Garde, 1910-1925* (Middletown: Wesleyan University Press, 1975), 4. For a particularly good overview of the shattering of the boundaries between "high" and "low" art, see Kirk Varnedoe and Adam Gopnik, *High and Low: Modern Culture and Popular Art* (New York: MOMA, 1990).

[21] It should be noted that the Dadaists, in their revolt against high culture's hostility to mass culture, did not just embrace American popular culture. Like the Cubists before them, the Dadaists used brochures, catalogues, illustrated magazines, advertising material and newspapers in their art and were also much fascinated by European manifestations of popular culture, especially the French pulp fiction series *Fantomâs*. See Varnedoe and Gopnik (1990) and Robin Walz, *Pulp Surrealism: Insolent Popular Culture in Early Twentieth-Century Paris* (Berkeley: University of California Press, 2000).

urban-technological landscape and its mechanical development, had a
significant liberating effect on many American writers and provided a
strong sense of legitimization of the use of contemporary American
materials in their art. As Dickran Tashjian pointed out: "While a few
American artists seized upon the formal experimentation of Dada, the
majority discovered the freedom of new subject matter, particularly
the machine and its industrial-urban environment, construed by
Dadaist and American alike to be peculiarly American."[22]

In his classic account *Skyscraper Primitives* Tashjian discusses the
aesthetics of several American artists – dubbed "skyscraper primitives"
by Gorham B. Munson in 1924 – who responded to the European avant-
garde's celebration of America's culture and technological landscape.
Although the book is somewhat hampered by the author's determination
to establish too direct or even causal a relationship between the historical
Dada movement and the American avant-garde of the 1910s and 1920s,
his book served an important groundbreaking function.[23] It is unfortunate
that Coates was not included in his account: *The Eater of Darkness*, after
all, is one of the most ambitious comments on the efforts to create
literature out of the "terrifically alive"[24] phenomena of American
culture, and responds both to the Dadaists' formal experiments and to
their suggestions about literary content. Set in New York City, his novel
contains reproductions of advertising signs and slogans, newspaper
articles and headlines, shopfronts, a page from a detective novel, chunks
of a filmscript, an excerpt from a "Scotland Yard Docket," and it
recreates the cacophonous and kaleidoscopic life of the metropolitan,
technological landscape in an innovative literary style. The novel's racy
plot, which revolves around the invention of a futuristic x-ray machine,
is responsive to the European avant-gardist "machine aesthetic," an
aesthetic in which machine technology was seen as an agent that
would encourage revolutionary change in both art and society, which
drew many avantgardists towards America's technological
environment.

The novel's construction is of special interest because it reflects
how Europe's fascination for America was based not on the real

---

22 Tashjian, *Skyscraper Primitives*, 7.
23 For similar criticism, see Milton A. Cohen, *POETandPAINTER: The Aesthetics of
E.E.Cummings's Early Work* (Detroit: Wayne State University Press, 1987).
24 Edmund Wilson, "The Aesthetic Upheaval in France: The Influence of Jazz in
Paris and Americanization of French Literature and Art," *Vanity Fair*, 17 (February
1922), 49.

nation, but on the representations of American culture dispersed by the American mass media and culture industry. In this, Coates managed to avoid the mistake made by self-proclaimed American Dadaists such as Malcolm Cowley and Matthew Josephson who (in the verdict of Waldo Frank) were unaware that in their celebratory appropriation of America they were "reflecting not even America's surface, but Europe's thirsty reflection of our surface."[25]

Coates, by contrast, allowed the novel's plot to be explicitly dictated by a French girl whose imagination had been formed by her exposure to popular culture (especially pulp fiction and silent movies) and the tabloids. As Coates outlined *The Eater of Darkness* to the Guggenheim Foundation: "[The novel's] plot is a fantasy developed along Nick Carter lines, [which] tells what a girl in France (who has read of New York only in the tabloids and the sensational fiction) imagines is happening to her lover, when he goes there. It is, naturally, a moviesque hodge-podge of murder, armored cars, x-ray bullets and bank hold-ups."[26] Thus, the book's protagonist becomes caught up in the most improbable, fantastically adventurous circumstances, which causes the book to become very amusing indeed.

The butt of Coates' jokes, however, is not the French consumer of American popular culture, but the popular culture industry itself. The author made his points by joyfully transforming the stylistic and narrative conventions that underlie popular fiction, thus exposing it as a series of formulaic clichés that reduce human life to fixed role-patterns, stereotypical characters and predictable dramatic incidents. Thus we find that the cold-blooded criminal Picrolas experiences passionate feelings of love for the protagonist (Charles); that the detective is attempting to solve the crime he himself committed; that the heroine of the story is a prostitute; and that Charles himself is totally unfit for the role of Hero. Morally unsound, subject to fits of unreasonable violence, a mass-murderer and a rapist, Charles nevertheless has to act according to the hero-formula. An element that adds considerable interest to the novel's scheme is that its protagonist is aware of the manipulation of his character by his French lover (and, incidentally, by the author, one Robert Coates). Lacking a stable fictional characterization, he functions as a puppet on a string,

---

[25] Waldo Frank. "Seriousness and Dada," *1924*, 3 (September 1924), 70-73. Reprinted in Frank's *In The American Jungle* (New York, 1937), 131.
[26] Robert M. Coates, Application for John Simon Guggenheim Award, 1928 (John Simon Guggenheim Memorial Foundation, New York City).

subjected to other people's creative whims,[27] and imprisoned by the French girl's imaginings about life in America. In this manner, Coates lightfootedly indicated how the then current popular representations of American culture hampered Europe's understanding of America and, in essence, violated the free will and identity of the individuals thus represented.

Although Coates profited from the suggestions that Dada offered, he was not at all cheering on the European infatuation with things American. In fact, despite its hilarious surface, the novel strongly suggests that its author balked at the fact that the European avant-garde saw oppositional value in the country that he had abandoned as culturally and spiritually arid. In addition to his mockery of the modes of popular fiction that European members of the avant-garde rejoiced in, Coates' particular use of the machine in his novel questions the machine aesthetic's utopian notion that society could be transformed through technological development: Coates' machine is an instrument of mass destruction, which is used to electrocute dozens of people. Also, in his recreations of New York's urban-technological life, Coates focussed on the danger of mental collapse, urban loneliness, and the dehumanizing effects of mass life. At the same time, however, the novel amply illustrates how the appropriation of the American metropolitan landscape could generate radical artistic change – which was, to Coates, a cause for rejoicing in its own right.

Yesterday's Burdens: **Robert Coates and the 1930s**
Coates returned to the United States in late 1926 and joined the *New Yorker* staff as a writer of the famous "Talk of the Town" column, working alongside James Thurber and E.B. White, both of whom became close friends of his and of his first wife, the sculptor Elsa Kirpal. In 1930 he published his much celebrated historical work, *The Outlaw Years: The History of the Land Pirates of the Natchez Trace, 1800-1835*, which became the Literary Guild Selection for August of that year. With the money, Coates started building a house in the country, in Gaylordsville, Connecticut, and left New York City. At that time, he began to develop "the most intricate plans" for a new novel

---

[27] A particularly amusing example occurs when Charles himself becomes confused by the different styles and genres that Coates employs to describe his adventures and is proud when he chooses the right jargon in the right situation: "Charles's heart leaped proud within him. It had not, after all, been a wrong guess. He had made it a toss-up between scenario-writing and detectives" (*The Eater of Darkness*, 95).

about life in New York City – his greatest artistic challenge – which was to become "a sort of mixture of dissertation, narrative, and autobiography."[28]

A product of the 1920s, Coates continued to attach great value to the novel as a work of art in the politicized decade that had just begun. His continued concern for literary form, however, was not prompted by a commitment to art-for-art's sake, but arose directly from the writer's conviction that the novel, although a self-contained work of art, should reflect society and illuminate its life and that of its members. Coates rarely spoke explicitly about his methods, but his belief in the unequivocal relationship between form in art and form in society can be gleaned from an unpublished novel, "Bright Day," which Coates worked on from 1934 until 1942. In it, the writer Amberman – a character modelled on Robert Coates himself, and no doubt named after his stunning mass of orange-red hair – points out that, to him, "the art-form is, inevitably, no more than the esthetic embodiment of the social form of the life it expresses."[29] Coates defended his continued concern for literary form in an era of grave social and economic problems in a letter to his friend, the critic Kenneth Burke:

> [It is] the attempt to find an appropriate form ... that slows us all up so much nowadays. And I don't mean that in too purely "esthetic" a sense, either. Look, for instance, at the trouble our proletarian writers are having in trying to find a "form" for a novel about a strike ....
> "Form" I might add, is really only "true expression" isn't it?[30]

With *Yesterday's Burdens*, which took the author three years to write, Coates endeavored to create an "aesthetic embodiment" of New York City that would express the social, psychological and existential conditions of metropolitan life. As such, New York does not just feature as the setting, but plays a central role as a powerful determinant of literary form and narrative style: all is geared to express the intensely demanding aspects of the city for the artist. The effect, as one reviewer noted, is one of intense exasperation:

---

[28] Robert Coates to Gertrude Stein, June 16, 1931, Gertrude Stein papers, Beinecke Library, Yale University.
[29] Robert M. Coates, "Bright Day," unpublished manuscript, Robert Coates papers, American Heritage Center, University of Wyoming, Laramie.
[30] Robert Coates to Kenneth Burke, April 3, 1935, Kenneth Burke papers, Pattee Library, Penn State University.

> Here is a man with the sensitive instincts of a poet flung willy-nilly
> into the complicated environment of this modern world. Like
> innumerable sensitive and less expressive spirits, he is overwhelmed
> by it. He regards escape as both impossible and undesirable.[31]

The style Coates used to convey the urban scene in *Yesterday's Burdens* is similar to that used in the sketches of urbanity that were scattered throughout *The Eater of Darkness*. Indeed, the writer had not just emerged from Paris a skillful observer and an expert in pastiche. More importantly, out of the "various modern influences" that he encountered, he distilled a distinctive urban literary style.

Coates' sketches are rare evocations of the sights, sounds and systems of New York City, as well as intriguing portraits of the dire psychological effects of metropolitan mass life, especially loneliness, the loss of human contact, the loss of humaneness, and the danger of mental collapse in America's sign-encoded and technology-regulated climate. The thoughts, emotions, moods, and associations rising up from the inner world of the individual urban dweller are never allowed to interact meaningfully or coherently with the continuous material onslaught from the world outside: both are shown to simply accumulate to the breaking point. The most notable stylistic and syntactical device that Coates used to convey how the two different worlds abut each other, is the use of double, even triple, parentheses. The device is a happy one: the parentheses prove remarkably well-suited to express the chaotic process of accumulation and disruption of auditory and optical input and to convey New York's continuously discontinuous interaction with the human mind and sensibility. Note how, in the following example from *The Eater of Darkness*, the electric advertising sign is included as a powerful eye-catcher, and is perceived to wink "maliciously":

> At an immeasurable distance across
> Fifth Avenue where (a whirr (the chatter of
> traffic   GOLDBAUM & BIRNER   enmoil-
> ing) of red-   SILKS   yellow axles)
> winked maliciously into a building-window
> (through the poignant moment of disparition)
> as New York again had swooned smotheringly

---

[31]   Florence Haxton Britten, "Everyman of the Modern Age," *New York Herald Tribune*, December 17, 1933.

over him (her face drowning) irremediably
(into the freckled sides of the Flatiron Building).[32]

Although the style that Coates employed leaned heavily on the several avant-garde and modernist techniques that he had become acquainted with in Europe, the jolty, chaotic amalgam of literary styles that he created is idiosyncratic and quite unique.[33] The combination of surreal and hallucinatory imagery, the inclusion of mass material, the parentheses, the interrupted, unfinished sentences, the use of the colon and semi-colon, and the progressive form of the verb, as well the frequent absence of main clauses – all are Coates' unique property. The use of the progressive form might recall Gertrude Stein's style, but the progressive is here employed to convey the tempo, the constant speed of modern life, rather than a "prolonged present."[34] His continuously interrupted, unfocussed texts do not produce the "circular, infinitely slow movement" that characterizes Stein's "continuous present,"[35] but convey instead the highly agitated state of mind and overworked sensibility of modern man.

The inclusion of various mass materials in his text – advertising slogans, brand names, newspaper headlines, markers in subway stations, traffic signs as well as fragments of conversations and remarks – was essential to the writer's aim to document the city. Partly, the function of this material is mimetic. Coates' impressive city-pictures – frequently wholly exempt of any narrative sequence and replete with public materials – follow each other as in a verbal slide show. Together they form a collage of images that "ma[k]e a sound to the eyes," as Gertrude Stein once described Coates' sense-impressions, and which she, as an experimenter in "prose painting" herself, had good reason to admire.[36] Above all, however, Coates' urban sketches

---

[32]   Robert M. Coates, *The Eater of Darkness,* 121.
[33]   For more detailed analyses of Coates' urban style, see M.H. Roza, "Robert Myron Coates in the 1920s and early 1930s: The Impact of Dada and the Development of a Distinctive City Fiction," *Oasis*, Working Paper No. 41 (October 1999), 15-17 and "Lost in 'The Dada City': The New York City Fiction of Robert M. Coates," in *The American Metropolis: Image and Inspiration*, eds H. Krabbendam, M. Roholl and T. De Vries (Amsterdam: VU University Press, 2001), 123-34.
[34]   See, for instance, Richard Bridgman, *Gertrude Stein in Pieces* (New York: Oxford University Press, 1970), 97.
[35]   *Ibid.,* 52.
[36]   Gertrude Stein, *The Autobiography of Alice B. Toklas* (New York: Harcourt, Brace and Co., 1933), 244; Bradbury uses the term "prose painting" in relation to Gertrude Stein in *Dangerous Pilgrimages*, 263.

seek to explore the impact of the unpredictable forces at work within urban modernity – forces of which the mass material that the author used are merely surface manifestations: mass media, crowds, commercialism, technological developments, and social engineering. All of these are shown to affect the atmosphere and mood of American life and to play upon the sensibility, psychology and actions of its citizens. In all, Coates' city-scapes are more expressionist than reportorial and can be compared to John Dos Passos' rendition of the city in *Manhattan Transfer* (1925). More heavily citational and fragmented than Dos Passos, however, the artistic effect of some of Coates' work can be more profitably compared to certain works of the American abstract artist Stuart Davis.

In addition to literary style, Coates also surrended the novel's formal aspects to the demands of the modern city that he was so intent on recreating in his work. Having studied New York and its life thoroughly, the author concluded that the condition of city-life – especially the disappearance of the separate individual on the one hand, and the pluralization of the self on the other – necessitated a new approach to characterization. In a similar way, the transient and intractable life of the urbanite had effectively taken away the novelist's recourse to a tractable plot, making it nearly impossible for the writer to write, except in the fragmentary, improvisatory, impressionistic collage-style that is employed in many parts of the novel. This is indeed one of the points that *Yesterday's Burdens* was to make: Coates described the novel as "basically an attempt to express the disintegrative aspects of modern city life, particularly as affecting the artist."[37] Indeed, New York City appears to orchestrate the work of fiction, dictating and finally usurping plot, character and description. Coates offers little hope for the future of the metropolitan novel. At the end, the writer has effectively been silenced. Having lost his sole would-be protagonist in the urban maze, he withdraws, leaving the reader on a note of sad resignation: "I never saw him again."

The aesthetic consequences of Coates' conviction that "the novel must derive its form from the form of social order he describes"[38] are

---

[37] Robert M. Coates, Application for Guggenheim Fellowship, 1935 (John Simon Guggenheim Memorial Foundation, New York).
[38] Robert M. Coates, "A Greek Named Pete," *The New Masses* (August 31, 1939), 24. A review of William Saroyan's *Little Children*.

explicitly communicated to the reader by the highly self-conscious narrator-cum-writer of *Yesterday's Burdens*:

> "But let me tell you about this book I'm trying to write, in between bouts of book- reviewing.... It's a novel, or rather a novel about a novel, or perhaps one might better describe it as a long essay discussing a novel that I might possibly write, with fragments of the narrative inserted here and there, by way of illustration or example .... I have this young man, Henderson, and the process would seem to be to take him to the city and there lose him, as thoroughly as possible. Or at least reverse the usual method, and instead of seeking to individualize him and pin him down to a story, to generalize more and more about him – to let him become like the figures in a crowd, and the crowd dispersing."[39]

The self-referentiality of the novel, as well as the author's deliberate manipulation of his fictional character in the novel as a whole (an element that we also saw in *The Eater of Darkness*), anticipates certain postmodern, or late modern, self-referential techniques. Indeed, when the novel was republished in 1975, it was hailed as an "interesting, very quiet forerunner to some contemporary Players with their players (like Barth, Fowles)."[40] Malcolm Cowley, too, considered the author's "cards-on-the-table attitude towards the art of fiction" to be "prophetic."[41] It should be borne in mind, however, that Coates was not so much commenting on the phenomenon of fiction (as opposed to reality), as on the difficulties that he encountered while executing his craft. As a result, as Phelps has argued, the impression that arises from Coates' fiction is one of "a besetting, often harassing mixture of feelings toward his art, of devotion and dogging anxiety."[42] While Phelps' observation is discerning indeed, the mixture must be said to be considerably lightened up by the author's casual conversational tone and the curious throwaway attitude of, almost, carelessness with which, on occasion, he surprises the reader.

---

[39] Robert M. Coates, *Yesterday's Burdens* (New York: Macaulay, 1933), 42. The quotation marks are in the original.
[40] Anonymous review, *Choice*, 12 (September 1975), 838. See also Donald Phelps, "Passionate Precision: The Fiction of Robert Myron Coates," *Pulpsmith*, 6/4 (Winter 1987), 162.
[41] Malcolm Cowley, – *And I Worked at the Writer's Trade*, 94.
[42] Donald Phelps, "Passionate Precision," 162.

When an author's style appears to be out of time, he is not necessarily ahead of it. While he may, in effect, be anticipating certain literary techniques and developments (as Coates very much seems to be doing), the past should not be ignored as a source for explanations. To understand the intention that underlies Coates' willful confusion of the realms of art and life, note should be taken of the author's enthusiasm for the works of Anthony Trollope (which Gertrude Stein, incidentally, sent him by the caseload), who took the Victorian tendency to address one's audience a decided step further, and obtained, in the words of an offended Henry James, "a suicidal satisfaction in reminding the reader that the story he was telling was only, after all, make-believe. He habitually referred to the work in hand (in the course of that work) as a novel and to himself as a novelist, and was fond of letting the reader know that this novelist could direct that course of events according to his pleasure."[43] It would appear that Coates, by addressing his readers directly, was less interested in exposing his fiction as fiction in order to question the knowability of reality or the usefulness of language as a descriptive tool, than in establishing a bond, in the nineteenth-century fashion, with his audience. In the early 1950s, Coates explicitly expressed his longing for a harmonious relationship between the artist and his public in a letter to Malcolm Cowley:

> It's quite true that in our time [1920s] we considered the reading (and buying) public – in fact, principally the buying public – to be insensitive and incompetent, and so had to develop a principle of success-by-failure to justify ourselves; and true too that no such problems ever bothered Trollope or Dickens …. But I know it did bother Courbet and Rembrandt, and the whole point is, I think, that we, like they, worse luck!, just didn't happen to be living in one of those wonderful Golden Ages they talk about, when the buying public and the artists could go beautifully hand in hand.[44]

Coates' notion of "success-by-failure" originated in the early 1930s: in an unpublished notebook related to the composition of *Yesterday's Burdens*, the author suggests that although he was passionately convinced of the necessity of artistic renewal, he was, in fact, a willy-nilly experimentalist:

---

[43]   Henry James, *The Future of the Novel: Essays on the Art of Fiction*, edited and with an introduction by Leon Edel (New York: Vintage Books, 1956), 6.
[44]   Robert Coates to Malcolm Cowley, August 21, 1951, Malcolm Cowley papers, Newberry Library, Chicago.

This is no time for artists, anyway. [Great] time for artists is in a fixed society, one that has reached or is just reaching its apex. Then fixed esthetic form is possible (form in art a mirror of form in society). Now I truly believe that we are in a paradoxical state where to be truly good one must be in a certain way bad. Galsworthys, Whartons, Glasgows, etc., writing in traditional forms are bad, but good. Steins, Joyces, etc. are good, but bad because experimental, foundering.[45]

Ironically, Coates' attempts to establish a rapport with his public and explain his deviations from the classical ideal of a fixed aesthetic form, fell largely on deaf ears: *Yesterday's Burdens* did not sell at all well and neither, for that matter, did *The Bitter Season*. In fact, sales were so bad that the author later referred to his novels as "a sheer waste, financially."[46]

Yesterday's Burdens was published by Macaulay's Publishing Company in New York – the same company that had brought *The Eater of Darkness* to the American public. By that time, however, the firm was losing money and its earlier interest in avant-garde writing was drawing to an end. The book was published with "misgivings" and Malcolm Cowley believed that "most of the first and only printing was sold cheaply as overstock."

Probably, Coates' artful book suffered from being launched at a historical moment that had little concern for aesthetic considerations. In addition, Lee Sherman, the head of Macaulay at that time, was much bothered by the book's downbeat title. Coming in 1933, at the depth of the Depression and with the New Deal in its first phase, the novel seemed incompatible with the atmosphere of hopeful anticipation, however faint, of a less burdensome future. Sherman tried to persuade Coates into changing the title: "This year," he told Coates, "nobody wants to hear about yesterday's burdens or any other burdens. Can't you find something upbeat and catchy?" [47] Robert Coates, who was shy but stubborn, refused to change his title to match Sherman's intuition about the public's need for relief.

Interestingly, Sherman's request was not as far-fetched or public-oriented as it may sound: with *Yesterday's Burdens*, Sherman found

---

[45] Unpublished manuscript material, related to the composition *Yesterday's Burdens*, Robert Coates papers.
[46] Robert Coates to Kenneth Burke, March 31, 1958, Kenneth Burke papers.
[47] Malcolm Cowley, Afterword to *Yesterday's Burdens*, 268.

himself confronted with a novel of several dimensions, one which ranged in content from the exalted to the ludicrous, and in atmosphere from profound and somber to slapstick and vaudeville. Indeed, the book's title might well be said to raise false expectations, or to needlessly emphasize the book's darker side. Ironically, the writer stuck to his title precisely because, to him, it uncovered the tragic dimension to the novel that he, while writing it, had not even been aware was there:

> ... all the while I was writing that book I was convinced it was a cheerful, almost a funny book, and I was honestly surprised when, after I turned the [manuscript] in to Macauley [sic] Company, Izzie [Isidor] Schneider there said something to me about it's being very sad –said it, too, as if we both knew that had been my intention. It hadn't, and yet the title expressed that, without my knowing it.[48]

Coates' initial failure to see the sadness inside his book reminds us that he belonged to what Ann Douglas referred to as "the most theatrical generation in American annals,"[49] the group of sharp-witted and often hard-drinking writers and performers that included Dorothy Parker, S.J. Perelman, Robert Benchley, E.B. White, James Thurber, F. Scott Fitzgerald, Eugene O'Neill, Edmund Wilson, Thomas Wolfe, Edna St. Vincent Millay, Ring Lardner, Hart Crane, Louise Bogan and many more, who pressed their cultural mark on Manhattan of the 1920s.[50] Although these individuals were strongly committed to lifting the genteel veil of Victorian make-believe and to tell the "terrible" truth, they had a remarkably strong penchant for drama. As Douglas pointed out: "If the stated goal of 'terrible honesty' was the facts, its route there was pure theater."[51] The Pierrot-like effect of this stance, caused perhaps by an incapacity to treat life wholly seriously and the tendency to laugh problems away, is part and parcel of Coates' novel, and was so deeply ingrained in its author that it could fool even himself.

---

[48] Robert Coates to Kenneth Burke, March 16, 1946, Kenneth Burke papers.
[49] Ann Douglas, *Terrible Honesty,* 55.
[50] A publication that is worth mentioning in this context is *Whither, Whither, or After Sex What?*, a curious, somewhat excessive "symposium to end symposiums" by Kenneth Burke, Robert Coates, E.E. Cummings, Corey Ford, Matthew Josephson, Edmund Wilson, and others, which was published by Macaulay in 1930.
[51] Ann Douglas, *Terrible Honesty,* 55.

Aware of the theatrical inclinations of his peers, critic Edmund Wilson referred to his generational group as "The All Star Literary Vaudeville," and defined his fellow writers as "comic monologuists, sentimental songsters and performers of one-act melodramas."[52] Wilson assessed the literary situation bitterly: "We have the illusion of a stronger vitality and a greater intellectual freedom, but we are polyglot, parvenu, hysterical and often only semi-literate."[53] Although intended as an uncomplimentary tag, Wilson's phrase helps the reader to understand the paradoxical mood of *Yesterday's Burdens*; the tag aptly conveys the contrast between the exhilarating, even manic, joyfulness and the deep seriousness that exist side by side in Coates' fiction; the bathos and the pathos rolled into one flippant, essentially opaque, form. It also neatly encapsulates the problematical relationship in Coates' novel between the writer's explicit and sophisticated aestheticism, his modernist commitment to the autonomy of art, and the insistent avant-gardist appropriation of elements of mass and popular culture in his work.

Certainly, Coates himself loved vaudeville, and frequently visited Harlem nightclubs, burlesques, and performances of Jimmy Durante, often accompanied by his friend Nathanael West.[54] Indeed, many moderns considered popular entertainment, with its playful sensuality, emotional honesty and refreshing absence of Victorian prudery and snobbery, not only a democratic, but an authentic art-form – one that was greatly preferable to the "scented merde"[55] and the rehearsed sterility of high art. These were the values that Coates celebrated in a 1924 essay on the National Winter Garden,[56] a small but renowned vaudeville theatre that was favorably discussed by the critic Edmund Wilson in the mid-1920s[57] and featured in the work of Hart Crane[58]

---

[52] Edmund Wilson, "The All-Star Literary Vaudeville," reprinted in *The Shores of Light: A Literary Chronicle of the Twenties and Thirties* (New York: Vintage Books, 1952), 247.

[53] *Ibid.*, 246.

[54] Jay Martin, *Nathanael West: The Art of His Life* (London: Secker and Warburg), 237-38.

[55] E.E. Cummings, "Poem, or Beauty Hurts Mr. Vinal" (1922), lines 15-20: "i do however protest, anent the un/-spontaneous and other wise scented merde which/greets one (Everywhere Why) as divine poesy per/ that and this radically defunct periodical."

[56] Robert M. Coates, "Don Juan of Second Avenue, Or the Glory That Still Is the East Side of New York," *The New York Times Magazine*, May 25, 1924.

[57] Edmund Wilson, "Burlesque Shows," reprinted in *The Shores of Light*, 274-81.

[58] Hart Crane, "National Winter Garden," in "The Bridge," part 3, section V.

and E.E. Cummings.[59] Certainly, the characteristics of popular culture were diametrically opposed to the Puritan values that the late-Victorian American middle-class (especially its female members) had cultivated, and which were thoroughly researched and violently denounced during the early decades of the century.[60]

Frequently the use of popular or "low" culture, as well as the adoption of unconventional, unaesthetic material by such American moderns as Cummings, Crane, Williams and, in the 1930s, West, is attributed to these writers' exposure to the aesthetics of the historical avant-garde, especially the Dadaists.[61] As we saw, Robert Coates witnessed Dada activities in Paris in the early 1920s, and there is little doubt that he took courage from their iconoclastic stance toward high art. Many elements in his work that might be traced to Dada, however, may have come naturally to its author. Coates had a strong inclination toward the absurd, a fascination for American popular culture, a distaste for America's commercial life, and in New York was positively surrounded by the manifestations of mass and popular culture. Also, the mixture of "high" and "low," and the use of non-literary material in his fiction – both of which could be attributed to Dada influence – was almost intuitive for a man whose tastes and habits were described by James Thurber, Coates' friend at *The New Yorker*, as follows: "[Robert Coates] likes 'The Saturday Evening Post,' Bach fugues, Negro blues, Jimmy Durante, the poetry of Hart Crane, Mahonri Young, enjoys reading dictionaries, histories of Ireland, Flaubert, trade journals, the printing on cans of preserved vegetables, the Graphic [and] old [newspaper] clippings about Gerald Chapman."[62] More importantly, Robert Coates and the other writers

---

[59] E.E. Cummings, "National Winter Garden Burlesque," *The Dial*, 68/1 (January 1920).

[60] Frederick J. Hoffman, *The Twenties: American Writing in the Postwar Decade* (Revised Edition. New York: The Free Press, 1965), 30-31; 146-47. Ann Douglas argues that the modern generation directed its revolt primarily at the values championed by the white, middle-class matriarch who had acquired cultural power during the late-Victorian era. See Ann Douglas, *Terrible Honesty*.

[61] For Crane, Cummings and Williams, see Tashjian, *Skyscraper Primitives*. For a fairly detailed analysis of the influence of surrealism on Nathanael West, see Jonathan Veitch, *American Superrealism: Nathanael West and the Politics of Representation in the 1930s* (Madison and London: University of Wisconsin Press, 1997).

[62] James Thurber, "Are Coates Necessary?" Clipping from the *Springfield, Mass. Union*, August 6, 1930, Gertrude Stein papers, Box 146, Folder 3390. The reference to Gerald Chapman, it should be noted, is relevant to *The Eater of Darkness*. Chapman, a hold-up man and a murderer, was much in the news during the early

and poets mentioned above used the manifestations of American culture not, as the Dadaists did, for the purpose of contrasting them with European values or to express a sense of revulsion at a moribund civilization, but to explore the possibilities to create an indigenous American art.

In his second novel, Coates used several forms of popular culture – vaudeville, slapstick, comic strips, cartoons and the advertising industry – for this purpose. If in his earlier novel he had spoofed popular culture's representations and misrepresentations of human action, the author increasingly came to realize that the manifestations of popular culture were, in fact, distorting mirrors of American society whose grotesqueries had a much greater bearing on reality than anyone might like to admit and could be used as such in his fiction.

Coates' point of view may profitably be compared to that of Nathanael West, who was in many ways a kindred spirit. The two writers met in 1933, shortly after Coates, who was "one of West's earliest appreciative critics,"[63] had reviewed *Miss Lonelihearts* in *The New Yorker*.[64] They immediately hit it off. As Coates recalled: "somehow [we] became, instantly, friends from the moment we met." Over the years, they became "close, very close friends."[65] West frequently came to Coates' country-home in Gaylordsville, Connecticut, to hunt, bringing his dog Danny, who, after West's tragic death in 1940, came to live there.[66] Regularly, Coates stayed at the Sutton Hotel in New York City of which West was the manager and upon which he (West) conferred "a special glamour and a place in the literary history of the thirties" – in addition to Coates, West's guests included Sid and Laura Perelman, John Sanford, Quentin Reynolds, Edmund Wilson, Lillian Hellman, Dashiell Hammett, James T. Farrell, and Erskine Caldwell.[67] When West moved to Hollywood,

---

1920s. Coates dedicated his novel to him, among eighteen other individuals and institutions.

[63] *Twentieth-Century Views on Nathanael West: A Collection of Critical Essays*, ed. Jay Martin (Englewood Cliffs, New Jersey: Prentice-Hall, Inc., 1971), 175.

[64] Jay Martin, *Nathanael West: The Art of His Life* (London: Secker and Warburg, 1970), 191-92. Robert Coates, "Messiah of the Lonely Hearts," *The New Yorker*, 9 (April 15, 1933), 59.

[65] Robert Coates to Jay Martin, August 4, 1966, Jay Martin Papers, Huntington Library, San Marino.

[66] Jay Martin, *Nathanael West*, 224-25; James F. Light, *Nathanael West: An Interpretive Study* (Evanston: Northwestern University Press, 1971), 116.

[67] Jay Martin, *Nathanael West*, 159

Coates visited him there. Sadly, some months before West's violent death in the car-crash on December 22, 1940 that also killed his wife Eileen McKenney, Coates and West had been planning a trip through California and Mexico together – a trip that would involve an adventurous journey by rowboat down the Colorado river. West was greatly looking forward to it. As he wrote his friend: "I'm still feverishly planning that trip of ours – it fills my every day-dream." [68] The trip, however, did not materialize on time, and Coates could not help feeling: "I wish! I wish! If I had gone out, and had been on that last trip, I might have been driving, or Eileen, with Pep [West] and me sitting in back talking, and, well … there it is."[69] The closeness of their friendship is suggested by Coates' feeling that Laura Perelman, West's sister, took to him as a kind of "surrogate brother" after his death.[70]

Both writers had an acute interest in popular culture. Discussing West's oeuvre, Coates identified slapstick as an important source for the tragicomical scenes that fill his fiction: "Slapstick weighed upon him heavily. The goofy guy (versus the fast-talking gagster who punctuates his jokes by hitting the innocent over the head) was a symbolic figure for him."[71] Comic strips and cartoons were likewise interpreted as apt symbols and reflections of the modern cultural and social state of affairs. West famously referred to *Miss Lonelihearts* as "a novel in the form of a comic strip," a description that revealed, as Jonathan Veitch pointed out, that its author was "alive to the pathos – more often, bathos – of Being as it is grotesquely contorted within the cartoonish dimensions of mass culture."[72]

Coates had a similar view of mass life. In a section of *Yesterday's Burdens*, entitled "125th Street Comic Strip," he exposes to view mass man's transgressions of the thin dividing line between pathos and bathos by explicitly linking human behavior to Harry Hershfield's

---

[68] See Nathanael West to Robert Coates, May 26, 1939, Nathanael West papers, Harry Ransom Humanities Research Center, University of Texas at Austin.
[69] Robert Coates to Jay Martin, July 22, 1966, ellipsis in the original, Jay Martin papers, Huntington Library, San Marino.
[70] Robert Coates to Jay Martin, August 4, 1966, Jay Martin papers.
[71] Robert Coates to Mr. Schneider, June 6, 1952, quoted in Jay Martin, *Nathanael West,* 263.
[72] Jonathan Veitch, *American Superrealism,* xix.

"Abie the Agent," Carl Ed's "Harold Teen," and Frank Willard's "Moon Mullins."[73]

Coates brought his insights into the tragicomical implications of mass man's habitual descent into the ludicrous to bear especially on his treatment of the narrator's loneliness – a deleterious psychological effect of mass life that was an important preoccupation for Coates – and his efforts to overcome his solitude. Throughout *Yesterday's Burdens*, the narrator is caught in a regulated and anonymous mass environment, where he is bombarded with information whose relevance is dubious at best. Coates allows his narrator to invest fully in the ideas proposed by the phenoma of mass culture that surround him. A highly sensitive individual, he fails to realize the impersonal, essentially dehumanized status of the endlessly reproduced products of the culture industry, and insists on finding human traits where there were never meant to be any. His attempts to establish human contact with the lifeless phenomena of mass capitalist culture are pathetic in the extreme:

> I was intensely interested in Miss Elizabeth Godwin of Roslyn, L.I., a young lady whom I had never seen, but whose name and specimen of whose handwriting – "Marlboro, America's finest cigarette" – confronted me from the seat-back before me whenever I rode on a Fifth Avenue bus.
>
> I was worried too, about Little Orphan Annie, who had gotten herself lost again, and this time so thoroughly that it seemed that Daddy Warbucks might never find her; and there was a young man on the Chesterfield ads whose tired eyes met mine with a look of such utter hopelessness, as he raised them from his littered desk and announced, "I'm working and smoking overtime. Hence a *milder* cigarette," that I felt an almost personal responsibility for his plight.[74]

The narrator's craving for emotional nourishment through human contact becomes increasingly grotesque as his search for "Henderson," the novel's would-be protagonist and Coates' alter-ego besides, leads him deeper and deeper into the anonymous crowd. Caught there, and overwhelmed by a desire to belong, he falls victim

---

[73] For information on these comic strips, see for instance Coulton Waugh, *The Comics* (New York: MacMillan Company, 1947), 63-67 and 80-94.

[74] Robert Coates, *Yesterday's Burdens,* 192-93.

to an obsessive need to adapt or conform to mass values and norms.[75] Paranoia increasingly overwhelms the initially harmless flâneur, until he is finally transformed into a stalker. At the risk of appearing perverse, the narrator offers suggestions of how "true intimacy" may be wrenched from unsuspecting strangers – a state of affairs that would appear in much later fiction, for instance Saul Bellow's *Seize The Day* (1956).

The cartoon-like aspects of the narrator were not lost on Coates' close friend during the 1930s, the writer and cartoonist James Thurber, to whom, in fact, *Yesterday's Burdens* is dedicated (and whom Coates, in his dedication, pronounced to have "helped a lot"). Thurber made several unpublished drawings while reading the book,[76] in which he depicted the narrator (easily recognizable as Robert Coates) as a befuddled little man – one of Thurber's favorite types – dwarfed and helplessly overwhelmed by the confusions of modern mass life.

Indeed, the humor in *Yesterday's Burdens* bears a close resemblance to the peculiar type of laughter that, largely thanks to James Thurber, characterized the magazine *The New Yorker*. In an excellent essay on Harold Ross's brainchild, Dwight Macdonald defined it as "the humor of the inadequate,"[77] and singled out James Thurber as the originator of the genre. In an attempt to outline the superiority of the magazine's (and Thurber's) humor, Macdonald pointed out that its success was derived from the inadequacy of the observer who, instead of violating cultural or social norms, reveals the inadequacy of these norms by exposing their doggedly incomprehensible arbitrariness:

> Typically, [*The New Yorker* humor] establishes a relationship between a rational observer and an irrational person or phenomenon – so far the classical formula. But the observer is ineffectual, and the comic

---

[75] Coates' worries about the human desire to conform are also displayed in *The Eater of Darkness*: "[Charles] was walking up Fifth Avenue: the pistoning men, aptly moving, glozed with women as with oil. They were all taking themselves so seriously. The moment past, Charles Dograr made himself serious. He swung his arms like the rest. He masked a face of 'It's 4:37 now and I've got to be at the offices of the Hydraulic Compression and Resurfacing Company 999 West 48 Street at 11:30' over his whimpering soul." Note how Coates heightened the automaton-like performance of the men which Charles Dograr conforms to by the use of machine imagery.
[76] The drawings survive in the Malcolm Cowley papers.
[77] Dwight Macdonald, "Laugh and Lie Down," *Partisan Review*, 4 (December 1937), 44.

object is not only irrational but also overpowering, so that for all his perception, the observer is unable to cope with the object. Thus, the humorist also becomes a source of amusement, and humor is drawn as much from the insufficiency of the norm as from its violation.[78]

The situation outlined by Macdonald frequently occurs in *Yesterday's Burdens*. Coates' narrator is either dwarfed by the raging, man-made spectacle of modernity or reduced to an intimated and flabbergasted automaton as he succumbs to the regulations required for the several technological systems – the subway, the Elevated, traffic – to operate efficiently.

Coates lamented humanity's utter dependency on regulations, and delighted in the prospect of the collapse of regulating systems. His desire for anarchy is the theme of two of Coates' best-known stories, the delightful and oft-anthologized "The Law"[79] and "Will You Wait."[80] In *Yesterday's Burdens*, however, man is powerless to resist the forces of urban social engineering, although the author does allow one of the supernumeraries in his novel to raise a futile voice of protest. The scene is an interesting one, and powerfully suggests the loss of communication and human purpose in New York's sign-encoded mass environment. The setting of the scene in question is a platform along the circular subway connection between Times Square and Grand Central Station, which Coates succinctly identified through a literal, almost plastic, representation of the system's signs:

> Next train—
> > Arrow to the left.
> Next train—
> > Arrow to the right.
> Watch your step
> > Getting on and off trains.

On the platform, the reader witnesses a young man shouting, "I am organizing a revolution!" to the startled passers-by. The reader's assumption that the desired revolution is of a political nature – as would be expected in a novel from the 1930s – is flouted when the young man continues his speech on the train:

---

[78] *Ibid.*, 48-49.
[79] Robert M. Coates, "The Law," *The New Yorker*, 23 (November 29, 1947), 41-43.
[80] Robert M. Coates, "Will You Wait," *The New Yorker*, 26 (June 17, 1950), 24-26.

"I am organizing a revolution." And then, continuing more didactically: "As distinguished more merely revolving. Don't you ever get tired of whirling round and round? Don't you ever weary of going back and forth?"[81]

With one subtle stroke, Coates makes it abundantly clear that, like Nathanael West, he was much "less interested in the masses than in the phenomenon of 'mass man.'"[82] Coates' young man is not beset by economical problems, but seeks to put a stop to what Thomas Pynchon would later refer to as "yo-yoing," the senseless, purposeless, absurd shuttling through the city, which Pynchon, like Coates, found epitomized in that same circular subway connection.[83] Needless to say, the young man is unsuccessful in drawing attention to his plight. The crowd disembarks, leaving him staring at the advertisements that remain:

> All too soon the journey ended and (the young man his eyes clicking ratchet-like: as with a surprising unanimity (everyone: the girl with the pink hat the little man in the corner seat the gray the (smugly the fawn-colored top-coat, the) stout lady discontentedly the stout man. You would have seen) everyone arising crowding to (the doors rubberly sliding, to) the platform and) the car swept suddenly bare: only LUDEN'S Little Doctor in UNEEDA Candy Form Maiden Form REMember Formamint For Me WHO smiling their bright imperative smiles. It really does whiten the teeth![84]

Although Coates and West agreed that there was something uproarious about mass life and the individual caught within it, and, as a result, tended to approach the essentially serious subject matter of their work through humor, they did not want to make light of the situation. It should be noted, however, that Coates' humor was never as savage or wry as that of West, nor his laughter as bitter. There was, indeed, a crucial difference between the two men and their fiction.

---

[81] Robert M. Coates, *Yesterday's Burdens*, 131.

[82] Jonathan Veitch, *American Superrealism*, xiii.

[83] Cf. for instance: "One morning Profane woke up early, couldn't get back to sleep and decided on a whim to spend the day like a yo-yo, shuttling on the subway back and forth underneath 42nd Street, from Times Square to Grand Central and vice versa" (Thomas Pynchon, *V.* [Philadelphia and New York: J.B. Lippincott Company, 1961], 37).

[84] Robert M. Coates, *Yesterday's Burdens* (New York: Macaulay, 1933), 128.

Coates, despite bouts of intense gloominess, was essentially an optimist. West, on the other hand, was "a fatalist, and a coolly pessimistic one at that," as Coates himself defined him.[85] In fact, it was this dimension of West's fiction that Coates found objectionable: in his review of *Miss Lonelihearts* in 1933 Coates had been disconcerted by the fact that West's characters seemed to him to "cavort in an emotional and spiritual vacuum"[86] and had considered the book's fault to be "a little too much insistence on the futility of things" – an insistence which he termed "unhealthy" in an introduction to the novel in 1949.[87] Certainly, Coates' appraisal of the human situation was less bitter, and much less severe than West's. As a consequence, he was not aroused to such intense feelings of indignation, or such biting satire and resorted primarily to an attitude of burlesque to cover up his real feelings of sadness and deep mental confusion.

The perceptive critic Kenneth Burke was aware of the seriousness beneath the novel's frequently flippant surface and expressed his joy that his friend was "not just a playboy after all."[88] The term "playboy" was in use at that time to refer to the liberal "Bohemian vagabonds" of the 1920s who retained their "cheerful, bourgeois-shocking inclinations" in an age that seemed to call for an infinitely more serious approach to society on the part of the writer.[89] Indeed, despite its jokes and flippancy, *Yesterday's Burdens* is severely critical of America's ruthless promotion of consumerism, even in the face of the nation's deep economic depression. Research material likewise reveals that Coates was intensely worried about the power of the advertising industry to reach and manipulate countless people.[90] So

---

[85] Robert M. Coates, "The Four Novels of Nathanael West, That Fierce, Humane Moralist," *New York Herald Tribune Book Review* (May 19, 1957), 5.

[86] Robert M. Coates, "Messiah of the Lonely Hearts," *The New Yorker*, 9 (April 15, 1933), 59.

[87] Robert Coates, "Introduction" to *Miss Lonelihearts* (1949). Also, in his article for the *New York Herald Tribune*, in 1957, Coates complained that "a trace of sadism" ran through West's fiction, which he felt became "a little uncomfortable."

[88] Coates quotes Burke's comment back to him in Robert Coates to Kenneth Burke, June 22, 1934, Kenneth Burke papers.

[89] See Daniel Aaron, *Writers on the Left: Episodes in American Literary Communism* (New York: Octagon Books, 1974), 199.

[90] Coates was also worried about the consequences of America's consumerist outlook for the development of art. A delightful piece that reflects this concern is his essay "How Much A Word?" (*The New Yorker*, 4 [November 17, 1928], 101-03; reprinted in *The Bookman*, 72/3 [November 1930], 269-70) in which he proposes a

much so, in fact, that "sometimes" he felt "more worried about the 'smoother cigarette' than about Hitler" and hoped that someone would line out the "correlations between Hitler's technique and our own advertising and commercial-propaganda techniques, and the similarities between their aims and the points of view toward the 'masses.'"[91]

In his novel he voiced his distaste for America's consumer culture in several formal experiments which used the nation's capitalist markers. In a fascinating and brilliant example, a young depression-struck couple is hopelessly attempting to make plans for their future. Lacking all means to build a home of their own, they project their desire for comfort and protection onto the urban landscape that surrounds them:

> Let this be our chamber, then, this endless avenue: this pavement our couch and this stony firmament our sky, wide and starry with:

	I. FREEDMAN & CO.	
R		**WIENER & KATZ**
E		**ACME**
I	**RAU**	**PANTS**
S	**FASTENER**	**CO.**
E	**CO.**	
R		
BROS.		**MAX GAMSA, Inc.**
	"GAYTOWN" CLOTHES	

---

business arrangement for magazines in which authors are paid by the word on the basis of a Stock Market list:

Domestic	Opened	Closed
Ambiance	...............$0.14	0.15
Anodyne .	...............$0.22	0.16
Burgeon	...............$0.22	0.03
Moue	...............$0.27	0.25
Moo	...............$0.02	0.02
(...)		
Foreign		
German, misc.		
(Ewigkeit, Ach! etc.)	........$0.18	0.12
French, misc. (Rue, Hein,		
Bah! Cocotte)	...........$0.10	0.23
English, misc. (Right-o!		
Ruddy, etc.)	...........$014	0.15

[91]   Robert Coates to Kenneth Burke, August 20 [1941], Kenneth Burke papers.

HERO SHIRT
                    ROTARY
                    SHIRT
Jos. J. Siegel
STOUTS and SLIMS

"GROTTOMAID" NECKWEAR
M   E   R   O   D   E

Let BAYUK CIGARS be our flaming sun.
Let LUNA HOSIERY shed its brooding light upon us.
Let THE HOME OF PUSSYWILLOW CHOCOLATES be our
home too.
Let ANNIN & CO unfurl their banners above us as we go
marching, bearing our bitterness proudly unrelentingly past the
(grim-walled, the) METHODIST BOOK CONCERN.[92]

The form is magnificent. Interestingly, Coates' formal experiment is an
exact translation into art of David Nye's description of the "slippage
between signifier and signified" that he considered to be in place in
New York City in the mid-1920s:

> Here was a literal universe of signs. Each insistently proclaimed a
> particular man-made product. Each was an overdetermined signifier
> for a product that was obviously part of the capitalist system of
> production and distribution. Yet no sign was ever seen alone; each
> was a part of an overwhelming impression produced by the
> constellation of citylights. Just as so many individual skyscrapers
> became a great signifier, advertising signs collectively became a
> great signifier, an important cultural marker.[93]

Indeed, the efforts of Coates' characters to try and make the
advertising signs mean something which they were never intended to
mean is what creates the greatest poignancy in this scene. Typically,
his characters' despair is played down by the absurdity of their
hopeless desires: again, Coates balances on the thin line between
pathos and bathos. Nevertheless, through his recreation of the electric
cityscape of New York City, he creates a powerful critique of the fact

---

[92] Robert M. Coates, *Yesterday's Burdens*, 219-20.
[93] David Nye, *American Technological Sublime* (Cambridge: MIT Press, 1994),
195-96.

that although, as the urban sociologist Louis Wirth observed in 1938, "there is virtually no human need which has remained unexploited by commercialism,"[94] the most basic of human needs – a home – is left unheeded. In social content, Coates' ironical juxtaposition of poverty and the promise of abundance can be usefully compared to the equally ironic images produced during the Depression by social photographers, such as Dorothea Lange's 1939 photograph of "two hoboes walking up a dusty road, next to a billboard that says, 'NEXT TIME TRY THE TRAIN—RELAX,'" or Margaret Bourke-White's 1937 image of "folks in a breadline, patiently waiting beneath a billboard proclaiming 'THE WORLD'S HIGHEST STANDARD OF LIVING.'"[95]

As Coates' literary rendering reveals, the writer became increasingly interested in an art with social and political relevance, and, like so many of his fellow writers and artists in the 1930s, developed communist sympathies. Thus, Coates attended two of the American Writers' Congresses (in April 1935 and June 1937) and became involved with The League of American Writers – an association of writers dedicated to "the preservation and extension of a truly democratic culture" which had been established at the first American Writers' Congress.[96] In 1936, he occupied a position on the editorial board of the *LAW Bulletin*,[97] together with Kenneth Burke, Henry Hart, Rolfe Humphries, Bruce Minton (pseudonym of Richard Bransten) and Dorothy Brewster, and was "active in the election campaign" of 1936 "as member of the Independent Committee for Browder and Ford."[98] In addition, in 1938, Coates contributed to "Writers Take Sides," thus giving his public support for the elected

---

[94] Louis Wirth, "Urbanism as a Way of Life," *American Journal of Sociology*, 44/1 (July 1938), 22. Coates successfully spoofed the advertising industry's exploitation of human needs in a humorous article, "Do You Offend?" *The New Republic*, 86 (April 8, 1936), 246-47.

[95] Rita Barnard, *The Great Depression and the Culture of Abundance* (Cambridge: Cambridge University Press, 1995), 4.

[96] Description of the League of American Writers in descriptive essay accompanying The Archives of the LAW, Bancroft Library, Berkeley. For a more detailed outline, see Granville Hicks, "Call for an American Writers' Congress," *The New Masses* XIV (January 22, 1935), 20; Daniel Aaron, *Writers on the Left*, and Franklin Folsom, *Days of Anger, Days of Hope: A Memoir of the League of American Writers 1937-42* (Niwot, Co.: University Press of Colorado, 1994).

[97] Franklin Folsom, *Days of Anger, Days of Hope,* Appendix G.

[98] *LAW Bulletin*, 4 (October, 1936), 4, the Archives of the LAW, Bancroft Library, Berkeley.

government of Spain.[99] Finally, also in 1938, he signed his name to a letter, probably circulated by Malcolm Cowley,[100] requesting writers to sign in "defense of democracy," against the "fascist attempt to wreck the solid socialist achievement of the Soviet Union," and as a protest against the suppression of "the truth" by the "fascists" at the Moscow trials.[101]

In the final analysis, however, the entire political spectacle struck Coates as abstract and alien to him as an individual and, especially, as an artist. In 1932, for instance, Coates signed his name to the pamphlet "Culture and the Crisis" – a pamphlet that encouraged its readers to vote for the Communist Party of William Z. Foster and James W. Ford[102] – but after he had made his own vote, his reaction, in a letter to Kenneth Burke, reveals that his faith in politics in general and the Communist Party in particular, was low indeed:

> I feel a little gaga today. Having just found my way through a maze of tables with solemn fellow-citizens sitting at them polling booths, more tables, etc., and marked X's opposite the names of a number of people about whom I know nothing at all and care less. It's the first time I've ever voted, but I hope I did everything right. How, as far as that goes, could one do wrong in particular, when the whole thing is wrong? But it just occurs to me that I forgot to fold up my ballot in the proper way, so I'll have to hurry down and fold it properly, otherwise my vote won't count.[103]

---

[99] Franklin Folsom, *Days of Anger, Days of Hope,* 30 and Appendix G.

[100] See Edmund Wilson to Malcolm Cowley, October 20, 1938, published in *Edmund Wilson: Letters on Literature and Politics, 1912-1972*, ed. Elena Wilson (New York: Farrar, Straus and Giroux, 1977), 309-10.

[101] A copy of the circular, dated April 2, 1938, is among the papers of Kenneth Burke at Penn State University. Burke was requested to sign the statement and send it to a man called Toni Michael. The circular was indicated to have already been signed by Robert Coates, Malcolm Cowley, Stuart Davis, Marc Blitzstein and Paul Strand. Evidently, Coates, like Cowley and Burke, naively took the official accounts of Russia about the trials at face value and condemned those who tried to escape the sentence that the Russian government felt they deserved. For an account of Malcolm Cowley's political stance, see for instance, Hans Bak, *Malcolm Cowley: The Formative Years* (Athens: University of Georgia Press, 1993), 475. For Burke, see Donald Parker and Warren Herendeen, "KB & MC: An Interview with Kenneth Burke," in *The Visionary Company: A Magazine of the Twenties* (Summer 1987), 97.

[102] See Daniel Aaron, *Writers on the Left,* 196-98, and Jay Martin, *Nathanael West,* 31-32.

[103] Robert Coates to Kenneth Burke, no date [November 1932], Kenneth Burke papers.

Coates believed that "for the artist, *qua* artist ... any choice of active political doctrine," must always be a "choice of [two or more] evils."[104] In *The New Masses*, he elaborated on his attitude towards the writer-in-society as follows: "I believe ... that the artist can function in many ways in revolutionary or other struggles, and active participation in politics or in warfare is only one them." With characteristically dismissive candor he added, "At least, we all say so, and it's usually very comforting."[105]

Although Coates' political sympathies were decidedly on the left and he was greatly concerned about the effects of consumer capitalism, he never considered art a weapon in the class war and subscribed to the belief that in "times of change ... it is the artist's sole duty to record the changes, not to influence them."[106] As a dutiful reporter, Coates did partake of the era's "general ambition ... to articulate the low and genuine" and revealed that "ordinary level of human reality" that much proletarian writers demanded should be recognized.[107] Indeed, many of his short stories from the 1930s have a distinct social emphasis. Sharing Thurber's belief that "art does not rush to the barricades,"[108] however, he dealt with such "proletarian" themes of urban poverty, unemployment, and homelessness as unemphatically and authentically as possible.[109] In fact, Thurber held

---

[104] See Robert Coates to Kenneth Burke, September 1, [1934], Kenneth Burke papers.

[105] Robert M. Coates, "A Greek Named Pete," *The New Masses* (August 31, 1939), 24.

[106] Unpublished manuscript material, related to the composition of *Yesterday's Burdens*, Robert Coates papers.

[107] Marcus Klein, Introduction to *Albert Halper's Union Square* (1933; Detroit: Omnigraphics Inc., 1990), xvii, xxi.

[108] James Thurber, "Voices of Revolution," 77.

[109] *The New Yorker* was careful to keep its socially-oriented stories in line with Harold Ross' conviction that his magazine "was not designed to stem tides, join crusades, or take political stands" (James Thurber, *The Years with Ross* [London: Hamish Hamilton, 1959], 150.) During the 1930s, the magazine rejected several of Coates' stories which dealt with proletarian themes. For instance, the grimness of a class struggle story such as "Meet God With Pride," which describes a bankrupt young couple's resort to suicide as the only dignified solution, was deemed unacceptable (see Katharine White to Maxim Lieber, February 10, 1936 [*New Yorker* records, New York Public Library]). Likewise, *The New Yorker* was unwilling to place "Not This Time," a story about poverty, because of Harold Ross's fear of the mediocrity that had come to envelop themes usually addressed by proletarian writers. As William Maxwell reported: "What bothers [Ross] especially is the poor-house

that proletarian writers like Joseph North and Albert Halper, whose social reporter fiction he considered wholly unconvincing, might "profit by an examination into the way Robert Coates or St. Clair McKelway handles such pieces. I can tell you that their observation and writing is hard, painstaking and long."[110]

In several chapters of *Yesterday's Burdens*, too (especially in the chapters "The Ballad of the Bowery" and "Sunday Morning on Fifth Avenue"), Coates addresses social mishaps which counterbalance the preoccupation with the Self that marks other portions of the novel. His effective use of the New York vernacular in other parts of the novel ("Elissen Mae wadja Ma say wen ya cmin lass niyut?" … "Less get a cross a street ssa guy follin us – "[111]) and his recognizable, though frequently somewhat caricatural vignettes of the sleazier aspects of ordinary New York life reveal that Coates had his eye trained on the people, and caused one critic to refer to Coates as Reginald Marsh's "graphic peer."[112] Above all, however, Coates considered the social situations of the decade that he felt obliged to report on in his novel as artistic challenges to resolve. The moral necessity to report on social conditions was subservient to his main aim: to create innovative art to match an ever-changing society. This was the obligation that Coates had to himself, and which he phrased as follows: "Every artist, starting on a project, should have among his main aims, to do the work in a new way, a way no one has done before. The main feeling the artist should have to sustain him is the knowledge that there is at least one thing he can do better than anyone else. Otherwise, why try?"[113]

---

theme which has been done, he says, far too many times by bad writers to stand up even when a good writer tackles it." (William Maxwell to Robert Coates, December 22, 1939 [*New Yorker* records, New York Public Library].)

[110] James Thurber, "Voices of Revolution," *New Republic* (March 25, 1936). Reprinted in *Collecting Himself: James Thurber on Writing, Writers, Humor and Himself*, ed. Michael Rosen (London: Hamish Hamilton, 1989), 76.

[111] Robert M. Coates, *Yesterday's Burdens*, 136, 137

[112] John Chamberlain, "Books of the Times," *The New York Times* (December 6, 1933), 6.

[113] Robert Coates, "Notes for a Non-Existent Dictaphone: Dictaphone—Art," n.p., n.d. [1940s?], Robert Coates papers.

Works by Robert M. Coates

The Eater of Darkness, Paris: Contact Editions, 1926; New York: Macaulay, 1929.

The Outlaw Years: The History of Land Pirates of the Natchez Trace, New York: Macaulay, 1930.

Yesterday's Burdens, New York: Macaulay, 1933.

All The Year Round: A Book of Stories, New York: Harcourt, Brace, 1943.

The Bitter Season, New York: Harcourt, Brace, 1946.

Wisteria Cottage: A Novel of Criminal Impulse, New York: Harcourt, Brace: 1948.

The Farther Shore, New York: Harcourt, Brace, 1955.

The Hour After Westerly, and Other Stories, New York: Harcourt, Brace, 1957.

The View From Here, New York: Harcourt, Brace, 1960.

Beyond the Alps: A Summer in the Italian Hill Towns. New York: Sloane, 1961.

The Man Just Ahead of You, New York: Sloane, 1964.

South of Rome: A Spring and Summer in Southern Italy and Sicily, New York: Sloane, 1965.

E.E. CUMMINGS AND MARION MOREHOUSE:
THE LATER YEARS

RICHARD S. KENNEDY

My book, *Dreams in the Mirror: A Biography of E.E. Cummings*, contains a fairly full portrait of Marion Morehouse and her life over a thirty-year period.[1] This treatment of her was not easy to put together because of a great many obstacles that were placed in my way as I tried to create the story of E.E. Cummings' life. The principal obstacle was Marion Morehouse herself, for she did not want a genuine literary biography of Cummings to be written, at least not until long after his death and until the erosion of time would have smoothed away some of the rough surfaces and obscured many of the details that might have caused posterity to be critical of him. When I first approached her by letter in 1963 and sent her a copy of my recently published biography of Thomas Wolfe, she was decisively dismissive, stating that it was far too soon after his death (1962) for biographical investigation. I think now that the fact that I was a professor of English teaching at Wichita State University in Kansas was at this point two strikes against me, for she was scornful of people west of the Appalachians and very snobbish in her view of non-prestigious academic institutions.

She became more cordial when I moved East to teach at Temple University in Philadelphia in 1964 – and actually gracious after I arranged a meeting for her with William Jackson, Director of the Houghton Library at Harvard, to purchase the Cummings papers for the library. Still she maintained her opposition to a biography, telling

[1] New York: Liveright, 1980. The present article is in some ways a supplement to my book, for it draws upon Cummings' Notes in the Houghton Library that had been restricted from research until 1991. For permission to quote from the unpublished writings of E.E. Cummings in this article I am grateful to George Firmage, agent for the E.E. Cummings Trust, and to Leslie Morris, Curator of Manuscripts at the Houghton Library, Harvard University. Call numbers are given for quotations from the Cummings Collection at Houghton Library. This article appeared in an earlier, different and less accurately footnoted form in *Spring, The Journal of the E.E. Cummings Society*, New Series, Number 5 (Fall 1996), 8-17. I wish to thank the editor, Norman Friedman for permission to reprint part of this material.

me to wait another five years. Before her death in 1969, I visited her four times, but whenever I would ask her a specific question about some feature of her life, she would raise a warning finger against my inquiry. However, she did allow me to do a study of Estlin's father, Edward Cummings, and supplied me with two boxes of his notes and sermons before the Cummings papers were shipped to the Houghton Library. It was not until after her death that I was able to begin my real biographical research.

As a result of her reticence about herself, my gathering of information about her had to start with the facts set down in her obituary, a course which gradually raised questions in my mind about the persona she had created for herself during her lifetime. For instance, I discovered that there was no record of her birth in South Bend, Indiana, on March 9, 1906, as the obituary stated. Nor was there any record for 1904 or 1905, which I checked in case she had chopped off a year or two, as people in the theater or the fashion industry are wont to do. In Edward Steichen's photograph of her, made for *Vogue* Magazine in 1925, she was supposedly only nineteen years old; yet she looks much older.[2]

My inquiry about her school records also led nowhere. St. Anne's Academy in Hartford, Connecticut, where she supposedly was educated, never existed. Nor was there any record of her at St. Anne's School, a parochial school for French-speaking students in Hartford. Nor any record at Mount St. Joseph's Academy, to which Sister Maria Michaud of St. Anne's referred me. Other walls of mystery surrounded the facts about her early life. Marion's sister, Lillian Cox, who still lived in Hartford, did not reply to my letters. Nor was it possible to reach her by telephone, because she had an unlisted number. Her New York lawyer, Philip Rice, would not intercede for me, although he had given me her address. I began to wonder about what family secrets were being protected. Further, when I began my research at Houghton Library, I discovered that Marion had closed off research for twenty-five years to a portion of Cummings' "Personal Notes." This material included the journals and notebooks that Cummings had accumulated from the 1930s to the end of his life – the period in which Marion had lived with him.

---

[2] For the photograph, see Richard S. Kennedy, *E.E. Cummings Revisited* (New York: Twayne, 1994), 112.

It was not until 1978 when I interviewed Aline Macmahon, who had known Marion in the 1920s in New York, that I obtained any information about Marion's early life.[3] It seems that she had come to New York from Hartford, perhaps with Lillian, when she was very young, hoping to get into the theater, and she lived at first by her wits and her beauty. For example, she and a friend (or perhaps Lillian) used to go to the west side piers when the big ocean liners were about to sail and crash the bon voyage parties – an extra young girl or two was always welcome. Since Marion was very tall, she had a hard time finding roles to play on the stage, although her height and beauty were very suitable for work that she secured as a showgirl in the Ziegfield Follies. Lillian, an attractive blonde, was also a showgirl for Ziegfield.

A note in E.E. Cummings' journal mentioned that Marion's "real debut" in the theater was as "a snooty Claire [Standish] in *Ladies of the Evening* by Milton Herbert Gropper."[4] She was not listed in the part when the play opened in December 1924, but since the play had a long run, she may have been a replacement. At some point, she was sent by the Neighborhood Playhouse Theater to an acting school that it had established in Pleasantville, New York, under the supervision of Richard Boleslavsky. It was here that she and Aline Macmahon became friends.[5]

By 1925, she had become a fashion model and was appearing in *Vogue*, photographed by Edward Steichen. She was, Steichen declared, "the greatest fashion model I ever shot."[6] Not only was her high-waisted, long-legged figure ideal for modeling work, but her training in the theater helped her adapt to any role that her costume required.

She was still finding small dramatic parts in the early 1930s. She was the "Second Corinthian Woman" in *Lysistrata*, which opened in Philadelphia in 1930 and caused such a sensation that its opening in New York was delayed for several weeks. She was performing in a play (no record of the name) on June 23, 1932, when she and Cummings first met, introduced by Patti and James Light, who had directed Cummings' play, *Him*. After a late dinner at Felix's, one of Cummings' favorite restaurants, Marion did not hesitate to spend the

---

[3]   Much of the material in this article is drawn from interviews I had with many of Cummings' friends in the 1970s.
[4]   bMS Am1892.7 (222), Summer 1946.
[5]   For further details about Marion's early life, see *Dreams in the Mirror*, 337.
[6]   Edward Steichen, *A Life in Photography* (New York: Doubleday, 1963).

night with this charming, somewhat bewildering poet.[7] He sent her a love note and a huge bouquet of flowers the next day.

It was the beginning of a long, occasionally troubled, but solid relationship. Since Cummings was ten or twelve years older than she was, twice divorced, somewhat embittered by the world he lived in, and always in precarious economic circumstances, it was not easy for Marion to stick with him. But the love she brought him in 1932 pulled him out of the deep discouragements that he had suffered from his earlier marriages and from the lack of recognition that he had endured in the literary world. In return, he loved her as much as his self-centered existence allowed. Things took a decided upturn for this couple in the spring of 1933 when Cummings was awarded a Guggenheim Fellowship and was able to take Marion to Europe for a year, where they lived in Paris, met many of Cummings' friends in the arts, and traveled to Italy and Tunisia. Marion had never had such an exciting and glamorous experience in her life.

Marion once mentioned that she and Estlin were married in 1933, but the Bureau of Vital Statistics in New York State shows no evidence of this, although I had the records searched from 1932 to 1934. Since a couple of Cummings' friends had offered the opinion that Marion and Estlin were never married, I finally came to the conclusion that they had a common-law marriage and that it began to be established in the summer of 1934 when Cummings brought her to Joy Farm and introduced her as his wife to all the residents of the Silver Lake area whom he had known since childhood.

As the years went by, they remained together, living in New York at the same address, but their marriage had its peculiarities. Their New York home, 4 Patchin Place, was actually two separated areas. Marion occupied a first-floor apartment – sitting room, bedroom, kitchen, and bath – while Estlin spent most of his time in a studio on the third floor, where he slept, painted, read, and pounded away with two fingers on his typewriter. He went to the bathroom down the hall, which was shared by a tenant of another room. When he went downstairs, he was visiting "chez Marion,"[8] where he spent part of the day and evening with her, chatting, having tea or drinks, entertaining visitors, and occasionally sharing her bed. They left notes for each other when they went out.

---

7   bMS AM1892.7 (236), ca. November 1, 1959.
8   bMS Am1892.7 (225), October 1948.

But their love for each other was very deep. Over and over in his journals, Cummings kept comparing his experiences in his three marriages and always with the same theme: in his first, he idealized Elaine Thayer; in his second, he found sexual fulfillment with Anne Barton; but with Marion, he discovered genuine love and was loved in return. "What a wonderful girl M is!" he jotted in his notebook in June 1950. "'May I be worthy of her' is my prayer (feeling in the deep of my spirit Dante & his lady)."[9] On January 13, 1954, he wrote: "Marion is different from any girl I've ever loved in one (above all) respect – a spiritual generosity or upward sweetness; which is close to forgiveness – a noble psychic kindness to the man who tries but fails to please her."[10] Even as the years went by, he was continually seeing her anew. One day in the fall of 1953, when he was at Lloyd Frankenberg's apartment, Marion returned from a matinée and Estlin reacted with surprise and gratitude to her sudden appearance: "looking up I saw someone *young, lovely & gifted with beauty* – as a deer in a glade, unconscious of anyone else, is beautiful."[11] As Marion's love for Estlin developed and strengthened, it is best expressed by what she told him in March 1945: "I want to please you" and "I'll give you everything always."[12]

In one of his journal notes, for Christmas 1948, Cummings quoted Browning's lines from "One Word More":

> God be thanked, the meanest of his creatures
> Boasts two soul-sides; one to face the world with,
> One to show a woman when he loves her.[13]

This alteration between a public face and a private face was not only true for Estlin but also for Marion – indeed their friends observed this was true of the two of them as a couple, for they sometimes allowed their true selves to emerge and at other times erected barriers beyond which even intimate friends could not pass. Cecily Angleton recalled that when, fresh out of Vassar, she first met them she was "transported" by their presence. The atmosphere they created was "absolute magic." Estlin's conversation was brilliant; Marion was

---

9   bMS Am1892.7 (228).
10 bMS Am1892.7 (232).
11 bMS Am1892.7 (235).
12 bMS Am1892.7 (221).
13 bMS Am1892.7 (226).

utterly gracious. Cecily arranged for them to spend the winter with her
and her parents in Tucson, Arizona, for Marion was recently out of the
hospital after a long and dangerous struggle with rheumatoid arthritis.
During their stay in Arizona, they "wove a spell" with their charm,
beauty, and wit. "It was the best talk I ever heard," Cecily
remembered. This was a common impression felt by many of their
friends.

Yet despite Cummings' personal magnetism and Marion's
stunning beauty, others found them not easily approachable. Helen
Stewart, long a young disciple of Cummings, said they were "touchy
people." You did not drop in on them. Even an old friend might find a
chilly welcome. (This probably applies to Marion, who had mixed
feelings about the young women who were devoted to Cummings.)
They were "both very demanding people" in their expectations of
friends. They were "not casual in their relations with others." You did
not interrupt them to carry on a conversation "if they were on a long
discourse of some sort." (This probably has reference to Estlin, who
was given to long ex cathedra pronouncements in his later years.)
Aline Macmahon thought that they lacked "tendresse."

In her manner, Marion often played a very "queenly" role. As
Evelyn Segal remembered it, she "held court." In her social views, she
posed as a "monarchist" and an "aristocrat" and often offered her
opinions with hauteur. Like many people lacking in educational
background, she enjoyed looking down on others – working-class
people or people outside their social circles – in order to elevate
herself. Yet she could be kind, helpful, sympathetic, even gracious to
individuals who paid court to her. With close friends she was warm
and lively and a welcoming hostess for tea at Patchin Place or for
weekends at Joy Farm, their summer place in New Hampshire.

This existence of a private side often became the public side in
Cummings' treatment of Marion. He liked to play the role of "Little
Estlin," the "non-hero," the *petit garçon* who was totally dependent on
Marion, who dominated and commanded. On social occasions with
friends, he would often defer to her for her authoritative opinion.
Indeed, at times her matter-of-fact views were more sound than his
poetic flights or irrational fulminations, for she had more common
sense than he did and often advised him wisely when he had abruptly
turned down an offer or avoided making a decision.

The bonds of a common-law marriage are looser than those of a
legalized union. Cummings shied away from full admission of their

marital situation. Once on November 16, 1950, when he was flying home from a poetry reading, he took out an insurance policy naming Marion as beneficiary. "Relation?" asked the insurance agent. "None," Cummings replied. Then taken aback by his own statement, he sheepishly added, "a friend."[14] Even toward the end of his life, the harness of marriage seemed to chafe him. On July 3, 1962, in Silver Lake, two half-clad, sexually vibrant, young women "grazed" him in the aisle of the general store. At that moment, Marion walked in. "Admiring the beauties of nature?" she inquired. He recorded his response in his notebook: "next to being cuckolded, I ponder, the worst thing is perhaps to be husbanded." "And I can't help admiring the expertness with which she plays her part. ... The merest tinge of irony was all she needed to bring me to heel. Marvellous."[15]

Marion felt likewise somewhat free in their semi-official relationship. Since she was so extraordinarily beautiful in face and svelte in body ("Marion had no corners," said Sophie Treadwell), she always attracted men and enjoyed their homage. She felt justified in sharing her beauty and allowed herself occasionally to drift into love affairs. In the late 1930s, she had an extended affair of the heart with Paul Rotha, a British film-maker, during the period he was working in New York. Cummings became aware of the situation and broke it off. He was very hurt, but after he consulted with Fritz Wittels, his psychoanalyst, he and Marion became reconciled, and their love was stronger than ever. Later, when she was in England, she had a brief fling with A.J. (Freddy) Ayer, the logician, a professor of philosophy at Oxford and one of Cummings' friends who was intellectually and politically his complete opposite.

However, the fact that she always remained with Cummings was clear evidence of how devoted she was to him – for the two of them usually teetered on the edge of financial desperation.[16] On the morning of January 4, 1938, for instance, they had less than a dollar between them and no prospect of any of the patronage handouts they frequently received from Estlin's wealthy friends such as Sibley Watson or

---

[14]   bMS Am1892.7 (228).
[15]   bMS Am1892.7 (238).
[16]   They were able to have their summers at Joy Farm in New Hampshire only because Cummings' mother paid the taxes on the property. She also paid the rent at 4 Patchin Place most of the time, and she sent Cummings a monthly "allowance" from his father's estate.

Stewart Mitchell. They could only look forward to a dinner invitation that awaited them that evening.[17]

One summer, when Helen Stewart's brother Dr. Walter Stewart and his wife sublet 4 Patchin Place for a few weeks while Estlin and Marion were up at Joy Farm, they were appalled at the state of the furnishings in Marion's apartment – the sagging couch, the chair with its legs tied together with string. Their servant, Lena, who came in to clean up, said "Oh Helen, I have never seen such poverty." In his journal, Estlin mused, "With Marion there was no question of money"; she was "unworldly." After years together, and especially after her long period of hospitalization with arthritis, they felt that "money and society are trivial."[18]

Her devotion was often tested, however. In the last two decades of their life together, when Estlin suffered from osteo arthritis in his back and legs, he had to wear a metal-braced corset, which he called "The Iron Maiden," to support his back. His intermittent pains were such that he had to take Nembutal in order to sleep. His condition made him irritable, full of complaint, and generally hard to live with. At one point, Marion decided to separate from him and went to consult with Wittels, who apparently advised her to put up with her neurotic partner for her own good as well as his. She returned home and they were reconciled. The state of Estlin's health increased his jaundiced view of the world in general and of the United States in particular, so that his youthful individualism had now altered, making him into an anti-social curmudgeon constantly critical of the political scene and the post-World-War II changes in American society.

But Marion's greatest trials began when Cummings began to go through a late "mid-life crisis," in which he worried about his aging, his declining sexual powers, and his inability to make progress on a play he was writing. He began to think he needed rejuvenation through a sexual escapade with a young girl. In his pocket notebook in February 1950, he considered what he would do if Marion were to die, and he happened to leave it where she read his entry. She reacted with hurt and outrage, accusing him of wishing she were dead. Once again, she decided on separation and strode out of the apartment leaving him stewing with guilt. But she returned later and calmed down. Estlin was relieved but felt unjustly treated, "Damn this woman who has such

---

[17]   bMS Am1892.7 (113).
[18]   bMS Am1892.7 (222), 125-26.

power over me," he confided to his notebook, utterly oblivious to the injury that he had caused.[19]

As early as 1947, he was smitten by a young woman named "Jackie," whom his fellow poet, Theodore Spencer, had brought over for tea. Later, he was reading Browning's "The Statue and the Bust," which made him feel that he should take action and seek her out – to seize the moment or else suffer for his inaction as Browning's failed lovers did.[20] This inclination eventually led to a somewhat comic episode in April 1948, on an evening when he and Marion attended a gallery opening and later had dinner and "quantities of Scotch" at the apartment of Dorothy Case, another of Cummings' long-time disciples. After Marion left to go home, Cummings' alcoholic state urged him into making advances to Dorothy and the two of them ended up in her bed. When he returned home, he found he had left "The Iron Maiden" behind. The next day he awoke with a villainous hangover, full of remorse, and told Marion all about it. Exasperated with him for making such a fool of himself with one of their best friends, she was nevertheless forgiving and even volunteered to telephone Dorothy about the overlooked "Maiden."[21]

Cummings' state was not much helped by the fact that over the next three years he began to experience sexual impotence from time to time. To make matters worse, when he and Marion consulted their family physician, Dr. Peters, about it, the doctor blithely suggested the King David treatment, namely, that a sixteen-year-old girl could probably fix him up.[22] Although this was a joke and an assurance that there was nothing physically wrong with the patient, Cummings took it under serious consideration.

Two years later, when Cummings was giving the Norton non-lectures at Harvard, he and Marion had a group of students to tea one afternoon. On this occasion, a blonde Radcliffe student named Ann Grant gave him "a look." His response: "feel shock: as if by lightning ... realize this is love's 'arrow' – am really wounded!"[23] He became obsessed with this young woman, although he never made any overtures to her at all. His journal is full of speculations and meditations about "la blonde," until she became a symbol of what he

---

[19] bMS Am1892.7 (227).
[20] bMS Am1892.7 (223), January 1947.
[21] bMS Am1892.7 (225), April 26, 1948.
[22] bMS Am1892.7 (229), January-February 1951.
[23] bMS Am1892.7 (231), February 19, 1953.

needed to restore his virility, to rekindle his creativity, and even to cure his bad back. But he remembered his consultations with Fritz Wittels, now dead, who had always counseled him to stay with Marion and warned him that at his age young women were a bad idea.

Long after they left Harvard, he continued to mull over a "last opportunity" with one young woman after another, blonde or not, who happened to cross their path briefly, either in New York or in New Hampshire. When he began to be afflicted by heart fibrillations, he interpreted them guiltily as punishment for his fantasies of infidelity to Marion. Nevertheless, his yearnings and notions about sex with a young girl did not cease. His notebooks are full of considerations about "la bl." She became such an *idée fixe* that he even discussed the problem with Marion, with his son-in-law Kevin Andrews, and with his old friend Hildegarde Watson. Marion became tired of the whole matter and told him that he should "go uptown and find as many blondes as [he] wanted."[24]

Marion's love for Estlin was still able to weather this kind of childish fear of old age and mortality. In 1955 when Estlin underwent surgery for a rectal polyp at Rochester Memorial Hospital while she remained in New York, she told him, "It was very strange while you were away. I hope you'll let me die first."[25]

But, of course, with his greater age and all his ailments, he did die before Marion, on September 3, 1962. Jere Knight told me that after his death, Marion would wake every morning weeping. Aline Macmahon reported to me that Marion did not stop weeping for weeks. Her love for this brilliant, very exasperating man, one of the unique artists of our century, continued to be quite present and real until her own death on May 18, 1969.

After my book *Dreams in the Mirror* was published in 1980, I received a letter from England one day from Paul Rotha. He told me of his love for Marion and how he had wanted to marry her but that she had refused his offer. She told him that she could not leave Cummings. Rotha informed me that he was dying of cancer, and he asked me if he could have a copy of the photograph by George Hoyningen-Huene that had appeared in my book. I sent him the photo, and he replied in a letter of thanks:

---

[24]   bMS Am1892.7 (232), April 6, 1954.
[25]   bMS Am1892.7 (233), May 13, 1955.

Am better now but alas cannot walk far. However I keep as busy as possible .... Looking back on it all now, I think that Marion made a great personal sacrifice when she decided to remain with E.E. You see, I admired her not only for her remarkable beauty but also for her intelligence. My only memento of her today is a pair of platinum cufflinks which she gave me just before we parted in March, 1938. I have worn them many times in sundry countries but no longer have any use for them. I shall, of course, keep them and have said what they were in my will ....

If ever you are in NYC and visit "21" (if it still exists), you will find Marion's and my initials carved on a wood tabletop which I think was in a downstairs bar. Another spot we visited a lot was Bleek's, the "Herald Tribune" bar in Times Square. But we met in so many places including the flat of a friend of hers in, I think, 53 East. We spent a number of nights there.[26]

Some years later I reported this surprising correspondence to Jere Knight, for she and her husband Eric had introduced Rotha to the Cummingses. She scoffed at Rotha's story, telling me that he was already married at the time and was a notorious womanizer. Nevertheless, he wrote me as he did, and I was genuinely moved by his request. "Truth sits on the lips of dying men," as the saying goes. The impact of Marion's beauty upon men was, perhaps, more than another woman could understand.

---

[26] August 28, 1981.

MARTHA GELLHORN (1908-1998):
FEMME FATALE OF AMERICAN LETTERS

INEZ HOLLANDER-LAKE

[T]he kids have discovered me, while previously, I languished in the literary shadows. But after all my books have always been reviewed and the size of the reviews changed only as the size of all reviews changed – I doubt if I will have a larger public now than the one I've always had .... I'm beginning to feel condescended by this why-hasn't-anyone-noticed-her-before-stuff.
Martha Gellhorn, Letter to Bill Buford,
December 14, 1987

When Martha Gellhorn died on February 15, 1998, she was, in the first place, remembered as the third and only wife who dared walk out on her legendary novelist-husband, Ernest Hemingway. Since she was a prolific journalist and author of five novels, fourteen novellas, two collections of short stories and one play, she considered it an insult to be mentioned as a footnote to Hemingway's life. As one of the first female war correspondents, who reported from the front lines of nearly all the wars the twentieth century has known, she made an invaluable contribution to that most dangerous brand of journalism, war reporting. Unfortunately, her death went almost unnoticed in the country of her birth. "A loner by temperament," who lived the "postwar ex-pat's life and relished never quite belonging,"[1] Gellhorn became better known in Britain where she commuted between a flat in London's Cadogan Square and a cottage on the Welsh-English border. Upon her death, the British newspaper *The Independent* decided to establish a Martha Gellhorn-prize for young war reporters, and Bill Buford, former editor of the English quarterly *Granta* paid her the highest tribute by arguing that Gellhorn "is not a travel writer or a

---

[1]   Bill Buford, "Life and Letters: The Correspondent," *New Yorker* (22 and 29 June 1998), 96.

journalist or a novelist. She is all of these, and one of the most eloquent witnesses of the twentieth century."[2]

Because so few assessments have been made of her work thus far, a brief survey of the author's life and oeuvre seems appropriate. Since Gellhorn never took her own short stories very seriously, calling them "bilgers" and "stylish junk,"[3] I will exclude them here and concentrate on the longer fiction instead. While Gellhorn's versatility as a journalist, cultural critic, novelist and short story writer make it difficult to decide upon her place in literary history, the author's prime achievement seems to have been her drive for artistic and political independence. Nonetheless, because she was a remarkable female voice in a predominantly male world, Gellhorn's cigarette-smoking, pants-wearing New Womanhood was heartily embraced by feminists. Although feminism was an essential part of her being and oeuvre, Gellhorn denounced the label:

> Feminists nark me. I think they've done a terrible disservice to women, branded us as "women writers." *Nobody* says "men writers" and before we were all simply writers. This "woman" tag leaves one seemingly apt only for women readers which is hardly my idea of my audience.[4]

---

[2]   Bill Buford in Rick Lyman, "Martha Gellhorn, 89, Pioneering Female Journalist," *New York Times*, 17 February 1998, *New York Times Online*, Online, 6 July 1998.
[3]   Martha Gellhorn, *The View from the Ground* (New York: Atlantic Monthly Press, 1988), 111.
[4]   Gellhorn quoted in Nicholas Shakespeare, "Martha Gellhorn," *Granta* (Summer 1998), 217. For a considerable period, besides a handful of articles, there were no books on Gellhorn with the exception of Carl Rollyson's unauthorized biography, *Nothing Ever Happens to the Brave: The Story of Martha Gellhorn* (1990). Gellhorn eluded the "academic kook" and said in an interview that "A writer should be read, not written about. I wish to retain my lifelong obscurity" (Jane O'Reilly, "Hemingway Was Her Greatest Mistake," review of *Nothing Ever Happens to the Brave* by Carl Rollyson, *New York Times Book Review*, 30 December 1990, *New York Times Online*, Online, 6 July 1998). On reading Rollyson's work Gellhorn commented: "Rollyson's book is almost a paean of hate; Hemingway would have adored it. And Rollyson would have never bothered with me, except for Hemingway. It has made me sick to read it with horrid care, noting the lies, inaccuracies, etc. for future use. He has used, as a narrative, a rewording of all my printed work and he transposes my fiction directly into my life with weird effects" (Martha Gellhorn to Bill Buford, 26 August 1990, in Buford, "Life and Letters," 105). In late 2003, as the present volume was going to press, a new biography, based on Gellhorn's papers at Boston University, appeared: Caroline Moorehead, *Gellhorn: A Twentieth-Century Life* (New York: Henry Holt and Co, 2003); published in Great Britain as *Martha Gellhorn: A Life* (London: Chatto and Windus, 2003).

Born on November 8, 1908, in St. Louis, Martha Ellis Gellhorn was the daughter of a well-to-do gynecologist. Her mother was a suffragette and social reformer who, early on, raised her daughter's political awareness by taking her to rallies and protests. When she found out that the nuns would not teach the young Martha anatomy, she co-founded a progressive co-educational school which "scandalized the conservative community. 'You'd have thought she was trying to open a brothel,' Ms. Gellhorn later remembered."[5]

Dropping out of Bryn Mawr, Gellhorn persuaded the Holland-America Line to give her free passage to Paris in return for advertising copy. Unlike some of her more successful countrymen who had crowded the Left Bank already, Gellhorn "absorbed a sense of what true poverty means, the kind you never chose and cannot escape, the prison of it. Maybe that was the most useful part of my education ... all in all, standing room at ground level to watch history as it happened." Failing to become a foreign correspondent, she returned to the United States in 1934 and joined the FERA (Federal Emergency Relief Administration) to travel around the country and report on citizens' homelessness, unemployment and poverty. Eleanor Roosevelt, who had been reading some of her reports, invited her to a White House dinner where Gellhorn was seated next to the President: "Mrs. Roosevelt, being somewhat deaf, had a high sharp voice when talking loudly. She rose at the far end of the table and shouted 'Franklin, talk to that girl. She says all the unemployed have pellagra and syphilis,'" Gellhorn recalled. Despite this embarrassing incident, Gellhorn befriended the Roosevelts and even stayed in the White House to write her first novellas after she quit the FERA.[6]

Gellhorn's eye-witness accounts for the FERA were the foundation for the four novellas which were later published under the title *The Trouble I've Seen* (1936). H.G. Wells was so impressed with the novellas that he wrote a preface for the book, lauding the young author's "lucidity and penetration." The four gloomy tales, all dealing with characters who see their dreams dashed and their lives limited by the Depression, are extraordinary in their telling detail and quiet understatement. Reminding the reader of Theodore Dreiser, Frank Norris and other masters of the naturalist school, the proletarian tales show the early signs of Gellhorn's disenchantment with big business

---

[5]   Gellhorn quoted in Rick Lyman, "Martha Gellhorn, 89, A Pioneering Female Journalist."
[6]   Martha Gellhorn, *The View from the Ground*, 68, 71.

and big government. Frustrated with capitalist America, Gellhorn left for Spain in 1937.[7]

When she arrived in Madrid as *Collier*'s war correspondent, the Spanish Civil War was in full swing. After a failed marriage to the French pacifist Bertrand de Jouvenel, she met up with Ernest Hemingway who held court in the much-besieged Palace Hotel. They became lovers and married in 1940; they shared a villa in Cuba but would finally divorce in 1945. According to Jane O'Reilly,

> Ernest Hemingway was [Gellhorn's] greatest mistake. The glorious partner of her days covering the Spanish Civil War turned into the fraudulent, drunken competitor of World War II, a poseur who even stole her job as correspondent for *Collier*'s.[8]

Gellhorn claimed she left the marriage because she got tired of her husband's jealousy and bullying:

> There is nothing worse than being married to a jealous man .... It took me a long time to realize that I was being bullied when he kept saying my stuff was no good and that it was all just an accident because I was a pretty young girl.[9]

Finally, Bernice Kert ascribed their discord to the fact that "during the Spanish Civil War and World War II, [Gellhorn] was not only more aggressive but also braver. She walked out on him because she thought he was playing the hero without really being one."[10]

Gellhorn's bravery was indeed extraordinary. After dodging bullets in war-torn Madrid, she joined British pilots on their bombing raids over Germany and stowed away on a hospital ship to witness D-Day up close as a stretcher-bearer on Normandy's beaches. She was there, too, when the first Allied troops liberated Dachau. The sight of the skeletal survivors who were picking at their lice behind the barbed

---

[7]   Martha Gellhorn, *The Novellas of Martha Gellhorn* (1991; New York: Vintage, 1994).

[8]   Jane O'Reilly, "Hemingway Was Her Greatest Mistake."

[9]   Gellhorn quoted in Rick Lyman, "Martha Gellhorn, 89, Pioneering Female Journalist."

[10] Aaron Latham, "Papa's Mother and Wives," review of *The Hemingway Women* by Bernice Kert, *New York Times Book Review*, 17 July 1983, *New York Times Online*, Online, 6 July 1998.

wire had a lasting impact on her view of Nazism, the Germans and Israel's desire for autonomy.

Although Gellhorn had great difficulty reporting from the front lines, being a woman ("The US Army PR officers, were a doctrinaire bunch who objected to a woman being a correspondent with combat troops"[11]), she deplored what war reporting had become:

> They [military leaders] realized the power of the press and have been controlling it ever since .... Look at the Gulf War. If you wanted to go out and say to a soldier, "How is it, kid?" you had to bring a minder so the kid says nothing .... It seems to me that they feed war reporters at these ridiculous briefings in the ballroom of hotels miles from anywhere. I think we have to educate the reading public to realize that they are getting crap. [12]

Some of Gellhorn's World War II experiences went into three major works, her first novel, *A Stricken Field* (1940), her third novel, *The Wine of Astonishment* (1948; republished as *Point of No Return* in 1989), and a play, *Love Goes to Press* (1946; reprinted in 1995), which she co-authored with Virginia Cowles, another war correspondent.

Dedicated to Ernest Hemingway, *A Stricken Field* is the story of Mary Douglas, American journalist and obvious alter ego of Gellhorn herself. At the book's opening she arrives in Prague shortly after the Munich Pact and just before the *Anschluss*. Czechoslovakia is overrun by refugees from Sudetenland and while Mary's male colleagues lounge about their hotel rooms, believing that there is nothing worthwhile to report, Mary goes out, visits refugees' shelters and decides that writing about the situation is not enough; she persuades the British Lord Balham and French General Labonne to talk to the Czech Prime Minister about a two-week-delay of deportation so that the refugees will have more time to seek asylum in other countries.

These efforts fail, as does Mary's painstaking attempt to get her refugee-friend, Rita, out of the country. Rita and her boyfriend Peter run an underground network for refugees but Peter is seized by the Gestapo. In an unlikely attempt to be with him the last few hours of

---

[11] Martha Gellhorn, *The Face of War* (1959; New York: Atlantic Monthly Press, 1988), 86.
[12] Gellhorn quoted in Rick Lyman's "Martha Gellhorn, 89, Pioneering Female Journalist."

his life, Rita manages to penetrate Gestapo headquarters from whose cellar she is able to eavesdrop on Peter's torturous interrogation. Losing all hope about Peter's survival, Rita walks back into the rainy streets of Prague and has herself arrested, too.

Meanwhile, Mary prepares to return to Paris and is persuaded to smuggle out a stack of eye-witness accounts of Nazi atrocities. Reading through the papers, she realizes that the truth in war is "propaganda" to some:

> if I called Tom and Thane [fellow journalists] and everybody and let them make copies, they couldn't use it. I can't use it. We wouldn't be believed. We'd be accused of propaganda, the way we always are. She thought: safe people will not believe this and who will dare to publish it?[13]

Ironically, this would be Gellhorn's own fate when, reporting on the suffering of the Vietnamese during the Vietnam War and questioning America's motives for the war, only one American paper (the *St. Louis Post-Dispatch*) bought her pieces and the Saigon regime denied her a visa to return to Vietnam. However, Hugh Cudlipp, then editor-in-chief of the British *Daily Mirror*, applauded her for being the first war reporter "who had finally made sense of the war, who saw it, as Martha would say, 'from the ground.'"[14]

Although Gellhorn accused Hemingway of "mythomania" as he liked to make his heroes larger than life, in *A Stricken Field* Mary assumes a larger role than the one that has been assigned to her. For someone who has been through the Spanish Civil War, her naiveté is startling; possibly, she is the embodiment of the kind of humanitarian that Gellhorn may have aspired to be herself but could not be because of the professional distance she had to keep as a journalist.

The other characters are not quite convincing either and the dialogue between Mary and her colleagues seems stilted and dated. But this debut novel has some virtues, too. Although the plot is not very intricate, there are some truly suspenseful scenes, such as the ones in the Gestapo basement and Mary's airport departure. Also, considering that the novel was published as early as 1940, one should

---

[13]   Martha Gellhorn, *A Stricken Field* (New York: Duell, Sloan and Pearce, 1940) 286-87.

[14]   John Pilger, [column remembering Martha Gellhorn], *New Statesman*, 20 March 1998, 17.

praise the book for its sharp political instinct about the realities of Hitler's regime. Gellhorn's powerful prose, describing the overall atmosphere and misery of a city that is about to be occupied, underscores this. The novel's dour realism derives from the author's actual war reporting as well as the possible influence of Hemingway's paratactic and matter-of-fact style:

> I would tell how I heard the children sing once in Spain, in Barcelona, that cold and blowing March when the bombers came over faster than wind, so that it would all happen in three unending minutes, but if you saw them they were hanging in the sky not moving, slow and easy, taking their time, you'd think, not worried about anything. But usually the planes were higher than you could see or hear, and suddenly the streets beneath them fountained up, in a deep round echoing underground all-over-the-sky roaring that seemed never to finish, and the windows bent inward and the furniture shook on the floor and in the stillness afterwards you would hear one voice, wild and thin and alone, crying out sharply, and then silence.[15]

Gellhorn was certainly aware of her husband's legacy:

> he did liberate English prose from mandarins like Henry James and Edith Wharton. He freed everyone into being able to write about what they felt. After Ernest it was possible to use ordinary words. He only used the words he knew, but he had his poetry. Plainspeak and cadence.[16]

Both war novels, *A Stricken Field* and *Point of No Return*, feature masculine prose. This is also where the author's feminism comes in, for not only does Mary speak and write like a man, she acts like one, too. In fact, she has more courage than her male counterparts who lounge about the hotel in a kind of 1920s alcoholic stupor.

Mary is an Amazon in a world of weak males and her character would be recreated in *Love Goes to Press* (1946), a comedy that stars two female war correspondents whose courage and independence make them stand out as true-blue early feminists. Jane Mason and Annabelle Jones are the butt of jokes before they arrive at the Italian Press Camp of Poggibonsi. However, when Jane arrives – soon followed by Annabelle, who recently divorced her journalist-husband

---

[15] Gellhorn, *A Stricken Field*, 82-83.
[16] Gellhorn quoted in Nicholas Shakespeare, "Martha Gellhorn," 230.

Joe Rogers because he (like Hemingway) stole all her stories – she is, like Annabelle, glamorous and feminine but also competent and courageous. Together, they subvert the stereotype that such women lose their femininity because they are doing a man's job. On top of their attractiveness, they are vulnerable in matters of the heart: Jane falls in love with the PR officer Philip Brooke-Jerveaux and Annabelle has a weak spot for her former husband Joe when she runs into him again at Poggibonsi. But like truly independent women who refuse to sacrifice their individuality and career for the sake of marriage, they end up preferring another war to another husband. Thus, while Annabelle puts Joe out of her mind for good when she finds out he has appropriated another of her leads, Jane backs out of Philip's marriage proposal when she learns that he is a country squire who only lives for horses and hunting:

> [Jane to Annabelle]: "Well, have you any idea what it [life with Philip in Yorkshire] means? It means getting flung from half-wild horses while they leap over gates like swallows. Then you lie in a field until you rot. They never thought of a field dressing station. Or else you're cowering in a wet little box on a lake, speechless in the middle of the night, waiting for some silly ducks to show up. Or for real fun you go fishing somewhere in Scotland in a blinding snowstorm."[17]

In her sensitive afterword to the play's 1995 edition, Sandra Spanier observed that *Love Goes to Press* has the feminist theme in common with such 1940s movie classics as *His Girl Friday* (1940), *Woman of the Year* (1942) and *Adam's Rib* (1949). Like the play, these movies portray intelligent women who "out-man" their mates and colleagues "at [their] 'own game'"; but unlike these (man-made and man-produced) movies that "end happily ever after," the play was truly ahead of its time and "an important piece of women's literary history" because it "was written by two New Women and their idea of 'happily ever after' does *not* include their mates."[18]

After the war, Gellhorn returned to the U.S. and traveled cross country in 1947. This gave rise to the article "Journey through a Peaceful Land" which first appeared in *The New Republic* in June and August of 1947. The article shows that Gellhorn experienced a deep

---

[17]   Martha Gellhorn and Virginia Cowles, *Love Goes to Press* (1946; Lincoln: University of Nebraska Press, 1995), 69.
[18]   Sandra Spanier, "Afterword," *Love Goes to Press*, 84-85.

sense of alienation: coming from a wasteland of war, she could neither relate to America nor her countrymen:

> After all the miles ... there is still no conclusion to draw from driving through America. It is beautiful and strange. It has also a great quality of unreality, because the reality of most of the world now is hunger and desolation, gutted houses and factories ... the hopelessly repaired clothes, the cracked shoes and the wretched allotment of coal. I do not see how anyone can make that reality clear to Americans, because they have not felt it and experience is not communicated through the mind.[19]

The harshest war reality to convey was the existence of the concentration camps. Gellhorn's visit to Dachau had affected her so much that she put the experience in a novel that may well be her best work. *Point of No Return* (1948) is a journey from innocence into experience and Hell. Jacob Levy, a Jewish soldier and typical innocent abroad, finds himself in an infantry battalion in Europe during the last few months of the war. Unlike many of his fellow soldiers, he survives the Battle of the Bulge and the journey across Germany but when he visits the Dachau death camp that has just been liberated by Allied troops, he breaks down completely.

Confronted with the hidden extermination agenda of the Nazi's, Levy is greatly disturbed by the camp's gas chambers, ovens and pile of "naked, putrefying, yellow skeletons." On his way back to the army base he is overcome by feelings of revenge and steers his jeep into a small crowd of German pedestrians, killing them all, while (once again) surviving himself. Recovering in the army hospital, he admits to his guilt and expects to pay for the crime with his life: "Once in his life he had done something, of his own will, for nobody he knew, not caring what became of him after, and it was no use." While Levy is well aware that evil will not redeem evil, towards the novel's conclusion, he hopes to be reunited with his Luxembourg fiancée Kathe and wishes to continue his life in spite of his crime.[20]

Although the novel ends on a slightly more positive note, the story seems to imply that there are no victors in war. While Levy and his

---

[19] Martha Gellhorn, "Journey Through a Peaceful Land," *The View from the Ground*, 88.
[20] Martha Gellhorn, *Point of No Return* (1948; Lincoln: University of Nebraska Press, 1989), 284, 322.

commander Lieutenant Colonel John Dawson Smithers may survive, their exposure to battle, death and concentration camp evils turns them into embittered individuals who have reached a point of no return in their lives. Quite literally this means that both Levy and Smithers cannot return to their hometowns because – like Gellhorn experienced herself – they fear that the relatives and friends they left behind will not be able to truly understand what they have seen and experienced; thus Levy cannot return to his middle-class parents in St. Louis; instead, he dreams up some pastoral cabin in the Smoky Mountains, away from people, civilization and war. Likewise, Smithers finds himself caught in a vacuum: "in the end, he belonged nowhere; he wouldn't be any worse off in a foreign country."[21]

Dorothy Brock, Red Cross nurse and lover of Smithers, also loses her innocence to experience (and final indifference). In fact, when Smithers makes love to her for the first time, he is baffled by her lack of feeling:

> Smithers was shocked and hurt. Whores acted like this, only at least they'd say something agreeable while they were about it. And he knew she wasn't a whore, she was a nice girl, she had come from a good family. They checked up on all these Red Cross girls before they let them join. It was awful to think American girls got like this, just wanting it the way the man would.

In the end, Brock's hardening and apparent promiscuousness do not only seem to come from her experience in war, but also from her essential feminism. One even hears Gellhorn's own feminist voice coming through when Brock argues that war is a male invention:

> "Men don't love women, you know .... Sex, yes, that's different. But not love them. Or else how is it they can always invent something that finishes any life a woman could be happy in? Like wars and concentration camps and whatever they'll think up next? I know the men get massacred while they're about it but I tell you, honestly, that's their nature."[22]

Just as Levy, the emotional, young and gullible soldier, is paired up with the rational, older and skeptical Smithers, so the experienced and

---

[21] *Ibid.*, 252.
[22] *Ibid.*, 74, 316.

independent Brock is contrasted with the innocent and helpless Kathe. Kathe's fall from innocence is brought about by sexual awakening; the "Liberator," Levy, brings both the experience and hurt that a war romance involves. In this way, the four main characters are all changed people by the end of the novel and herein lies the book's strength. While the plot may be straightforward and simple, the characters are convincing and illustrate, one by one, how deeply war scars man and his psyche.

Another outstanding quality of the novel is its realism. Although Gellhorn had never traveled with an actual infantry battalion, she manages to convey truthful and lifelike situations, without ever becoming sentimental. The war novel is a difficult genre if one has not been a soldier oneself; a war novel by a woman is all the more remarkable as it is a rarity in American literature. However, it does not stand out as a woman's book: *Point of No Return* portrays a man's world in a man's language. As with *A Stricken Field*, the novel's prose has a sober but highly effective Hemingwayesque echo.

The novel's only defect may be its ambivalent ending: both author and characters seem to condone Levy's vengeful act. The killing of the Germans is wrong but in the novel their deaths hardly seem to matter. This is disturbing unless, of course, the author seems to suggest that, after the Holocaust, man is essentially condemned to repeat the same evil. Gellhorn, who tended to take a dim view of humanity after all the horrors she had witnessed in her lifetime, does seem to imply this in her 1989 afterword of the book:

> Various adaptations of Dachau thrive in some ninety countries now. It has been a splendidly successful model: the State declares that crimeless people, any people, are enemies of the State. Then the State locks them up, starves them, tortures them or "disappears" them, the language of our time. The Nazi formula for war has also been copied, in the needless wars, large and small, that have raged every year since 1945. *Schrechlichkeit*, frightfulness. Standard operational procedure nowadays; no rules; anything goes. I see Lieutenant Colonel Smithers' battalion as the last fortunate soldiers.[23]

Between the light-weight *Stricken Field* and the masterful *Point of No Return*, Gellhorn published *Liana* (1944), a mediocre novel that, with its Caribbean setting, seems to have been based on the years the

---

23   Martha Gellhorn, "Afterword," *Point of No Return*, 331.

author spent with Hemingway in Cuba. At the time, Hemingway told Gellhorn that *Liana* was "not bad for a Bryn Mawr girl" but meanwhile wrote his mother saying that *Liana* was better than anything he had written.[24]

Liana is a beautiful mulatto girl who, through her marriage to the unsympathetic French planter Marc Royer, rises above her milieu and race. The marriage is an unhappy one; while Royer merely needs Liana to satisfy his sexual appetite, Liana has opted for the marriage because she wants to escape the poverty of her childhood. Much to the resentment of the black servants, she tries to be like a white wife and dresses and runs the house accordingly, but, rejected by both blacks and whites, she ends up being no more than a bored and isolated concubine.

This changes when the French refugee and the island's schoolteacher Pierre Vauclain is hired to give Liana private reading lessons. The two fall in love and the affair sets off a chain reaction of betrayal: when Royer finds out, he feels betrayed and convinces Vauclain to return to France to join the war. Vauclain agrees under the condition that Royer will provide for Liana after his departure. Liana, who had hoped to flee to Martinique and start a new life with Pierre, feels betrayed by her lover when she overhears the cold and calculating talk the two men have regarding her future. Out of spite, she writes him a cold farewell letter. Upon reading the letter Vauclain, in turn, feels betrayed as he thought he meant more to Liana; he does not know, however, that Liana sees no way out and kills herself.

Liana's fate underlines the book's feminist (and imperialist) theme: the marginalization of the black woman by the white male. Liana is not viewed as a full individual but as an object that can be bought (Royer offers Liana's mother money for her hand in marriage), "sold" (Royer's deal with Vauclain) and discarded (Vauclain's shameless leave-taking after having promised their elopement). Uneducated and unemancipated, the girl is not only a slave of her white masters but she is also a typical "tragic mulatto" in that she is ultimately an outcast of both the white and black communities.

Aside from this interesting theme, *Liana* is a somewhat predictable novel. The book's setting is alluring and enchanting but its characters lack both the depth and development of a Levy or Smithers. As someone who was compulsive about the truth and doubtful about

---

[24]   Gellhorn quoted in Nicholas Shakespeare, "Martha Gellhorn," 230.

"invention," Gellhorn may have struggled more with the composition of *Liana* than with that of *Point of No Return* or *A Stricken Field*. After all, writing from the perspective of a war correspondent or a soldier must have been easier than adopting the point of view of a mulatto woman. Some critics have even argued that Gellhorn's exceptional talent and instincts as a facts-gathering and truth-telling journalist limited her story-telling ability as a novelist. "I'm not a natural novelist because I can't invent," Gellhorn declared towards the end of her life.[25]

In the 1950s Gellhorn traveled to Poland to write about the new communist generation and visited Israel at the time of the Suez crisis. Since London became the most permanent of her residences she also wrote on English politics, while becoming overtly disgruntled with McCarthy's communist witch hunt in her own country. In the 1980s and 1990s she even believed that a new McCarthyism had taken root "in the Moral Majority, in countless right-wing organizations [and] in Fundamentalist Christianity."[26]

After the productive and eventful 1940s, the author hit a dry spell in the 1950s, when, besides raising her adopted son George Alexander (Sandy) on her own, she only published short stories and the novellas-collection, *Two by Two* (1958). Not much is known about Gellhorn's third and brief marriage to *Time*-editor T.S. Matthews but her skepticism of marriage, "a terrible institution that should be suppressed," is clearly present in her novellas-collections, *Two by Two* and *Pretty Tales for Tired People* (1965), as well as in her fourth novel *His Own Man* (1961). Interestingly, Gellhorn went from war reporting and war novels to the war between the sexes in her next works. In her novellas marriage is never fulfilling but always a confining power struggle in which one partner drives the other away by wanting or exerting too much control. The only marriage that has some potential is destroyed by actual war: in "Till Death Us Do Part" war photographer Bara and his only and true love Suzy both get killed by sniper bullets.[27]

Critics of these novellas argued that they were too much like English drawing-room dramas. Though they are light fare reminding one of P.G. Wodehouse, the two novellas "Till Death Us Do Part" and

---

[25] *Ibid.*, 234.
[26] Martha Gellhorn, *The View from the Ground*, 158-59.
[27] Gellhorn quoted in Rick Lyman's "Martha Gellhorn, 89, Pioneering Female Journalist."

"For Better For Worse" are interesting because, like its author, their characters derive their identity and life from war. Ironically, although war means death to many, war means life to some: while Andrea blossoms on the front and withers in peacetime, the war journalists in "Till Death" dread peacetime as a "curious coma. ... Bara said ... that it was going to be very hard to get used to peace."[28]

The *Pretty Tales*-novellas and *His Own Man* are significant for their underlying feminism. While the trials and tribulations of marriage are still the focus of attention in these tales, the women characters strike out on their own more often and are considerably more independent than their female contemporaries. Contrary to the conventional Liana-story in which the woman is victimized and abandoned, these stories show that deceitful men ultimately receive a taste of their own medicine. Thus Theodore Ascher in "The Clever One" is found sobbing in his bathroom after his third marriage hits the rocks and the adulterous Robert Hapgood in "The Fall and Rise of Mrs Hapgood" has a nervous breakdown when his "faithful" wife Faith runs off to France and starts an affair of her own.

His Own Man, which could well have been another novella in the *Pretty Tales*-collection, repeats the feminist nemesis theme. Ben Eckhardt, Lost Generationeer, American scholar and eternal bachelor, breaks up with women the moment they declare their love for him. However, he is finally dumped himself when the two women he is dating simultaneously find out that marriage is out of the question for Ben; Jessica takes her revenge by having his baby and excluding him as a father and Liz simply leaves him to pursue her life of opulence abroad. Contrary to the novel's title, the two heroines become "their own women" while Ben is left behind humiliated and emasculated:

> He was not a new man with a new life ahead. He was a nearly middle-aged man with the same old life. It was the life he had invented and loved; he had reveled in it, considered himself fortunate, unique: his own man. Ben tried to remember what it was like long ago, in the golden age before he met Jessica and Liz. He tried to remember happiness. He covered his eyes with his hand, as if shielding them from harsh light, and wept without a sound.[29]

---

[28]   Martha Gellhorn, *The Novellas of Martha Gellhorn* (1991; New York: Vintage, 1994), 292.
[29]   Martha Gellhorn, *His Own Man* (New York: Simon and Schuster, 1961), 188-89.

Gellhorn's last novel, *The Lowest Trees Have Tops* (1967), is set in Mexico and narrated from the viewpoint of a critical Susanna who recounts the stories of the eccentric, colorful and, at times, misbehaving expatriates. Unlike similar and popular travel stories of today, such as Peter Mayle's Provence series, *The Lowest Trees* does not expose the quirkiness of the locals but pokes most fun at the expatriates, worst of whom are Susanna's fellow Americans. Thus upon the arrival of three American couples whose lives have been wrecked by the McCarthy trials, one of the American residents complains that Communists and other "riff raff" will taint the town's character. Susanna then teases that Jews are on their way, too:

> "My God, don't tell me there are Jews, too?" "Yes," says Susanna, "Haven't you heard? A whole train load. From Auschwitz, so they say."

Ironically, the supposed "Reds" turn out to be the dullest people who merely stand out for their homesickness and yearning for American apple pie and white Christmases.[30]

Regardless of all the odd characters who land in San Ignacio del Tule, the sleepy community is a model Gellhornian town as it does not tolerate bigotry and other forms of narrow-mindedness. As soon as a hostile element invades town, such as for example the rabble-rouser Mrs. Hatfield or the anti-Semitic Englebachs, the town rallies together and, like a catalyst, drives the foreign element out while preserving its own integrity and character.

The book is of a lighter genre than Gellhorn's earlier fiction but it splendidly conveys both the author's biting sense of humor and her talent as a seasoned expatriate observer. Her only book of travelogues, *Travels with Myself and Another* (1979), and her distinctive last novella *The Weather in Africa* (1978) were acclaimed for the same reason. Travel was Gellhorn's passion and like war, it electrified her and made her feel alive: "I have only to go to a different country, sky, language, scenery to feel it is worth living."[31]

Traveling all over the globe and living in Cuba, Italy, Mexico, Kenya and finally Britain, Gellhorn preferred exile to a life in the U.S.

---

[30] Martha Gellhorn, *The Lowest Trees Have Tops* (New York: Dodd, Mead and Company, 1967), 33.
[31] Martha Gellhorn to James Fox, 3 July 1986, "Life and Letters: The Correspondent", 99.

Sickened by the Vietnam War and the Nixon years, she became ashamed of carrying a U.S. passport and even blamed the writer's block she was experiencing in the 1970s on the on-going war in Vietnam. When the war did end, "prison gates ... opened, I walked out into a wide world where I could see to the horizon in all directions. I wrote two books, one after the other; my life took shape."[32]

Well into her seventies, the veteran journalist was still traveling (and snorkeling) in faraway places and writing for the common good. Whether they were Welsh miners on strike, women protesting nuclear proliferation or political prisoners who survived the gruesome torture chambers of El Salvador, they were heard by Gellhorn. In 1990 the eighty-one-year old writer traveled to Panama shortly after the American troops had left: "as long as I am around I have to keep on with the record, how things really are, as near as I can find out."[33]

Although she thought she had hit a "golden plateau" and was all "set for a spiffing old age,"[34] in 1992 her worsening eye-sight stopped her from using the typewriter and made her fear she had to give up her other lifeline, travel, too. Yet, feisty and chain-smoking until the very end ("It bores me all that health stuff"[35]), Gellhorn, who had seen so much death and destruction in her lifetime, anticipated her own end with her characteristic valor and understatement:

> Limbo is a new country to live in and not one I would gladly choose. At present there's no escape and one must always remember that it's worse for the men at sea ...[36]

A month later Martha Gellhorn was dead. Although she would probably have resented the label herself, she was the *femme fatale* of American Letters *par excellence*. Her oeuvre, both non-fiction and fiction, should be remembered and reconsidered for its exceptional heroism, feminism and virtue.

---

[32] Martha Gellhorn, *The View from the Ground*, 329.
[33] Gellhorn quoted in Nicholas Shakespeare, "Martha Gellhorn," 226.
[34] Martha Gellhorn to Victoria Glendinning, 8 July 1996, "Life and Letters: The Correspondent," 109.
[35] Gellhorn quoted in Rick Lyman's "Martha Gellhorn, 89, Pioneering Female Journalist."
[36] Martha Gellhorn to Paul Theroux, 13 January 1998, "Life and Letters: The Correspondent," 109.

Works by Martha Gellhorn

Novels
A Stricken Field, New York: Duell, Sloan and Pearce, 1940.
Liana, New York: Scribner's, 1944.
Point of No Return, 1948; Lincoln: University of Nebraska Press, 1989.
His Own Man, New York: Simon and Schuster, 1961.
The Lowest Trees Have Tops, New York: Dodd, Mead, 1967.

Novellas
The Novellas of Martha Gellhorn, 1991; New York: Vintage, 1994 (includes: *The Trouble I've Seen* [1936], *Two by Two* [1958], *Pretty Tales for Tired People* [1965] and *The Weather in Africa* [1978]).

Play (by Gellhorn and Virginia Cowles)
Love Goes to Press, 1946; Lincoln: University of Nebraska Press, 1995.

Short Stories
The Heart of Another, New York: Scribner's, 1941.
The Honeyed Peace, New York: Doubleday, 1953.

Non-Fiction
The Face of War, 1959; New York: Atlantic Monthly Press, 1988.
The View from the Ground, New York: Atlantic Monthly Press, 1988.
Travels with Myself and Another, New York: Dodd, Mead, 1978.

READING SIGNS: EPISTEMOLOGICAL UNCERTAINTY AND THE SOUTHERN GROTESQUE IN FLANNERY O'CONNOR'S *WISE BLOOD*

SUSAN CASTILLO

The Southern novelist Flannery O'Connor once remarked that all of us are grotesque in one way or another, though we rarely realize this about ourselves, and that indeed what is considered normal is often grotesque, while the grotesque itself is the stuff of everyday reality. An example of this are the bizarre road signs which flank Southern highways and which are a source of endless delight for the semiotician. Though it would be difficult to choose a favorite (serious contenders would be "Do not shoot from highway," "Get Right with God," and the truculent "Don't mess with Texas"), this critic's personal choice is "Read Signs," spotted near Pelahatchie, Mississippi. Clearly, there is a logical contradiction at work here; if one does not read signs, one is hardly likely to be galvanized into doing so by reading the one in question.

As a person who was born and raised in the American South, I have always been a bit bemused by the to-do over what critics (particularly those who hail from points north of the Mason-Dixon line) call the Southern Grotesque. The abundance, in texts by Southern writers, of references to the distorted, freakish, and absurd elements which seem to be woven into the texture of everyday life are, as any Southerner can attest, not mere stylistic devices but rather Aristotelian mimesis of the first water: Southern life really *is* like that. One could of course argue that distortion, freakishness and absurdity are not exclusive to the South, and indeed one does encounter them in the work of writers from other regions. The uniqueness of the Southern Grotesque, however, is its moral dimension; writers such as Flannery O'Connor and Eudora Welty chronicle these qualities not only with amusement but with a certain compassion devoid of sentimentality. The South of the Southern Grotesque is a Bakhtinian Carnival of crazed businessmen, sinister hairdressers, serial killers, con artists, mad housewives desperately seeking redemption. It is, in short, a reasonably accurate and plausible rendering of Southern reality.

In this essay I shall begin by sketching the characteristics of what has come to be known as the Southern Grotesque. I shall then go on to analyze Flannery O'Connor's novel *Wise Blood.*

Colonial texts describe the South as "a delicate garden, abounding with all kinds of odoriferous flower" where making a living demanded "no toil or labor."[1] In a certain sense, subsequent Southern fiction attempts to come to terms with the contradictions between this pastoral vision of the South as idyllic agrarian dream and the historical reality of a patriarchal culture which relied on the extensive use of slave labor. One thinks, for example, of Mark Twain's *Huckleberry Finn* and the contrast between the idyllic world of Huck and Jim on the raft floating down the Mississippi and the sordid world of redneck reality on the banks of the river. The Southern Agrarians, including writers and critics such as John Crowe Ransom, Allen Tate, Robert Penn Warren and Donald Davidson, reaffirmed pastoral agrarian values and denounced what they perceived as the sordid values of an economy based on industry and commerce. Anne Goodwyn Jones, in her marvelously titled study *Theory and the Good Old Boys*, has analyzed the profoundly reactionary attitudes underlying the Agrarian movement, which, one may note, included no women writers.

Perhaps for this reason, it is in the texts of certain Southern women writers that this division between idyllic pastoral dream and crude historical, economic and political realities is most clearly apparent. One can thus argue that the style which critics call the Southern Grotesque is in reality a reaction on the part of certain Southern writers to the discrepancy between the vision of the South as ante-bellum pastoral Arcadia on the one hand and the crude historical realities of a patriarchal, racist society.

The word "grotesque" is itself derived from the Old Italian *grottesco*, odd or extravagant, and was originally used to describe the paintings decorating the walls of a grotto or cave. Webster's *New Twentieth-Century Unabridged Dictionary* describes it in the following terms:

> fruit, etc. 1. in or of a style of painting, sculpture, etc. in which forms of persons and animals are intermingled with foliage, flowers, in a fantastic design; 2. characterized by distortions or striking

---

[1]   See *The Literatures of Colonial America: An Anthology,* eds Susan Castillo and Ivy Schweitzer (Oxford: Blackwell, 2001).

incongruities in appearance, shape, manner, etc.; fantastic, bizarre; 3. ludicrously eccentric or strange; ridiculous, absurd.

Thus, the grotesque is characterized by the juxtaposition of contradictory elements or genres, meant to produce a feeling of alienation or de-familiarization in the reader or spectator in order to present a reality characterized by radical discontinuity, devoid of significance, in which human beings attempt to create meaning in a world which is disjointed and senseless. The German theorist Wolfgang Kayser has suggested that the grotesque is based on a vision of this estranged world:

> Suddenness and surprise are essential elements .... We are so strongly affected and terrified because it is our world which ceases to be reliable, and we feel that we would be unable to live in this changed world. The grotesque instills the fear of life rather than the fear of death. Structurally, it presupposes that the categories which apply to our world view become inapplicable. We have observed the progressive dissolution ... the fusion of realms which we know to be separated, the abolitions of the law of statistics, the loss of identity, the distortions of natural size and shape, the suspension of the category of objects, the destruction of the personality, and the fragmentation of the historical order. The grotesque is a play with the absurd ... an attempt to invoke and subdue the demonic aspects of the world.[2]

The grotesque is thus an aesthetic of extremes. There is indeed a tradition of the grotesque in American literature, dating from the convoluted autobiographies of the colonial period, going on to the work of Charles Brockden Brown and Edgar Allan Poe, and later in that of Ambrose Bierce and Sherwood Anderson. Indeed, F. Scott Fitzgerald's description of the bizarre party guests of Jay Gatsby in *The Great Gatsby* is a tour de force of the grotesque, as are the tormented characters which people the fiction of Nathanael West. But it should be said that the South, as a region and a culture of extremes characterized by decadence and by racial and social fragmentation, is especially fertile soil for this genre.

---

[2]   Wolfgang Kayser, *The Grotesque in Art and Literature*, trans. Ulrich Weisstein (Bloomington: Indiana University Press, 1963), 184.

Thus, as critic Erwin Panofsky suggests, the grotesque is ultimately an art of acceptance and reconciliation of contradictory possibilities.[3] Indeed, it represents a certain recognition of the fact that amid the essentially chaotic nature and violent nature of the universe, it is the perception of the individual that orders and gives meaning to reality. At the same time, however, it should be kept in mind that an essential condition of the grotesque is its comic nature. Gilbert Muller has pointed out that

> ... the subject matter of the grotesque – the raw material which creates the vision – is always potentially horrible, but the treatment of this material is comic: this explains the peculiar complexity of tone, combining both horror and the ludicrous, which characterizes the grotesque as an art form. But our laughter at grotesque figures is always tinged with uneasiness and a certain sense of guilt at our own amusement.[4]

It is this guilty pleasure that distinguishes the grotesque from the surreal; in surrealism, the realm of the irrational is viewed with wonder. In the Southern Grotesque, however, the irrational and the arbitrary are seen as part of the fabric of everyday life.

Thus, characters in a fiction of the grotesque are always contradictory, with more than a little of the absurd. One encounters Trickster figures, clowns, demons, fanatics, pranksters. The bodies of many characters in this type of fiction are often grotesque or deformed. The grotesque plot is characterized by exaggeration, comic melodrama, the juxtaposition of the horrible and the ridiculous.

Flannery O'Connor was one of the most skilled practitioners of the style which has come to be known as the Southern Grotesque. This was not by accident; in her essay "The Grotesque in Southern Fiction" she states that the kind of fiction which can accurately be called grotesque is so because of a directed intention on the part of the author.[5] After discussing the confinements and limitations of the

---

[3] Cf. Erwin Panofsky, *Gothic Architecture and Scholasticism* (Latrobe, Pennsylvania: Archabbey Press, 1951), 64.

[4] Gilbert Muller, *Nightmares and Visions: Flannery O'Connor and the Catholic Grotesque* (Athens, Georgia: University of Georgia Press, 1972), 7.

[5] Flannery O'Connor, "The Grotesque in Southern Fiction," in *Flannery O'Connor: Collected Works*, ed. Sally Fitzgerald (New York: Library of America, 1988), 815.

realist and naturalist traditions and invoking Nathaniel Hawthorne's distinction between novel and romance, she goes on to state:

> If the writer believes that our life is and will remain essentially mysterious, if he looks upon us as beings existing in a created order to whose laws we freely respond, then what he sees on the surface will be of interest to him only as he can go through it into an experience of mystery itself. His kind of fiction will always be pushing its own limits outward .... Such a writer will be interested in what we don't understand rather than in what we do. He will be interested in possibility rather than in probability. He will be interested in characters who are forced out to meet evil and grace and who act on a trust beyond themselves – whether they know very clearly what it is they act upon or not .... (815-16)

Later in the same essay, she adds that a novelist should be characterized not by his function but by his vision.

Flannery O'Connor's dark visions were not always fully understood by her contemporaries. When her first novel, *Wise Blood*, appeared, one obtuse critic declared that the author dwelled on degeneracy in "an insane world, peopled by monsters and submen,"[6] concluding that the protagonist, Hazel Motes, was not credible because he was "a poor, sick, ugly, raving lunatic." John Simons, reviewing it in *Commonweal*, dismissed it as "a kind of Southern Baptist version of *The Hound of Heaven*,"[7] while *Time* magazine, with its usual inane glibness, saw it "as if Kafka had been set to writing the continuity for L'il Abner."[8] In recent decades, however, and particularly after 1980, the outpouring of critical studies on O'Connor's work have assured her status as one of the major writers of twentieth-century American fiction.

O'Connor's debut novel, *Wise Blood*, is, by any standard, an extraordinary achievement. The reader first encounters Hazel Motes, its protagonist, traveling by train to the city of Taulkinham. He is

---

Subsequent references to this work (to be included parenthetically within the text) are to this edition.

[6] Isaac Rosenfeld, "To Win by Default," review of *Wise Blood*, by Flannery O'Connor, *New Republic* (7 July 1952), 19-20.

[7] John Simons, "A Case of Possession," review of *Wise Blood*, by Flannery O'Connor, *Commonweal* (27 June 1952), 297-98.

[8] "Southern Dissidence," anonymous review of *Wise Blood*, *Time* (9 June 1952), 108-10.

described as a young country bumpkin of about twenty, with a broad-brimmed preacher hat, wearing a loud blue suit with the price tag still attached. At first glance, it would seem that O'Connor is setting him up as a figure of fun, but there is something dark and forbidding about Hazel, and death is woven into his story at every turn. On the journey he encounters Mrs. Hitchcock, a garrulous matron, who tries to look into his eyes, described as having "the color of pecan shells" (3) and who notices that "the outline of a skull under his skin was plain and insistent." As he lies in his berth on the train, Hazel is haunted by memories of death:

> In his half-sleep he thought where he was lying was like a coffin. The first coffin he had seen with someone in it was his grandfather's. They had left it propped open with a stick of kindling the night it had sat in the house with the old man in it, and Haze had watched from a distance, thinking: he ain't going to let them shut it on him; when the time comes, his elbow is going to shoot into the crack. His grandfather had been a circuit preacher, a waspish old man who had ridden over three counties with Jesus hidden in his head like a stinger. When it was time to bury him, they shut the top of his box down and he didn't make a move .... Haze had had two younger brothers; one died in infancy and was put in a small box. The other fell in front of a mowing machine when he was seven. His box was about half the size of an ordinary one, and when they shut it, Haze ran and opened it up again. They said it was because he was heartbroken to part with his brother, but it was not; it was because he had thought, what if he had been in it and they had shut it on him. (9-10)

Though Hazel had thought of becoming a preacher like his grandfather, his Army experience had convinced him that in fact he has no soul. He is nonetheless haunted by the image of Christ, described as moving from tree to tree in the back of his mind, "a wild ragged figure motioning him to turn round and come off into the dark where he was not sure of his footing, where he might be walking on the water and not know it and then suddenly know it and drown." (11)

On arriving in Taulkinham, Hazel is assaulted by an apparently meaningless barrage of blinking neon signs: "PEANUTS, WESTERN UNION, AJAX, TAXI, HOTEL, CANDY" (15). Following yet another sign ("MEN'S TOILET. WHITE") to the segregated toilet, he sits in the cubicle (which he chooses because of a sign on the door with "the large word WELCOME, followed by three exclamation points and something like a snake" [15]) and studies the obscene inscriptions on the sides and door. Finally, he notices a scrawled sign advertising the services of Mrs. Leora Watts, a local prostitute, "the friendliest bed in town" (16), and decides to flee from Jesus by actively embracing sin.

Hazel thus makes a beeline to Mrs. Watts' house. She is a figure straight from a painting by Hieronymous Bosch, with yellow hair, greasy pink skin and small pointed teeth flecked with green. After informing her that he is not a preacher, Hazel proceeds to lose his virginity, albeit in highly unsatisfactory and guilt-ridden fashion. He nonetheless continues to feel that he is being stalked by Christ.

On his second evening in Taulkinham, Hazel encounters three figures who will figure prominently in his private drama. He meets the first, Enoch Emery, a country boy like himself, as they watch a demonstration of a miraculous potato peeler. Enoch is one of the doppelganger figures who populate O'Connor's fiction; he is a vision of Hazel's darker side. At the same time Hazel catches sight of a blind man, who seems to be a preacher and who has allegedly blinded himself as an act of faith. He is led by a young girl, who gives Hazel a pamphlet titled "Jesus Calls You," which is yet another sign (21). When the blind man urges him to repent, Hazel replies defiantly that he does not believe in sin, that Jesus does not exist, and shouts to the crowd which has assembled that he is going to preach a new church, which he calls "the church of truth without Jesus Christ crucified."

Shortly after this incident, Haze decides to buy a car, perhaps because of his compulsion to flee from the danger of unconditional faith. After buying a decrepit car, he cruises at high speed down the highway, until he is obliged to slow down by a truckload of chickens. The slow pace at which he has to drive leaves him vulnerable to glimpses of the menacing signs which flank the highway: "WOE TO THE BLASPHEMER AND WHOREMONGER! WILL HELL SWALLOW YOU UP?" (42). Despite his frantic efforts to pass the truck and escape from these signs, he is literally brought to a halt by yet another sign: "Jesus Saves." To this, Hazel reacts by reiterating the doctrine of Original Sin, that this sin has come for any person before the whore mongering and the blasphemy. He adds, "Jesus is a trick on niggers" (43).

In an attempt to escape from his Christ-ridden conscience, Hazel then goes to the local zoo in order to find Enoch Emery and through him to locate the mysterious blind preacher and his daughter. He encounters Enoch in a landscape of the absurd, a municipal swimming pool flanked by a hot dog stand called the Frosty Bottle in the shape of

an Orange Crush soda. There, he and Enoch ogle a local woman, who
again resembles a gargoyle out of a medieval nightmare:

> The woman was climbing out of the pool, chinning herself up on
> the side. First her face appeared, long and cadaverous, with a bandage-
> like bathing cap coming down almost to her eyes, and sharp teeth
> protruding from her mouth. Then she rose on her hands until a large
> foot and leg came up from behind her and another on the other side
> and she was out, squatting and panting .... Her hair was short and
> matted and all colors, from deep rust to a greenish yellow. (47)

Enoch then agrees to reveal the whereabouts of the blind preacher
and his daughter, if Hazel will agree to see something which he insists
on showing him. Hazel, in exasperation, agrees. Enoch tells him of his
"wise blood," a kind of visceral pre-verbal knowledge which provides
him with premonitions:

> Enoch's brain was divided into two parts. The part in communication
> with his blood did the figuring but it never said anything in words.
> The other part was stocked up with all kinds of words and phrases.
> (49)

These premonitions, though non-verbal in nature, are nonetheless
interpreted by Enoch as signs impelling him to act:

> " . . . when I saw you at the pool, I had thisyer sign."
> "I don't care about your signs," Haze said. (52)

Nonetheless, Hazel allows Enoch to take him to the zoo, where he
is shown what appears to be a piece of mop with an eye (actually an
owl). Vision, as has been stated, is all-important in O'Connor; indeed,
one of the only things Hazel had taken along when he went to war
were the glasses of his pious mother, "in case his vision should ever
become dim". (13) To the sinister all-seeing eye of the owl, Hazel
repeats desperately, "I AM clean" (54). Enoch then presents him with
yet another sign, graven in concrete: "MUSEVM". Inside the museum,
he shows Hazel a shrunken three-foot man in a glass case. At this
vision of a diminished humanity, of the jesus with a small j of the
Church without Christ, Hazel throws a rock at Enoch and runs away in
terror. Here it could be argued that Hazel Motes is fleeing not only
from religion but from his own sexuality; indeed, religion and

sexuality are often conflated in Southern culture. His car is a getaway car in the most literal sense; his escapes, ostensibly from his relentless consciousness of God, invariably follow episodes involving women leading him into carnal temptation. This occurs first of all with Leora Watts. Later Sabbath Lily Hawkes, the daughter of the false blind preacher Asa Hawkes, entices him into bed, provoking another getaway. Despite his protestations that he believes in nothing, Hazel is confident of his car's ability to whisk him away from the danger of faith in religion or in women, and it is in his car that Hazel's dark side emerges in earnest. As Laura Kennelly has observed, it is dangerous to feel pity for an O'Connor character, precisely because the author often uses it to trap the reader into a sentimental empathy based on condescension. It is usually at this point that she pulls the rug from under the reader and the reader's preconceptions by having the pitied character do something revolting or morally repugnant.[9] This is certainly the case with Hazel Motes: just as we are beginning to empathize with his existential quest, he uses his car as murder weapon, running repeatedly over the defenseless body of Solace Layfield, an evangelical competitor weirdly similar to himself, who has tried to steal the idea of the Church Without Jesus, but who despite this really does believe in Christ:

> The man didn't look so much like Haze, lying on the ground on his face without his hat or suit on. A lot of blood was coming out of him and forming a puddle around his head. He was motionless all but for one finger that moved up and down in front of his face as if he were marking time with it. Haze poked his toe in his side and he wheezed for a second and then was quiet. "Two things I can't stand," Haze said, "– a man that ain't true and one that mocks what is. You shouldn't have ever tampered with me if you didn't want what you got." (115)

It is only when a bullying highway patrolman pushes his beloved car (the only thing in which he seems to have real faith) over an embankment that Haze deliberately blinds himself[10] in order to

---

[9]   Laura B. Kennelly, "Exhortation in *Wise Blood*: Rhetorical Theory as an Approach to Flannery O'Connor," in *Flannery O'Connor: New Perspectives*, eds Sura P. Rath and Mary Neff Shaw (Athens: University of Georgia Press, 1996), 156.

[10]   The idea of blindness as a prerequisite for insight is present, for example, in the story of St. Paul's temporary blindness during his conversion experience on the road

recover his original purity of vision. Shortly thereafter, he dies while fleeing from his landlady, the terrifying rationalist Mrs. Flood, yet another predatory, sexually threatening woman.

The Southern Grotesque world of Flannery O'Connor is characterized by an aesthetic of liminarity. Its denizens inhabit a fluid realm in which conventional borders are effaced or erased or shrouded in mystery, in which ontological or epistemological certainties no longer exist. The usual boundaries between human beings, animals, plants and even objects are seen as tenuous. Examples of this abound in the text: the women on the train are "dressed like parrots" and one of them has a "bold pea-hen expression" (7); Leora Watts, the prostitute, has "a grin as curved and sharp as the blade of a sickle" (37); the cheeks of the false blind preacher, Asa Hawkes, are streaked with lines that give him "the expression of a grinning mandrill" (20); the bears in the municipal zoo are compared to sedate matrons seated face to face, having tea. But these perceptions are never fixed, never constant. Enoch Emery is described at first as "a friendly hound dog with light mange" (23), but when he spies on the woman at the swimming pool, his image takes on more sinister connotations:

> She had a stained white bathing suit that fitted her like a sack, and Enoch had watched her with pleasure on several occasions. He moved from the clearing up a slope to some abelia bushes. There was a nice tunnel under them and he crawled into it until he came to a slightly wider place where he was accustomed to sit. He settled himself and adjusted the abelia so that he could see through it properly. His face was always very red in the bushes. Anyone who parted the abelia sprigs at just that place, would think he saw a devil and would fall down the slope and into the pool. (45-46)

This acts to reinforce in the reader the sensation that the world of the physical real is mysterious and unknowable, populated by demons and malevolent objects, where nothing is what it seems and nothing remains what it apparently is for very long. Descriptions involving reflections, mirrors and polished surfaces occur throughout the text, but the images they reflect back are distorted. When Hazel goes to Leora Watts' room, he sees her reflection, slightly distorted, in a

---

to Damascus (as O'Connor herself states), in the Oedipus myth, and in the tradition of the blind poet, represented by Homer.

yellowish mirror; when he buys the car, he sees the sinister blasphemous boy he meets on the used car sales lot through the car windows: "The two window glasses made him a yellow color and distorted his shape." (38)

As Hazel goes around the city, preaching (unsuccessfully) the Church without Christ, he proclaims his belief that "it was not right to believe in anything you couldn't see or hold in your hands or test with your teeth." But this narrow positivistic view of reality is ultimately unsatisfactory, and does not enable Hazel to operate any more successfully in the world. The unreliable evidence of his senses induces him into error, over and over, with his mistaken recognition of the porter on the train, and his idea that the sexually aggressive daughter of Asa Hawkes is an innocent child; as well, he is blind to Asa's false blindness. O'Connor skewers the Church without Christ, and its positivist refusal to accept whatever it cannot see, in the advice Asa's daughter Sabbath receives when she writes to newspaper columnist Mary Brittle:

> Then she answered my letter in the paper. She said, "Dear Sabbath, Light necking is acceptable, but I think your real problem is one of adjustment to the modern world. Perhaps you ought to re-examine your religious values to see if they meet your needs in Life. A religious experience can be a beautiful addition to living if you put it in the proper perspective and do not let it warp you. Read some books on Ethical Culture." (67)

For O'Connor, this is what the Church without the vision of Christ Crucified and without faith in the Resurrection amounts to: a fashion accessory, an addition to living divorced from the meaning of life itself.

The secular world portrayed in Flannery O'Connor's Southern grotesque novels is one of radical epistemological uncertainty. Names are unreliable; Hazel's competitor, the evangelical con man Hoover Shoats, calls himself Onnie Jay Holy. It is a nightmare world, devoid of meaning; each of Hazel's epiphanic moments is precipitated when he is unable to interpret the signs which constantly crop up in neon, on pamphlets, on roadside billboards. And yet it is when he finally surrenders to the realization of the limitations of his senses by the radical act of physically blinding himself, that he gains a measure of tortured peace. As his landlady looks at his dead face, she glimpses in the blackness of the burned-out sockets where his eyes once were a tenous, receding point of light.

"HOW ROUGH CAN EDITORS BE?":
CONRAD AIKEN, EDWARD DAHLBERG,
AND KARL SHAPIRO IN A LITERARY ROW

DIEDERIK OOSTDIJK

The "tranquilized fifties" – in Robert Lowell's famous phrase[1] – were not particularly conducive to literary fights or arguments of any sort. The New Criticism ruled supreme in such quarterlies as *The Hudson Review, The Kenyon Review, Partisan Review*, and *The Sewanee Review* and its critics were wary of personal attacks or subjective criticism. In fact, in the 1930s they had reacted against a conservative trend of impressionist and nationalistic reviewing and now endorsed an objective mode of criticism, mostly devoid of biographical and historical context. The poem or story itself and its structural relations were the object of their study. Close textual interpretations had become commonplace and emotional denunciations or praise were rare. Randall Jarrell was one of the few critics who openly introduced his own opinions into his arguments; it was he, also, who first stressed the shortcomings of "The Age of Criticism."[2] Still, Jarrell was a voice crying in the wilderness and he only had a few allies.

Karl Shapiro, a poet of Jarrell's generation, was one of them. This young Pulitzer Prize-winning poet from Baltimore had published in all of the foremost academic quarterlies and was revered by Allen Tate, but he was nevertheless impatient with the New Criticism, as is evident in his *Essay on Rime*, a witty commentary on contemporary poetry written in iambs. In his second, and more serious, critical book, *Beyond Criticism*, Shapiro declared, against the grain, that he preferred "good subjective gusto" in literary criticism.[3] At the time of this bold statement, in 1953, Shapiro was editor of *Poetry: A Magazine of Verse*, the only major literary journal in the United States

---

[1]   Robert Lowell, "Memories of West Street and Lepke," *Life Studies* (London: Faber and Faber, 1959), 57.
[2]   See Randall Jarrell, *Poetry and the Age* (1955; London: Faber and Faber Limited, 1973), 71-92.
[3]   Karl Shapiro, *Beyond Criticism* (Lincoln: The University of Nebraska Press, 1953), 72.

which did not primarily devote itself to criticism. *Poetry*'s chief task was to introduce new poetic talent, Shapiro had explained in his first editorial, and he did not want to compete with the literary quarterlies.[4] Instead of asking professional critics to review or write articles in *Poetry*, he mainly invited other poets to evaluate their peers. What resulted was the "most distinguished and lively [prose section] in the history of the magazine," if not to say controversial.[5]

A series of incidents marked Shapiro's brief tenure as editor of *Poetry*, which lasted only five years, from 1950 to 1955. Besides rubbing some of *Poetry*'s Board members the wrong way – most notably Ellen Borden-Stevenson, ex-wife of Presidential candidate Adlai Stevenson – Shapiro's relationship with a number of poets also came under fire, due to his unorthodox prose policy. Hugh Kenner, a virtually unknown critic at the time, whom Shapiro admired and who appeared frequently in *Poetry* during Shapiro's editorship, wrote an annihilating review of Delmore Schwartz's disappointing volume *Vaudeville for a Princess* in 1950. Even though Shapiro was friendly with Schwartz and a few months earlier had given him one of *Poetry*'s annual prizes, he decided not to suppress the article, but invited a number of people to write a more positive article to counterbalance Kenner's. In the end, after John Berryman and others refused, a review by William Van O'Connor was juxtaposed to the one by Kenner, the latter being superior in both clarity and poise. Shapiro sent Schwartz an apology, but the damage was already done and Shapiro's "relations with Schwartz, which had never been of the best, suffered considerably."[6]

A year later Shapiro solicited a review of Carl Sandburg's voluminous *Collected Poems* from William Carlos Williams. Perhaps Shapiro was "critically naive not to know what Williams was going to do," as he explained in an interview, but Williams wrote the most devastating review of Sandburg's career, which certainly damaged his reputation.[7] Still, Williams' crushing verdict was not exactly

[4]   Karl Shapiro, "The Persistence of *Poetry*," *Poetry*, 76/2 (1950), 89-91.
[5]   Joseph Parisi, "The Care and Funding of Pegasus," *The Little Magazine: A Modern Documentary History*, eds Elliott Anderson and Mary Kenzie (Yonkers: The Pushcart Press, 1978), 225.
[6]   Karl Shapiro, "A 75th Anniversary Celebration: *Poetry*, 1912-1987," speech delivered at Modern Poetry Association, First Chicago Center, Chicago, 30 October 1987.
[7]   Michael Anania and Ralph J. Mills, Jr. "Karl Shapiro: An Interview on Poetry," *The Little Magazine: A Modern Documentary History*, 200.

surprising. Sandburg and Williams had often been compared as followers of Whitman who wrote in the American grain. Tired of this analogy, Williams asserted his independence by claiming that Sandburg's poems "show no development of the thought, in the technical handling of the material, in the knowledge of the forms, the art of treating the line."[8] The implication is that Williams was not just milking the success of his early years as Sandburg was, and that instead he was "still searching out the new prosodic forms that fitted the new world around him," as Reed Whittemore suggests.[9]

On several occasions Shapiro has made it seem as if these literary rows just befell him, as if he was accidentally stuck in the middle of two opposing camps each with an ax to grind. However, he was not quite that innocent. Shapiro could have sent these negative reviews back to the authors asking them to tone down a little, as his successor Henry Rago was apt to do. The reason why he never did is probably because he must have secretly enjoyed stirring up the literary world. This is after all the man who, because he felt their literary estimation did not strike with their records, claimed that T.S. Eliot's *Four Quartets* was "a deliberately bad book" and who called Henry Miller the "greatest living author."[10] Randall Jarrell was not far from the truth when he wrote that "Shapiro loves, partly out of indignation and partly out of sheer mischievousness, to tell the naked truths or half-truths or quarter-truths that will make anybody's hair stand on end; he is always crying: 'But he hasn't any clothes on!' about an emperor who is half the time surprisingly well dressed."[11] Shapiro reveled in pronouncing the unexpected or unpopular statement and the same prankishness that Jarrell notes can be witnessed in the way he edited the prose section of *Poetry*.

The most shocking review was yet to come, however. In February 1953, *Poetry* printed "A Long Lotus Sleep," by Edward Dahlberg, a fairly long review, for *Poetry*, of Conrad Aiken's autobiographical narrative *Ushant*. Shapiro had been on cordial terms with Aiken ever

---

[8] William Carlos Williams, "Carl Sandburg's Complete Poems," *Poetry*, 78/6 (1951), 350.
[9] Reed Whittemore, *William Carlos Williams: Poet from Jersey* (Boston: Houghton Mifflin Company, 1975), 318.
[10] Karl Shapiro, *In Defense of Ignorance* (New York: Random House Inc., 1960), 57, 313.
[11] Randall Jarrell, *The Third Book of Criticism* (New York: Farrar, Straus and Giroux, 1971), 331.

since 1945. Newlywed, Shapiro, who had just been discharged from the army, rented Aiken's Model-A Ford that year and the two would continue to meet, for instance at the Library of Congress where they were both Fellows of American letters. When Shapiro became editor of *Poetry*, he regularly kept in touch with Aiken to solicit poems, to discuss the possible sale of *Poetry*'s archives, or just to exchange literary tidbits. A few months before Dahlberg's infamous article appeared, Aiken had shared his anger with Shapiro about a review that had appeared in *The New York Times Book Review*. A short quotation from his work had contained four typographical errors and one added word. "How rough can editors be?" he had asked Shapiro rhetorically.[12]

Ushant was, in more than one sense, the culmination and a "synthesis of the tendencies" of Aiken's career.[13] Aiken had originally begun outlining the book in 1933, but had quickly abandoned the process because it was too difficult.[14] He finally completed *Ushant*, on his third attempt, in 1951 when he was sixty-two years old and serving as Poetry Consultant at the Library of Congress. Even though he died more than twenty years later in 1973, this was his last major prose book. A few volumes of poetry appeared in the intervening years, including his *Selected Poems*, but it was evident that the bulk of his life's work was over. Stylistically, *Ushant* was also the highlight of his literary life. Starting with *The Jig of Forslin* in 1921, Aiken had for years continued to experiment with Freudian psychology and autobiographical forms in a loose poetic prose mode and in *Ushant* he tried to bring his long-lasting self-analysis to an end.

The title of *Ushant* refers to a dragon-shaped island off the coast of England which Aiken saw each time he traveled back and forth to that country. Besides symbolizing his bicultural nature, as Aiken calls it, the title is also a pun on "you shan't," either a metaphor for the Ten Commandments or the acquiescence that you will not attain your life's ambitions. *Ushant* is a fairly dense and complex autobiography without a clear chronological order. Only gradually is the reader able to discern how the narrative shifts from one formative moment in the

---

[12] Conrad Aiken to Karl Shapiro, 27 October 1952, *Poetry* papers, University of Chicago.
[13] Jay Martin, *Conrad Aiken: A Life of His Work* (Princeton: Princeton University Press, 1962), 227.
[14] Conrad Aiken to C.A. Pearce, 15 March 1952, in *Selected Letters of Conrad Aiken*, ed. Joseph Killorin (New Haven: Yale University Press, 1978), 300-301.

life of D., Aiken's alter ego, to the next. The most central event in Aiken's life, which set in motion his quest for identification, was the murder of his mother by his father and his father's subsequent suicide in his hometown of Savannah, Georgia. Aiken, who was just eleven years old when this happened, found the bodies and notified the police. After this tragic experience Aiken moved in with an uncle and aunt in Massachusetts and was separated from his siblings who were taken elsewhere.

Aiken's *Ushant* fits in a long tradition of American autobiography as a confessional and spiritual quest for self-knowledge. Aiken seems aware of working within such a tradition and *Ushant* is sometimes reminiscent of other, older New England autobiographies, from the Puritans to *The Education of Henry Adams*. In another sense, however, it is not conventional at all. Only those elements of Aiken's life are discussed which "brought about a deepening of his awareness."[15] Neither time nor space is wasted on quotidian details and even the people that Aiken meets are treated symbolically rather than as persons of flesh and blood. Aiken's wives become numbered Loreleis and literary peers are transformed into the Tsetse, the Farouche John, and Rabbi Ben Ezra, for T.S. Eliot, John Gould Fletcher, and Ezra Pound, respectively. Shapiro was particularly amused by the portrait of Eliot and, in a note to Aiken, he congratulated him on *Ushant* which, he said, was "fascinating and beautifully done. I hope the Tse Tse sits."[16]

Anyone thinking that such a praising letter entailed a positive review in *Poetry* was to be deceived. In October 1952 Shapiro mailed out a copy of *Ushant* to Edward Dahlberg, who had asked to review it a few months earlier. In a talk that Shapiro gave on *Poetry*'s 75th anniversary, he feigned surprise that Dahlberg, whom he described as "an Old Testament guru," "had been lying in wait for Aiken for years and was now about to bushwhack him."[17] True, Shapiro was hardly familiar with Dahlberg's work, but he had regularly received letters from Dahlberg up to this time which made the impending attack not unpredictable. Dahlberg had urged Shapiro to make "Poetry rebel ground, like The Little Review, or Seven Arts, or the Dial at its best" and had claimed that if he was running a literary magazine his

---

[15]   Martin, *Conrad Aiken*, 228.
[16]   Karl Shapiro to Conrad Aiken, 17 November 1952, *Poetry* papers.
[17]   Karl Shapiro, "A 75th Anniversary Celebration: *Poetry*, 1912-1987."

"touchstone would be ATTACK."[18] Similar to Shapiro, Dahlberg was bored with The New Criticism and cautioned him not "to allow Poetry Magazine to be a parnassian adjunct to the academic doctors of small knowledge."[19]

Shapiro came in contact with Dahlberg after printing a devastating review of his book *The Flea of Sodom*, in January 1951, by Edouard Roditi, a Sephardic Jew with also American and Turkish roots. Significantly entitled "Prophet or Pedant", Roditi's review presented Dahlberg as one of several writers, such as D.H. Lawrence, Henry Miller, Kenneth Patchen, Ezra Pound and Thomas Wolfe, who had succumbed "to some of the habits of totalitarian thought."[20] Roditi stopped short of calling Dahlberg a Fascist, but the article, which hardly went into *The Flea of Sodom* and centered around Dahlberg's bad spelling and semi-learned allusions to ancient Greek literature, did not leave much to the imagination. Dahlberg's response, "How Do You Spell Fool," which was more than twice the length of Roditi's piece, came two months later. Dahlberg countered that some of the world's best writers were bad spellers and denied strongly the allegation of being a Fascist.

Shapiro thought it was only fair to let Dahlberg reply and, though personal and thunderous, his answer was not foul. Perhaps Shapiro imagined that he had found another reviewer who did not shun controversy and who wrote with subjective gusto. During the following months their correspondence increased and Dahlberg submitted poems – his poem "For Louis Zukofsky" featured in *Poetry*'s August 1951 issue – as well as articles on Shakespeare, which Shapiro refused because it did not deal with contemporary poetry, and on William Carlos Williams. Dahlberg also tried to introduce Shapiro to some poets he felt were neglected at the time, for instance Basil Bunting and Louis Zukofsky. Shortly afterwards, Shapiro printed two reviews of Bunting's latest work and later even solicited "The Spoils" from this British modernist who was living in Persia. Shapiro was not too keen about Zukofsky, but promised to look more closely at his work which Dahlberg urged Zukofsky to send to *Poetry*.

---

[18]   Edward Dahlberg to Karl Shapiro, 23 March 1951 and 13 February 1951, *Poetry* papers.
[19]   Edward Dahlberg to Karl Shapiro, 17 March 1952, *Poetry* papers.
[20]   Edouard Roditi, "Prophet or Pedant," *Poetry*, 77/4 (1951), 236.

Whatever kinship Shapiro may have had with Dahlberg as far as their attitude to criticism was concerned, he could still not have been prepared for what arrived on his desk next, which was more vicious than anything Shapiro himself ever wrote. As Dahlberg's biographer Charles Defanti writes, in writing on Aiken's autobiography Dahlberg had "seized the opportunity to outdo himself completely in the writing of virulent criticism."[21] In his first two paragraphs, Dahlberg claimed that *Ushant* was a "homesick, water book" and "an archive of piddling obscenities, and ... a loose-anecdotal recollection of puerile eroticisms."[22] While Aiken confesses to a number of extramarital affairs and flings, which are sometimes described in detail, Dahlberg overstates his case here. Not unlike Shapiro in his criticism, Dahlberg has the tendency in "A Long Lotus Sleep" to stretch the truth to denounce Aiken's work which he finds too highly appreciated.

Dahlberg's severest allegation, however, was that *Ushant* was "an ill-conceived cento."[23] He suggested that Aiken's style was at times indistinguishable from that of John Dos Passos, T.S. Eliot, Henry James, or Ezra Pound, and that he had pilfered their works in order to write *Ushant*. This exaggerated charge was obviously below the belt, but Dahlberg also accused Aiken of being cerebral, chagrined, obscure, and pretentious, which is closer to the truth. *Ushant* is in many ways a high-modernist work, composed at a time when American poetry was about to change. Dahlberg's review of *Ushant*, in which he urged writers to "return to the näive [*sic*] heart, without minding what is banal and average, and relating it in clear sentences," showed the direction in which he felt literature ought to go and did indeed go.[24] Unfortunately, the many personal rebukes and exaggerations of his review caused these prophetic statements to go unheard.

Dahlberg also specialized in autobiographical writing, albeit of a different kind, but he was much less successful than Aiken. Between 1936 and 1950 he only featured twice in literary magazines and the "meager reception" of *Do These Bones Live* put him in a slump.[25] By

---

[21] Charles L. Defanti, Jr., *The Wages of Expectation: A Biography of Edward Dahlberg* (New York: New York University Press, 1978), 185.
[22] Edward Dahlberg, "A Long Lotus Sleep", *Poetry*, 81/5 (1953), 313.
[23] *Ibid.*, 316.
[24] *Ibid.*, 320.
[25] Fred Moramarco, *Edward Dahlberg* (New York: Twayne Publishers, Inc., 1972), 23.

the 1950s Dahlberg had started to reassert himself, however. In 1950 *The Fleas of Sodom* came out, which, although negatively reviewed in *Poetry* and in only two other magazines, was an indication that he was fighting his way back. *Poetry* was the only major journal which published his work in the early 1950s, but soon Dahlberg would be picked up by Paul Carroll and Irving Rosenthal of the suppressed *Chicago Review* and the newly formed *Big Table*. With his work appearing side by side with that of William Burroughs and Jack Kerouac, who were quickly making a name for themselves, Dahlberg was gaining a new audience and could feel that he was finally on the rise.

Dahlberg, by no means a modest person, must have felt that this attention was long overdue. His "throbbing ambition to become America's greatest author" coincided with "personal, and mostly illogical vendettas" with anybody who thought ill of him, such as Edouard Roditi or contemporaries he perceived as competitors.[26] It is plausible that Dahlberg saw Aiken as "an interloper in the field" of autobiographical narrative who needed to be wounded.[27] Aiken's pride in his New England heritage and his Harvard education probably also stung Dahlberg who was born out of wedlock, was mostly raised in orphanages, and was an autodidact who despised formal education. "A Long Lotus Sleep" is not only an attack on Aiken, but a raid on mythic Beacon Hill; at least two pages of his review are aimed at Henry James. To Dahlberg, Aiken represented everything he himself was not and this partly accounts for his angry diatribe.

Shapiro reacted in a surprisingly positive manner to the review, supplying the title and calling it "extremely good," even though he realized that printing it would end his friendship with Aiken, and he was right.[28] Aiken reacted furiously in a letter to Shapiro on March 2, claiming that "90% of his [Dahlberg's] quotes from USHANT are inaccurate, garbled, or distorted" and suggesting that the allegation of plagiarism could be libelous.[29] An alarming number of mistakes, amounting to two pages, which were listed in *Poetry*'s Corrigenda section in June 1953, had indeed crept into Dahlberg's review. The staff of *Poetry* had apparently not checked Dahlberg's review well enough, for it was further marred by curious omissions and additions

---

[26]   Defanti, *The Wages of Expectation*, 150.
[27]   *Ibid*, 185.
[28]   Karl Shapiro to Edward Dahlberg, 4 December 1952, *Poetry* papers.
[29]   Conrad Aiken to Karl Shapiro, 16 March 1953, *Poetry* papers.

in quoting from *Ushant*. While several letters of protest arrived at the *Poetry* office, Shapiro apologized to Aiken, although he emphasized that as a matter of policy *Poetry* gave reviewers the freedom to express whatever their opinions might be. By now, however, he was starting to doubt Dahlberg's honesty.

Katharine Garrison Chapin and Rolfe Humphries were among those who contacted *Poetry* to object to Dahlberg's review. A poet who was married to Attorney General Francis Biddle and a Board member of *Poetry* to boot, Chapin "was tempted to resign" but rescinded after Isabella Gardner, associate editor under Shapiro, changed her mind after a long talk.[30] Chapin, however, did counter Dahlberg's venomous commentary on *Ushant* in an emphatically praising article in *The Sewanee Review*. Rolfe Humphries, a poet and critic who was anything but an advocate of Aiken's work, expressed his disapproval of Dahlberg's tone and ceaseless insults in a letter to Gardner.[31] Later, when Shapiro asked him to elaborate on these comments for possible publication, Humphries turned down this request saying that he did not consider the case important enough to expatiate on it. Yet, he did stress that he appreciated Shapiro's open policy and conceded that it was sometimes difficult to know where to draw the line.[32]

Of the dozen letters or so that *Poetry* received about the incident, Shapiro decided to publish the one by Elizabeth Pollet because he felt it most clearly stated what was wrong with the Dahlberg review. At the time Pollet was married to Delmore Schwartz, who knew what it was like to be raved over by Shapiro and subsequently run over in *Poetry*. Pollet charged in her pithy two-page communication that Dahlberg's "remarks about the book are astonishingly false."[33] Aiken's sexual escapades, which Dahlberg made so much of, represented a mere fraction of the entire autobiography, she argued, and his suggestion that Aiken's landscapes were indiscriminate from each other was ludicrous to her. Pollet also denounced Dahlberg's incorrect reference to Socrates, claimed that he was "blind to the

---

[30] Katharine Garrison Chapin to Karl Shapiro, 20 August [1954], Karl Shapiro papers, University of Texas at Austin.
[31] Rolfe Humphries to Isabella Gardner, 25 February 1953, *Poetry* papers.
[32] Rolfe Humphries to Karl Shapiro, 12 March 1953, *Poetry* papers.
[33] Elizabeth Pollet, "Communication," *Poetry*, 82/3 (1953), 176.

wonderfully poetic visuals," and concluded that no one "would know from Mr. Dahlberg's review what Mr. Aiken's book is like."[34]

Still other letter writers had asked Shapiro to formally express his regret to Aiken in *Poetry* or, at least, give a statement explaining *Poetry*'s puzzling policy. When Shapiro sought out the opinion of Hayden Carruth, his predecessor as editor of *Poetry*, on the matter, Carruth advised against a public apology or explanation: "it would be a pity and bad policy besides, for you to apologize to Aiken or anybody else." Carruth went on to say that Dahlberg was a distinguished writer and his remarks on *Ushant* were not arrived at in a flippant or ill-considered manner. Admitting that he did not know all the circumstances, he believed that backing down would not be just to Dahlberg and would be disadvantageous for *Poetry*. Moreover, the review was humorous and spirited and what *Poetry*, which had been close to folding a few years earlier, needed above all was to get away from the morbidity of the rest of the literary world.[35]

Shapiro nevertheless resolved that an editorial, only his second at that point, was in order to relieve some of the tension. "Does *Poetry* Have a Policy?" immediately followed Pollet's indignant letter and was a well-balanced outline of *Poetry*'s intentions. Shapiro reiterated that *Poetry*'s foremost goal was to publish a monthly anthology of the best poetry it could lay its hands on and that the reviews it published were of secondary importance. The magazine had never professed to print well-wrought criticism, which it left to the literary quarterlies with their "operating-table approach."[36] Instead, it promoted subjectivity in criticism to negate that dominant trend in American literature, but did not tell the reviewer which side to choose:

> *Poetry* does not favor edited literary criticism or party-line criticism or laboratory criticism. Systematic and impersonal criticism does not seem to us to belong to literature, but to science and philosophy. We take the view that literary criticism should be subjective (but certainly not *ad personam*), passionate, humanly decent, and stylistically unique: we are inclined to judge a piece of criticism by how well it is written and not how "right" it is. *Poetry* does not attempt to legislate about poetics.[37]

---

[34] *Ibid.*, 177.
[35] Hayden Carruth to Karl Shapiro, 4 April 1953, *Poetry* papers.
[36] Karl Shapiro, "Editorial: Does *Poetry* Have a Policy?" *Poetry*, 82/3 (1953), 179.
[37] *Ibid.*, 178.

Shapiro ended by saying that, to the best of his knowledge, Dahlberg's errors and misquotations were neither deliberate nor serious. While he regretted that some readers had taken offense at Dahlberg's tone, Shapiro believed that Dahlberg, who told Shapiro that his review was not a personal attack, apparently did not see another way of expressing his objections.

Shapiro's clear emphasis on *Poetry*'s editorial line did not put an end to the matter, nor did it convince Aiken that the injustice was undone. Aiken, who accused Shapiro of showing "a tendency to run with the hare and hunt with the hounds" continued to hold a grudge and felt he was damaged for good.[38] In the 1910s, when Harriet Monroe was editor, Aiken had a spell during which he had nothing accepted by *Poetry*, except some poems he had sent under an assumed name, and he was now beginning to suspect that there was a pattern of maltreatment by the magazine towards him. When Shapiro did not accept poems by the seventeen-year-old Jay Martin, who later wrote an important study of Aiken's work, Aiken assumed that it was because he had sent them and called Shapiro dishonest.[39] Shapiro had judged that the poems, which *The Kenyon Review* later also rejected, were remarkable for a person Martin's age, but not altogether accomplished enough to be put in *Poetry*. It is not astonishing that Aiken's resentment lingered on, even though he sometimes took his suspicion too far.

Dahlberg, who had much less to complain about, also felt shortchanged by Shapiro's behavior. He had warmly received his review and then suddenly suspected that Dahlberg had covert reasons to pan *Ushant*. Dahlberg tried to convince him of his clear conscience and was outraged that Shapiro thought he was embittered and jealous. Dahlberg put forward his poor eyesight to explain the misspellings and misquotations and assured Shapiro once again that he "would not garble any one's book for the purpose of destroying or praising it."[40] Dahlberg indeed had notoriously bad vision and was entirely blind in one eye. In the long run, Dahlberg's rancor towards Shapiro faded somewhat, although he never forgot Shapiro's accusations. Yet, Dahlberg must have realized that Shapiro offered to print Dahlberg's

---

[38] Conrad Aiken to Karl Shapiro, 27 March 1953, *Poetry* papers.
[39] Conrad Aiken to Karl Shapiro, 9 June 1953, Conrad Aiken papers, Henry E. Huntington Library.
[40] Edward Dahlberg to Karl Shapiro, 26 March 1953, *Poetry* papers.

work at a time when few others did and deserved some of his gratitude. In 1958 he told William Carlos Williams that "Karl Shapiro is one of the very few people, and poets, editing a magazine who is not vindictive or revengeful, but, on the contrary, is very kind, and even merciful to those who labor for wind, and the vanity of vanities we call poems."[41]

Aiken was not quite so forgiving. *Poetry* continued to solicit manuscripts from him and also invited him to lecture in Chicago and to write a review of E.E. Cummings' poems. Aiken politely declined these requests, usually claiming that he was too busy. However, in July 1953 he admitted to Isabella Gardner, who tried to soothe both parties in this conflict, that his real reason for refusing was that he was still shocked by the Dahlberg review, Shapiro's "twofaced whitewashing" of it in his editorial, and *Poetry*'s troubling lack of policy which led to "unprincipled sensationalism."[42] Gardner came to Shapiro's defense in a long letter to Aiken saying that Shapiro was "entirely direct & candid, clearly unprejudiced, ready & able to oppose injustice, and certainly wholly devoid of malice" and that his editorial was "a long overdue, much needed statement of policy."[43] The following summer Gardner visited Aiken on Cape Cod in her native Massachusetts to explain *Poetry*'s position further, but it was evident that this wound would not heal. Aiken never published in *Poetry* again.

Shapiro himself was also affected by the affair. Even though he was pretty much left alone in editorial matters by *Poetry*'s Board of Trustees and only Katharine Garrison Chapin objected, some may have been concerned that such literary rows squandered *Poetry*'s clean and respectable reputation. An even more worrying prospect for Shapiro was that poets, such as Aiken, would become so livid that they ignored *Poetry* altogether and this was potentially dangerous for his policy to secure the best new poems for the magazine. Also, he was losing literary friends fast and his policy made his more enemies than allies. Shapiro was still committed to subjective criticism and would continue to be so for the rest of his career, as is evident from his later collections of essays *In Defense of Ignorance* and *To Abolish*

---

[41] Edward Dahlberg to William Carlos Williams, 1 July 1958, in *Epitaphs of Our Times: The Letters of Edward Dahlberg* (New York: George Braziller, 1967), 203.
[42] Conrad Aiken to Isabella Gardner, 27 July 1953, Isabella Gardner papers, Washington University, St. Louis.
[43] Isabella Gardner to Conrad Aiken, 3 August 1953, Conrad Aiken papers.

Children and Other Essays, but he did begin to wonder whether "it would be best to publish no criticism except favorable criticism" in order to avoid "poisonous backfires."[44] The review of *Ushant* was sure enough the last big controversy involving *Poetry*'s prose section. Soon, Shapiro delegated much of its responsibility to his associate editors Nicholas Joost and Henry Rago who were both more careful not to ruffle too many feathers.

For a brief period in the 1950s, Shapiro had tried to break the dominance of The New Criticism which held sway in the literary quarterlies of the day. "There has never been an age in which so much good criticism has been written," Randall Jarrell rightly wrote about this time, but he quickly added that too much of it appeared in magazines.[45] While he was editor of *Poetry* Shapiro opposed this trend in literature by making sure that at least half of each issue was devoted to poetry and the other half to subjective reviewing instead of objective criticism. This attempt was usually successful and it created the most stirring prose section in *Poetry*'s astonishing history. Printing Dahlberg's review of *Ushant* without having spotted the many inaccuracies of his piece seems the only demonstrable fault Shapiro made, even though it is arguable whether Dahlberg's tone was not offensive as well. In all other cases, Shapiro's behavior was not all that outrageous. He was only promoting that the "reading of new works should be done with good subjective gusto, not with a manual of criticism in hand."[46]

---

[44] Karl Shapiro to Hayden Carruth, 26 March 1953, Hayden Carruth papers, University of Vermont.
[45] Randall Jarrell, *Poetry and the Age*, 72.
[46] Karl Shapiro, *Beyond Criticism*, 72.

POSTILLION FOR PEGASUS:
ISABELLA GARDNER AND *POETRY*

MARIAN JANSSEN

"I am excited by these. Please stop by the office some day."[1] These words, written to the poet Isabella Gardner (1915-1981) in the summer of 1951 by Karl Shapiro, Pulitzer Prize winner and editor of *Poetry* from 1950 to 1955, not only signaled the first acceptance of Isabella Gardner's poetry by that prestigious magazine of verse, but also marked the beginning of her intense editorial association with it. At the time, Gardner was still a virtually unknown poet who had only been published in *Furioso* (1939-1953), a truly little magazine. To be accepted by the magazine that was regarded as "that mythical dreamland for young poets" and which T.S. Eliot had called an "American Institution," marked her coming of age as a poet .[2]

Although Gardner had written poems as a child and teenager, she had stopped writing after her finishing school in Virginia, because "I felt I was too facile."[3] Instead, she had pursued a career as a comic actress, studying with the famous Thorndike sisters in London and touring with 1930s stars such as Gloria Swanson, Estelle Winwood, and Clifton Webb. It was during one of these tours that, in Chicago, she met and, in 1944, married her second husband, the theater photographer Maurice Seymour, a Russian Jewish immigrant. Heavily involved in left-liberal causes, taking care of her two small children, and hosting guests like Paul Robeson, Gardner unexpectedly found herself writing verse again at the end of the 1940s. Insistently encouraged by Oscar Williams – according to Robert Lowell America's best anthologist – she started sending out poems. Seymour had to take a back seat to poetry (and an occasional man) and the marriage deteriorated rapidly, being dissolved

---

[1]   Karl Shapiro to Isabella Gardner [summer 1951], quoted in Isabella Gardner, "Postillion for Pegasus," unpublished, undated manuscript, Karl Shapiro papers, University of Texas at Austin; Gardner's poems were "The Panic Vine," Cadenza," "The Last Trump," and "Cowardice."

[2]   M.L. Rosenthal, *Poetry*, 151/1-2 (1987), 218.

[3]   Isabella Gardner to Judy Bartholomay, February 9, 1974, Isabella Gardner papers, Washington University, St. Louis.

in 1950. Soon after, she married Robert Hall McCormick III, scion of one of Chicago's wealthiest families.

It was at this point in her life that Gardner received Karl Shapiro's summons. "After tremulously telephoning for an appointment," she found herself in the "private dusty burrow" of the *Poetry* offices, where Shapiro, who thought she "was a fine poet and felt that he had discovered her ... asked her if she would be interested in reading for the magazine."[4] Gardner was "*terrified*," protesting her "ignorance ... [,]self-imposed non-reading of most contemporary poets, ... [and] lack of college education."[5] Why indeed did Shapiro ask this inexperienced housewife to decide all by herself which of the over three hundred poems the magazine received per week to return and which to submit to him for final judgment? In the second part of his autobiography, *Reports of My Death* (1990), and in interviews Shapiro has protested that the fact that Gardner was a "Boston Brahmin beauty heiress poet" and Mrs. Robert Hall McCormick III to boot – or, in her own words, "Mrs. Rich Bitch poet" – had nothing to do with his request.[6] But Shapiro was not quite truthful, for the precarious financial situation of the magazine preyed continuously on his mind and he knew full well that with Gardner on board, *Poetry* could easily tap into new sources of Old Money. Besides, it seemed to him she would feel at home with the Bryn Mawr and Vassar socialites who performed *Poetry*'s secretarial duties for free. Then, too, he was well aware that she had great publicity value; for instance, she was offered $1000 (two months of Shapiro's salary) for a cigarette commercial – which she turned down.

Though suspicious of Shapiro's reasons for asking her, Gardner wished so ardently to be involved with poets and *Poetry* that she agreed to become its first poetry reader, without pay. Realizing Gardner's advertising potential, *Poetry*'s new publicity director immediately sent out a press release, informing editors of society pages of the blue-blooded pedigree of *Poetry*'s new volunteer. Isabella Gardner felt "deceived and betrayed" and decided to quit.[7] By summarily firing his publicity director – which landed him in a lot of trouble with *Poetry*'s

---

[4]   Isabella Gardner, "Postillion for Pegasus"; Karl Shapiro, *Reports of My Death* (Chapel Hill, N.C.; Algonquin Books, 1990), 58.
[5]   Isabella Gardner to Judy Bartholomay, February 9, 1974, Isabella Gardner papers; Isabella Gardner, "Postillion for Pegasus."
[6]   Shapiro, *Reports of My Death*, 59; Isabella Gardner to Lee Gardner, 18 March 1955, Robert Gardner papers, private collection.
[7]   Shapiro, *Reports of My Death*, 59.

Board of Trustees – Shapiro managed to convince her to stay on. But, then, he knew that he "had struck gold."[8]

If Shapiro had hoped that Gardner would become a patroness to *Poetry* – just like her godmother, Isabella Stewart Gardner, the founder of Boston's Fenway Court, had been to Henry James and John Singer Sargent – he was not to be disappointed. A month after her acceptance, Gardner's husband was already offering the use of the brand-new Mies van der Rohe buildings on Lake Shore Drive for a benefit for *Poetry* "to conduct tours of the premises [*sic*], have a cocktail party or anything else we wished."[9] A few years later, when *Poetry* was homeless, McCormick offered the magazine, rent-free, "either the Roanoke Building or the McCormick Building, and you can feel that those are available as soon as you want them, just give me a little notice so that I can get the space fixed up for you."[10] This was in 1954, when that "incredibly vain + destructive" Ellen Stevenson, President of *Poetry*'s Board of Trustees, ex-wife of the Democratic presidential candidate, and owner of the Arts Center where the magazine was then housed, had tried to "to put the magazine into receivership + take over" – she had even put Oscar Williams "in an empty room next to the Poetry offices," so that Shapiro and Gardner "suspected he might be Ellen's candidate for Karl's job."[11] When her ploy failed, she resigned and threatened to throw the magazine out overnight. Moreover, as Shapiro had hoped, the McCormicks gave generously to *Poetry* and got their relatives and friends to donate as well, while Gardner helped raise considerable sums of money by organizing readings by public personalities such as Edith Sitwell. Also, Gardner made the worksheets of Dylan Thomas' thirty-fifth birthday poem – which she had bought to support him – available to *Poetry*'s Thomas issue (November 1955) and, that same month, gave them to be auctioned at the first annual "Poetry Day," a lucrative benefit with Robert Frost as its main bait.

If less tangibly, Gardner's work as its first reader benefited *Poetry* much more. Even after moving to her new Mies van der Rohe house in Elmhurst, she came in religiously every day of the week, six hours a day,

---

[8]   *Ibid.*, 58.
[9]   Modern Poetry Association, minutes of the meeting of trustees, October 20, 1951, *Poetry* papers, Newberry Library, Chicago.
[10]   Modern Poetry Association, minutes, June 14, 1954, *Poetry* papers, Newberry Library. In the end, thanks to its new President, Stanley Pargellis, *Poetry* moved to the rent-free attic of the Newberry Library, of which he was the head librarian.
[11]   Isabella Gardner to Robert and Lee Gardner, undated, Robert Gardner papers.

to work her way through "the mountain of manuscripts."[12] It can safely be said that Gardner spent much more time working for *Poetry* than its editor, as Shapiro, in order to provide for his wife and three children, often held down three jobs simultaneously. In addition, Shapiro, though keeping final editorial say, was away teaching and writing almost a third of his time in charge. "[A]n angel ... stuck in [a] broomcloset," Gardner proved to be such a diligently independent reader, that Shapiro, in "his big carpeted office," was soon "staring out of the window into Lake Michigan and feeling foolish and in a sense out of work."[13] In early 1952, he had already reported to the Trustees that Gardner was a "major addition to the volunteer staff," adding that she preferred "to perform the duties of first reader of the manuscripts anonymously; consequently her name has never appeared on the masthead of the magazine."[14] But in July 1952, Gardner was mentioned as assistant, and in April 1953, as associate editor: by that time she apparently felt so certain of her true value to the magazine that she no longer feared being misused as a moneyed decoy.

If part of the "incredible" number of poems that came in was the work of well-meaning amateurs, "stuff by illiterates, or the kind of thing that gets in newspapers about your grandmother," which Gardner could screen and weed out easily, it was nevertheless amazing how, without being abreast of the contemporary poetry scene, she selected from the remaining manuscripts so sensibly that Shapiro "relied on her opinion and her taste very much and ... never questioned her," usually following her suggestions for publication.[15] Usually, but not always. When Gardner's sister-in-law wanted to submit a poem, Gardner warned her: "If I *love* it + Karl is just *dubious* we would have to turn it down," which Shapiro proceeded to do.[16]

Whereas in this case Shapiro was probably right, he was less sensitive than Gardner with respect to a number of promising poets. It was mainly thanks to her that Philip Booth, John Logan, and Galway Kinnell came to publish in *Poetry* when they first started out. The latter,

---

[12] Shapiro, *Reports of My Death*, 58.
[13] Karl Shapiro to Nicholas Joost and Sue Neil, March 5, 1954, *Poetry* papers, University of Chicago; Shapiro, *Reports of My Death*, 71.
[14] Modern Poetry Association, report of the editor to the trustees [1952], *Poetry* papers, Newberry Library.
[15] Karl Shapiro, interview with the author, February 20, 1990.
[16] Isabella Gardner to Lee and Robert Gardner, Christmas 1954, Robert Gardner papers.

for one, submitted large batches of poems, which Shapiro, in spite of Gardner's advocacy, turned down, indiscriminately using, as was his custom, printed rejection slips. This might have thoroughly discouraged Kinnell, had not Gardner written him long letters, commenting extensively and positively on his work, and again and again encouraging him to submit. Finally, in December 1953, he broke through with "The Wolves" and from then onwards appeared more or less regularly, although Shapiro never really recognized his talent. Writing also on behalf of Gardner, Henry Rago, *Poetry*'s acting editor in 1955, practically begged Shapiro, who was teaching at Berkeley, to accept something by Kinnell, or, at the least, to let *them* turn him down:

> Now: we don't want to pepper him with rejections; it seems much better to reject everything in one batch, especially if in the same letter we can be accepting something .... Even if you want to reject all of it, please send it back to us, so that we can put it in with the stuff here. If you want to accept something, so much the better; again send everything to us, if you will, and let us write the acceptance from here, and then slip the other stuff back to him very quietly.[17]

Even after Gardner had left *Poetry*, in September 1955, Kinnell continued sending poems to her, asking for advice. And she did more: at the height of her own (short-lived) fame during the late 1950s, she helped him select poems for a book, had his poems retyped at her expense (as "a token of faith"), and wrote many publishers on his behalf – though it was not until 1960 that Kinnell broke into print with *What a Kingdom It Was*.[18]

Gardner's relationship with the very Catholic John Logan was similarly nurturing. In January 1953, he wrote to Gardner that he was

> sad that you will not publish my second-rate poems because unfortunately that is probably the only kind I am now writing. But it is a joy to know that if I find the strength and the time to do something better you are willing at *Poetry* to help find an audience .... I am very pleased that you like my shorter lyrics ... because I love to write them and though

---

[17] Henry Rago to Karl Shapiro, January 31, 1955, *Poetry* papers, University of Chicago.

[18] Isabella Gardner to Galway Kinnell, June 7, 1954, Galway Kinnell papers, Indiana University.

publishers are interested in the longer more dramatic things it is hard to touch them with the lyrics.[19]

One of the two poems that comprised Logan's first appearance in the magazine two months later was the lyric "Spring Chill," which, however, paled beside his ecstatic, exalted "Mother Cabrini's Bones."[20] In his review of Logan's first book, *Cycle for Mother Cabrini* (1955), Stanley Kunitz, though finding Logan's religious motivation "too bristling for my taste" and the climax of this particular poem "as overwrought as it is over-italicized," nevertheless saluted him for his "force and admirable control" and "unmistakable authority."[21]

Desiring his aspiring fellow American-Irish poet-friends to share her "kindness" and "careful criticism" as well as, obviously, hoping to get them published, Logan kept mentioning their work in his letters to Gardner.[22] Where no such promotion was necessary in Kinnell's case, she needed some convincing with respect to Paul Carroll. Carroll finally appeared in March 1955 with "Un Voyage à Cythere," a surprisingly controlled classicist poem – with references to Alpheus, Arcady and all – particularly in view of Carroll's sponsoring of the Beats during his provocative editorships of *Chicago Review* and *Big Table* less than five years later.[23] Carroll appeared only this once during Gardner's years with *Poetry*, but, as with Logan and Kinnell, her detailed and reassuring reactions to his submissions fostered his latent talent and made him a life-long, devoted friend.

Among many others who were enriched by Gardner's appreciative criticism of their work were new writers as different as the powerful, poised New England poet Philip Booth ("she gave me some of the earliest, warmest responses") and rough Beat poet Gregory Corso ("Thank you for a beautiful helpful letter. 'Mental muscle' – yes, how right you are"), but also established ones like Richard Eberhart ("I'm glad you liked the poem. ... Karl didn't think it had my idiom (should readers become too accustomed to an idiom?") and Theodore Roethke ("Here are some different final versions – of the sequence you liked. ... I always will cherish your phrase about their being 'the very voice of

---

[19]   John Logan to Isabella Gardner, January 26, 1953, Isabella Gardner papers.
[20]   John Logan, "Spring Chill," *Poetry*, 81/6 (1953), 350-51.
[21]   Stanley Kunitz, "Five Points of the Compass," *Poetry*, 88/3 (1956), 183, 184, 185.
[22]   John Logan to Isabella Gardner, August 18, 1953, Isabella Gardner papers; John Logan to Isabella Gardner, May 19, 1954, Isabella Gardner papers.
[23]   Paul Carroll, "Un Voyage à Cythère," *Poetry*, 85/6 (1955), 319.

love.'")[24] These explicit acknowledgments come from sprawling, simultaneously literary and intensely personal letters that Gardner came to receive from these poets to whose submissions she reacted so extensively, impassionedly, and encouragingly.

Consequently, they continued to submit, as did poets like Reuel Denney, Ruth Herschberger, and Barbara Howes, all of whose work Gardner actively solicited. This was in contrast to Shapiro's practice, as he generally trusted the mail to bring in the manuscripts. He made an exception, though, for *Poetry*'s fat fortieth-anniversary issue, which consisted of solicited poems only. Gardner, too, invited contributions for this occasion, sometimes using her Old Money connections, as in writing to T.S. Eliot, a Harvard chum of her father's. Eliot unfortunately had "absolutely nothing in the desk which I could offer" and he refused to act as a judge for the best poem in the anniversary issue, as "he didn't want to be put in the position of judging his contemporaries in a competition."[25] Ezra Pound, whom Gardner also approached, did not appear either, but the editors could be justly proud of a double special issue amounting "to an anthology of the latest poems of many of the foremost living poets," among them Elizabeth Bishop, E.E. Cummings, Robert Graves, Randall Jarrell, Archibald MacLeish, Marianne Moore, Theodore Roethke, Wallace Stevens, and William Carlos Williams.[26]

Another special issue, on Dylan Thomas, took the joint exertions of *Poetry*'s editor, two acting editors, and Gardner as associate editor to finally come into being. They probably decided to launch this issue as a spin-off of Thomas' profitable benefit lecture for *Poetry* in the spring of 1952. But as early as January 1953, Shapiro called it a "rather abortive plan."[27] Instead of submitting, as promised, new poems to *Poetry*, Thomas had "borrowed" Shapiro's two copies of D.H. Lawrence's *Collected Poems* and reneged on reviewing a rhyming dictionary, which he had also taken. Irritated, Shapiro wrote to R.M. MacGregor at Thomas' American publisher, New Directions: "I wish I knew who was actually in charge. Oscar [Williams] is one of the impressarios but

---

[24] Philip Booth, interview with the author, October 20, 1989; Gregory Corso to Isabella Gardner, November 18, 1954, Isabella Gardner papers; Richard Eberhart to Isabella Gardner, July 19, 1954, Isabella Gardner papers; Theodore Roethke to Isabella Gardner, January 24, 1954, Isabella Gardner papers.
[25] T.S. Eliot to Isabella Gardner, June 12, 1955, Isabella Gardner papers; Karl Shapiro to Wallace Fowlie, August 27, 1952, *Poetry* papers, Chicago University.
[26] The editors, "Announcement," *Poetry*, 81/1 (1952), A.
[27] Karl Shapiro to R. M. MacGregor, January 23, 1953, *Poetry* papers, University of Chicago.

apparently there is a man in England, various publishers and friends. It
takes a lot of people to take care of Thomas."[28] MacGregor explained the
complicated situation with respect to Thomas' agents, some of whom
were not on speaking terms with each other, and tried to temper
Shapiro's annoyance: "I expect that there is no point in trying to trace the
two copies of D.H. Lawrence's COLLECTED POEMS. If you have ever
seen Mr. Thomas looking for his other shoe of a morning, you will
realize that his attitudes towards impedimenta are not exactly
acquisitive."[29] Mollified, *Poetry*'s staff invited Thomas for another
lecture in the autumn, perhaps hoping to acquire new work – but this was
not to be. On November 5, 1953, with Shapiro in Rome on a six-month
Guggenheim grant, acting editor Nicholas Joost wrote to him that
"apparently Dylan Thomas is critically ill in New York and is not
expected to pull through. ... We just managed to get back our cards,
announcing the lecture, which were out at the University Press."[30]
Thomas died four days later and so, instead of celebratory, the issue
became commemorative. In order to distinguish it from the mass of
memorial tributes that were appearing, Joost and Gardner discussed a
"workshop" issue, consisting partly of Thomas worksheets owned by
Stevenson and Gardner and of a "really good essay on Thomas' method
of composition." In view of Oscar Williams' close relationship with
Thomas, Joost felt he had to ask him first for an essay – even if he
preferred Wallace Fowlie – but he balked at having the notoriously
quarrelsome Williams as guest-editor, too: "I think you [Shapiro] ought
to do the issue as editor; I see no reason to bring anybody else in, as the
staff are quite capable of producing the whole thing with a modicum of
or indeed no outside aid and advice."[31] A month earlier Gardner had
asked Williams to be guest editor, but she soon agreed with Joost as
Williams' "impractical" ideas included "25 pages of *testimonials* from
other poets (ugh) and 40 pages of work-sheets ... and the advertising to
be keyed to the Dylan theme!"[32]

---

[28]   Karl Shapiro to R. M. MacGregor , January 23, 1953, *Poetry* papers, University of
Chicago.
[29]   R.M. MacGregor to Karl Shapiro, February 5, 1953, *Poetry* papers, University of
Chicago.
[30]   Nicholas Joost to Karl Shapiro, November 5, 1953, Karl Shapiro papers, Library
of Congress.
[31]   Nicholas Joost to Karl Shapiro, January 29, 1954, *Poetry* papers, University of
Chicago.
[32]   Isabella Gardner to Karl and Evalyn Shapiro, undated, Isabella Gardner papers.

Williams was shelved, but, because of other urgent matters, the issue had to be put on a backburner. For when Gardner left for a holiday in Mexico in February, as Joost did not do first readings of poetry, Shapiro, in Virginia, was snowed under with "another thousand or so manuscripts," forwarded with her "condolences" by Sue Neil, *Poetry*'s secretary.[33] In March, Neil could report that "Belle [Gardner] is back so the great mailings will be cut appreciably," but after Shapiro's own return to Chicago in late March, other matters received priority: plans for the continuance of a bi-monthly *Poetry* radio program together with WFMT radio, a lecture program in cooperation with the University of Chicago (organized by Gardner, Denney and an assistant dean), as well as plans for publication of a *Poetry* index and anthology (of which Gardner was to be an editor).[34] Soon, due to the break-up with Ellen Stevenson, the magazine had to move to new quarters, and, partially prompted by his vexation at the constant obstruction of the Board of Trustees, Shapiro started looking for a different job, telling Neil in October that he might accept a Berkeley visiting lectureship. In that same letter he mentioned Thomas:

> I talked to Ellen Stevenson the other day, believe it or not, about some of her property which we apparently transported in great haste. Ellen seems to think that we have some of her Dylan Thomas manuscripts. But Belle and I today went through the Thomas papers and discovered none of Ellen's. Do you have any recollection of the Thomas manuscripts belonging to Ellen ever being in the office, in the exhibit case, or do you recall Ellen taking them home? Any information will be appreciated by us and the F.B.I.[35]

Shapiro did leave for Berkeley in January 1955, having appointed Rago as acting editor, but, as had been the case with Joost, still reserving all final editorial decisions for himself.

Almost three years after its germination, Rago wrote a long, pessimistic memo about the Dylan Thomas issue, which had now

---

[33] Sue Neil to Karl Shapiro, February, 9, 1954 , Karl Shapiro papers.
[34] Sue Neil to Karl Shapiro, March 3, 1954, Karl Shapiro papers; in the end the lecture series was terminated and the radio program was continued, and it was not until 1963 that the *Index to Fifty Years of Poetry: A Magazine of Verse, Volumes 1-100, 1912-1963* (New York, NY: AMS Reprint Company) compiled by Elizabeth Wright, was published; the anthology, edited by Joseph Parisi, finally appeared in 1987 as *Poetry*'s 75th Diamond Jubilee issue, *Poetry*, 151/1-2.
[35] Karl Shapiro to Sue Neil, October 4, 1954, *Poetry* papers, University of Chicago.

dwindled to "a good, honest, busy, living issue of the magazine, with Dylan Thomas' name prominent on the cover." At this time, the editors were only sure of a Thomas photograph, an elegy especially written for *Poetry* by Edith Sitwell, Gardner's – but not Stevenson's – Thomas worksheets, and a prose piece pledged by Shapiro. If the promised microfilms of unpublished Thomas manuscripts yielded some good new Thomas poems and if Roy Campbell, one of Thomas' friends, delivered a high-class article, the issue, padded by fifteen pages of general poetry, might just avoid becoming merely a "souvenir brochure."[36]

For a while, correspondence from California to Chicago concentrated on Shapiro asking Rago's and Gardner's advice on his prospective successor, on enclosed poems "for you and Belle to look over," and on young West Coast poets like Michael McClure: "I think he is talented and may be something of a discovery. However, I want you and Belle to help me decide."[37] By the end of May, Rago had received both Shapiro's and Campbell's contributions, more came in over the summer, and the Thomas issue finally appeared under Rago's editorship, in November 1955, two months after both Shapiro and Gardner had officially resigned.

Edith Sitwell's "Elegy for Dylan Thomas," which out-Thomased even the five previously unpublished poems from 1933 by the Bard himself, opened its poetry section, which was complemented by work by the Welsh poets David Jones and Vernon Watkins.[38] The three reviews all dealt with Thomas and encompassed the gamut of his creative output. Parker Tyler, in praising Thomas' script, *The Doctor and the Devils*, fulminated, as was his wont, against Mammon: "he might have anatomized film-scripting into an exact and sacred art regardless of that tomb of false pretenses: the box-office."[39] Gene Baro somewhat qualified the general hype about *Under Milkwood* by questioning the play's "enduring value"; and Brewster Ghiselin thought that "[t]hose who have been baffled in their reading" would find Elder Olson's *The Poetry of Dylan Thomas* "immensely helpful," but sharply criticized the many defects due to the unseemly haste with which the book had been published after

---

[36] Henry Rago to Karl Shapiro, February 14, 1955, Karl Shapiro papers.
[37] Karl Shapiro to Henry Rago, May 28, 1955, Karl Shapiro papers; Karl Shapiro to Henry Rago and Charlotte Miller, May 7, 1955, Karl Shapiro papers.
[38] Dylan Thomas' poems were "Out of a War of Wits," "This Is Remembered," "Shiloh's Seed," "Before We Mothernaked Fall," and "The Almanac of Time."
[39] Parker Tyler, "Then Was My Neophyte a Scriptist," 118.

Thomas' death.[40] In his Laurentian "Dylan Thomas" – for Rago "the most intelligent analysis of [Thomas] I have seen so far" – Shapiro described Thomas' death as "the cause of the most singular demonstration of suffering in recent literary history."[41] This "derivative, unoriginal, unintellectual poet," jamming his "personality and vitality ... into his few difficult, half-intelligible poems" became, Shapiro argued, through the force of his emotion, "the first modern romantic."[42] Shapiro particularly admired Thomas because he "did the impossible in modern poetry. He made a jump to an audience which, we have been taught to believe, does not exist."[43] Where Shapiro saw Thomas as "a male Edna St. Vincent Millay, or perhaps a Charlie Chaplin," Roy Campbell found him "very manly, a[th]letic, and a great runner, though there was something wrong with his reflexes and he never learned to fight, which was a great pity in one so extremely aggressive and pugnacious."[44] This exemplifies the tone of his "Memories of Dylan Thomas at the B.B.C.," which remained, even after Rago had "cut two-thirds of it away," "a letdown: too much R.C. and not enough D.T."[45] The eight pages dedicated to Thomas' worksheets may have been worth their weight in gold to the Thomas aficionado, but did not add much to the surprisingly varied, exciting quality of this special issue.

Gardner had actually spent her last day at the *Poetry* office excerpting "a meager 10 or 12 pages" from the seventy Thomas worksheets, as she wrote her brother. "I felt no real pangs at leaving *Poetry*. I think I stayed too long but had promised Karl to. Henry was friendly but obviously panting to get rid of me. I shall miss only the contact with working poets. The coming upon + encouraging of talent."[46] In one of the very few letters Gardner ever typed, written in September to Shapiro, she was more explicit about her departure:

> I came back from my heavenly weeks in Edgartown prepared to work through the month of August but Henry's anxiety to get me out of the office was almost funny. I didn't mind in the least as you can imagine,

[40] Gene Baro, "The Orator of Llaregubb," 119; Brewster Ghiselin, "Critical Work in Progress," 119.

[41] Henry Rago to Karl Shapiro, May 25, 1955, Karl Shapiro papers; Karl Shapiro, "Comment: Dylan Thomas," 100.

[42] Shapiro, "Comment: Dylan Thomas," 103, 101.

[43] *Ibid.*, 109.

[44] *Ibid.*; Roy Campbell, "Memories of Dylan Thomas at the B.B.C.," 111.

[45] Henry Rago to Karl Shapiro, May 25, 1955, Karl Shapiro papers.

[46] Isabella Gardner to Robert and Lee Gardner, undated, Isabella Gardner papers.

but he was far from friendly in any genuine sense of that word. I scraped my things together, dumped my old red slippers in the wastebasket and scrammed. I tried to say that I had enjoyed "working" with him, that I would love to drop in at the office once in a while for coffee and talk; but he didn't even say "please do" or words to that effect. I can think of nothing I[']ve done to offend him, though I know he articulately resented letters I got from poet friends etc. ....

You say Henry is the "best man available for the job." I do not agree. As long as I am on the Board my loyalty is to Henry and I will protect his interests. Mostly because I feel it is important to have a Board member who is sympathetic to and understanding of editorial problems. Also I think Henry [h]as integrity (without doubt) I like him, mildly but genuinely, I think he is good and kind, and a fairly good poet .... But there are at least a dozen poets, young and promising, or older and distinguished who are certainly "available" in the sense that they would joyfully undertake to edit Poetry for two years at a crack. Cal Lowell? Roethke? Maybe not Wilbur because he has children. Donald Hall? I don't think that to qualify as available the poet needs must be a Chicagoan. You were not. And if a Chicagoan is desirable (and I do not feel this is true) then Reuel Denney is ... warmer, more gifted, and more imaginative.[47]

This letter smacks of sour grapes, but is understandable in view of Rago's low behavior towards Gardner the day she left *Poetry* after having devoted over four years of her life to it. In her letters to others, Gardner remained loyal to Rago and a few weeks later wrote Richard Eberhart that she was "*sure* he'll do well." She explained that she had "wanted to [leave] for more than a year but stayed on because Karl asked me to wait until he also could resign."

It "was suggested in a sub rosa sort of way," she continued, "that I edit with a capital E when Karl was to leave but I am *both* inadequate (grossly) and unwilling."[48] An earlier letter by Julia Bowe, member of the Board of *Poetry*, partly corroborates this: "She and I agree that it would be unfair to Henry not to propose him as a candidate for editor after the fine work he has been doing. She talks of resigning but can be talked into staying on for a while until things become more stable."[49] But there was never any really serious thought of making Gardner editor. In an interview in 1990, Shapiro emphasized that "[i]t probably was

---

[47] Isabella Gardner to Karl Shapiro, September 28, 1955, Isabella Gardner papers.
[48] Isabella Gardner to Richard Eberhart, October 24, 1955, Richard Eberhart papers, Dartmouth.
[49] Julia Bowe to Karl and Evalyn Shapiro, undated, Karl Shapiro papers.

because the magazine had sort of half criticism and half poetry ... and I can see that I would not have asked her because of that gap in that part of her interest." But, then, he himself "felt inept at the handling of criticism, so that I hired ... people like Wallace Fowlie ... and Hugh Kenner ... I needed someone as criticism editor."[50] In spite of this and all his many public statements against criticism, Shapiro, in truth, was a lively, prolific critic, if an inconsistent and idiosyncratic one, who would get wholeheartedly involved in critical skirmishes. Gardner, on the other hand, for all her sensitive, precise reading of her contemporaries' poems and her great ability to spot their weaknesses and strengths, hardly read criticism and could not care less about the differences between fighting factions such as the New Critics, the Chicago School of Critics and the like. Also, for all her acuity with respect to new poems and poets, Gardner disliked taking final editorial decisions: "Nick [Joost] just came in and tells me I must choose single-handed six pages of poetry by Dec. 30th. I hate to do so without your o.k. especially as there's so little thats [*sic*] good."[51] Finally, in view of the fact that *Poetry* continuously teetered on the brink of insolvency, the magazine needed a manager, taking care of administrative problems, finances and fund-raising. If Shapiro himself was not a good manager by any standards, Gardner, perhaps because of her Boston Brahmin upbringing, trust fund, and Bohemian nature, was totally incompetent in that respect. In all then, in spite of her immense contribution to the renewed fame of *Poetry* during Shapiro's editorship, she certainly could not have become a second Harriet Monroe, even had she wanted to.

But Gardner no longer wished to be involved in the magazine anyway. She could not get along at all with Shapiro's successor, Rago, a serious, conservative Catholic theologian, who wrote very abstract poetry and "used to brag about the fact that his family, who were funeral directors, were the ones who buried the Capone gang, whenever they shot each other."[52] Shapiro "didn't particularly care for his poetry" either and had, in fact, first asked another Catholic, John Frederick Nims, to succeed him, but Nims at that time could not give up his duties at Notre Dame: he was to be *Poetry*'s editor from 1978 till 1983.[53] Comparing Rago, "pedantic ... non-emotional ... essentially a professor," to Gardner, Shapiro stressed that his successor accepted "poems for the magazine

---

[50]   Karl Shapiro, interview with the author, February 20, 1990.
[51]   Isabella Gardner to Karl and Evalyn Shapiro, undated, Isabella Gardner papers.
[52]   Karl Shapiro, interview with the author, August 18, 1990.
[53]   Nims was visiting editor in 1960-1961.

that I never would, that had a great deal of classical literary background; they were ... literary things. Whereas her poetry ... is quite personal and even though she keeps her emotions in check, there is an awful lot of emotion sort of boiling under the surface."[54] It is no wonder that these two people, poles apart, wished to sever their connection as soon as possible. Anyway, Gardner's main reason for leaving was that without Shapiro *Poetry* had lost its attraction. If Shapiro slightly overstates the impact of his considerable charms on Gardner in *Reports of My Death* – she "loved him all her life and would have been happy to be his wife if he had asked" – she had certainly fallen under his spell:

> Aside from having been to me, long before I met him, a kind of talisman poet by virtue of his truth, grace and acuity, Karl was a wonderful editor to ride postillion to. He ... has charity, clarity, acute judgment and courage. His respect for other human beings engaged him to his own cost where a lesser man, editor and poet might have withdrawn from engagement.[55]

News of Gardner's departure triggered comments and commiserations from the poets she had befriended. Philip Booth had "heard the very bad thing that you are leaving Poetry this fall" and felt "lonely ... knowing that you are leaving who always read my poems best."[56] John Logan was "sorry you are leaving *Poetry*. The magazine needs your taste. But I suppose it has taken too much of your blood." In his first issue, Henry Rago briefly thanked Gardner: "It is a sadness to announce the resignation of Isabella Gardner, who will be missed by countless contributors as the wise and helpful associate editor she has been."[57] Karl Shapiro had the last word when, about a year later, he briefly returned to his editorship of *Poetry* in his correspondence with Gardner:

> I feel hostile to [Rago] at this point. He's been quite the big shot. I'm a dilly at picking people for jobs: Ellen, Stanley [Pargellis] and Henry .... Still, POETRY is good. I always liked it better when I wasn't on it. Not meant as a remark about your job. You did the bulk of the work for years.[58]

---

54   Karl Shapiro, interview with the author, August 18, 1990.
55   Karl Shapiro, *Reports of My Death* 59; Gardner, "Postillion for Pegasus."
56   Philip Booth to Isabella Gardner, August 21, 1955, Isabella Gardner papers.
57   Henry Rago, "A Statement by the New Editor," *Poetry*, 87/1 (1955), 39.
58   Karl Shapiro to Isabella Gardner, Isabella Gardner papers.

Starting out, in 1951, as an insecure, unknown poet without the literary connections she craved, thanks to her indefatigable dedication to the nation's most famous poetry magazine, Isabella Gardner had moved to the center of a large literary circle and had made lifelong friends. *Poetry* greatly increased her self-confidence and boosted her career, but after four years of volunteering, she had become weary. While an apprentice poet, she had shunned reading her contemporaries for fear of being influenced too much, but since she had become Shapiro's helpmate, some 40,000 poems had passed through her hands and she was feeling stale. Kinnell, who himself had sent a considerable number of these poems over the years, understood:

> I am sorry for *Poetry*'s sake that you have left it. And it must be a loss to Henry Rago. But for your own sake I suspect it is for the good. Too much reading of one's contemporaries is never an advantage.[59]

Apart from starting to suffer from writer's block because of this, Gardner simply had hardly any time left for writing, as next to *Poetry* she had her children, husband, and house to take care of. Notwithstanding the pressures on her time, she had nevertheless succeeded in publishing her first and most famous book, *Birthdays from the Ocean*, in March 1955. *Birthdays*, on the whole, received rave reviews and sold out quickly. All this rendered it natural and timely for Isabella Gardner to sever her ties to *Poetry* and stand on her own two feet.

---

[59] Galway Kinnell to Isabella Gardner, September 5, 1955, Isabella Gardner papers.

NABOKOV'S UNWANTED CHILDREN:
LOLITA AND THE WRITERS OF THE OLYMPIA PRESS

JAAP VAN DER BENT

Vladimir Nabokov's relationship and eventual falling out with the first publisher of *Lolita*, Maurice Girodias of the Paris-based Olympia Press, has often been written about. So often, in fact, that in his book about the postwar literary scene in Paris, *Paris Interzone: Richard Wright, Lolita, Boris Vian and Others on the Left Bank, 1946-1960*, James Campbell decided upon a ruse. Aware that he could hardly skip an account of the clash between the Russian-American novelist and the French publisher, but reluctant to cover ground that had already been trod by others, Campbell boiled down a ten-year affair to a twelve-page collection of quotations: from letters and articles by Nabokov and Girodias themselves, but also from Graham Greene, the American publisher Walter Minton, Vera Nabokov and others who, to varying degrees, were involved in the fray.[1]

It is not clear whether Campbell's decision to present his material in this particular fashion was his first choice. He may have been forced to apply this strategy because almost concurrently with *Paris Interzone*, John de St. Jorre published *The Good Ship Venus: The Erotic Voyage of the Olympia Press*, a thorough investigation of Girodias and his activities, which includes a substantial chapter on Nabokov's and Girodias' "lolitigation."[2] While Campbell's elliptic account is amusing reading for those who are already somewhat in the know, one has to turn to *The Good Ship Venus* for a description of Nabokov's and Girodias' doings (and the latter's undoing) which is not only full-fledged and immensely readable, but which also manages to throw some new light on the matter.

---

[1]   James Campbell, *Paris Interzone: Richard Wright, Lolita, Boris Vian and Others on the Left Bank, 1946-60* (London: Secker and Warburg, 1994), 183-95.
[2]   John de St. Jorre, *The Good Ship Venus: The Erotic Voyage of the Olympia Press* (London: Hutchinson, 1994), 121-60. The term "lolitigation" was coined by Nabokov in a letter to Girodias, March 10, 1957, printed in Vladimir Nabokov, *Selected Letters 1940-1977* (San Diego: Harcourt Brace Jovanovitch, 1989), 210.

As the books by Campbell and St. Jorre helped to make more widely known, the Olympia Press was a small English-language publishing house founded in Paris in 1953 that managed to survive until the mid-1960s.[3] Its owner was Maurice Girodias, son of the English-born Jack Kahane, himself the owner of a small press in Paris in the 1930s, the Obelisk Press, which brought out books and booklets by writers like Henry Miller, Anaïs Nin, Lawrence Durrell, and even James Joyce. After the Second World War Girodias decided to follow in his father's footsteps, and by the mid-1950s the Olympia Press had published not only work by Samuel Beckett, Guillaume Apollinaire, the Marquis de Sade and Jean Genet, but also Nabokov's *Lolita*.

Even after numerous essays and articles on Nabokov's European connections have been published, it is still not quite clear why Nabokov decided to take his chance with Girodias when he was unable to find an American publisher for *Lolita*. In fact, as John de St. Jorre has revealed, it is not unlikely Nabokov could have had the book published in America after all, if only he had grabbed one of the chances he was offered. It is true that in early 1950s America, under pressure from McCarthy's anti-communist witch-hunt, most publishers were reluctant to issue an unconventional and in some respects shocking book like *Lolita*. However, at least one publisher – Roger Straus of Farrar, Straus and Young – turned out to be eager to publish the novel, if only Nabokov would give up his demand that the book should be published under a pseudonym. When Nabokov, afraid that publication under his own name might harm his position as a Professor at Cornell University, insisted on the use of a pen name, Straus backed out. In the end it was only Barney Rosset of the recently established Grove Press who was willing to publish *Lolita* with a pseudonym. Nabokov, however, decided upon another strategy and, through a European literary agent, approached Maurice Girodias.

This was a course of action Nabokov came to regret almost immediately, and which would continue to plague him for some time to come. In the first place it soon turned out that Girodias was not the most reliable person to do business with: to the great annoyance of Nabokov, who claimed to "write for [his] pleasure" but to "publish for money,"[4] Girodias was frequently reluctant to tell him how *Lolita* was doing in financial terms. Moreover, Girodias had a bee in his bonnet about

---

[3]   The Paris Olympia Press largely closed down in 1965, after which Maurice Girodias continued to publish erotic books in New York City from 1967 to 1974.
[4]   Cf. John de St. Jorre, *The Good Ship Venus*, 145.

censorship; already shortly after he had published *Lolita* he attempted to engage the book and its author in his struggle to attain complete freedom of the press: that of the press in general, but especially that of the Olympia Press. Nabokov, however, did not want to be caught up in Girodias' attempts in this particular area. Not only was he wary of *Lolita* becoming a *succès de scandale*, he had also found out that Girodias' activities as a publisher had moved in a direction which was hardly compatible with his own aristocratic inclinations. Unable to resist the urge to earn a fast buck, by 1954 Girodias had started to publish a series of dirty books (DBs, as they were also called): pornographic novels which were written to order by a number of British and American writers who were part of the large expatriate community in postwar Paris. As a consequence, when *Lolita* was issued by Girodias in September 1955, Nabokov's favorite found itself in the company of volumes with suggestive titles like *White Thighs*, *The Whip Angels* and *Rape*.

All in all and in spite of the fact that Nabokov was genuinely pleased that *Lolita* had finally found a publisher, he had enough reason to be disgruntled with Girodias and his press. He certainly made no attempt to disguise his low view of most of the work that was issued by the Paris publisher. In an article published in 1967, in which Nabokov is still trying to come to terms with Girodias (who by then had relocated to the United States), Nabokov refers explicitly to Olympia Press' "obscene novelettes which Mr. Girodias was hiring hacks to confect with his assistance."[5] He goes out of his way to explain why he was unwilling to back up Girodias in his fight with the censors ("I did not see how my book could be treated separately from his list of twenty or so lewd books"), and stresses the differences – "in vocabulary, structure and purpose (or rather absence of purpose)" – between *Lolita* and Girodias' "much simpler commercial ventures, such as *Debby's Bidet* or *Tender Thighs.*"[6] While it is unlikely that anyone will rank Nabokov's masterpiece with Girodias' erotica, the highly derogatory terms which Nabokov used to damn the latter tend to obscure the fact that, as this essay will point out, at least some of Girodias' "lewd books" are not devoid of artistic merit. At the same time it will be interesting to see how – while Nabokov was trying to extricate himself from the Olympia Press – some of its more talented "hacks" wasted no time in appropriating

---

[5] Vladimir Nabokov, "Lolita and Mr. Girodias," *Evergreen Review*, 45 (February 1967), 38.

[6] *Ibid.*, 40.

Nabokov and his work. By using elements from that work in their own "much simpler commercial ventures," they created further ties between the author of *Lolita* and the Olympia Press, of which Nabokov himself in all likelihood was not even aware.

One of the first Olympia Press authors to become acquainted with *Lolita* was Alfred Chester. Chester, born in 1928 in Brooklyn, New York, was a highly talented and precocious writer whose relatively short life was marked by tragedy and madness. His problems were partly the result of the fact that at the age of seven, due to scarlet fever, he lost all his hair. While his parents wanted to cover up their son's infirmity by forcing him to wear a wig, Chester's baldness continued to be a source of anxiety throughout the rest of his life; it almost certainly contributed to his becoming addicted to drink and drugs, and thus also to his early death in 1971. By then Chester, after many peregrinations, was living in Jerusalem, far from the New York literary scene on which he had briefly starred in the early 1960s, when magazines like *Commentary* and *Partisan Review* published his highly personal and iconoclastic book reviews that were widely read and discussed. Even then, however, most readers were unaware of the fact that Chester had also written a superb first novel, *Jamie Is My Heart's Desire* (1956), and strikingly original stories, collected in *Here Be Dragons* (1955) and *Behold, Goliath* (1964). Even his masterpiece, *The Exquisite Corpse* (1967), failed to make its mark, which only helped to increase the speed of Chester's downfall.

Still, Chester's beginnings as a writer had seemed promising, also on a personal level. As a student at New York University in the late 1940s he not only kept in touch with soon-to-be-famous Truman Capote, but he had also befriended budding writers like Cynthia Ozick and Edward Field, who would always remain loyal to him. After having set sail for Paris in 1951, Chester quickly fell in with the many expatriates that were crowding the French capital. At the Hôtel de Verneuil, a home away from home for many artists and writers, Chester met James Baldwin and a number of Dutch writers who had also come looking for freedom and inspiration in Paris. One of the writers from Holland, the poet Hans Andreus, became close enough with Chester to portray him in a novel, the quite autobiographical *Denise*, published a decade after the events portrayed. Strikingly enough, *Denise* (1962) already seems to hint at Chester's mental instability. With a poet's intuition or perhaps merely by chance, Andreus has divided Chester's most striking features among two characters: a man referred to as "nummer Een en Twintig" ("number

Twenty-one," after the number of his hotel room) and an equally nameless "Jewish-American pianist and composer,"[7] clearly based on the "darkly-handsome Israeli piano student"[8] who was Chester's lover at the time. "Een en Twintig" is described as "a young American, Jewish, gay," born in Brooklyn; as a "promising writer"[9] he is the author of "a modern type of ghost story, bitingly intelligent, but with a childlike quality that entails a belief in gnomes"[10] (a description which fits Chester perfectly and also indicates that Andreus was familiar with Chester's writing). On the other hand, it is the pianist in *Denise*, also Jewish-American, who is wearing Chester's "orange-red wig."[11] One scene in *Denise* especially, in which "Een en Twintig" and the pianist are very much at odds with each other, conveys the uncanny feeling that Andreus was already aware of the split in Chester's personality that would ultimately be his undoing.

In those early days in Paris Chester still managed to keep afloat, however. Of course there was always the question of money, even though living in Paris at the time was relatively cheap. Chester's monetary problems were partly solved when, like many Americans (and others) in Paris, he became a writer for the Olympia Press. For the then munificent sum of $500 he contributed a volume entitled *Chariot of Flesh* to Girodias' Traveller's Companion Series, which was published under the pseudonym Malcolm Nesbit. Before actually sitting down to write his erotic potboiler, Chester took his cue from one of Olympia Press' main men, the Scottish author Alexander Trocchi. Like Chester, Trocchi had settled in Paris in 1951, where he had become involved in the publication of a little magazine called *Merlin*, whose seventh and last issue would be financed by Girodias. As the editor of *Merlin*, by 1954 Trocchi had already been partly responsible for the Olympia Press publication of Samuel Beckett's *Watt* (1953), Austryn Wainhouse's weird novel *Hedyphagetica* (1954), and the British poet Christopher Logue's first volume of poetry, *Wand and Quadrant* (1953). These and a number of other books helped to give Girodias' publishing house a respectable façade which in the years to come would be hard to uphold,

---

[7] Hans Andreus, *Denise* (Amsterdam: U.M. Holland, 1962), 111.
[8] Edward Field, "The Mystery of Alfred Chester," first published by the *Boston Review* in 1997. Printed from the internet: http://www-polisci.mit.edu/BostonReview /BR18.2/field.html.
[9] Andreus, *Denise*, 110.
[10] *Ibid.*, 125.
[11] *Ibid.*, 111.

because also by 1954 Trocchi had already become actively engaged in Girodias' scheme to publish a series of profitable erotic novels. Apart from a sexually stirred-up version of Trocchi's first serious piece of fiction, *Young Adam*, 1954 also saw the publication of Trocchi's first two full-fledged pieces of erotica, *Helen and Desire* and *The Carnal Days of Helen Seferis*, both (like *Young Adam*) published under the pseudonym Frances Lengel. *Helen and Desire* bore a marked resemblance to Daniel Defoe's *Moll Flanders*, and it was in fact Trocchi's firm belief that a writer of erotica's best bet was to model his efforts on fiction that had stood the test of time: "Take a book you like and add the fucking," were his words when Chester asked him how to write a pornographic novel.[12]

Acting on this piece of sound advice, Chester decided to model his dirty book on one of Vladimir Nabokov's lesser known novels, *The Real Life of Sebastian Knight* (1941). In this book a narrator who is only referred to as "V" sets out on the trail of his half-brother, Sebastian Knight, a brilliant young novelist who has recently died at the age of thirty-six. "V," of Russian descent but now inhabiting Paris, plans to write a biography of Sebastian; in fact, Nabokov, with his usual flair for double-entendre and irony, creates the impression that this biography may very well be the book we are actually reading. Because "V" only knew his half-brother somewhat more intimately when they were young, and because Sebastian is a rather enigmatic figure, "V" has considerable difficulty in tracking down the facts of Sebastian's existence. The latter's love life in particular is puzzling to "V," but with ups and downs and the help of a highly incredible detective he is finally able to locate and talk to the woman who brought about Sebastian's downfall.

Chariot of Flesh is a similar tale of detection. Its narrator, an American in Paris called Howard Cunningham, is eager to find out more about a woman with whom he had a brief but passionate fling twenty years before, and who disappeared from his life immediately afterwards. After having read about the death of this woman, Baroness Carla Arvon, in a Paris newspaper, he presents himself at the Arvon mansion. There Carla's daughter hands him a letter in which Carla herself – aware of the fact that Howard had never lost interest in her – gives him the names of six people who will be able to tell him what has happened to her since her one and only meeting with Howard. It is especially the list of names

---

[12] Ira Cohen, "Our Ancestor Alfred Chester," in Alfred Chester, *Head of a Sad Angel: Stories 1953-1966*, ed. Edward Field (Santa Rosa: Black Sparrow Press, 1990), 364.

in the letter that establishes a striking similarity between *Chariot of Flesh* and *The Real Life of Sebastian Knight*, because in the latter a similar list allows "V" to acquire more knowledge about his half-brother. However, while *The Real Life of Sebastian Knight* is a playful and enjoyable investigation into the tricky nature of biographical and autobiographical writing, *Chariot of Flesh* does not rise above the level of the average dirty book. Each step in Howard Cunningham's quest for truth is primarily the occasion for another description of Howard's sexual adventures with the people who were mentioned in Carla's letter. Some of these descriptions are very graphic and more openly erotic than similar Olympia Press publications of the same period. Therefore it is perhaps appropriate that for this particular project Alfred Chester chose the pen name Malcolm Nesbit: its reference to the English author of children's books, Edith Nesbit, serves to remind us that *Chariot of Flesh* is not a book for children, nor for the prim and proper.

According to Patrick J. Kearney's bibliography of the Paris Olympia Press, the first edition of *Chariot of Flesh* was printed in May 1955.[13] That same month contact was established between Maurice Girodias and Vladimir Nabokov, who was still casting about for a publisher who would not be adverse to publishing *Lolita* with a pseudonym. In early June 1955 a contract was signed by Girodias and Nabokov's agent in Paris, Doussia Ergaz, and shortly afterwards *Lolita* entered the editing process at the Olympia Press. In the course of this process, which immediately caused friction between author and publisher, Alfred Chester almost certainly served as copy-editor of Nabokov's manuscript.[14] As this activity must have taken place in the summer of 1955, *Lolita* will not have affected the writing of *Chariot of Flesh*. However, after it had been published in September 1955, *Lolita* made an indelible impression on some other Americans who had also taken up residence in Europe: Terry Southern and Mason Hoffenberg.

Southern, later to become famous as a novelist and screenwriter, was among the early American expatriates in Paris: between 1948 and 1950 he occasionally attended lectures at the Sorbonne on the GI Bill, at the same time making his first attempts as a prose writer. In the course of the 1950s Southern frequently commuted between Paris, New York and Geneva, where his wife Carol was a teacher at the United Nations nursery school. Mason Hoffenberg, with whom Southern would

---

[13]   Patrick J. Kearney, *The Paris Olympia Press* (London: Black Spring Press, 1987), 50.
[14]   Edward Field to author, March 3, 1999.

eventually write *Candy* – one of the best known books to come out of the Olympia Press – was more of a fixture in Europe. In the early 1950s Hoffenberg belonged to a group of bohemian intellectuals in Greenwich Village that was described by Jack Kerouac in *The Subterraneans* (1958), in which Hoffenberg appears as a character called Jack Steen. Backed by the GI Bill he too moved to Paris, where he quickly made himself at home among the other expatriates, and where he also married a French woman, Couquite, with whom he had three children. Although Hoffenberg was able to contribute an occasional poem to Princess Marguerite Caetani's fancy art magazine *Botteghe Oscure*, he was unable to make much headway in the fiction he also wanted to write – that is, until he too discovered the Olympia Press and its practices, which suddenly enabled him to write two erotically charged novels in quick succession: *Until She Screams* (1956) and *Sin for Breakfast* (1957).

For the first of these two books, published under the name Faustino Perez, Hoffenberg clearly heeded Trocchi's advice to take another novel's plot and to improvise on it. In fact, one can detect echoes of several well-known novels in *Until She Screams*. The book opens with a confrontation between a Mexican fieldworker called Miguel and his highborn and beautiful mistress, Countess Inez De Cordoba. Their meeting is vaguely reminiscent of the relationship between Lady Chatterley and her gardener, although Hoffenberg's "peon" ends up being sexually humiliated by his mistress in a manner that would be completely out of character in the work of D.H. Lawrence.

With an abrupt transition the second chapter takes us to even more familiar territory. It describes the goings-on in a Mexican household consisting of Senor Carlos Lopez and his wife Maria, who has a nineteen-year-old daughter from an earlier marriage. The daughter's name, Lolita, would have been enough to establish a link between Hoffenberg's DB and Nabokov's masterpiece, but this connection is made even more explicit when it becomes clear that Senor Lopez for years has been doing to his stepdaughter what Humbert Humbert in a different era and in a different setting can only bring about with great difficulty. In Humbert Humbert's view this difficulty is largely due to the continual presence of his wife, Lolita's mother, which is why it becomes increasingly tempting for him to kill her. In a similar manner Lopez begins to harbor thoughts of getting rid of Maria. This is not because she is an obstacle to his affair with Lolita (Maria hardly ever seems to notice what is going on between her husband and her daughter), but because she does not allow Carlos to smoke his marijuana cigars in peace.

Hoffenberg's frank references to drugs are an outstanding feature of the book, and also a very funny one, especially when the author introduces hipster jargon of the 1950s into the novel's nineteenth-century setting. This is the case when Carlos has come to know Miguel and wants to share one of his marijuana cigars with him:

> He [Carlos] began to feel positively friendly. "Do you pick up?," he asked.
> "What's that?"
> "Smoke the weed," Senor Lopez explained.
> "I don't know what you mean."
> "I'll show you later." That was nice too. It would be good to have someone else to smoke with.[15]

A passage like this is in line with Hoffenberg's playfulness, which also comes out in his tendency to engage in formal experiments. After having introduced and combined two story lines in the first three chapters, in the fourth chapter he introduces even a third group of characters: a number of young blind girls in a Roman Catholic convent who are in the process of discovering their own sexuality, while they are at the same time – unable to see what is going on behind their backs – the victims of their perverted teacher, Don Fernando. Hoffenberg pulls the strings in his novel in such a way that – after Senor Carlos has got rid of Maria – both he and Miguel end up at the convent. There they abuse some of the blind girls, which inspires Miguel to take revenge on his mistress. Her last words in this entertaining novel, which is at least partly a clever send-up of *Lolita*, are "Miguelito ... I love you" (150).

A year after *Until She Screams*, in 1957, Mason Hoffenberg published a second DB in Olympia Press' Traveller's Companion Series, this time using the pseudonym Hamilton Drake. The book, *Sin for Breakfast*, describes the experiences of a young American in Paris, Trent, who is troubled by the apparent frigidity of his girlfriend, Vivian, who hardly ever allows him to sleep with her. As it turns out, however, Vivian is only too willing to make love with other men, including Trent's friend Oliver. After Trent has caught the two in the act, he decides to change his course of action: instead of constantly begging Vivian for sexual attention, he now bends his eyes to other women. The

---

[15]   Mason Hoffenberg, *Until She Screams* (New York: Olympia Press, 1968), 42.

first with whom he is able to become intimate happens to be Oliver's girlfriend, Margot, a beautiful and lively eighteen-year-old who earns a large amount of extra money by writing pornography for a Paris publisher called Ben. Margot convinces Trent that writing may be a sensible occupation for him as well and she loses no time in introducing him to Ben. At Margot's suggestion, she and Trent also decide to use each other as guinea pigs and to try out sexual acts on each other, with the aim of making their writing more inspired and convincing. With this idea at the back of their minds the two go out on the town, for instance visiting a riotous art students' ball, until Margo gets cold feet and no longer wishes to endanger her relationship with Oliver. An even greater shock for Trent is his discovery of some secret notebooks Vivian has been keeping in the meantime which describe her sexual adventures not only with Oliver, but with a whole range of men, including complete strangers. These revelations are unbearable for Trent, who tries to commit suicide by swallowing a large amount of pills. He survives, however, and recovers consciousness in the company of Vivian, who claims that she has loved him all along and that the notebook pages he has been reading are not based on reality but part of a novel she has just completed.

Vivian's ruse is, of course, reminiscent of the excuse which Humbert Humbert comes up with when Lolita's mother has discovered the diary in which Humbert has described his feelings about Charlotte and Lolita:

> "You are crazy, Charlotte. The notes you found were fragments of a novel. Your name and hers were put in by mere chance. Just because they came handy."[16]

Although elsewhere in *Sin for Breakfast* Hoffenberg does not allude to Lolita, the book's artifice frequently rivals that which is found in a large part of Nabokov's work, including *The Real Life of Sebastian Knight.* We saw how in that book Nabokov tricks us into believing that his protagonist, "V," has written the very book we are reading. Hoffenberg successfully aims at a similar effect, when towards the end of the book Trent puts down the pen with which he has apparently been writing the account we have read so far. Of course we should have been warned that Hoffenberg might attempt to fool us, because Trent's account included several references to a strange character called Faustino Perez, the author

---

[16] Vladimir Nabokov, *Lolita* (Paris: Olympia Press, 1960), 98.

of a novel called *Until She Screams*, much admired by Margot who claims that it is "the best book in [Ben's] series – a parable with a Mexican setting – it's brutally frank."[17] But Hoffenberg's ingenuity does not stop here. After having deceived us about the nature of Trent's writing, he opens a further Nabokovian trapdoor beneath our feet when – in the last thirty pages of the novel – Trent gradually turns out to be merely a character in a book written by his girlfriend Vivian, a dirty novel entitled *Sin for Breakfast* which she plans to publish under the pseudonym Hamilton Drake.

Hoffenberg's structural playfulness is not the only saving grace of *Sin for Breakfast*. At times the book quite convincingly captures the atmosphere of postwar Paris and the kind of life led there by American and other expatriates. Margot's "room in a little hotel on the rue de Verneuil" (36), for example, can only refer to the hotel close to the Seine, the Hôtel de Verneuil, which accommodated Baldwin, Chester and other foreigners temporarily settled in Paris. More detailed and enlightening is Hoffenberg's description of the goings-on at the office of Ben's small publishing venture, which is closely modeled on the Olympia Press and the way it was run by Maurice Girodias and his limited staff. Still, if Nabokov ever laid eyes on Hoffenberg's depiction of Girodias, he must have laughed heartily – or perhaps not at all – at the positive and altruistic, but probably also tongue-in-cheek, presentation of his Paris publisher:

> Ben's office was within walking distance and, on the way, Margot briefed him [Trent] as to what his attitude should be with the publisher.
> "He's not at all what you might think," she explained, "not commercial, not interested in getting rich and the hell with everything else. He has two interests: one is helping new writers to develop, and the others is to fight the taboo on treating sex truthfully in books. After all, there is something odd in the fact that writers are forbidden to deal with what's probably the most important single subject in existence. People like Kinsey and Havelock Ellis make an attempt to report on people's sex habits, of course, but there's a big difference between that kind of dry, statistical, case-history approach, and the sort of living description that a novelist can get. Don't you think so?"
> Trent was fully in accord.
> They arrived at this point. She steered him into a building and they walked up a flight of stairs and entered a door. The office seemed

---

17 Mason Hoffenberg, *Sin for Breakfast* (New York: Olympia Press, 1967), 67.

modern and efficient. Two remarkably pretty girls sat behind desks and clattered sporadically on typewriters. (65-66)

Especially graphic and captivating, however, is Hoffenberg's description of the art students' ball which *Sin for Breakfast*'s four main characters – Trent, Vivian, Oliver and Margot – attend in "some huge, dimly lit, old room – perhaps an abandoned livery stable – reached through a succession of alleys and little doors, in which hundreds of fantastically costumed figures jumped and screamed – some obscure ball smacking of the Black Mass and orgiastic riot" (113). This passage introduces Hoffenberg's lively version of an event which has become legendary among the Paris expatriates and which helped to establish Alexander Trocchi's reputation for devilry and daring. One July evening in 1954 Trocchi and his associate and lover Jane Lougee, together with other writers associated with *Merlin* and its rival magazine *The Paris Review*, took part in an all-night party organized by Paris art students. In an interview with Allan Campbell and Tim Niel in 1995, George Plimpton – founding editor of *The Paris Review* – commented on the event, which may very well also have been attended by Mason Hoffenberg:

I remember we went to the Quat'z Art ball once. The whole city is sort of turned over to this bacchanal once a year, in July, and the students of the various *ateliers*, I think there are six of them, and their guests, go to this great dance hall in the Avenue Wagram. They lock the doors. There's a big band that plays way up in the eaves somewhere .... Most of the people are naked. We were asked by the *atelier* who had invited us to put on some sort of a spectacle, up on the balustrade of one of these boxes, like in an opera house .... Jane was to lie on the front of this box and when the lights came on her she'd be completely naked and Alex would then appear from the darkness and couple with her .... Alex was rather nervous about this but he had thought up the idea. He was down drinking when the time came and he rushed up this little stair to get into position and, being a tall man, he knocked his head against a sort of overhang, knocked himself almost unconscious and toppled down so that when the search lights focused on the box, they illuminated Jane lying, naked on the box railings. I was there with a fan, in the background, sort of like an Egyptian scene. But no Alex .... The lights moved on to something else. Alex was very upset. He thought that one of us should have taken his place ... which I thought was very gentlemanly of him indeed.[18]

Although Hoffenberg's two novels have their merits, it is not surprising that the Olympia Press erotica did not appeal to Nabokov's sophisticated taste. Judging from the fact that he hardly ever refers to them, one may safely assume that he never actually perused any of the efforts by Chester, Southern, Hoffenberg or other Olympia Press stalwarts. The exception should have been *Candy*, co-written by Hoffenberg and Southern, and first published in 1958, with the name Maxwell Kenton on the familiar green cover of Girodias' Traveller's Companion Series. Like *Lolita*, *Candy* became both a best-seller and a major and protracted source of aggravation between the authors and their publisher. Moreover, the monetary success of the book almost immediately threatened the friendship between Hoffenberg and Southern, who had been on excellent terms while concocting *Candy*.

Based on Voltaire's *Candide*, *Candy* describes the erotic adventures of a young and attractive American girl, Candy, whose romantic notions about those who are in need cause her to end up in the eager hands of – among others – an African American, a hunchback, and a Puerto Rican crook. After she has sought refuge in a religious order, she is raped by a rather too "fatherly" priest. Candy then tries to find peace of mind in Buddhism, but at the end of the book finds herself literally crushed by a statue of Buddha, the stone tip of whose nose has entered her vagina. Some of the scenes in *Candy* are so extravagant that it is not always quite clear what Hoffenberg and Southern are up to, but to a large extent *Candy* can be read as an extremely funny and biting satire of certain aspects of American middle-class life, which is something that can be said about *Lolita* as well.

This superficial similarity is of course not enough to establish a firm connection between *Candy* and *Lolita*. However, it can hardly be denied that Candy, although seemingly more ingénue than Nabokov's heroine, at times behaves as if she were Lolita's twin sister. This may very well have to do with the fact that both Hoffenberg and Southern were great admirers of Nabokov's masterpiece. Is it therefore too farfetched to suggest that *Candy*'s creators chose the name Candy not only because of its similarity to Candide, but also because Nabokov himself in *Lolita* at least once draws the reader's attention to that same name? Not long after

---

[18]   *A Life in Pieces: Reflections on Alexander Trocchi*, eds Allan Campbell and Tim Niel (Edinburgh: Rebel Inc., 1997), 73-74.

he has moved in with her, Humbert Humbert's unlucky American wife, Charlotte, is eager to find out what her husband has hidden in the locked drawer of his imitation mahogany table. Humbert is able to ward off this first attack, which leaves Charlotte standing with Humbert's copy of "Volume C of the *Girl's Encyclopedia*" in her hands, turning its pages from "Campas, Canada, Candid Camera" to "Candy."[19] Slightly more than sixty pages further on, when he is sixty pages closer to losing track of his darling, Humbert recalls how in the course of their travels across the U.S. he would occasionally buy Lolita a piece of candy at a garage: "and hardly had I turned my back to go and buy this very Lo a lollipop, than I would hear her and the fair mechanic burst into a perfect lovesong of wisecracks" (160). A wisecrack the authors of *Candy*, aided by Girodias' assistant and editor Miriam Worms, came up with themselves when their book was suppressed by the Paris Vice Squad, was to retitle it *Lollipop*. This new – and temporary – title not only allowed Olympia Press to go on selling the book while it was banned, but was almost certainly a further reference and a tribute to Vladimir Nabokov. Although the latter was eager to jump the "good ship Venus," as John de St. Jorre called the Olympia Press, it is not only Nabokov's own *Lolita*, but also the writing of Chester, Southern and Hoffenberg, that will forever keep him on board.

---

[19] Nabokov, *Lolita*, 94.

THE ALMIGHTY'S OWN PURPOSES:
ALFRED KAZIN'S *GOD AND THE AMERICAN WRITER*

RENÉ VERWAAIJEN

Men grown desperate may assign an ulterior purpose to events the true magnitude of which their hearts and minds cannot encompass. Abraham Lincoln's second inaugural address, for instance, has been seen as the supreme instance in modern American history of a chief executive relying on a religious interpretation of his torn nation's fate. It features prominently in Alfred Kazin's *God and the American Writer* (1997), which stands as the grand finale of a distinguished career in American letters. The book is remarkable for its unabashed identification with Lincoln as a man of reason building a wholly personal religion on his gradual but persistent understanding of the national tragedy during the Civil War.

Kazin's career started out on the ebullient faith of many radicals in the 1930s that the cultural commonwealth was finally within reach. *On Native Grounds* (1942) was proof of both Kazin's unusual talent and his sympathy for the radical social aesthetics of *The Seven Arts* just prior to the First World War, but for many critics it too emphatically worked around the extremes in contemporary American literature of, on the one hand, high aesthetic experiment in the social void and, on the other, cultural Communism, of unsparing naturalist exposé and nationalist celebration. These critics objected that the historical hopes for creative America painted by Kazin were carefully modulated by the unusual range of his rhetorical gifts. "Criticism Between the Poles," for instance, the only chapter in *On Native Grounds* to come to grips with ideology and contemporary criticism, was condemned by one critic as a composite "formalist monster," its purpose apparently being to bolster the cultural Left and to dismantle the aesthetic theory of the New Criticism. In actual fact, as Kazin's *Starting Out in the Thirties* (1965) was to show, he was driven by nostalgia for a time before "the age of Hitler" when, as one of its reviewers noted, people lost their temper arguing about Marx as they did about Schönberg and Joyce.[1]

---

[1]   Lionel Trilling to John Crowe Ransom, 10 December 1942, John Crowe Ransom

The rise of totalitarianism in Europe as well as the slow filtering down of the Holocaust into the common consciousness, however, were to strike at the root of experimental, progressive programs for art and life. Stalin, Hitler and Mussolini sought a previously cherished cultural ideal, perfection, for their societies through socio-political systems of their own devising, and in the process destroyed millions of people. In a 1962 interview with Robert B. Silvers, Kazin admitted that at the time of writing *On Native Grounds* he had underestimated the extent to which the age had turned against the notion of the writer as a free individual creator. He believed the work of reactionary writers like Louis-Ferdinand Céline, whose protagonists, "strangers," manifestly no longer believed in any of the traditional hopeful expectations for man, were a case in point. A decade or so later, reviewing the modernist literary heritage, Kazin once more traced the presumed loss of social vision among modernist writers and exposed the fundamental mistake made by their audience in believing that these writers' ideas could restore order to twentieth-century society:

> The original basis of modernism ... was exactly and especially the aim that *art* could *not* accomplish. Which was why the idea of the masterpiece as a teacher and inspirer of humanity, a force for change, died out.
> The basic reason why *we* in the last twenty years of this century cannot believe in masterpieces is the failure of conservative and reactionary thinkers – modernists all: Eliot, Lawrence, Pound, Yeats, Mann, Pasternak, Mandelstam, Woolf, Proust, et cetera – to affect the modern age that they hated so bitterly.[2]

Their reactionary views have now been amply documented, and Kazin himself made valuable contributions in this regard, presenting the modernists as dour traditionalists ill-accustomed to liberal society. He argued, however, that even though they represent an attractive alternative to our anxious civilization "obsessed by its vulnerability" through their belief in the subtlety of form, the example of Louis-Ferdinand Céline has

---

papers, Tennessee State Library and Archives, Nashville; Louis Kronenberger, "The Thirties: Frayed Collars and Large Visions," *Atlantic Monthly*, 217 (January 1966), 79-81.
[2] Kazin, "The Critic as Creator," *Horizon*, 4 (July 1962), 98-103; Kazin, "We See from the Periphery, Not the Center: Reflections on Literature in an Age of Crisis," *World Literature Today*, 51 (Spring 1977), 187, 188.

made clear that "even in the late 1920s the real problem of literature was to surmount disintegration by expressing it *fully*." Céline exposed modern man's illusion of total mental freedom in relation to the world to be lived in and acted upon. Next, Samuel Beckett extended this radical skepticism about the power of language to express the anguish of the human condition by inventing "verbal equivalent[s] of silence." To Kazin, these writers showed that "language in our time is an effort, not a rhetorical triumph; it is a confrontation, is not and cannot hope to be an example of that self-confidence once known as 'style'."[3]

Kazin had long since been convinced of the radical insufficiency of language. He first outlined the concept in the postscript to the 1955 edition of *On Native Grounds*, arguing that the epic American literature of the nineteenth century – he must have had Melville's *Moby-Dick* in mind – provided an image of great philosophical interest to postwar Europeans: that of "man's awareness of himself moving through an utterly new situation." At mid-century, however, the American writer was himself facing a crisis of creative faith and, for all of his popularity in Europe, did not present much of a model for Europeans shattered by the experience of the most destructive war in history. If anything, he was reduced to making "solitary raids on the inarticulate," hoping to dissolve the world's "strangeness" and to establish insights from his precarious sense of the true nature of things.[4]

Kazin's disappointment with the failure of postwar writers to establish a *rapport* with their world and so gain a creative hold on their experience led him to undertake a revaluation, in *An American Procession* (1984), of a succession of nineteenth-century writers, thinkers first and foremost,[5] whose unrivalled sense of selfhood signified a moral-philosophical framework promising salvation through expanding consciousness. Mark Shechner has made a case for viewing Kazin as the Melvillean "isolato" ecstatically seeking connections with the ancient genius of American writing by facing the conclusive evidence of his own heart and mind. Indeed, by Kazin's own account Melville forms the center of gravity of *An American Procession*, and on several occasions he praised Melville's almost nihilist hubris and willingness to be driven back upon the mind's despair when trying to fix its relation to Nature. More particularly, *An American Procession* makes

---

3   Kazin, "We See from the Periphery, Not the Center," 190, 192.
4   Kazin, "Postscript" to 1955 edition of *On Native Grounds*, 408.
5   Kazin, Journals, 10 July 1982, Alfred Kazin papers, Berg Collection, New York Public Library.

an ultimate attempt to project a redemptive vision, of a supreme consciousness of both self and its inextricable relations with the Other, through an extraordinary devotion to language, straining to reach "a precision of definition and perfection of style." But Kazin does so from a radically different perspective than the modernists, who saw language as unified consciousness countering the fragmentation of modern culture. His stylized critical narrative rather makes it the nearest analogue to experience, and the experience he traces in *An American Procession* is that of the classically tragic American self towards the end of this "ghastly century" confronting the epic of its growth and concluding that it continues to be baffled by the divisions of life in the modern era. At the end of *Writing Was Everything* (1995), Kazin typically exclaims "But where – how – is the writer to be found who will have the inner certainty to see our life with the eyes of faith and so make the world shine again?"[6]

It is this absence, too, that marks *A Lifetime Burning in Every Moment: From the Journals of Alfred Kazin* (1996). Much as *An American Procession* sets up a myth of American consciousness in order to "explain it from within," so the resolution of *A Lifetime Burning* presents a self inspecting its secular progress – previously documented in a series of three "personal histories" – and turning inward. The theme of Kazin's quest has become religious. And is creative still. Marshall Berman's review of *A Lifetime Burning* notes its polyphonic structure, with Kazin's style increasingly resembling that of the modernist writers "letting the voices resound and interact, not demanding resolution, just letting go."[7] Not demanding it, perhaps, but certainly anxious for it. *A Lifetime Burning* reflects an aging critic's burning desire to achieve faith at the conclusion of a lifetime of struggle, to command supreme attentiveness to the mystery of being, of existence itself. Several commentators have indicated that *A Lifetime Burning* is the result of fairly heavy editing by the author, but Kazin's notebook material in the Berg Collection of the New York Public Library shows that the book has been organized around a carefully developing religious sensibility. The question of religion, or rather faith, dominates its later sections, and

---

[6]   Mark Shechner, "Rhapsody in Red, White and Blue," *Nation*, 238 (June 23, 1984), 759-61; Kazin, Journals, 22 November 1981: "The titans of the book are really Melville, by the force of his Intellect, and Whitman, by the force of his love"; Shechner, "Rhapsody," 760; Kazin, *Writing Was Everything* (Cambridge: Harvard University Press, 1995), 152.
[7]   Marshall Berman, "In the Night Kitchen," *Nation*, 262 (May 6, 1996), 14.

Kazin often turns to prayer as the peace available through the heart's final reconciliation with the contrasts of existence. *A Lifetime Burning* presents a religious vision, but Kazin remains first and foremost a secular skeptic with a personal metaphysics of redemption.

That personal vision informs *God and the American Writer*, which presents Abraham Lincoln as the moral and literary genius whose absence from the contemporary scene Kazin lamented in *Writing Was Everything*. Indeed, Kazin's totally sympathetic interpretation of Lincoln's spiritual growth offers more than just evidence of moral and intellectual kinship: it provides the riveting drama of the late twentieth-century American-Jewish literary spectator establishing connections with the nineteenth-century mind at the center of the national destiny. It is twentieth-century selfhood defining itself in terms of nineteenth-century nationhood. But then the men had common roots: both Lincoln the presidential candidate debating pro-slavery senator Douglas on the strength of his humanism and young Kazin basing the first critical history of American literary realism on the social hopes fomenting during the early years of the new century are representatives of the Enlightenment tradition of reason. Both experienced a deep crisis – Kazin went through a period of profound personal turmoil after the publication of *On Native Grounds* – before recognizing the limitations of their original faith, transcending these, and developing their myths of American experience and consciousness, of nationality and self.[8] Tracing the tragic evolution of Lincoln's political position, Kazin in fact reclaims that particular quality of mind for his own age.

The background to Lincoln's emergence as a visionary and authoritative statesman, Kazin points out, was in all respects inauspicious. The Lincolns were poor white trash from the Midwest with no first-hand experience of the slavery question that was to throw Abraham into national prominence. He was equally exceptional by personal inclination: whereas his parents and stepmother sought spiritual sanction by joining the Baptist Church, and while pro-slavery Southern interests and abolitionist Northern idealists and clergymen increasingly resorted to high moral principle and invocations of the Bible to support their cause, Lincoln did not trust Divine intervention in human affairs so much as the exercise of a "cold, calculating, unimpassioned reason." From the first, he staked his political fate on preserving the Union by all

---

[8]   See Shechner's argument in "Rhapsody" that *An American Procession* presents a "myth of American consciousness."

means, even if this meant tolerating slavery in the Territories. This, according to Confederate Vice-President Alexander Stephens, was the only type of "religious mysticism" Lincoln allowed himself.[9] Reason, the mainstay of Lincoln's law practice, self-reliance, strength of mind and hard work were his guiding principles, Thomas Jefferson and George Washington his models. He distrusted passion; it troubled him personally, and he believed it would be the ruin of the nation.

Writing to Kentuckian Albert G. Hodges, who was worried about the President's move to enlist ex-slaves in the Union forces, Lincoln on April 4, 1864 justified his decision by stating his own powerlessness in the matter: "I claim not to have controlled events, but confess plainly that events have controlled me." The fledgling President in 1861 could not have anticipated anything like the ruthless march of events that was actually to take place, for he never expected a holy war to be fought over slavery, and responded promptly to the South's taunt at Fort Sumter, for the South had to be kept from nationalizing its "peculiar institution." Before long, however, as the war took a course all its own, he was to become deeply conscious of the limitations of the human will. But most of all he was to grow convinced that the conflict itself was about the emancipation of men generally and that the effort to save the Union, as he said as early as 1861, meant to ensure freedom for all. And since the North did not wish to see slavery extended to its territory, this won him its support. The War was a "People's contest," he claimed, indicating that neither side could claim the absolute justness of its cause. Accordingly, Lincoln considered it presumptuous for anyone to enlist God in the support of the war effort when He so adamantly refused to bestow His favors on either of the parties locked in battle. With Grant finally clearing the Mississippi at Vicksburg in 1863, Lincoln rather thanked "all. For the great republic – for the principle it lives by and keeps alive – for man's vast future – thanks to all."[10]

The war experience was soaked in religious sentiment. New England was fiercely abolitionist and the Transcendentalist clergy relied on Scripture to claim total emancipation, yet Lincoln dispassionately noted that the Emancipation Proclamation did not benefit a single slave in the Rebel states. Kazin points out that both sides felt they were *living* Scripture, and in rampant, righteous patriotism, Julia Ward Howe's "Battle Hymn of the Republic" easily outdid anything in the South,

---

[9] Quoted in Kazin, *God and the American Writer* (New York: Knopf, 1997), 123.
[10] *Ibid.*, 126.

which put up a vociferous defense of its cause as providential, sacred and just. The strident moralism of the people even eclipsed the priests' professional stake in the issue.

Such militant conviction and self-justification contrasted violently with the slow, painful process of recognition that Lincoln was to go through. Only as the war continued to wreak havoc did he begin to see that slavery was the crux of the issue. Unaffected by the mob sentiment that beset the issue, he had early on held out hope for a magnanimous compromise with the South and focused his strategy on not committing the Territories to an overtly antislavery position. So strong was his genuine belief that this was feasible that, when Generals Frémont and Hunter captured portions of Rebel territory during the early stages of the war and proposed the immediate emancipation of all slaves, he held back. Nor did he wish at any time during the conflict to alienate the border states. As late as March 4, 1865, with Grant's victory at Appomattox little more than a month away, he refused to use the military option against states like Louisiana, hoping to get them back into the Union, and held in the second inaugural that "the progress of our arms ... is, I trust, reasonably satisfactory and encouraging to all. With high hope for the future, no prediction in regard to it is ventured."

Kazin's fascination with the second inaugural centers around the fact that Lincoln refrained from official triumphalism and self-righteousness, and that he countered Southern attacks on the alleged absurdity of the Declaration of Independence with "his supreme emblem of reason, [which] was to go back to what was self-evident." Rather than accept bigoted supernaturalism as his guiding light, he continued to be inspired by events as they unfolded their moral necessity to him. Such good sense comported ill with the religious bigotry and moral fanaticism inspired by the Christian promise of salvation as the war continued to rage. What saved Lincoln was his "perfect confidence in his own [unimpassioned] mind" and his "religious independence." From the first, he had been the perfect inversion of Emerson's faith in man's inborn divinity rivaling the gods, but the second inaugural registers Lincoln's deep wonder that the war may after all have been revealing God's purpose.[11]

Kazin reminds us that God was as much contested territory in 1861-65 as the slave territory was and the Bible still an authoritative interpretation of Americans' existence. Both sides used it extensively as a source of justification, defending their holy cause while seeking

---

[11]   *Ibid.*, 131.

evidence of God's interventions on the battlefield. Stalwarts of a religious tradition, both sides used Old and New Testament texts to point up the conflict's religious dimensions, beyond the social and economic. Distorted notions of sin accordingly reigned on both sides of the issue: "The appeal to righteousness and the sense of moral guilt were more vehement and impassioned than anything Germans expressed over Auschwitz, Russians over the Gulag, Americans over the 'wasting' of peasant hamlets in Vietnam."[12]

If slavery was sin, "the Negro" came to dominate the issue in a moral sense. The cultural drama of the second inaugural to Kazin, however, is precisely that it announces the start of "modern history in America," because it emancipates the Negro from his all too symbolical status and turns him into an autonomous agent, to become an urgent and divisive social issue in real life. Yet, Lincoln's move carried religious sanction, for God was the only language to reach both parties, even though He favored neither: "The prayers of both could not be answered, that of neither has been answered fully. The Almighty has his own purposes." This is America's chief executive instructing the nation about the "mighty scourge of war" from within a wholly religious context, and the second inaugural constitutes in fact a conversion experience in its own right. Lincoln, who initially searched out any opportunity for political compromise, here surrenders to the supreme insight that division will and must remain at the heart of the Union, that there is no true north to guide him or anyone else on American soil. He must have understood that emancipation achieved by political means did not signify the Negro's total liberation in a social sense, for the latter would in all likelihood continue to be subject to bigotry and lingering hatred. The war's outcome, as it slowly emerged in early March 1865, surely left some doubt in Lincoln's mind about God's revealed purpose, but he took things elegantly and refused to give any indication as to which party in his view could claim greater intimacy with God's special Providence:

> In his torturing responsibility to the nation, to the future democratic government in the world, Lincoln had come through a terrible experience to submit to a power higher and greater than anything his political ambition had prepared him for. Now he felt himself responsible before God for whatever he did and said to guide the nation.
>
> The most compelling sentence to me of the second inaugural is the one that leads to the essence of the speech in the fourth paragraph. There

---

[12] *Ibid.*, 133.

is a troubled searching here of God's will, a startling admission by a man who was as self-trusting in religion as he was in law and the art of writing. *The Almighty Has His Own Purposes.* And it has all he has to say with any confidence about God's will.[13]

Writing on the occasion of the centennial of the Civil War in 1961, Kazin laid the groundwork for this view. He recalled that Lincoln had believed neither side "anticipated that the *cause* of the conflict might cease with or even before the conflict itself should cease." Even the President of the Confederate States, Jefferson Davis, had admitted that abolition was inevitable. There was a *non sequitur* in the slavery view that Lincoln was quick to spot: was it possible for anyone to be truly free if democracy were contradicted? This silenced even the Northerners who were not against slavery. "The Negro" was a crucial issue because he was not consciously so in most people's minds:

> So long as he was a slave, no one else in America was really free. As soon as people even anticipated his freedom, they had to look further and anticipate his becoming a citizen like themselves. So Allan Nevins is right when he says, at the end of his conclusive review of the events leading up to the Civil War, that the war broke out over slavery *and* the future status of the Negro in America. Look around you.[14]

How much Lincoln himself was aware of this became evident when he acted on the insight, threw off his official reserve and countered Kentucky's refusal to accept compensated emancipation by enlisting freed slaves in the Union Army.

On several occasions Kazin pointed out that there was a literary boon in the conflict that emerged only over time and in unexpected quarters. For while the South expediently rationalized the worsening military situation and presented itself as a martyred civilization "baptized in blood," a movement arose to counter so much self-righteous sacredness – which, to be sure, was cultivated on both sides of the issue, certainly also in the North. The self-righteousness was present, for instance, in H.D. Thoreau's strident criticism of the slave party based on a "majestically simple rhetoric" of moral indignation which, despite

---

[13] *Ibid.*, 131, 137.
[14] Kazin, "And the War Came," in *Contemporaries* (Boston: Little, Brown, 1962), 83.

Thoreau's regained popularity since the1960s, even today constitutes a wholly non-political stance.[15] In that respect, Thoreau was untypical of the Northern tradition of reform moralism as represented by William Lloyd Garrison, John Greenleaf Whittier and Ralph Waldo Emerson. He was, in Kazin's view, a mere crank, and incomparably less effectual as an instigator of personal revolutionary consciousness than Emerson, for one.

In the South, something rather more complex offset the shrill moralism of the abolitionists. In "The Generals in the Labyrinth," a review of a number of books about and memoirs of the Civil War published in the early 1990s, Kazin wondered just what the South had fought for and concluded that it was the outdated institution of slavery, a Darwinian flaw in modern social reality. No ulterior motives could explain why the South so desperately wanted to go to war when it was clear that it could at all times force the new Northern president Lincoln to compromise on the point of slavery. For one thing, it controlled the political arena in the decades leading up to the war, it controlled the Army, the Presidency and even the Supreme Court. What more could it have wished for to be able to spread slavery across the Union or successfully pursue secession? The reason was simply that the South did not understand the direction history was taking. Kazin paints a telling contrast between Generals Grant and Lee: whereas Grant (like Sherman and future presidents Hayes, Garfield and McKinley) epitomized "the man who has risen" – William Dean Howells' definition of the legendary modern American[16] – Lee was the representative of an embattled, entirely retrospective and aggressively self-righteous culture of honor and high principle (even when surrendering at Appomattox he had to remind Grant, who kept reminiscing about the old Army life they shared, that he had come to surrender). When appointed Jefferson Davis' military adviser, Lee wrote to his sister that he saw no intelligible purpose in the conflict looming and would gladly be spared the trouble of his intervention. This Southern archetype was not a man hoping to form a new society in the shell of the old or engaging the new socio-political reality emerging in the North as a field of opportunity. Kazin concluded that

---

[15] *Ibid.*, 74.
[16] "The alternation of disaster and triumph in Grant's life is typical enough of American life and the business cycle" (Kazin, "The Generals in the Labyrinth," *New Republic* [February 18, 1991], 63).

Lee was, even at the outset of the war, a figure of the past .... [He] triumphed as a strategist in a war that he did not expect to win. He was an anachronism even in his own eyes .... The South stood in the way of history.[17]

And so it forced the threatened Union into a conflict it never desired. So much for the myth of the South as a martyred civilization.

By an equally subtle line of reasoning, Kazin dispelled the myth of the North's rapacious carpetbagger mentality, which was frequently used in the South to foment a war morale in the years leading up to 1861. He saw the myth in the figure of Grant, amiably conducting conversation with Lee at Appomattox yet totally a man of purpose, not the product of nostalgia. Meeting with Bismarck at the 1878 Congress of Berlin, Grant admitted initially having had little grasp of the deeper moral and social issue of slavery underlying what clearly seemed to be a political conflict. It was a good thing the war was not decided very early on by his hard-driving commanders Sherman and Sheridan, he added, because many people formerly indifferent to slavery – he himself and Sherman not the least among them – had gradually come to see how much of a blight it really was. At Appomattox he acknowledged to himself that the real cause of the war had been slavery, not the Rebellion. The war had in fact been a tremendous revolution in the North destroying the political compromise of tolerating slavery in the South.

Writing on the occasion of the first centennial of the Civil War, Kazin hinted at the real significance of Grant's war experience:

> The inescapable fact is that if you look at the passionate writing that helped to bring the war about, that in turn came out of the war, and that, among Southerners at least, has never ceased to come out of the war, you can see why even the endless debates between American historians as to the causes of the war seem dry and inconclusive by contrast with the torment of principle, the convulsion of experience.[18]

Such convulsion of experience, he argued, was clearly the prerogative of a sizable portion of Northerners, and perhaps also of a few sensitive Southern minds restricted from political influence on the grounds of sex,

---

[17] *Ibid.*, 63. General Alexander described the Southern aggression as follows: "We had the right to fight, but our fight was against what might be called a Darwinian development – or an adaptation to changed and changing conditions – so we need not greatly regret defeat" (*ibid.*, 65).
[18] Kazin, "And the War Came," 71.

office or temperament. It certainly characterized Lincoln the war president, who on July 4, 1861 apparently entertained little doubt about the cause of the war being waged and his own role in it, telling Congress:

> This is essentially a people's contest .... It is a struggle for maintaining in the world that form and substance of government whose leading object is to elevate the condition of men – to lift artificial weights from all shoulders.

He still believed the South to be committed to the cause of progress. His outlook was to change radically within three years, however, and (as we have noted) in April 1864, shattered by the prolonged conflict, he humbly accepted the chastening impact of the war experience: "I have not controlled events, and confess plainly that events have controlled me." Perhaps more than anyone else Lincoln showed that the stated objective of preserving the Union could never have been achieved by a rational political strategy and that the issue was infinitely more complex and tragic, capable of solution only piecemeal and by a spiritually harrowing process. The President who during the early stages of the war had by and large lost his firm belief in his executive power to solve the conflict, by 1864 held out an eloquent vision of hope for the future. This involved no less than a return to "our ancient faith" contained in the spirit of '76 and the Constitution.

This was Lincoln's supreme defense against the reactionary views of human nature held by the proslavery factions. But it was ultimately his willingness to be guided by the unsettling experience of the war that led him to the higher levels of intensity that dominated the Congressional debates about slavery prior to the war. Southern fanaticism, in Congress as well as in literature and on the battlefield, was largely inspired by the accountability the South felt to the God Who it was convinced would interpose on its behalf. Kate Stone, a Southern woman who never regretted the abolition of slavery, used words to the effect, that "The great load of accountability was lifted."[19] The South had a terrible burden of guilt to redeem.

Interpretations of the war and its origins by historians and others laid the groundwork for theories of human nature featuring in American literary discourse at mid-century. A case in point was Kazin's review of Robert Penn Warren's *The Legacy of the Civil War: Meditations on the Centennial*, in which he criticized Warren for his tendency to theologize

---

[19] *Ibid.*, 74.

man's unstable moral constitution. Kazin condemned Warren's outlook for being ideologically of a piece with the myth of Southern history embodying Man's Fall. He associated it with nostalgia for the past as a realm of innocence and rejected Warren's "pragmatism" as an attempt to theorize about the human contradictions that manifested themselves on both sides of the war issue as the killings went on and to unify these within the concept of man at war with himself. Thus, Kazin felt, it became impossible for Warren to say "'Yes' to life – not just to the 'open' life that Warren praises, but to the life in every man, whether he is an abolitionist or a slaveholder."[20]

It was not customary for Southerners, nor for writers, to be sure, to picture themselves having lost every providential connection with God, as did Robert Penn Warren. A great deal of self-searching was done in Southern homes by those whose moral dignity kept them from falling for secessionist demagogy and fire-eating military fanaticism. In *A Diary from Dixie*, Mary Chesnut, the wife of James Chesnut, Senator of South Carolina and Confederate Secretary of the Navy, exemplified the detachment and moral seriousness of which many who were pressed hard by the official political line were still capable:

> Just as we today cannot help noticing the contrast between the grand but often abstract principles announced by New England Intellectuals and the concrete defiance, courage, and desperation of Southerners fighting on their home grounds, so Mrs. Chesnut's ingrained social sense, her ability to convey the concrete human style of the people she is talking about, above all her attention to the truth of any human experience apart from the cause in which it is enlisted, give certain passages in *A Diary from Dixie* the stamp of universal experience that we value most in literature.

While Northerners of a certain moralistic bent prided themselves on their special relationship with the Lord and claimed they could read His intentions in the terrible conflict, many Southerners, particularly women, became increasingly disillusioned with the grand abstractions used to bolster official support for the Confederacy. They had seen social relations even in their own homes change during the decade or so that the war had been brewing and could not now understand the war party's insistence that the white masters and their black slaves must forever occupy separate spheres within the same social system. In their turn,

---

[20]   Kazin, "The Southern 'City of the Soul,'" *Contemporaries*, 184.

Southern slave owners were not up to the admission that society, even theirs, was inevitably and continuously subject to change, and it was a rare voice such as Senator L.Q.C. Lamar's of Mississippi that could be heard saying after the war that the fundamental "mistake made by the Southern defenders of slavery was in regarding it as a permanent form of society instead of a process of emergence and transition from barbarism to freedom."[21]

Obviously, it was difficult for many on either side to step down from their cherished convictions about human destiny, nor did the political situation promote such conversion experiences. Yet, Kazin argued convincingly that Southern writers, having a lot to explain and account for, not least to themselves, had been more fertile in rendering the fullness of life:

> Only when you put together the constant pressure on the Southerner from his religion, his property, and his need to play the great lord can you begin to understand why Southern writers have always taken the opposite line from Thoreau's majestically simple rhetoric – why they have gone deeper, have been more subtle and complex in their rendering of human conduct than the abolitionist writers were .... [I]t was Southern novelists and poets and diarists who came up against the complex human relationships of slavery.[22]

This was the literary treasure available to those who stopped rationalizing their own interests as God's Providence and admitted, like Lincoln, that the Almighty's purposes take no account of the human will.

---

[21] Kazin, "And the War Came," 79.
[22] *Ibid.*, 74.

SAUL BELLOW AND THE ACTUAL

JAN BAKKER

Old age, Bellow was born in 1915, tends to increase detachment as well as an urge for economy. This can not only be seen in the reduced size of Bellow's recent books – *The Theft*, *The Bellarosa Connection*, *The Actual*, and *Ravelstein* never exceed the novella format – but even more so in the treatment of his familiar subject matter, in particular his continuous search for what really matters in the world, which yields such a fascinating variety of forms in his major novels. In these novels the principal character is usually caught between two actualities: on the one hand, the world of the "reality instructors," the people who run and rule the world, the big personalities, and on the other, the world of the spirit, "the noumenal department," presided over by philosophers, writers, and artists, people who set great store by thought and feeling.

In *The Adventures of Augie March* and *Seize the Day*, for example, the main characters at first try to live in accordance with the world of these reality instructors, the destiny-molders, but fail. Realizing the value of the noumenal department, they reject the actuality of these people's craving for power and their money-grabbing zeal, without reaching, however, a viable alternative. In the end Augie still feels himself a wandering Columbus, while Tommy Wilhelm knows that the world's actuality is not the Stock Exchange, but that thought and feeling should be given their appropriate place. The question, how precisely, remains open.

In *Henderson the Rain King*, we watch the Bellow protagonist as a full-fledged man of action, but in this novel, too, the noumenal department gains in importance as a reflection of a more satisfying version of the world's actuality. Facts, the panacea of the reality instructors, are not enough. One needs, as Henderson learns, the imagination to convert them into the actual. If not, the actual becomes unreal, and therefore a danger, since actions based on unreality are apt to bring out the killer in man, resulting in death and destruction.

Both *Herzog* and *Mr. Sammler's Planet* explore this danger, presenting and rejecting two solutions: detachment from "the ordinary and the finite," or an escape into insanity, the kind of insanity illustrated by the actuality of New York, in fact, a new kind of cultural barbarism. There is, however, a third solution, as Mr. Sammler comes to believe, one that may solve the problem of man as both a killer and a moral person: imitate "archetypes of goodness," and practice this long enough for it "to take on." However, if this solution is to change the world's actuality, created by our reality instructors, it is necessary to believe that "a desire for virtue is no accident," a belief that presupposes a sense of "the mystic power of mankind," a force clearly belonging to the noumenal department. In the end both Moses Herzog and Artur Sammler come to the conclusion that if there is anything worth pursuing, it is the spirit, as kept alive and enhanced by the activities of writers, artists, and philosophers. This provides the necessary leaven to make "the actual" livable.

But what if these activities which produce works of art – actually referred to by Citrine in *Humboldt's Gift* as "matters of the spirit" – are ignored by the public? The public which, according to Corde in *The Dean's December*, lives in a distorted world of "false description and non-experience," created largely by the modern mass media, which Corde holds responsible for bringing forth "modern public consciousness." It is a state of mind, he believes, that prevents the public from knowing what is really going on in the world in which "the actual" of power and money as pursued by the Zaehners and the Spanglers determines the course of history. Corde believes that it is mainly a question of language: if there is something wrong with the public's sense of "the actual," it is because there is something wrong with the way it is articulated. But if it is precisely this, a question of language, he is faced with the problem of proving that language is not merely a matter of communication, or aesthetics, but also something profoundly moral. For only if this is so, can he defend the noumenal department, ignored by the public as a result of its distorted sense of reality, and denied by the hard-headed Zaehners and Spanglers because it might undermine their power. Corde has his doubts, but in the end he decides to continue his crusade to try and change, in his capacity as a journalist, "the actual" of life in Chicago, which he thinks hides a real threat to his fellow Chicagoans' humanity.

Like *The Dean's December, The Actual*,[1] one of Bellow's more recent shorter works, is also set in Chicago, the toughest city in the U.S.A.

---

[1]   *The Actual* (New York: Viking Penguin, 1997). All page references are to this edition

But unlike Corde, Harry Trellman, the narrator and Bellow's chief spokesman in this novella, is no longer outraged by the city's high crime rate, the corruption, the injustice, the ruthless power politics. Bellow's alter ego seems no longer to be concerned with that aspect of Chicago's actuality. As he remarks at the very beginning of the story, "The usual repertories of stratagems, deceits, personality rackets, ringing the changes on criminal cunning, are hardly worth examining." What Trellman – Jewish, spiky black hair, round eyes, thick lips – does find worth doing is "to settle unfinished emotional business." That is why, now in his sixties and semi-retired, he has returned to his hometown Chicago. It is what still connects him with the early Bellow believers in the noumenal department, an impression confirmed after we have learned more about Harry Trellman's personality. For despite the fact that Harry, a dealer in antiquities, has also made a pile by rather shady and ruthless activities in Burma and Guatemala, he often sounds rather more like an Artur Sammler or an Albert Corde than an associate of his new acquaintances in Chicago, the Adletskys, the Heisingers, the Wustrins, wealthy representatives of the class of Bellow's reality instructors. For, as Trellman gets to know them better, he soon recognizes them again for what they really are – "commonplace persons," who "were lacking in higher motives" (42). Although by now he has reached the stage in which, as he says, he is prepared to make his peace with his species, he still cannot help making judgments. When at Frances Jellicoe's dinner party he notices Cressy, a banker, that refuses to pose with her and her ex-husband (a drunk and a loser she wants to make socially acceptable again), he calls him a man who has "a condom over his heart." Completing his disapprobation in general terms, he adds "there is nothing human about bank officers" (14).

Trellman's most damning statement about the Adletskys, the Heisingers, the Wustrins, the kind of people that in the earlier major novels also used to provoke the Bellovian ire, is to be found in the following passage:

> They were run-of-the-mill products of our mass democracy, with no distinctive contribution to make to the history of the species, satisfied to pile up money or seduce women, to copulate, thrive in the sack as the degenerate children of Eros, male but not manly, and living, the men and women alike, on threadbare ideas, without beauty, without

and will be given parenthetically in the text.

virtue, without the slightest independence of spirit – privileged in the way of money and goods, the beneficiaries of man's conquest of nature as the Enlightenment foresaw it and the high-tech achievements that have transformed the material world. Individually and personally, we are unequal to the scope of these collective achievements. (42-43)

But even for these people Trellman preserves his "habit of watching for glimpses of higher capacities and incipient powerful forces" (43), which again links him firmly to the perceptive and sensitive, or even oversensitive, protagonists of Bellow's earlier novels, the Josephs, Leventhals, Augie Marches, Tommy Wilhelms, Herzogs, Sammlers, Citrines, and Cordes.

It is also at the Frances Jellicoe party that Trellman meets the man who sets into motion what little plot the novella contains: Sigmund Adletsky, one of the "heavy-money Yids," a Chicagoan "noble," a true representative of "the powers of darkness and the secret rulers of the world." A retired owner of airlines, mines, electronics laboratories, Adletsky, a small man in his nineties, is now very old and very rich. In fact, his wealth is so "profound" that it "can have no adequate human equivalent" (16-17). Apart from a shift in priorities due to old age that has mellowed him, made him more temperate than in his "angry, impatient, intolerant" early days, his wealth may explain why he has given up the reality instructor's business (though his sons and grandsons "still report to him"), and has become interested in his wife Siggy's "circuit." Therefore, what he needs is a different type of adviser, not on business, but on social and psychological matters, on matters of taste, too. It is a wish not easy to fulfill, since "there aren't too many observant people around." But when he sees that besides himself only Harry Trellman has noticed what is going on between Frances Jellicoe and Cressy at her party, he knows he has found one, "a first-class noticer," and Trellman, who despite his reservations has taken a liking to the little, "shrunken" guy, agrees to join Adletsky's "braintrust."

Trellman, who looks Japanese (Adletsky's comment), not like a Chinese as he himself always thought, is soon able to give his first advice. The Adletskys need someone to help them in their negotiations to buy a great duplex apartment on East Lake Side Drive; someone also capable of appraising the value of the chairs, sofas, carpets, bedsteads, even the drapes, the furniture in short, which is to be included in the sale. Dame Siggy, as Adletsky calls his wife (also past ninety, with standards of behavior still dating "from the days of Franz Josef"), does not want the stuff, but Bodo Heisinger, the owner of the apartment, a toy-manufacturer and a man "hard for his buyers," insists. Trellman recommends Amy Wurstin, an interior decorator, and therefore the right person to help out the Adletskys, but also the woman for whom he has returned to Chicago in order to settle unfinished emotional business with her. It is Amy he had fallen in love with as a high-school kid, whom he has never stopped loving since, and in whom he had invested "half a century of feeling," of "fantasy, speculation, and absorption, of imaginary conversation." No matter that a decade ago, when he happened to run into her under the El tracks, he had failed to recognize her. But then she was a woman "as gray-faced as a maid-of-all work," beset by marital worries, actually in "full ruin," and thus in "the real world," while he was not, and only remembering her as she had been when she was fifteen, with "fully feminine thighs, the gloss and smoothness of sexual maturity on the cheeks and in the brown gaze: she transmitted messages of which she may not even have been aware." When they embraced and kissed in the park, "the odor of the damp fur" (Amy's raccoon coat) was much stronger than the powder she used (Coty's face powder), a smell Trellman had never forgotten for the rest of his life, just as he had never forgotten "the ungainly sexiness of her movements and her posture" (17-21). Odors, especially female odors, have always fascinated Bellow.

The question that worries Trellman now is why he had not married her, although he had loved her as she had loved him, and why her first husband had been Berner, a man who had gambled away his raincoat factory, and then disappeared, after which Amy had divorced him. Was this perhaps because Berner had never made "theoretical statements"? Trellman had always made too many, a bad habit which from the beginning had always "come between him and Amy" (60). But then he was the university type, studious, an "odd-ball," as Amy said, somebody who in his early days had been a Marxist, even "a sort of revolutionist" (71). And why had her second husband been Jay Wustrin, Trellman's high-school friend, a one-time socialist, anarchist, later a not very distinguished lawyer, but always a swinger, a women-chaser, and a bit of a comedian? Was this perhaps because Jay immediately saw that "there's potential, there's action in that girl" (21)? All Trellman had seen was Amy's respectability, so that at the time it made him believe that the feelings he had for her were "sheer

kitsch," and "kitsch didn't sort well with the advanced forms of personal development [he] was after" (72). So how could he fall for what
looked such a "petty-bourgeois broad"?

The difference between appearances and "the actual" in the
novella's various characters emerges most clearly when we take a
closer look at the personalities of both Harry Trellman and Jay
Wurstin. Whereas Harry was actually an intellectual, despite his odd
looks, Jay, "an attractive man with a deliberate erotic emphasis in his
looks" (22), merely pretended to be one, and then only for purposes of
seduction. Whereas Harry had not come to court Amy after she
divorced Berner (Harry's excuse was he was just married himself),
Jay had married Amy, after divorcing his first wife, not in the first
place because he loved her, but because he needed another woman
who would look up to him. Harry had not taken the opportunity to
have sex with Amy in Palmer House (during a shower Jay had invited
him to share with them, a threesome that became a twosome when Jay
himself had to leave for a court appearance). The reason? The nature
of his love for Amy, "a tremendous feeling," simply forbade him to
turn their showery tête-à-tête into a "generic" product, an "any male
with any female" act. But when Jay, the compulsive seducer,
discovered Amy's one and only extra-marital escapade – no doubt
undertaken to get even with him, and holding him to his principle of
"free sexuality" – he had the encounter taped by an agency, cries and
moans included. This was not only to use the tape as proof of Amy's
adultery when he divorced her, so as to escape paying her alimony,
but also in order to play it to anyone who cared to listen, including
Harry Trellman, who had no use for it, and Madge Heisinger, who
thought she had.

In Harry and Jay we observe the "seeming" versus "the actual,"
appearances versus reality: Harry, believed to be "secretive," "uncha-
ritable," aloof, always keeping his own counsel; a liar all his life (his
strategy for survival), but who had never lied about what really
mattered, his love of Amy, which at first he had failed to recognize,
then never dared to claim, had put "in storage" instead, because, as he
thought, he was "too odd for Amy" (84) – and Jay, acting the famous
lawyer, but actually "clumsy with banks, interest rates, investments"
(41); attractive, sexy, "open," a zestful participant in the wave of
sexual liberation, believing that "there was no real eroticism that
didn't defy the taboos" (40), but who played a despicable trick on his
wife Amy when, humiliated by his own numerous infidelities, she

decided to break one of these taboos herself; Jay Wustrin, the fantast, whose seductions also included his clients, provided they were beautiful, and fascinating, and willing to set aside "the old morality and the old expectations and old rules" (39). Such clients included Madge, Bodo Heisinger's "problematic" wife, who therefore knew about the one glitch in Amy's otherwise exemplary life.

With the introduction of the Heisingers, the first of the two slim plotlines is taken up, and left dangling, since the use Madge wants to make of this knowledge is never worked out. The presence of this extraordinary couple contains echoes of some of Bellow's most hilarious and outrageous writing in such earlier novels as *Herzog, Henderson the Rain King, Humboldt's Gift*. Madge Heisinger, provocative, notorious, even "criminal," but very attractive, "a golden babe" (only the nose was wrong, "too full at the tip to be entirely feminine"), and always expensively dressed, reminds us of Madeleine in *Herzog*, equally ruthless and calculating, with the difference that the murder that blazes from her eyes is actually planned by Madge. The reason why Madge wanted her husband dead, is never revealed. Maybe because he was rich; not as rich as Adletsky, but he had done extremely well by anticipating children's changed taste for "hideous outerspace aliens, monstrously muscled and distorted" (37). Maybe because he resembled, as Amy thought, the type of man Jay Wurstin also belonged to: men whose strength was their "blunt masculinity," who demanded their women to look up to them; inventors, too, of "scenarios too histrionic to be translated into real terms" (40) that always served to dramatize or to advertise the image, a public image, of themselves (68). Whatever the reason may have been, Madge Heisinger had put out a contract on Bodo, hiring as the hitman Tom Bale, an old flame. But Heisinger knocked the gun out of his hand, and the guy ran. When he was apprehended by the police, he incriminated Madge. Both were convicted, and did three years. Then Heisinger, who wanted her back, withdrew his complaint. They were paroled, and Madge agreed to remarry him on condition that the man she had hired should go free too. She thought she owed him, the hitman, for having put him through the ordeal of three years in prison.

The story gets even more hilarious when Amy is told by Madge why Heisinger insists on the extra million dollars for the furniture, should the Adletskys decide to buy the apartment. The talk takes place when the Adletskys, bringing along Amy as their interior decorator, visit the Heisingers to discuss the terms of the purchase, and after

Madge, when tea is served, has deliberately poured Amy's tea in her lap. No accident this, but Madge's instant scheme to have a private word with Amy in the bathroom where she goes to clean up the mess, and where she is immediately joined by Madge herself. Here Bodo, Heisinger's impetuous wife, remembering the tape which entitles her to look upon Jay's unfaithful wife as a sister in public disgrace, tells Amy that the money for the furniture is to go to her, Madge, and why she needs it. Together with Tom, the hitman, she will start a divorce registry service, meant to provide in divorce cases all the essentials of housekeeping for either "the deprived husband or the stripped wife," and paid for by the gifts from family, friends, the company: more or less the opposite of a bridal registry. It would diminish worry and stress on the part of the divorcées and be profitable to the suppliers of this service, especially if they have Merchandise Mart contacts, as Madge has. Moreover, it "would give divorcées parity with brides," and in this way even have "a democratic flavor" (86).

Amy, who does not think much of the Heisingers' furniture – it is certainly not worth a million dollars – does not know what to make of Madge's proposition. Is she serious, mad, or what, and how could Madge think that she, Amy, would go for it, even suggest that she might want to participate in it? She decides to ask Harry Trellman. The absurd plan makes him laugh: it is obvious to them that like her husband Bodo, Madge, too, belonged to "the Jay Wustrin school of real-life-fantasy." But Amy wants advice, since she is inclined to think that as a business idea "it's not unimaginative." Trellman is quite willing to provide it, since it gives him an excellent opportunity to make once again one of his judgments, this time by pointing out to Amy that "to get some good, to extract it from so much bad" in the U.S. is usually "a business idea – the imagination of a profitable enterprise"(91). So far it has already brought profit to Bodo Heisinger, because by getting Madge and the hitman out of jail it has given him millions of dollars' worth in publicity, while presenting him to the public as both a brave, big-hearted, and loving husband. And the extraordinary idea of the divorce registry might turn out to be profitable as well. It would certainly be picked up by the newspapers, the TV people, maybe even arrest Oprah Winfrey's attention. The fashionable people, junior corporate employees, would become interested, even in a perverse way fascinated, when it got around that the initiators of the enterprise were the three members of "a scandal team," Madge, a jailbird, Tom, a hitman, and Amy, though looking "matronly" now, a notorious divorcée.

Trellman has put Madge's proposition in perspective, and apparently succeeded in making Amy realize that, if she accepted Madge's offer, she would indeed become part of a publicity circus. But, as she tells Trellman, it does not appeal to her. Bellow then abruptly drops this part of the story – he has made his point, and there is no need to go on – and he takes up his second, equally slight plot-line, though this time there is the suggestion of completion, albeit – supreme irony – in the traditional literary mode of a happy ending. It makes one think of Verdi, who in old age also unconcernedly ended *Falstaff* in an equally conventional musical mode, the time-honored fugue.

The place where Amy asks Trellman's advice, and where he himself subsequently starts to settle his "emotional business" with her, is, surprisingly, Adletsky's stretch limo, his monstrous car, big as "an oceanliner." Amy and Harry have frequently met in the past weeks, in restaurants, bars, cafés, to discuss business matters, chiefly Amy's, but always with people around, and this is the first time they are really alone. Adletsky, far from being the man who lacks observational skills – he must have been joking, as Trellman now realizes, when the billionaire recruited him for his brain trust – has guessed how much Amy means to his one-time adviser. So when he hears that she had to attend the exhumation and reburial of Jay at the Waldheim cemetery – a bad day for Amy – he asks Trellman to help and support her, promising to send the limo and his chauffeur to make it a little less burdensome to them. It shows that he has taken up his wife's "circuit" quite smoothly.

The reason for this exhumation and reburial is that Jay, who died five years after he had divorced Amy, was buried beside her mother, in a space in the family's plot intended for her father, who did not want it at the time (he would rather have the money) and who insisted upon selling it to Jay. The comedian in Jay Wustrin agreed to the buy; it was, as he used to joke, "like getting into a double bed with his mother-in-law" (who disliked, even hated him). Besides, was it not "a terrific story" for him to tell! What Jay, however, could not have expected was that Amy's father would outlive him, nor that after his own death his children (by his first marriage) would find the title to the grave in his bank box, and proceed to bury him there, beside Amy's mother. But Amy, anticipating the death of her father, now old and demented, thinks that when she has to bury him, he should lie there, beside his wife, not Jay, and that Jay's coffin must therefore be removed and be reburied between his own parents, in their own family's plot in another part of the cemetery. It is Chicago-like hilarity all over.

It is also in Adletsky's great black limo – warm and intimate inside, the weather cold and inclement outside – that the final assessments take place: Amy admits that she had given Harry serious thought as a suitor, that she was in love with him, but that she had never expected to see her love returned, "given the kinks of [his] high-level mental life," and that "there was not a chance that [he] could ever think well of [her]." Such things she had never told him before. And Harry Trellman acknowledges the sort of hold she had on him, telling her that "Other women were apparitions. She, and only she, was no apparition." She was the woman of whom he used to think that, if there had been a bare room in her house, it would have done him good "to go in and lie face down on the wooden floor ... " (83-84). Things he had never told her before. What they had been were "two dilatory people who had loved each other for forty years," yet they had not done much else apart from "discussing ottomans and wing chairs" (85). Even this exchange of assessments might never have taken place but for the exhumation of Jay's coffin – Jay, the man who had separated them, and who had now, before he would rise from his grave for two hours, finally brought them together again.

There is one thing, however, that Amy still needs to know: did he or did he not listen to her on the tape? Although a practiced liar, Harry Trellman is no longer able to hide the truth: yes, he heard the tape, screams and all. But, as he assures her, it had never changed his feelings for her, a lifetime of feelings, just as his elopement with Mary had not changed them, nor the fact that she had married Berner, and after that Jay. And now after forty years of thinking it over, he can only describe these feelings as "an actual affinity," and when asked by Amy to translate this into a language she understands (she has not forgotten how little use he always had for the way other people speak), he explains, "Other women might remind me of you, but there was only one actual Amy" (101). But, as Amy reminds him, his "affinity" was screaming on the tape, just as she was still married to Berner when she had shared the shower with him and Jay in Palmer House. To Trellman it no longer matters; this lies behind them, and all Trellman cares about is what he now understands to be the one essential experience in his life, his love for her, the only thing that is "actual."

When Jay's coffin is lowered into his new grave, Trellman looks into Amy's face, which "*was* the most amazing thing in the life of the world" (104), and does what he should have done forty years ago: he proposes to her. The suggestion is that she will accept, but whether she does so or not, is not nearly as important as his understanding of why he has finally made the proposal. So Bellow can leave this out. Plot, after all, is an artificial construct, and so everything else that does not directly bear on what results in Harry's final decision can be left out as well, including the big social ideas, so characteristic of Bellow's earlier long novels.

Alfred Kazin, in his insightful, though pithy review of the novella,[2] is not very happy about the absence of such an overriding idea in *The Actual*, complaining that it is not a book "in which top-heavy American wealth gets much scrutiny." There is, however, another way of looking at this. What could be an advance is that the distinction between the wealthy reality instructors and their socially and intellectually more perceptive counterparts, the typical early Bellow protagonist – Trellman in this case – is no longer as firm as it used to be. It has become blurred, more complex, but Bellow's language has remained profoundly moral, that is critical. Kazin's remark that Harry Trellman "is not much of a character," is also a bit puzzling in view of what Trellman himself has to say, quite persuasively, about "character": character, as Bellow (alias Trellman) believes, is primarily a social construct, and therefore always "compromising." More important is "nature," as it reveals itself in appearance, in posture, in everything that can be seen, heard, felt, smelled, and from which also issues something as indefinable as "the soul," finding, again according to Trellman, its richest expression in the human face. It is "character" versus "nature" that actually explains Harry's late recognition of Amy's forty-year long attraction for him, an element in the story that Kazin finds the weakest and least convincing part. Is this perhaps because he overlooks Harry's struggle to get rid of his dread of "kitsch," as well as his protracted reliance on a too theoretical approach whenever he has to deal with human affairs? It inevitably

---

[2] Alfred Kazin, "Struggles of a Prophet," *The New York Review of Books* (June 26, 1997), 17-18.

reminds us of another early Bellovian protagonist, Moses Herzog. This time, however, Bellow records it all with a marvelous, laconic economy, employing as of old his alter ego's self-conscious, comic pedantry to full dramatic and ironic effect. Add to this the ease and lightness with which he presents his new assortment of peculiar Chicagoans, plus the flavor of his idiosyncratic, descriptive detail, notably in the evocation of wintry Chicago – "the thick, dried urban gumbo of dark Lake Street" (19) – the city in which this time the enigma of Harry Trellman's delayed proposal is the captivating center of his story. Take all this into consideration, and one knows that the old master has pulled it off again.

BETWEEN PROMINENCE AND OBSCURITY: JEWISH-AMERICAN WRITERS AT THE CENTER OF A DECENTRALIZED LITERATURE

DEREK RUBIN

In October 2001 I attended an exhilarating three-day conference organized by the Program in Jewish Studies at Princeton University, entitled "Celebrating Jewish-American Writers." Sitting in an auditorium jammed with an eager audience, listening to poets and fiction writers reading from their work, to critics and scholars lecturing on Jewish-American writing, and to comic-book artists discussing Jewish culture, high and low – this to me, a visitor from afar, was a wonderful treat. I live in the Netherlands where, even though the occasional appearance of a Jewish-American author or critic will usually draw a sizeable audience, such events are few and far between. So, when a colleague at Princeton told me about the three-day conference featuring writers and artists and scholars as diverse as Max Apple, Susan Sontag, James Atlas, Daniel Mendelsohn, Grace Paley, Leslie Epstein, Art Spiegelman, Will Eisner, Morris Dickstein, James Young, Robert Pinsky, Alicia Ostriker, Thane Rosenbaum, Rebecca Goldstein, and many, many more – this was simply too good to be true.

Being on a visit to the U.S. at the time of the conference, I traveled from Boston to Princeton full of high expectations, and I must say these were largely met. From Melvin Jules Bukiet's chilling portrayal of the seething anger and the stifling sense of entrapment that dominate the lives of the second generation of Holocaust survivors like himself and Thane Rosenbaum to Morris Dickstein's astute analysis of the absence of politics and power as themes in Jewish-American fiction; from the mesmerizing cadences of Marge Piercy's poetry to the slapstick humor of Jonathan Wilson's fiction; from the telling comments and questions from the audience (many of them elderly Jews, who in person experienced the very stuff from which much of the literature discussed at this conference is made) to the informal conversations with writers and scholars over coffee and cake between lectures and readings – all of this made the Princeton conference a rich and varied learning experience.

And yet I left this event puzzled about one important issue. For the last twenty years or so the American academy has been troubled by the culture wars. The multicultural debate has been largely defined by identity politics, and various scholars have pointed out that in this context the Jews occupy an anomalous position in America. They have attained majority status, and as such they see themselves and are perceived by others as white, Euro-Americans. At the same time, they continue to maintain, and indeed often insist upon, their distinctiveness as an ethnic minority. David Biale, Michael Galchinsky, and Susannah Heschel, editors of the landmark book, *Insider/Outsider: American Jews and Multiculturalism,* point out that it is largely owing to "the consciousness Jews have of themselves as occupying an anomalous status [as] insiders who are outsiders and outsiders who are insiders"[1] that they "confront contemporary multiculturalism with great ambivalence, trepidation, and even hostility."[2] Yet, as critical and probing as some of the lectures and discussions may have been, none of these emotions concerning the position of contemporary Jews in multicultural America were evident at the three-day conference at Princeton.

Somehow, one had the feeling at this conference that it was Jews talking to Jews about Jewish literature. Not only were the speakers Jewish, but my guess is that most of us in the audience were Jewish, too. There were certainly very few African-American, Latino or Asian-American people present, and Yiddishisms were used freely on the understanding that we all knew what they meant. There was a general sense of shared values, of a common sensibility and sense of humor, and of being, well, almost among family. Now, as comforting as this might have been, it also perhaps explains why very few of the speakers at the conference felt the need to refer to the multicultural debate or to raise the thorny issue of identity politics and how this affects American Jews and their literature. Let me not be misunderstood. I lapped up every minute of this warm feeling of being part of one big *mishpocheh.* But the point I wish to draw attention to

---

[1] *Insider/Outsider: American Jews and Multiculturalism,* eds David Biale, Michael Galchinsky, and Susannah Heschel (Berkeley: University of California Press, 1998), 5.
[2] *Ibid.,* 4.

here is that the very sense of comfortable insulation and togetherness that pervaded the conference belied an important fact about the younger generation of post-acculturated writers, namely that as a group these writers at best occupy an exceedingly tangled and tenuous position on the American literary scene today.

For the sake of clarity, let me point out that when I say post-acculturated writers I am referring loosely to the younger generation (or perhaps one should say *generations*, since their ages vary widely) of Jewish-American writers of fiction, such as Pearl Abraham, Paul Auster, Melvin Jules Bukiet, Michael Chabon, Nathan Englander, Myla Goldberg, Myra Goldberg, Rebecca Goldstein, Allegra Goodman, Michelle Herman, Dara Horn, Nessa Rapoport, Lev Raphael, Jonathan Rosen, Thane Rosenbaum, Jonathan Safran Foer, Helen Schulman, Gary Shteyngart, Aryeh Lev Stollman, Jonathan Tel, and a host of others, as opposed to those famous and less famous older writers of the post-immigrant generation, such as Saul Bellow, Bernard Malamud, Grace Paley, Tillie Olsen, Isaac Rosenfeld, Philip Roth, and Delmore Schwartz.[3]

Given the title of the Princeton conference – "Celebrating Jewish-American Writers" – one can well understand the failure to address the uncertain status of the generation of younger writers, which after all represents the future of Jewish-American literature. Yet paradoxically it is important that we do so if we are to grasp their full significance in multicultural America and the potential importance of their contribution to the rapidly changing American literary canon. Let us therefore first take a brief look at the position of these writers on the American literary scene.

The position of the younger generation of post-acculturated Jewish-American writers on the American literary scene today can best be described as reflecting the anomalous insider/outsider status of

---

[3]   The distinction between "post-immigrant" and "post-acculturated" writers is Ted Solotaroff's. In his Introduction to *Writing Our Way Home* he rightly argues that, rather than speak of different cultural generations, "It makes more sense ... to speak of a post-immigrant culture that is coming to an end and a post-acculturated one that has been coming into being, along with much else that is new in our increasingly pluralistic society." See Ted Solotaroff, "The Open Community," in *Writing Our Way Home: Contemporary Stories by American Jewish Writers*, eds Ted Solotaroff and Nessa Rapoport (New York: Schocken, 1992), xv. Solotaroff's distinction is particularly useful because it avoids the inevitable imprecision of grouping Jewish writers by generational presence in America.

American Jews in general. That is to say, these writers find
themselves caught between the prominence of major writers within
the white, Euro-American mainstream of American literature and the
prestige of minority status afforded to black writers within the context
of American multiculturalism. Like the older generation of post-
immigrant Jewish writers these younger writers are certainly within
the mainstream of American literature in the sense that their work is
published by major publishing houses, such as Random House, Harper
and Row, Scribner, Norton, Knopf, Riverhead, Vintage, and St.
Martin's Press. Their stories appear in mainstream journals, such as
Esquire, The New Yorker, The Paris Review, and *Playboy,* or smaller,
prestigious journals such as *The Antioch Review, The Kenyon Review,*
and *Yale Review.* The work of many of these writers is reviewed in
major newspapers like the *New York Times* and the *Los Angeles
Times,* and a number of them have won important prizes. For example,
in 2001 Michael Chabon was awarded the Pulitzer Prize for his novel
The Amazing Adventures of Kavalier and Clay (2000);[4] Rebecca
Goldstein has been a MacArthur Foundation Fellow, and both she and
Allegra Goodman have received Whiting Awards. And then there are
the even younger, highly talented, debutants like Nathan Englander
and Jonathan Safran Foer, who enjoy national and even international
fame, at least in part, one suspects, because of the record advances
they received for their books.

However, in spite of the success of a few individual writers and
these general signs of prestige and mainstream status, unlike their
post-immigrant predecessors most of the writers of this younger
generation are not very well known among the general reading public.
In an essay published in 1997 as part of a milestone symposium on the
recent revival in Jewish-American fiction organized by *Tikkun*
magazine, Morris Dickstein pointed out that

> When [he] mentioned these younger writers in a lecture in London ...
> a well-known publisher quickly challenged [him]. Who were these
> people, he asked? "I'm in New York all the time and I haven't heard
> of them."[5]

---

[4]   Michael Chabon, *The Amazing Adventures of Kavalier and Clay* (New York:
Random, 2000).
[5]   Morris Dickstein, "Ghost Stories: The New Wave of Jewish Writing," *Tikkun* 12/
6 (November-December 1997), 35.

And I must say that my recent experience is very similar. Speaking to avid readers of fiction – literary scholars specialized in fields other than Jewish literature; scholars from other disciplines; and doctors, lawyers, and other professionals who read widely – I am often struck by the blank look on their faces when I talk about a generation of younger Jewish-American writers and I mention some of their names. But if the position of these writers within the mainstream of American letters is on the whole at best shaky, how do they fare as ethnic or minority writers? Thematically their fiction clearly constitutes a "Jewish Literary Revival," as the title of the *Tikkun* symposium suggests. Various critics have discussed the ways in which the work of many of these writers embodies the richly diverse Jewish cultural and religious revival that has occurred over the last two or three decades in the United States.[6] Indeed, some critics see this Jewish literary revival as a by-product of the multiculturalist movement's emphasis on identity politics. "In line with the wave of

---

[6]   See, for example, Morris Dickstein, "Ghost Stories," and "Never Goodbye, Columbus: The Complex Fate of the Jewish-American Writer," *The Nation*, October 22, 2001, 25-34; Andrew Furman, *Contemporary Jewish American Writers and the Multicultural Dilemma: The Return of the Exiled* (Syracuse, NY: Syracuse University Press, 2000), 16-19; Nessa Rapoport, "Summoned to the Feast," in *Writing Our Way Home*, eds Solotaroff and Rapoport, xxvii-xxx; and Solotaroff, "The Open Community," in *ibid.*, xiii-xxvi. I should point out that not all critics agree that a revival in Jewish fiction is taking place at present in the United States. The novelist and essayist, Cynthia Ozick, for one, has argued that, since for literature to be Jewish it must be morally didactic, the very notion of a "Jewish novel" is a contradiction in terms. See her "Promoting Virtue Through Learning," *Forward*, October 26, 2001, B1, B8. The critic and scholar, Ruth Wisse, who bases her criticism on traditional, orthodox Jewish standards, argues that the weaknesses in contemporary Jewish-American fiction reflect "the insufficiencies of American Jewish life" (Ruth R. Wisse, "Honest Reflections of Moral Collapse," *Forward*, October 26, 2001, B1, B8; see also her *The Modern Jewish Canon: A Journey Through Language and Culture* [New York: Free, 2000]). And finally there are those who claim that on literary grounds one cannot speak of a revival of Jewish-American fiction. For example, in a caustic (and to my mind unfounded) attack on younger Jewish-American writers, the critic Lee Siegel argued that "For the most part, rather than the heirs to Bellow and Roth and Mailer (and the New York Intellectuals at their best), today one sees younger American-Jewish writers who are more like characters straight out of the satirical fiction of Bellow and Roth and Mailer" (Lee Siegel, "Seize the Day Job," *Harpers Magazine*, March 2001, 79). For a well-argued reply to Siegel in defense of the younger generation of Jewish-American writers, see Andrew Furman, "The Exaggerated Demise of the Jewish-American Writer," *Chronicle of Higher Education*, July 6, 2001, 1-2.

identity politics in America," writes Dickstein for example, "there has
been a persistent search for roots among younger Jewish writers .... "[7]
Yet, in spite of the salient presence of Jewish themes in much of their
fiction, these writers are seldom recognized as fellow ethnic writers
within the context of American multiculturalism. For example, in
contrast to Asian American, Native American, African American and
Chicano literatures, courses in Jewish-American literature are rarely
offered by English departments at American universities and colleges.
Indeed, with Jewish-American literature as a specialty, a young
academic would have very little chance of being hired by an English
department at a major research university or top college in the United
States. And Jewish-American fiction is often excluded from
multicultural anthologies of American literature.[8]

Given that this younger generation of post-acculturated Jewish
writers belongs fully neither within the mainstream of American
literature nor within the rapidly growing body of multicultural
literature, one might wonder how one can possibly object to their
being boosted a little in the one place where they do belong fully,
namely, at a conference organized by a Jewish studies program and
aimed at "Celebrating Jewish-American Writers"? Why indeed should
a conference like this dwell upon their tenuous position on the

---

[7]
    Dickstein, "Never Goodbye, Columbus," 32. Indeed, publishers also seem to have
recognized the scope of this Jewish literary and cultural revival. The past decade or so
has seen the publication of numerous anthologies of Jewish-American writing. The
most important of these are *America and I: Short Stories by American Jewish Women
Writers*, ed. Joyce Antler (1990); *Writing Our Way Home: Contemporary Stories by
American Jewish Writers*, eds Ted Solotaroff and Nessa Rapoport (1992); *Nice Jewish
Girls: Growing Up in America*, ed. Marlene Adler Marks (1996); *People of the Book:
Thirty Scholars Reflect on Their Jewish Identity*, eds Jeffrey Rubin-Dorsky and
Shelley Fisher Fishkin (1996); *Making a Scene: The Contemporary Drama of Jewish-
American Women*, ed. Sarah Blacher Cohen (1997); *Sephardic-American Voices:
Two-Hundred Years of a Literary Legacy*, ed. Diane Matza (1997); *American Jewish
Fiction: A Century of Stories*, ed. Gerald Shapiro (1998); *The* Prairie Schooner
Anthology of Contemporary Jewish American Writing, ed. Hilda Raz (1998);
Neurotica: Jewish Writers on Sex, ed. Melvin Jules Bukiet (1999); *Jewish American
Poetry: Poems, Commentary, and Reflections*, eds Jonathan N. Barron and Eric
Murphy Selinger (2000); and most recently *Jewish American Literature: A Norton
Anthology*, eds Jules Chametzky, *et al.* (2001).
[8]
    For an interesting and insightful discussion of the exclusion of the younger
generation of Jewish-American writers from the mainstream and from the
multicultural curriculum, see Furman, *Contemporary Jewish American Writers and
the Multicultural Dilemma*, 1-21.

American literary scene? The answer, I believe, is that only by doing so can one appreciate fully the true significance of this generation of writers in multicultural America. In order to explain why this is so, it is helpful first to take a closer look at the broader position of Jews in general in multicultural America, or more specifically at the argument made by some scholars that the very conditions that have given rise to feelings of discomfort among many Jews in multicultural America point toward a possible resolution of what many Americans perceive as a crisis in American culture and society at large.

Multiculturalism, I am sure most of us would agree, has achieved a great deal politically, socially, and culturally for cultural minorities in the United States. In recent years, however, some progressive thinkers who otherwise support many of the aims of the multiculturalist movement have become increasingly critical of its having been largely dominated by an extreme form of particularism. The overemphasis upon a politics of identity, such critics argue, has resulted in a degree of cultural and societal fragmentation that they deem a threat to the democratic civic culture in America. One response to this divisive force within multiculturalism has come from post-ethnic or multiracial theorists, who argue that the rising rate of intermarriage and the increasing social and cultural mixing between different racial and ethnic groups in the United States make it necessary to go beyond the multicultural ideal, at least insofar as it is based upon a monolithic notion of racial and ethnic identity. For example, in his book *Postethnic America: Beyond Multiculturalism* David Hollinger offers a vision of America in which the constructedness of race and ethnicity is widely acknowledged, so that these are no longer perceived as being based solely upon primordial ties and inherited identity but also upon voluntary affiliation. In Hollinger's postethnic America the individual will be able to manifest freely any of the multiple facets of her or his identity, and the communities of descent that currently characterize much of multicultural America will be replaced by communities of consent.[9]

---

[9] David A. Hollinger, *Postethnic America: Beyond Multiculturalism* (New York: Basic, 1995). For important studies by other multiracial theorists, see Richard D. Alba, *Ethnic Identity: The Transformation of White America* (New Haven: Yale University Press, 1990); Paul R. Spickard, *Mixed Blood: Intermarriage and Ethnic Identity in Twentieth-Century America* (Madison: University of Wisconsin Press, 1989); and Mary C. Waters, *Ethnic Options: Choosing Identities in America* (Berkeley: University of California Press, 1990. The notions of "consent" and

While recognizing the utopianism of such a vision, especially for people belonging to cultural minorities in the United States, David Biale argues in an essay entitled "The Melting Pot and Beyond" that "Because they are now seen as white and are therefore capable of passing as other whites ... Jews ... are rapidly becoming a good example of just such a community of choice" as envisioned by Hollinger. "American Jews," Biale explains, "constitute a kind of intermediary ethnic group, one of the most quickly and thoroughly acculturated yet, among European immigrant ethnicities, equally one of the most resistant to complete assimilation."[10]

Given that the insider/outsider status of American Jews today renders their experience paradigmatic for a post-ethnic America, there remains the question of what bearing this has upon the literary significance of the generation of post-acculturated Jewish writers. Well, just as the position of the Jews in multicultural America can be taken to serve as a paradigm for a post-ethnic America, so too can much of the fiction being written by the younger generation of post-acculturated Jewish writers be seen as paradigmatic for what might be called a "post-ethnic literature." As I have argued in some detail elsewhere, in contrast to the post-immigrant generation's literature of alienation, or marginality,[11] which grew largely out of a sense of the overwhelming force of inherited identity and primordial ties, the fiction written by the post-acculturated generation of Jewish writers derives much of its strength from the interplay between a sense of the inescapability of inherited identity and an awareness of the contemporary American Jew's freedom to affiliate.[12]

"descent" are central to Werner Sollors' influential book *Beyond Ethnicity: Consent and Descent in American Culture* (New York: Oxford University Press, 1986).

[10]   Biale, "The Melting Pot and Beyond," 31. This essay of Biale's, the Introduction written by him and his co-editors, Michael Galchinsky and Susannah Heschel, and many other essays in the book *Insider/Outsider* were crucial to me in forming many of the ideas in this essay.

[11]   Although not all critics apply the term "marginality" precisely, I am using it here to refer to the hybrid experience of being partially assimilated into two cultures. In doing so, I am following the original sense in which the Chicago sociologist Robert E. Park defined marginality in his seminal essay "Human Migration and the Marginal Man," *American Journal of Sociology*, 33 (1928), 881-93.

[12]   See my essay "Postethnic Experience in Contemporary Jewish American Fiction," *Social Identities*, 8/4 (December 2002), 507-20. Although the focus of this essay is different from that of the present essay, I have drawn upon it where relevant.

There is a rich variety of works of fiction in which this source of creative tension figures in different and exciting ways. In some, the emphasis is on the sense of the inescapability of inherited identity set against the backdrop of American Jews' majority status. For example, in Paul Hond's highly accomplished debut novel *The Baker* (1997)[13] race and ethnicity intersect with social class and economic status to define the tumultuous relationship between a Jewish and a black family. And in Thane Rosenbaum's nightmarish depictions of the transgenerational transference of Holocaust trauma, his protagonists, in spite of their having grown up in America and their being fully Americanized, are dominated by their sense of the inescapability of their parents' victimization at the hands of the Nazis. Other works of fiction resist the hold of primordial ties by focusing upon the notion of Jewishness as a construct and as a matter of voluntary affiliation in present-day America. Anne Roiphe's *Lovingkindness* (1987) and Rebecca Goldstein's *Mazel* (1995),[14] for example, explore the experience of acculturated, secularized members of the older generation who are forced to come to terms with their children or grandchildren embracing Jewish orthodoxy. And Joshua Henkin's *Swimming Across the Hudson* (1997)[15] emphasizes the voluntary nature of Jewishness by exploring the intersection of ethnic and family ties through his portrayal of the relationship between an adopted son whose biological mother is not Jewish and his Jewish adoptive parents. And finally there is fiction that, like Allegra Goodman's brilliant collection of closely linked stories *The Family Markowitz* (1998), explores and dramatizes the complex and often contradictory interplay between a sense of the inescapability of inherited identity and an awareness of the possibilities of voluntary affiliation as a key factor in defining Jewish experience in present-day America.[16]

Let me offer, as an example, just a brief reading of Goodman's short-story cycle, since these closely linked stories, which portray the trials and tribulations of three generations of the Markowitz family,

---

[13]   Paul Hond, *The Baker* (New York: Random, 1997).

[14]   Anne Roiphe, *Lovingkindness* (1987; New York: Warner, 1997); Rebecca Goldstein, *Mazel* (1995; New York: Penguin, 1996).

[15]   Joshua Henkin, *Swimming Across the Hudson* (New York: Putnam's, 1997).

[16]   For a more detailed discussion of identity and affiliation in some of these and in other works of fiction by post-acculturated Jewish-American writers, see my essay "Postethnic Experience in Contemporary Jewish-American Fiction."

together form what is perhaps the most accomplished literary response thus far to the tensions and ironies of the anomalous position of American Jews today as they try to maintain a balance between their identity as Jews and as members of the white majority.

In these stories, rather than focus either on inherited identity or on voluntary affiliation as key factors in defining her characters' experience as American Jews, Goodman attempts to dramatize the complex and often contradictory interplay between the two. The Markowitz family prove to be a superb vehicle for this. First, there is elderly Rose Markowitz who, for example, refuses to let a rabbi preside over her second husband's funeral, because as a socialist he would not have wanted that; yet she is deeply upset when her son Henry, a lover of art and literature who manages a Laura Ashley store in Oxford, England, has a priest perform the wedding ceremony for him and his English wife, Susan McPhearson. Rose's view of Jewish identity as involuntary, as a fact of life that does not necessarily require confirmation through religious observance but that cannot and should not be denied, is highlighted by her attitude toward Henry's and Susan's wedding. Rose not only views this as an attempt on Henry's part to repudiate his Jewishness, but she even indicates to her other son, Edward, that she suspects Susan of pretending to be a Gentile, like a certain Mr. Winston, who Rose met on a cruise, and who she was convinced was really, as she puts it, "[a] Weinstein."[17] Although Winston would not admit to being Jewish, she was proved right when he inadvertently responded to a comment she made in Yiddish. Edward rejects as preposterous the idea of Susan's being Jewish. When he emphatically says to Rose, "'Susan McPhearson does not know Yiddish,'" Rose points out that neither does Edward (82).

Then there are Henry and Edward themselves, who exhibit vividly, if at times in extreme and often in comic form, many of the dilemmas, and contradictions experienced by post-acculturated American Jews. Henry is aptly described by Edward as having

> draped himself with cultures and collections. Developed the most complicated persona possible – the expatriate Brooklyn Jew in Oxford. The unaffiliated scholar and aesthete as businessman. (154)

---

[17] Allegra Goodman, *The Family Markowitz* (New York: Farrar, 1996), 81. Subsequent page references to this edition will be given parenthetically in the text.

Henry, who in spite of his marriage to Susan is in fact gay, has turned his back in contempt upon what he calls the "bourgeois pretension" (90) of his middle-class Jewish-American background. Yet he tells Edward, who in many ways has embraced the very values Henry has rejected, that he has always looked to him and his wife Sarah as constants in the midst of the turmoil and changes in his life (154-55). On the other hand, although Edward leads a seemingly stable life as a husband, a father of four children, and an established academic, he feels that, in contrast to Henry who he believes "has made himself at home in contradictions ... he, Ed, is completely at sea. At a loss" (154). As thoroughly acculturated, well-educated, and well-to-do American Jews, Henry and Edward have turned the old post-immigrant paradigm on its head, with all the ironies that this involves. Henry, with his love for beauty and European high culture, "has always chosen the Old World, just as Ed has chosen the New .... although, in fact, Henry is a businessman and it is Ed who works as a scholar" (168).

The ironies and reversals are just as complicated when we examine some of the intergenerational relationships in the book. For example, Edward's sense of being adrift makes him wish he could believe in God, yet he is upset that his eldest daughter Miriam, a student at Harvard Medical School, is becoming increasingly observant. He is ashamed, moreover, of the superficiality of his and Sarah's own brand of Judaism – they keep a semi-kosher home and attend temple services irregularly – yet he is angry with Miriam for rejecting what he calls their "pleasant suburban Judaism" (247) in favor of a strict orthodoxy. Estelle Kirschenbaum, Sarah's mother, is also upset about what she takes to be her granddaughter's religious extremism, yet at the same time she is worried that Sarah's and Edward's son Avi may be planning to marry his non-Jewish girlfriend from college. And, finally, Miriam's own orthodoxy undercuts the very openness of American society that has made it possible for her to embrace Judaism while remaining a member of the white majority. This is conveyed forcefully when she rejects Edward's universalistic interpretation of the Passover message of tolerance and identification with all oppressed minorities in favor of a strictly particularistic reading of the Haggadah, the book containing the liturgy for the Passover dinner, or Seder. In recounting the Israelites' suffering in Egypt and their subsequent liberation from slavery, Edward says:

> "We cannot ... say that we are truly free until the other oppressed people's of the world are free. We make common cause with all peoples and all minorities. Our struggle is their struggle, and their struggle is our struggle." (196)

To which Miriam responds: "It doesn't say a single word about minorities in here" (197). When Sarah comes to Edward's defense, saying "He's talking about the modern context," Miriam cuts her off, reminding her that this is a *Jewish* holiday: "What about the original context?" she asks. "As in the Jewish people? As in God?" (198).

The literary response in Allegra Goodman's fiction, in the works of fiction that I mentioned earlier, and in many other novels and stories by young, post-acculturated Jewish writers to the anomalous insider/outsider status of American Jews has been rich and varied. I have tried to argue here that the circumstances that have meant something of a crisis for many Jews in multicultural America are paralleled by the position of the younger generation of post-acculturated Jewish writers on the American literary scene. At the same time, these very circumstances have served as a vital source of creativity for these writers. One wonders, however, whether the work of this younger generation of writers will in time prove to be as relevant to members of the larger society as was that of their post-immigrant predecessors, those "specialist[s] in alienation," as Isaac Rosenfeld so tellingly referred to them, whose fiction, in dramatizing the experience of marginality, paradoxically moved them into the mainstream of American literature.[18] Potentially, this could very well

---

[18] In his well-known piece on "The Situation of the Jewish Writer" (1944), Isaac Rosenfeld attributed the significance of the Jewish writer in America to his being a "specialist in alienation" (123). Rosenfeld's essay is reprinted in *An Isaac Rosenfeld Reader*, ed. Mark Shechner (Detroit: Wayne State University Press, 1988), 121-23. Many critics have since recognized that the fiction written by post-immigrant Jewish-American writers derived much of its power from the ways in which it dramatized the experience of marginality. Indeed, various historians and critics have argued that this aspect of their work is the key to understanding how in the post-Second World War period Jewish-American writers of fiction came to be considered mainstream *American* writers. See, for example, Terry A. Cooney, *The Rise of the New York Intellectuals: Partisan Review and Its Circle* (Madison: University of Wisconsin Press, 1986), 15-17; Leslie A. Fiedler, "Saul Bellow" (1957), reprinted in *Saul Bellow and the Critics*, ed. Irving Malin (New York: New York University Press; London: University of London Press, 1967), 1-9, and his *Waiting for the End* (1964; New York: Stein, 1970), 65-88; Allen Guttman, *The Jewish Writer in America: Assimilation and the Crisis of Identity* (New York: Oxford University Press, 1971),

prove to be the case, for there is an important similarity between the position of post-immigrant and post-acculturated Jews in America. Just as the experience of marginality that characterized the post-immigrant culture was an age-old Jewish experience, so too is the anomalous position in which American Jews find themselves today. As Biale, Galchinsky, and Heschel point out, "one might argue that the Jews succeeded in surviving for so many centuries as a marginalized group precisely because they were able to establish themselves close to centers of power and negotiate between competing elite and popular forces."[19] Surely, then, should America move beyond multiculturalism toward becoming what Hollinger calls a "postethnic nation,"[20] we might find that the younger generation of post-acculturated Jewish writers, like those I have discussed here, have the very resources necessary for articulating the concerns of many Americans at large.

Biale notes that because American Jews are "At once part of the ... majority yet also a self-chosen minority, their very belonging to both of these categories undermines the categories themselves." He suggests therefore that, "Between the monoculturalists who wish to erase difference and the multiculturalists who see only difference, the Jews may still have a role to play in the definition of the American

---

134-37; Irving Howe, "Introduction," *Jewish-American Stories*, ed. Irving Howe (New York: Mentor-NAL, 1977), 1-17, and "Strangers" in his *Celebrations and Attacks: Thirty Years of Literary and Cultural Commentary* (London: Deutsch, 1979), 11-26; Alfred Kazin, "The Jew as Modern American Writer" (1966), reprinted in *Jewish American Literature: An Anthology of Fiction, Poetry, Autobiography, and Criticism*, ed. Abraham Chapman (New York: Mentor-NAL; London: New English Library, 1974), 587-96; Irving Malin, *Jews and Americans* (Carbondale: Southern Illinois University Press, 1965); Derek Rubin, *Marginality in Saul Bellow's Early Novels: From Dangling Man to Herzog* (Diss. Amsterdam: Vrije Universiteit, 1995) and "Postethnic Experience in Contemporary Jewish American Fiction"; Mark Shechner, *After the Revolution: Studies in the Contemporary Jewish American Imagination* (Bloomington: Indiana University Press, 1987); Alan M. Wald, *The New York Intellectuals: The Rise and Decline of the Anti-Stalinist Left from the 1930s to the 1980s* (Chapel Hill: University of North Carolina Press, 1987), 27-30; and Ruth R. Wisse, *The Modern Jewish Canon*, 70-91.

[19] "The Dialectic of Jewish Enlightenment," in *Insider/Outsider*, eds Biale, Galchinsky and Heschel, 5.

[20] By a "postethnic nation" Hollinger means "a democratic state defined by a civic principle of nationality in the hands of an ethno-racially diverse population and possessed of a national ethnos of its own" (*Postethnic America: Beyond Multiculturalism*, 132).

future."[21] Given that the current position of the younger generation of post-acculturated Jewish writers on the American literary scene reflects that of the Jews as a group within multicultural America, the same may hold for the role of these writers within the rapidly changing canon of American literature. Insofar as the distinction between mainstream and ethnic or minority literatures is at present in the process of being undermined under the influence of multiculturalism, Jewish writers may yet find themselves at the center of a decentralized literature. In order to see this, however, one needs to recognize that at present they are at best dangling between prominence and obscurity.

---

[21] "The Melting Pot and Beyond," in *Insider/Outsider*, eds Biale, Galchinsky and Heschel, 32.

TONI MORRISON'S TRICKSTERS

KATHLEEN M. ASHLEY

To propose to discuss tricksters in the novels of Toni Morrison may, on first consideration, appear uncontroversial. After all, is not this Nobel prize-winning author a noted champion of black culture, and is not the trickster a favorite folklore figure in both African and African-American literatures? In world mythologies, trickster gods preside over crossroads, commerce, and industry, symbolizing processes of transition, transformation and interaction, while in comic tales the boundary-crossing trickster is usually amoral, using brains and shape-shifting to outwit the more powerful in its world.[1] Morrison invites us to think about one of the most famous of these African-American tricksters, Br'er Rabbit, when she entitles her fourth book, *Tar Baby*. Countless literary critics have taken up the invitation to analyze the uses of folklore in Morrison's fiction – but with a surprising lack of critical consensus that has convinced me there is more to say on this subject.

Although I have long been an admirer of Toni Morrison's – reading and teaching her fiction at least since 1973 when *Sula* was published – the massive critical commentary (including the writer's own) that has grown up around her novels makes situating any new analysis a daunting prospect. Even more daunting are the literary and cultural politics that have accompanied Morrison's career as a black woman writer using folklore, myth, and African-American artistic forms to shape her stories. It is with some trepidation, therefore, that I undertake a reconsideration of her tricksters, a task that would appear

---

[1] While the scholarship on tricksters is extensive, the following studies offer a variety of perspectives on the meaning of this ubiquitous figure: Barbara Babcock-Abrahams, "'A Tolerated Margin of Mess': The Trickster and His Tales Reconsidered," *Journal of the Folklore Institute*, 11 (1974), 147-86; *Mythical Trickster Figures*, eds William Doty and William Hynes (Tuscaloosa: Alabama, 1993); Robert D. Pelton, *The Trickster in West Africa: A Study of Mythic Irony and Sacred Delight* (Berkeley: California, 1980); John W. Roberts, *From Trickster to Badman: The Black Folk Hero in Slavery and Freedom* (Philadelphia: Pennsylvania, 1989); Victor Turner, "Myth and Symbol," *The International Encyclopedia of Social Sciences* (New York: Macmillan, 1968), 576-82.

to engage once again the issue of folklore's role within African-American literary tradition. I propose, however, that we uncouple the automatic link between "tricksters" and "folklore," and that we use a broader range of anthropological theories to reach an understanding of the semiotic importance of tricksters in Toni Morrison's novels. I will be drawing first on the theories of structuralists like Claude Lévi-Strauss and Edmund Leach, extended in the writings of symbolic anthropologists like Victor Turner and Clifford Geertz.[2] These anthropological theories about the culturally cognitive work done by tricksters have been adopted by scholars of comparative religion and mythology and, most recently, by literary critics interested in the multicultural literatures of America. Therefore, far from being an unambiguous borrowing from folklore, the trickster is – I will argue here – the complex sign of Morrison's fictional and metaphysical ambitions. Morrison uses the trickster's fundamental characteristic of transgression to maneuver her readers into questioning moral and social categories and to pose alternate possibilities for interpreting the world.

   To remind ourselves how far the critical debate over African-American literary history has come and to situate my proposition that we take Morrison's tricksters as serious metasocial commentary, we might go back to 1973, to a review of *Sula* (Morrison's second novel) in the *New York Times* book review section. The patronizing (and one even might say racist) tone of just twenty-five years ago is instructive; the critic obviously had no idea that there was about to be an explosion of writing from black women authors that would transform the publishing and literary landscapes, nor that a combination of scholarly forces from the women's movement and African-American Studies would recover black women's writing from the nineteenth and early twentieth centuries. In her review of *Sula*, Sara Blackburn acknowledged Toni Morrison's artistic gifts but insisted that the novelist was wasting her time on inconsequential black, historically-distant topics: "Toni Morrison is far too talented to remain only a marvelous recorder of the black side of provincial American life." Presumably contemporary urban settings featuring white life were

---

2   Claude Lévi-Strauss, "The Structural Study of Myth," in *Structural Anthropology*, trans. Claire Jacobson and Brooke Schoepf (New York: Basic Books, 1963), 206-31; Edmund Leach, "Genesis as Myth," in *European Literary Theory and Practice*, ed. Vernon W. Gras (New York: Dell, 1973), 317-29; Clifford Geertz, *The Interpretation of Cultures* (New York: Basic Books, 1973).

what would have been worth writing about according to Blackburn, who advised Morrison that only by addressing "a riskier contemporary American reality" could she become an important novelist.[3]

Morrison might have been responding to just such a critique of her central subject matter, black life, when she commented in an interview:

> Critics generally don't associate black people with ideas. They see marginal people; they just see another story about black folks. They regard the whole thing as sociologically interesting perhaps but very parochial. There's a notion out in the land that there are human beings one writes about, and then there are black people or Indians or some other marginal group. If you write about the world from that point of view, somehow it is considered lesser. It's racist of course .... We are people, not aliens. We live, we love and we die.[4]

Morrison's "metaphysical ambitions" I take to be this desire to see her fictions about black people read as relevant to the social, spiritual, and artistic concerns of all people. Therefore, when Morrison employs trickster characters or trickster cosmology, we cannot simply label them as borrowings from black folklore; rather, we should examine Morrison's fictional purposes, which are usually complex and trickster-like themselves. African-American tricksters, in particular, are often interpreted sociologically – that is their trickery is understood to be the kind of power available to persons in a subordinate power position. I will argue instead for a primarily semiotic interpretation, in the sense that societies constitute their own boundaries by defining what is "other."[5] Trickster may be seen as a metaphor for "both the breakdown and the emergence of the

---

[3]   Sara Blackburn, review of *Sula*, *New York Times Book Review*, 30 December 1973, 3. See also the sexist comment by Mel Watkins, in a review of *Song of Solomon*, which he preferred to *The Bluest Eye* and *Sula* since it was not about "the insulated, parochial world of black women," but concerned a black male character ("Talk with Toni Morrison," *New York Times Book Review*, September 11, 1977, 50).
[4]   "Toni Morrison," *Black Women Writers at Work*, ed. Claudia Tate (1983), reprinted in *Conversations with Toni Morrison*, ed. Danille Taylor-Guthrie (Jackson: University Press of Mississippi, 1994), 160.
[5]   For a typology of various kinds of trickster theory, see my "Interrogating Biblical Deception and Trickster Theories: Narratives of Patriarchy or Possibility?" in *Reasoning with the Foxes: Female Wit in a World of Male Power*, a special issue of *Semeia (An Experimental Journal for Biblical Criticism)*, 42 (1988), 103-16.

classifications constituting culture," as Susan Stewart puts it.[6] I will
first look at some of the aspects of Morrison's novels that trickster
theory may illuminate, then take up *Sula* as her most extended
fictional version of a trickster universe.

Although I am suggesting we should uncouple the automatic
connection between trickster and folklore, Morrison does occasionally
use identifiable tricksters from folktales, but even in those cases her
appropriation is always a creative revision. Trudier Harris, in her
study of folklore and fiction in Toni Morrison's novels, has noted that
although the author "follows in the Chesnutt, Hurston, and Ellison
tradition by adapting folkloristic materials into her novels," we should
not "expect exact or consistent parallels between her usages and
folklore as it exists in historical black comunities." According to
Harris, Morrison "transforms historical folk materials" in a process
Harris terms "literary folklore."[7] But Harris goes further in claiming
that often in Morrison's works we "cannot tell where her imagination
leaves off and communal memory begins" – unlike the uses of
folklore in earlier authors, who tend to drop in nuggets of folklore that
differ in style from the rest of the narrative.[8] Rather, "Morrison
replicates the dynamic of folk communities by showing how people
interact with each other to shape tales, legends, rumors, and folk
beliefs"; the crazy war veteran Shadrack's institution of National
Suicide Day in *Sula*, for example, "is a dynamic event that reveals the
whole community's attitude toward Shadrack, his attitude toward
death, and the place of death in war and in the demise of one's
community – all of which are central to the texturing of the novel as a
whole."[9] In Harris' view, this is an innovation, folklore as fictional
process.

When we turn to specific trickster references, in *Tar Baby* for
example, Morrison appears to be citing the familiar tale of Br'er
Rabbit's encounter with a figure made of tar, but Morrison puts her
own spin on the tale when she writes:

---

[6]   Susan Stewart, *Nonsense: Aspects of Intertextuality in Folklore and Literature*
(Baltimore: Johns Hopkins, 1978), 62.
[7]   Trudier Harris, *Fiction and Folklore: The Novels of Toni Morrison* (Tennessee,
1991), 7.
[8]   *Ibid.*, 10.
[9]   *Ibid.*, 11.

It was a rather complicated story with a funny happy ending about the triumph of cunning over law, of wit over authority, of weakness over power. Its innocence and reassurance notwithstanding, it worried me. Why did the extraordinary solution the farmer came up with to trap the rabbit involve tar? Why was the rabbit's sole area of vulnerability having good manners? Why did the tar baby's silent complicity seem to be at once natural and obscene? Of the two views of the Brier Patch, the farmer's and the rabbit's, which was right? Why did it all seem so contemporary and, more to the point, so foreboding?[10]

Morrison describes her approach as "scratching" these familiar materials to see what new insights might emerge. In this process, one might say that Morrison plays tricks with the traditional African-American trickster tale.

Thus, while critics argue about who is the trickster and who the tar baby in the novel – for some, the uncouth young man Son is the tar baby,[11] while for others it is Jade, the liberated woman and ultra-sophisticated model[12] – Son is also considered "the classic trickster" by Craig Werner.[13] Werner analyzes Morrison's use of the Br'er Rabbit and tar baby myths not as an unproblematic embrace of African-American folklore but as a mechanism for exploring the multiplicity in any experience. What looks like an undesirable briar patch to one may turn out to be another's home.

The problem for readers has been that Morrison is not willing to give us easy answers; she is primarily interested in making us think through the options. Critical interpretations of *Tar Baby* seem to founder on choice between binaries – Son or Jadine, Eloe the black home or the white city, etc. – yet, if Morrison is employing trickster techniques, the issue is not a choice but an openness to alternatives that may challenge conventional conclusions. Readers seem to want to

---

[10] Quoted in Robert G. O'Meally, "Tar Baby, She Don' Say Nothin'," in *Critical Essays on Toni Morrison*, ed. Nellie Y. McKay (Boston: G.K. Hall, 1988), 36.

[11] See, for example, Valerie Smith's review of *Tar Baby* in the *Sewanee Review*, reprinted in *Critical Essays on Toni Morrison*, 37-39.

[12] See O'Meally's review of *Sula* in *Critical Essays on Toni Morrison*, 35, though the reviewer acknowledged that "Son is also Tar Baby-like: a trickster of many names, a piano player and a folktale spinner" (36).

[13] "For Son, masking is reflex response. Approaching all myths with caution, he attempts to keep his mind free to perceive the actual situation he understands to be shaped by a variety of mythic understandings" (Craig H. Werner, "The Briar Patch as Modernist Myth: Morrison, Barthes and Tar Baby As-Is," in *Critical Essays on Toni Morrison*, 164).

read the novel as a love story (which would imply that Son and Jadine must end up together), or a story about the discovery of self (which would necessitate that they go their separate ways). As Son at the end bounds away, rabbit-like, into the briar patch of the mythical island, Morrison does not tell us what choice he is going to make. She also leaves it up to her readers to decide how to judge Jadine's future.

Furthermore, critics have had difficulty in deciding which character they are supposed to identify with. In a Morrison story it is almost always difficult to pin down a "central character," because she tends to develop characters that operate in tandem: Sula and Nel, Milkman and Guitar, and in *Tar Baby* Jadine and Son.[14] Trickster-like, Morrison disrupts our expectation that there must be a central character whose fate represents the recommended solution to life's dilemmas. While characters like Nel or Milkman may ultimately have epiphanies, their novels remain open-ended, leaving each reader to determine the resolution to the plot line. These are the narrative and discursive traits that Gerald Vizenor, theorizing Native American literature, and most recently Jeanne Rosier Smith, writing on American ethnic literature, have identified as a kind of trickster "discourse" or trickster "aesthetics."[15]

Many of Morrison's most memorable characters, too, resemble trickster-transgressors by ignoring or deliberately violating social norms, especially sexual codes or gender expectations. Eva, Hannah and Sula in *Sula*, Pilate in *Song of Solomon*, and Jadine in *Tar Baby* are only the most obvious examples. Although the trickster of folklore is usually gendered male, with such characters Morrison seems to be exploring the somewhat different social implications when the trickster is a female, for whom nurturing rather than adventure is the norm.[16] Morrison also has adventurous, rule-breaking, lawless males in most of her novels, beginning with Cholly Breedlove in *The Bluest Eye* about whom Morrison has said that he is a "free man," free in his

---

[14]   See Robert Gran's essay, "Absence into Presence: The Thematics of Memory and 'Missing' Subjects in Toni Morrison's *Sula*," in *Critical Essays on Toni Morrison*, 90-103.

[15]   Gerald Vizenor, *The Trickster of Liberty: Tribal Heirs to a Wild Baronage* (Minneapolis: Minnesota, 1988) and Jeanne Rosier Smith, *Writing Tricksters: Mythic Gambols in American Ethnic Literature* (Berkeley: California, 1994).

[16]   As Trudier Harris comments with reference to uneasiness over Jadine, "African-American folk culture has not prepared us well for a female outlaw .... We can see traits of Stagolee in Milkman as well as in Son, but we have no models for accepting Jadine as a 'bad woman,'" *Fiction and Folklore*, 128.

head to "do whatever his whims suggested." He is the kind of person who is called a "bad nigger," using the adjective "bad" meaning both bad and good. "This is a man who is stretching ... ," Morrison says, "he's stretching, he's going all the way within his own mind and within whatever his outline might be. Now that's the tremendous possibility for masculinity among black men."[17] Sula's lover Ajax is another male who makes his own rules as he follows his desires with that sense of style and adventure, as is Guitar in *Song of Solomon*, also represented as "truly masculine in the sense of going out too far where you're not supposed to go and running toward confrontations rather than away from them ... taking risks."[18] With all these characters, both male and female, Morrison explores the trickster characteristic of adventurous boundary-crossing against which social limits may be defined.

Morrison creates forms of the ritual trickster in the healer-conjure woman figures like Ajax's adored mother in *Sula*, for whose spells her sons gathered "the plants, hair underclothing, fingernail parings, white hens, blood, camphor, pictures, kerosene and footstep dust that she needed."[19] In *Song of Solomon*, Milkman's aunt Pilate is also a "conjure woman" who uses her herbal magic to preserve his life at its outset and is crucial to the story of his maturation. Mysteriously marked by the absence of a navel and hence separated from normal relationships, Pilate is completely marginal to conventional bourgeois society, epitomized by her materialistic brother Macon. However, as with the ritual healer who transgresses social taboos to help the community, Pilate's life is one of nurturing and affirmation. As a cultural theorist might put it, what is socially marginal is often symbolically central to a culture – or to a novel.

---

[17] "Intimate Things in Place," interview with Robert Stepto reprinted in *Conversations with Toni Morrison*, 19. A precursor to Sula, the youthful Cholly is described as "Dangerously free. Free to feel whatever he felt – fear, guilt, shame, love, grief, pity. Free to be tender or violent, to whistle or wee. Free to sleep in doorways or between the white sheets of a singing woman. Free to take a job, free to leave it .... Free to take a woman's insults, for his body had already conquered hers. Free even to knock her in the head, for he had already cradled that head in his arms. Free to be gentle when she was sick, or mop her floor, for he knew what and where his maleness was .... He was free to live his fantasies and free even to die, the how and when of which held no interest for him. In those days, Cholly was truly free" (*The Bluest Eye* [New York: Pocket Books, 1970], 125-26).

[18] "Intimate Things in Place, " 20.

[19] Toni Morrison, *Sula* (1974; New York: Plume/Penguin, 1982), 126. All subsequent quotations are from this edition.

In her many revealing interviews Morrison has made no secret of
her desire to capture in her writing various features of Black culture,
and she has described those features in an essay entitled "Rootedness:
The Ancestor as Foundation":

> I don't regard Black literature as simply books written *by* Black
> people, or simply as literature written *about* Black people, or simply
> as literature that uses a certain mode of language in which you just
> sort of drop *g*'s. There is something very special and very identifiable
> about it and it is my struggle to *find* that elusive but identifiable style
> in the books.[20]

Morrison identifies among these characteristics the ability to create
the oral experience in print, especially as in the Black tradition oral
performance created a space for audience response. The story is to
appear spoken and the reader should be able "to *feel* the narrator" and
commentary by a communal chorus of some kind (such as the town in
Sula and *Song of Solomon*, or nature in *Tar Baby*). Most pertinently to
the argument of this essay, Morrison wants to represent a cosmology
that blends "acceptance of the supernatural and a profound rootedness
in the real world at the same time with neither taking precedence over

---

[20] "Rootness: The Ancestor as Foundation," in *Black Women Writers (1950-1980):
A Critical Evaluation*, ed. Mari Evans (New York: Anchor Books/Doubleday, 1984),
342. Morrison may be referring pejoratively to the prescriptions of the 1960s Black
Arts movement, for which "blackness resided in the use of black talk which they
defined as hip urban language" – in the formulation of Barbara Christian ("The Race
for Theory," reprinted in *Gender and Theory: Dialogues on Feminist Criticism*, ed.
Linda Kauffman [New York: Basil Blackwell, 1989], 225-46). Christian also
describes Black Arts Nationalist ideologues as condemning writing that was "not
black enough," as well as writers like Ellison and Baldwin who believed it was the
intersection of Western and African influences that "resulted in a new Afro-American
culture" (232). For a personally contextualized analysis of the aesthetic limitations of
the Black Arts movement, see also bell hooks, "An Aesthetic of Blackness," in
Yearning: Race, Gender and Cultural Politics (Boston: South End Press, 1990), 103-
13. In an extensive and theoretically sophisticated analysis of the history of "Black
Aesthetics, Feminist Aesthetics, and the Problems of Oppositional Discourse,"
Belinda Edmondson notes Toni Morrison's idiosyncratic disavowal of both feminist
and black aesthetics while affirming a black female aesthetic (*Cultural Critique*, 22
[Fall 1992], 87-88). Trey Ellis has coined the concept of a "New Black Aesthetic" as
a way of thinking about contemporary African-American artists, including Toni
Morrison, who deny "the old definitions of blackness, showing us the intricate,
uncategorizeable folks we had always known ourselves to be" ("The New Black
Aesthetic," *Callaloo*, 12 [Winter 1989], 233-43).

the other."[21] She believes she has been most successful at recreating this cosmology in *Song of Solomon*, a novel framed by men who "fly" in the opening and closing scenes and having at its heart the legend of the flying African great-grandfather who becomes the symbol of Milkman's search for his own identity as a black man.[22] The plot of *Beloved* is even more thoroughly permeated by the supernatural in the figure of the slain child's ghost that comes back to take over her mother's household.

Morrison's references to black cosmology in *Sula*, however, suggest that there is another, metaphysical, dimension to her concept of black cosmology. Her portrayal of black forms of belief in the supernatural that characterize the black town in Medallion's Bottom in the first half of the twentieth century is more than a celebratory representation of folk religion. A belief in omens and dream interpretation runs like a thread through the narrative, as one of the historical traits of black culture. But I am suggesting that Morrison wants her readers to entertain the proposition that this special understanding of cosmic powers might be relevant, as well, for other than black people.

Morrison's uses of trickster semiotic are one aspect of the cosmology she represents, one in which the western binaries – not only of natural and supernatural but also of good and evil – are challenged. Trickster metaphysics refuses moral binaries in favor of paradox; in the trickster universe, one must accept both good and evil, not choose between them. This point is most clearly articulated in *Sula*, in a description of the response of the folk living in the Bottom to bad fortune. Morrison has said that she intended to present an alternative to the Western concepts of good and evil in *Sula* by portraying the cosmology of black people who "thought evil had a natural place in the universe; they did not need to eradicate it."[23]

In *Sula*, when the title character returns to Medallion, Ohio, she is preceded by evil omens (a plague of robins) and proceeds to put her grandmother Eva in an old folks home, then seduce Nel's husband

---

[21] "Rootedness," 342.
[22] Gay Wilentz has analyzed the "Afrocentric discourse" of this novel in "Civilizations Underneath: African Heritage as Cultural Discourse in Toni Morrison's *Song of Solomon*," in *Toni Morrison's Fiction: Contemporary Criticism*, ed. David L. Middleton (New York: Garland, 1997), 109-33.
[23] "Toni Morrison," in *Black Women Writers*, reprinted in *Conversations with Toni Morrison*, 168.

Jude. The townsfolk consider her a witch, but Morrison explains that they did not drive her out of the community:

> In their world, aberrations were as much a part of nature as grace. It was not for them to expel or annihilate it. They would no more run Sula out of town than they would kill the robins that brought her back, for in their secret awareness of Him, He was not the God of three faces they sang about. They knew quite well that He had four, and that the fourth [that is, evil] explained Sula.[24]

As Deborah McDowell puts it, *Sula* "invokes oppositions of good/evil, virgin/whore, self/other, but moves beyond them, avoiding the false choices they imply and dictate."[25] According to McDowell,

> the narrative insistently blurs and confuses these other binary oppositions, blurs the boundaries they create, boundaries separating us from others .... *Sula* glories in paradox and ambiguity, beginning with the prologue, which describes the setting, the Bottom, situated spatially in the top. We enter a new world here, a world in which we never get to the "bottom" of things, a world that demands a shift from a dialectical either/or orientation to one that is dialogical or both/and, full of shifts and contradictions, particularly shifting and contradictory concepts of the self.[26]

To say this is to note that *Sula* is a text structured according to trickster principles of paradox that undercut our expectations and have therefore perplexed some critics.[27]

---

[24] *Sula*, 118.

[25] Deborah E. McDowell, "'The Self and the Other': Reading Toni Morrison's *Sula* and the Black Female Text," in *Critical Essays on Toni Morrison*, 80. See also the discussion by Terry Otten, *The Crime of Innocence in the Fiction of Toni Morrison* (Columbia: University of Missouri Press, 1989). Otten explores Morrison's claims that "Evil is as useful as good," and "Sometimes good looks like evil; and sometimes evil looks like good" (5).

[26] Deborah McDowell, "Boundaries: Or Distant Relations and Close Kin," in *Afro-American Literary Study in the 1990's*, ed. Houston A. Baker and Patricia Redmond (Chicago: Chicago, 1989), 60.

[27] A number of critics have pointed to the difficulty in morally categorizing Sula. Karla Holloway, for example, in a book co-authored with Stephanie A. Demetrakopoulos, thinks that the ambivalence of readers results from Morrison's own ambivalence towards this character: "I believe the dual nature of this woman comes because Morrison had not reconciled how she felt towards Sula as she created her"! *New Dimensions of Spirituality: A Biracial and Bicultural Reading of the Novels of*

Morrison explicitly creates a moral cosmology that is non-western, one in which good and evil are paradoxically intertwined. Thus, the townsfolk may label Sula as the epitome of evil, but her presence has the ironic effect of enabling them to become better: "They began to cherish their husbands and wives, protect their children, repair their homes and in general band together against the devil in their midst" (117-18). Conversely, when Sula dies, the community loses its virtue, which had been defined in opposition to her "evil." Without Sula to "rub up against," everyone reverted. "The tension was gone and so was the reason for the effort they had made" (153). There is more than just a strategy of ironic reversal to Morrison's delineation of Sula's effect on her community. Morrison uses what I am calling trickster semiotics to force her reader to reflect upon the categories of good and evil as defined not only by this black community but by all communities. For the reader, Sula is, in Lévi-Strauss' terms, "good to think with."[28] Like the other boundary-crossers and norm-transgressors in Morrison's fiction, Sula has a cognitive function in provoking what anthropologist Clifford Geertz calls "metasocial commentary,"[29] that is, consideration of a society's social categories and definitions.

Among the concepts that Morrison appears most interested in subverting is our definition of love. One could read her entire fictional corpus as a philosophical exploration of the complex idea of love, which ironically looks like its opposite. From her first novel, *The Bluest Eye*, to her latest, *Paradise*,[30] Morrison has created characters whose love is indistinguishable from violence, destruction, or death. The incestuous father Cholly Breedlove in *The Bluest Eye* is portrayed as trying to express his love for his daughter in the only way he knew how. Eva's burning of her son Plum in *Sula* likewise comes out of her despairing love for his damaged life, and for Hagar in *Song of Solomon* passion turns into murderous attempts against Milkman. The culmination of this motif must surely be Sethe's killing of her baby in *Beloved* in order to protect her from slavery. While these fictional

---

Toni Morrison (New York: Greenwood, 1987), 77. For a Jungian reading of Sula as trickster, see Nancy Tenfelde Clasby, "Sula the Trickster," in a special issue of *Lit: Literature, Interpretation, Theory on Toni Morrison*, 6 (1995), 21-34.
[28]   Claude Lévi-Strauss, "The Structural Study of Myth," 206-31.
[29]   Clifford Geertz, *The Interpretation of Cultures* (1973).
[30]   In late 2003, as this volume was going to press, Morrison published her latest novel, *Love*.

representations of love have both psychological depth and sociological implications, it seems to me that Morrison is challenging her readers to think beyond conventional categories of intention and behavior – to entertain the paradox of murderous or incestuous love. She also seems to be proposing through Sula's mother, the indiscriminately promiscuous Hannah, or the social marginals Circe and Pilate in *Song of Solomon*, or the inhabitants of the convent in *Paradise*, that we might see love and creativity in unlikely places if we are willing to abandon socially normative judgments about what constitutes acceptable behavior. If I am making Morrison sound didactic, then I am certainly giving a misleading impression, for she is one of the least explicit of writers, depending instead on her fictional characters to incarnate these paradoxical possibilities. But what I do want to suggest is that Morrison's aims go far beyond the representation of black social and cultural history as an end in itself.

Her boldness at challenging readers to take her tricksters as vehicles for their own philosophical and metasocial meditations on love is introduced in *Sula* in a passage where Sula teases Nel's husband – and her soon-to-be-lover – Jude about his complaints that a "Negro man had a hard row to hoe in this world" (103). Sula disagrees, in the process asking her listeners and readers to reconsider the definition of love:

> I don't know what the fuss is about. I mean, everything in the world loves you. White men love you. They spend so much time worrying about your penis they forget their own. The only thing they want to do is cut off a nigger's privates. And if that ain't love and respect I don't know what is. And white women? They chase you all to every corner of the earth, feel for you under every bed .... Now ain't that love? .... Colored women worry themselves into bad health just trying to hang on to your cuffs .... And if that ain't enough, you love yourselves. Nothing in this world loves a black man more than another black man. You hear of solitary white men, but niggers? Can't stay away from one another a whole day. So. It looks to me like you the envy of the world. (103-104)

Sula's satirical deconstruction of the world's "love" for black men amuses Nel and Jude and comically challenges our conventional ways of interpreting the world.

An even more challenging passage toward the end of *Sula* again raises the definition of love. In a speech to Nel on her deathbed Sula rehearses a litany of sexual transgressions that one critic, Cedric Bryant, has identified as Sula's "sneering" prophesy of the collapse of community coherence as well as its eventual acknowledgement of her oppositional role in helping define proper behavior.[31] However, I think that Professor Bryant has failed signally in understanding the semiotic import of the speech. Sula says:

> After all the old women have lain with the teen-agers; when all the young girls have slept with their old drunken uncles; after all the black men fuck all the white ones; when all the white women kiss all the black ones; when the guards have raped all the jailbirds and after all the whores make love to their grannies; after all the faggots get their mothers' trim; when Lindbergh sleeps with Bessie Smith and Norma Shearer makes it with Stepin Fetchit; after all the dogs have fucked all the cats and every weathervane on every barn flies off the roof to mount the hogs ... then there'll be a little love left over for me. And I know just what it will feel like. (145-46)

While the effects of Sula on the Medallion community are certainly ironic, Bryant has misread the tone of this particular speech, whose astonishing recital of sexual deviance and perversion can be read as Sula's vision of a community living according to the same trickster principles of category transgression that she had lived by.[32] Just as she had been accused of sleeping with white men – the ultimate imaginable violation of the Black community's moral boundaries – Sula pictures age, sex, kin, race and species boundaries breached in an experience of "love" that, far from being bitter or vengeful, is almost a utopian vision. Morrison tells us that Sula sighs when she says,

> Oh, they'll love me all right. It will take time, but they'll love me. The sound of her voice was as soft and distant as the look in her eyes. (145)

---

[31] Cedric Gael Bryant, "The Orderliness of Disorder: Madness and Evil in Toni Morrison's *Sula*," *Black American Literature Forum*, 24 (Winter 1990), 733-34.
[32] Another trickster type, the Fool in Shakespeare's *King Lear*, gives a speech with a satirical rehearsal of paradoxes as his summing up, which he calls "a prophecy" (*The Riverside Shakespeare*, eds Blakemore Evans, G. *et al.* [Boston: Houghton Mifflin, 1974], III,ii,81-94). I am indebted to Professors Filomena Mesquita and Teresa Tavares of the University of Coimbra, Portugal for the reference.

Although Nel is offended by Sula's unwillingness to distinguish between right and wrong, Sula challenges Nel to the end, asking as Nel walks out the bedroom door how she knows that she – rather than Sula – was the "good" one.[33]

Morrison's novel asks us to read the character Sula as a semiotic figure for the difference that constructs meaning or as the boundary-crosser that permits reflection upon the categories society has created for itself to order everyday living. There is critique here of the social categories of exclusion that define who can love whom, but it goes far beyond simple denunciation of the black community that had excluded her to become a meditation upon the outrageous possibilities of love. Ultimately, as Andrew Wiget has argued, trickster is a figure for possibilities that do not exist in society as we know it – but just might.[34] Trickster is not solely an expression of resistance to social constraints or oppression but a representation that it is only by going beyond those constraints, no matter how benign they may appear, that change can be envisioned.

Song of Solomon, the story of Milkman Dead's education in life (or *Bildungsroman*), ends with a final articulation of the unlimited possibilities of love by his aunt Pilate as she lies dying in his arms: "I wish I'd a knowed more people. I would of loved 'em all. If I'd knowed more, I would a loved more."[35] Milkman reaches maturity when he realizes that the only people who have unequivocally loved him were "both women, both black, both old. From the beginning, his mother and Pilate had fought for his life and he had never so much as made either of them a cup of tea."[36] At this point he is able to take responsibility for Hagar's loving him (literally) to death, by accepting a box of her hair from Pilate. But the most significant symbol of his manhood is his acceptance of the paradox represented by his best friend Guitar's love. Milkman thinks to himself, "perhaps that's what

---

[33] This scene introduces a motif reiterated later when Nel visits an aged Eva Peace in Sunnydale retirement home, and Eva keeps asking Nel how she and Sula had killed Chicken Little at the river. Nel insists that it was Sula, but Eva refuses to acknowledge the distinction: "You. Sula. What's the difference? ... Just alike. Both of you. Never was no difference between you." (168, 169).

[34] Andrew Wiget, "His Life in His Tail: The Native American Trickster and the Literature of Possibility," *Redefining American Literary History*, ed. A. LaVonne Brown Ruoff and Jerry W. Ward, Jr. (New York: MLA, 1990), 83-96.

[35] Toni Morrison, *Song of Solomon* (London: Piscador/Chatto and Windus, 1989), 336.

[36] *Ibid.*, 331.

all human relationships boiled down to: Would you save my life? or would you take it?" Only "Guitar was exceptional. To both questions he could answer yes."[37] The paradox represented by Guitar, and the other trickster-transgressors of Morrison's fiction, is that good and evil, love and hate, life and death, ultimately end up being difficult to distinguish. What Morrison offers her readers in such instances through trickster strategies is not the picturesqueness of folklore but semiotic challenge.

In a 1998 interview in *Le Monde*, given just after *Paradise* was published, Morrison named as one of her greatest achievements in this novel the obscuring of racial identity in the speech and description of her women characters.

> Des le depart, j'avais ce parti pris: que ces femmes ne puissent à aucun moment être identifiées par leur race. Je devais faire attention à ce qu'aucune de leurs paroles ne devoile leur couleur de peau. Cette contrainte de langage était pour moi un de extraordinaire liberation. Briser cette convention de l'identification raciale, c'était magnifique.[38]

As violator of the American literary convention that black people must be identified, above all by their speech patterns, Morrison herself played the role of trickster in *Paradise*, as she claims in this interview.

I would suggest in conclusion that Morrison has been playing the role of author-trickster from the beginning of her career in transgressing literary and political boundaries set for black writers in the United States by both white and black critics. In the terms made theoretically usable by Henry Louis Gates, Jr., Morrison "signifies upon" not just various literary traditions but also African-American folklore traditions.[39] Distancing herself from the Black Aesthetics movement of the 1960s and 1970s, as well as from militant feminism of the 1970s and 1980s, she has with quiet but articulate precision pursued her own vision and a fictional agenda that would place readers in the sometimes uncomfortable position of having to question

---

[37] *Ibid.*, 331.
[38] "From the beginning, I had an aim: that these women could not at any moment be identified by race. I needed to make sure that none of their speech revealed the color of their skin. This constraint of language was an extraordinary liberation for me. To break this convention of racial identification was magnificent" (Josyane Savigneau, "Morrison, la guerrière," *Le Monde des Livres* [Vendredi, 29 mai 1998], I. My translation.).
[39] Henry Louis Gates, Jr., *The Signifying Monkey* (New York: Oxford, 1988).

their cultural assumptions. Morrison's tricksters do not represent a nostalgic celebration of black folklore for its own sake, but become the means by which she challenges all her readers to understand the world in new ways. Like Ellison's Invisible Man, she appears to be saying, "Who knows but that, on the lower frequencies, I speak for you?"[40]

---

[40] Ralph Ellison, *Invisible Man* (1952; London and New York: Penguin Books, 1965), 469. For a complementary discussion of recent trends toward "Americanist" (as distinct from "African Americanist") readings of Morrison, see Michael Nowlin, "Toni Morrison's *Jazz* and the Racial Dreams of the American Writer," *American Literature*, 71 (March 1999), 151-74.

SITE OF PASSAGE: THE CITY AS A PLACE OF EXILE IN CONTEMPORARY NORTH-AMERICAN MULTICULTURAL LITERATURE

HANS BAK

For those having to actually live it, the drama of the multicultural experience has been acted out most visibly and searingly in the larger cities of North America. As numerous writers belonging to cultural and ethnic minorities (whether indigenous or immigrant, traditional or Third World) have testified, in a still swelling and canon-busting body of multicultural writing, the experience of becoming a part of the new multicultural America means first and foremost finding oneself an exile in the city. In most contemporary multicultural literature produced in Canada and the U.S. the city looms large as the primary site of personal, cultural and social dislocation: it is in the city that Native Americans ("urban Indians") fight out the bitter psychic traumas of cultural dispossession, that Puertoricans ("New Yoricans") seek to negotiate the ironic ambiguities of their intercultural positionings, that African-Americans (the oldest colonized minority) collide most sharply with both traditional immigrant groups like Southern or Eastern Europeans and more recent postcolonial immigrants from countries like India, the Philippines, Korea, or the Arab nations.

The multicultural city has been first and foremost the site of anger, the territory of racial strife and ethnic conflict, the arena for fighting out, in the streets or in the family, the politics of race and cultural or ethnic identity. But, of necessity, the city has also been the theater of interaction, dialogue and negotiation, of seeking to establish an intercultural middle ground as a prerequisite of survival. It has been the platform where the postcolonial struggle against oppression and for cultural empowerment has been waged most dramatically, where those seeking to lift themselves out of silence and invisibility have been brought most sharply into conflict with the "voiced" and the visible. Where the city becomes a multicultural collage or kaleidoscope – a contested and ever changing site of conflicting voices, cultures and beliefs – it permits itself to be read most effectively as a postmodernist arena of plurality, fluidity, discontinuity and difference, less a static mosaic than an ongoing process of ever-shifting interactions and dialogues between a multiplicity of voices and perspectives. Read from the perspective of those exiled from the dominant discourse (as we shall find, the city is in essence still, to borrow Tony Tanner's well-known phrase, "a city of words"), the city becomes the territory where the postmodern drama of irony and indeterminacy – of self, of language – most forcefully plays itself out.

From the vast literary landscape of urban multiculturalism I should like to hold up for closer inspection a select number of representative voices: taking my cue from Calcutta-born Canadian-American Bharati Mukherjee, I should like to explore the city as a "site of passage," a fluid and slippery zone of transition and transformation, in three pieces of contemporary urban fiction: Canadian-American author Clark Blaise' superb short story "A Class of New Canadians" (1973), on Montreal; *In the Skin of a Lion* (1987), a postmodernist reading of multicultural laborers in Toronto by Sri Lanka-born Michael Ondaatje, of mixed Dutch, British, Tamil and Singhalese descent; and *Indian Killer* (1996), a searingly realistic and anger-fed portrait of urban Indians in Seattle by Native American author Sherman Alexie.

For both Mukherjee and her husband Blaise crossing cultures and the concomitant sense of exile have been an experience from early childhood, charged with strong political, moral and existential resonance. Mukherjee, in particular, has made herself into a highly visible chronicler and highly vocal spokeswoman for the new multicultural America, the immigrants from India and other Third World nations who are being transformed by (and are in turn transforming) their new adopted land and culture. Having suffered in the 1970s the acute racism of Toronto and Montreal (where she was a full professor at McGill but found herself treated as a shoplifter and a prostitute), she and Blaise decided to move to the U.S. in 1980 and embrace the transformative possibilities of becoming American immigrants. Since then, in her numerous stories of the multicultural life in America, Mukherjee (who once described herself as "a four-hundred year old woman, born in the captivity of a colonial, pre-industrial oral cultural and living now as a contemporary New Yorker") presents the experience of being a transcultural exile in the city as first and foremost an exhilarating and transformative one: the city for her is par excellence a "site of passage" – the place where one passes from old to new culture, from old to new self: a fluid and sometimes slippery zone of transition and transformation, where one is forced to "straddle the seesaw of contradictions" and faces "the hurly-burly of the unsettled magma between two worlds," the old Hindu culture of a Brahmin Indian, drenched in myth and superstition, and the new American realities of popular culture, computer technology and female emancipation.[1]

For all her awareness of the dilemmas of the intercultural life, Mukherjee (in an essay bearing the Ellisonian title "An Invisible Woman") has sharply lashed out against Canada's official multicultural policy, as holding no guarantee against the racist treatment of people like herself belonging to "visible minorities."[2] In her stories likewise she has sharply exposed the fallacy of Canada's reputation for tolerance but practice of racism. "Tamurlane" (from her 1985 book of short stories *Darkness*) is the poignant story of Gupta, a crippled Tandoori cook in a Toronto restaurant, which also serves as the hiding place for illegal aliens, who, seeking refuge from racial violence in Bombay or Uganda, find themselves exposed to equally rabid racism in Canada. When the restaurant is raided by the Canadian Mounted Police, Gupta, "an artist with fish and fowl," whose lameness is the result of racist mugging (he was thrown onto the Toronto subway tracks), as a legal resident of Canada violently resists arrest, only to find that his Canadian passport offers no protection against the bullets of Canada's official police.[3]

Mukherjee has recurrently expressed strongly ambivalent feelings about the very notion of exile. Thus, she has condemned, in both essays and stories, the comforting if "mordant bite" of exile and the "ironic aloofness" of the expatriate who avoids the "messiness of rebirth as an immigrant" but insists on "clutching the souvenirs of an ever-retreating past."[4] Instead she has exuberantly embraced the transformative possibilities of "immigration" which she associates with her removal from Canada to the U.S.:

> If I may put it in its harshest terms, it would be this: in Canada, I was frequently taken for a prostitute or shoplifter, frequently assumed to be a domestic, praised by astonished auditors that I didn't have a "sing-song" accent. The society itself ... routinely made crippling assumptions about me, and about my "kind." In the United States, however, I see *myself* in

---

[1] "A Four-hundred-year-old Woman," in *The Writer on Her Work*, ed. Janet Sternburg (New York: W.W. Norton, 1991), II, 33-38.
[2] "An Invisible Woman," *Saturday Night* (March 1981), 36-40.
[3] Bharati Mukherjee, *Darkness* (1985; New York: Fawcett Crest, 1992), 100-108.
[4] Bharati Mukherjee, "Immigrant Writing: Give Us Your Maximalists!" *New York Times Book Review*, August 28, 1988, 28-29.

those same outcasts; I see myself in an article on a Trinidad-Indian hooker; I see myself in the successful executive who slides Hindi film music in his tape deck as he drives into Manhattan; I see myself in the shady accountant who's trying to marry off his loose-living daughter; in professors, domestics, high school students, illegal busboys in ethnic restaurants. It's possible – with sharp ears and the right equipment – to hear America singing even in the seams of the dominant culture. In fact, it may be the best listening post for the next generation of Whitmans ....

I have joined imaginative forces with an anonymous, driven, underclass of semi-assimilated Indians with sentimental attachments to a distant homeland but no real desire for permanent return. I see my "immigrant" story replicated in a dozen American cities, and instead of seeing my Indianness as a fragile identity to be preserved against obliteration (or worse, a "visible" disfigurement to be hidden), I see it now as a set of fluid identities to be celebrated. I see myself as an American writer in the tradition of other American writers whose parents or grandparents had passed through Ellis Island. Indianness is now a metaphor, a particular way of partially comprehending the world. Though the characters in these stories are, or were, "Indian," I see most of these as stories of broken identities and discarded languages, and the will to bond oneself to a new community, against the ever-present fear of failure and betrayal. The book I dream of updating is no longer *A Passage to India* – it's *Call It Sleep*.[5]

Feeling that immigration allows for a postmodern fluidity of urban identity, Mukherjee may well be unusual in her exuberant celebration of the possibilities of Whitmanesque fusion, but she is unambivalent in her commitment to transformation, not preservation: "my investment is in the American reality, not the Indian. I look on ghettoization – whether as a Bengali or as a hyphenated Indo-American in North America – as a temptation to be surmounted."[6] She is, likewise, uniquely sharp in her rejection of "the smothering tyranny of nostalgia," and in her fiction she shows us characters struggling, not always successfully, against the "tyranny of nostalgia" as they find themselves caught in the slippery amphibian realm between two cultures in the city. Thus, in a magnificent (and very Malamudian) story called "Nostalgia" – also from *Darkness*, and subsequently reprinted in *The Penguin Book of the City* (1997)[7] – Dr. Patel, a successful Indian psychiatrist at Queen's mental hospital in

---

[5] Mukherjee, *Darkness*, xiv-xv.
[6] "A Four-hundred-year-old Woman," 33.
[7] *Darkness,* 82-99, reprinted in *The Penguin Book of the City*, ed. Robert Drewe (Harmondsworth: Penguin, 1997), 300-18.

New York, begins to suffer under the combined strains of assimilatio-nism, an intercultural marriage and the recurrent experience of being attacked as "Paki scum" by his mental patients. Though he claims to be impervious to nostalgia, has made an American success (a luxurious home, a son at Andover and a Porsche) and become a millionaire by Indian standards, he is more deeply attached to his Indian background than he realizes: he still maintains a condominium in Delhi and in moments of crisis retains his belief in the miraculous interventions of the gods in the lives of mere mortals. The nostalgic attachment becomes his undoing when, in a mixed moment of "regret filtered through longing," he falls for the seductive charms of a beautiful young Indian woman, whom he spots in a store in "Little India," only to find himself framed and blackmailed by her uncle who needs a visa for an illegally resident relative. In vintage Malamudian fashion Dr. Patel suffers the wryly ironic twists of his intercultural fate.

Clark Blaise has likewise explored the cross-cultural ironies of dislocation and identity. In his book *Resident Alien* (1986) he has confessed to an obsession with self and place ("not just the whoness and whatness of identity, but the *whereness* of who and what I am"[8]) and for him, as for Mukherjee, urban localities have proved particularly slippery and treacherous zones of exile. In "A Class of New Canadians," one of his most frequently anthologized short stories, the American Norman Dyer, "semi-permanent, semi-political exile" in French-speaking Montreal, prides himself on being a connoisseur of the aesthetic splendor of the city: Blaise' treatment of his character's alienated, superficial understanding of the city's picturesque facade is rife with irony:

> Norman Dyer hurried down Sherbrooke Street, collar turned against the snow. "Superb!" he muttered, passing a basement gallery next to a French bookstore. Bleached and tanned women in furs dashed from hotel lobbies into waiting cabs. Even the neon clutter of the side streets and the honks of slithering taxis seemed remote tonight through the peaceful snow. *Superb*, he thought again, waiting for a light and backing from a slushy curb: a word reserved for wines, cigars, and delicate sauces; he was feeling superb this evening. After eighteen months in Montreal he still found himself freshly impressed by everything he saw ....
> Since leaving graduate school and coming to Montreal, he had sampled every ethnic restaurant downtown and in the old city, plus a few Levantine places out in Outremont. He had worked on conversational

---

8   Clark Blaise, *Resident Alien* (Markham, Ontario: Penguin Books Canada, 1986), 2.

French and mastered much of the local dialect, done reviews for local papers, translated French-Canadian poets for Toronto quarterlies, and tweaked his colleagues for not sympathizing enough with Quebec separatism. He attended French performances of plays he had ignored in English, and kept a small but elegant apartment near a colony of *émigré* Russians just off Park Avenue. Since coming to Montreal he'd witnessed a hold-up, watched a murder, and seen several riots. When stopped on the street for directions, he would answer in French or accented English .... [9]

Dyer's is the estranged spectator's aloofness, whose perception of the city barely penetrates behind or below its kaleidoscopic (and mostly bilingual) facade. Gazing into the window of exclusive men's shops, he is impressed by "the authority of simple good taste" (277) of clothes he could not afford to buy, but, dressed as he is in department store clothes, feels that he is as yet unworthy to embrace this summit of cultural elegance and assimilation. Teaching English as a foreign language to evening students at McGill, a job that as a recent PhD he knows is beneath him, he yet feels like Joyce in Triest and Nabokov in Berlin, "an omniscient, benevolent god" (278), self-enamored and patronizing, as he parcels out mastery of English to his multicultural body of students, exposing their ignorance of the language by reading them impenetrable samples of Faulknerian rhetoric. Dyer's supposition that Canada is by far superior as a culture and a nation to the imperialist and politically corrupt United States, and that mastery of English is the prerequisite to social and cultural success in multicultural Canada, is punctured by the remainder of the story, when he discovers to his horror that most of his pupils – a kaleidoscopic assortment of Greek, German, Russian, Hebrew, Polish, Spanish and French speaking immigrants – barely need English in their jobs, are absolutely insensitive to his political motives for preferring Canada to the U.S., and mostly look upon Montreal as a "site of passage" on their way to a real job in the U.S.. Deathblow to his assumptions (and his sense of Anglophone cultural superiority) is delivered by the Spanish Miguel Mayor, who to his horror not only tells him "Montreal is big port like Barcelona. Everybody mixed together and having no money. It's just a place to land, no?" (282), but is fated to acquire a good job in America on the basis of an application letter in hopelessly deficient English. Further, as a living denial of Dyer's belief

---

[9]   Clark Blaise, "A Class of New Canadians," in *A North American Education* (1973), reprinted in *The New Oxford Book of Canadian Short Stories in English*, selected by Margaret Atwood and Robert Weaver (Toronto: Oxford University Press, 1997), 277.

that one cannot lay claim to social and material success without the proper degree of cultural and linguistic assimilation, the Spaniard is dressed as if he had just walked out of the most expensive and tasteful men's shop in Montreal.

With relentless irony Blaise exposes the fallacy of the assumption of Anglophone cultural and linguistic hegemony in a new multicultural urban reality of Canada. He has implicitly underlined the degree to which the city of Montreal is a multilingual city filled with voices that no longer will be subservient to an English mother tongue.

Such themes are explored with much greater depth and complexity in Michael Ondaatje's superb city novel about Toronto, *In the Skin of a Lion* (1987). Though it is focused on the building of Toronto in the 1920s and 1930s, the novel offers us a decidedly contemporary postmodern perspective on the city as a contested terrain of conflicting voices, signs and communities. Ondaatje offers us a highly poeticized and richly metaphoric novel, in which the strongly foregrounded language ranges through a variety of discourses, from the starkly realistic to the highly sensuous and lyrical. Weaving together facts and fictions about the Toronto world of city-builders – architects, financiers, commissioners, laborers – the novel unfolds a rich tapestry of fragmented images and vignettes which conjointly depict the lives of city workers, while simultaneously it offers us a compelling meditation on the problems of urban representation (literary, historical, iconographic, epistemological, political). Thus the novel had best been seen as a piece of "historiographic metafiction" (in Linda Hutcheon's well-known phrase[10]), a self-referential act of literary and historiographical revisionism, in which Ondaatje seeks to do poetic justice to the anonymous masses of laborers who actually built the city, but whose historical contributions have mostly gone unrecorded; their lives have remained unwritten, they have remained silent in the public record of the city, without a voice in official urban historiography. Taking his cue from the American photographer Lewis Hine, Ondaatje highlights the gap between official and secret history and speculates:

> Official histories and news stories were always soft as rhetoric, like that of a politician making a speech after a bridge is built, a man who does not even cut the grass on his own lawn. Hine's photographs betray

---

[10] See Linda Hutcheon, *The Canadian Postmodern: A Study of Contemporary English-Canadian Fiction* (Toronto: Oxford University Press, 1988), 61-77.

official history and put together another family. The man with the
pneumatic drill on the Empire State Building in the fog of stone dust, a
tenement couple, breaker boys in the mines. His photographs are rooms
one can step into – cavernous buildings where a man turns a wrench the
size of his body, or caves of iron where the white faces give the young
children working there the terrible look of ghosts .... Official histories,
news stories, surround us daily, but the events of art reach us too late,
travel languorously like messages in a bottle.[11]

Like Hine, Ondaatje offers us a kaleidoscope of images, fragments and
signs which together pay poetic tribute to the hordes of workers whose
skilled labor, perseverance, self-sacrifice and heroism built two of
Toronto's city landmarks: the Bloor Street Viaduct and the Toronto
Waterworks. In doing so Ondaatje highlights, in what appears a
poeticized and aestheticized version of Upton Sinclair's *The Jungle*, the
death-defying acrobatics of the bridge workers, the unspeakable labor
conditions in the tunnels and the tanneries – in the process fully
humanizing the anonymous individuals, highlighting the artistry of their
skills and the heroic endurance of their silent lives filled with the risks of
accidents, disease and death through slow and unsuspected self-
poisoning:

> Dye work took place in the courtyards next to the warehouse. Circular
> pools had been cut into the stone – into which the men leapt waist-deep
> within the reds and ochres and greens, leapt in embracing the skins of
> recently slaughtered animals. In the round wells four-foot in diameter
> they heaved and stomped, ensuring the dye went solidly into the pores of
> the skin that had been part of a live animal the previous day. And the
> men stepped out in colors up to their necks, pulling wet hides out after
> them so it appeared they had removed the skin from their own bodies ....
> they had consumed the most evil smell in history, they were consuming
> it now, flesh death, which lies in the vacuum between flesh and skin, and
> even if they never stepped into this pit again – a year from now they
> would burp up that odor .... they would die of consumption and at present
> they did not know it .... Nobody could last in that job more than six
> months and only the desperate took it. There were other jobs such as
> water boys and hide-room laborers. In the open cloisters were the
> sausage and fertilizer makers. Here the men stood, ankle-deep in salt,
> filling casings, squeezing out shit and waste from animal intestines ...

---

[11]   Michael Ondaatje, *In the Skin of a Lion* (New York: Alfred A. Knopf, 1987), 145-46.
Subsequent references are to this edition and appear parenthetically in the text.

For the dyers the one moment of superiority came in the showers at the end of the day. They stood under the hot pipes, not noticeably changing for two or three minutes – as if, like an actress unable to return to the real world from a role, they would be forever contained in that livid color, only their brains free of it. And then the blue suddenly dropped off, the color disrobed itself from the body, fell in one piece to their ankles, and they stepped out, in the erotica of being made free. (130-32)

The contrast between the public and secret history of the city is emblematized in the contrast between city Commissioner Harris, Toronto's head of Public Works, and Nicholas Temelcoff, recent Macedonian immigrant and anonymous construction worker on the bridge. Harris' place in official history is fully assured: he belongs to the powerful and visible. Indeed, the Bloor Street Viaduct is his first brain child: "Before the real city could be seen it had to be imagined, the way rumors and tall tales were a kind of charting," and Harris has envisioned the bridge as a majestic enterprise, carrying not just cars and trains, but water from the east to the center of the city. He likes to watch the unfinished bridge from a distance, at night, just the outlines showing: "Night removed the limitations of detail and concentrated on form." Needless to say, he barely knows the individual workers, observing them from afar. Later, Harris envisions the "mad scheme" of the Toronto Waterworks, "the palace of purification" which necessitates the digging of a water-intake tunnel underneath Lake Ontario and which is "orchestrated" by Harris as a private dream, an "immaculate fiction" which, in the middle of the depression years, necessitates extravagant expenditures. In response to the public outcry, Harris quotes Baudelaire: "The form of a city changes faster than the heart of a mortal."

> Harris had dreamed the marble walls, the copper-banded roofs. He pulled down Victoria Park and the essential temple swept up in its place, built on the slope towards the lake. The architect Pomphrey modeled its entrance on a Byzantine city gate, and the inside of the building would be an image of the ideal city. The brass railings curved up three flights like an immaculate fiction. The subtle splay on the tower gave it an Egyptian feel. Harris could *smell* the place before it was there, knew every image of it as well as his arms – west wing, east wing .... Harris imagined a palace for it. He wanted the best ornamental iron. He wanted a brass elevator to lead from the service building to the filter building where you could step out across rose-colored marble. The neo-Byzantine style

allowed him to blend in all the technical elements. The friezes depicted stylized impellers. He wanted herringbone tiles imported from Sienna, art deco clocks and pump signals, unfloored high windows which would look over filter pools four feet deep, languid, reflective as medieval water gardens ....

He had sent Goss and his photographers down but he had not entered the tunnels himself. He was a man who understood the continuity of the city, the daily consumptions of water, the speed of raw water through a filter bed, the journeys of chlorine and sulphur-dioxide to the island filtration plant, the 119 inspections by tugboats each year of the various sewer outfalls .... This was choreography in 1930.

In those photographs moisture in the tunnel appears white. There is a foreman's white shirt, there is white lye daubed onto rock to be dynamited. And all else is labor and darkness. Ash-grey faces. An unfinished world. The men work in the equivalent of the fallout of a candle .... (109-11)

As this passage serves to illustrate, Ondaatje imagines the workers doing their work mostly in silence, invisibility or darkness: by night or in early morning darkness, in impenetrable fog, or in barely lit tunnels.

One of the most memorable scenes in the novel occurs when Commissioner Harris, enjoying one of his nightly visits to the bridge, observes a group of five nuns inadvertently step onto the unfinished bridge in windy darkness. While the nighttime workers, tied to halters, stand by helplessly, one of the nuns is ballooned off the edge of the bridge, and Harris is left staring "along the mad pathway. This was his first child and already it had become a murderer." By sheer miracle, however, unknown and invisible to any on top of the bridge, the falling nun is intercepted in mid-air by a man swinging from a rope under the central arch of the bridge, an "immaculate" act of "grace" perpetrated by Nicholas Temelcoff, at the price of a broken arm hanging loose from its socket. Nicholas saves the nun (and she him) in one of the novel's beautiful scenes of magic; for both this will turn out to become a self-defining moment.

Ondaatje thus introduces us to workingman Temelcoff, whose artistry in skilled labor expresses itself in the miraculous and death-defying acrobatics he perpetrates as he habitually throws himself off the bridge ("like a diver over the edge of a boat"), timing his fall perfectly to prevent his rope from breaking (no bunjy-jumping this), to swing floating between the three hinges of the crescent-shaped bridge. His is a symbolic position: freely floating under the bridge, he does essential work in linking the different parts together, but works and rests mostly in solitary silence, and often in the invisibility of fog or darkness. Ondaatje underlines the significance of the fact that, though there are over 4,000 archive photographs of the bridge under construction, Temelcoff remains well-nigh invisible: "the eye must search along the wall of sky to the speck of burned paper that is him, an exclamation mark, somewhere in the distance between bridge and river" (34).

In the story of Macedonian immigrant Temelcoff Ondaatje plays a poeticized postmodern variation on the traditional immigrant novel, exploring the complex interplay of language and power; silence and visibility; voice, history and identity. Temelcoff is the representative laborer, one of the voiceless and mute, whose tale is articulated by the novel and who is thereby given voice, record and identity. Most of his fellow immigrants – Macedonians, Bulgarians, Poles and Lithuanians – lack the dominant English language, and have been given artificial English names (as foreign as numbers) by labor agents. Since in public places they are forbidden to speak their native tongues, they have literally and metaphorically been condemned to silence. In their immigrant neighborhoods, accordingly, they lay off their false names and greet each other in the streets by their true countries: "*Hey Italy! Hey Canada!*" Ondaatje's Toronto thus becomes a silent cacophony of oppressed languages, voices and identities, in which language (English) equals power, and in which, conversely, to be without language is to be voiceless is to be powerless. As Temelcoff realizes upon arrival: "If he did not learn the language he would be lost." Ondaatje gives us memorable images of how the immigrants seek to master English through imitating popular radio-singers (Temelcoff speaks in the idioms of Fats Waller) and through following actors' lines in the local theaters: at popular performances a low droning echo of immigrant voices from the audience would accompany the actors' lines – once when a leading actor dropped dead on the stage, a Sicilian butcher was ready to take over, flawlessly. Where Temelcoff mostly withdraws into a private "vault of secrets and memories," later in the novel he is "sewn" back into history (and personal identity) as he is given back the "pleasure of recall" and the flood of stories in himself is released, as he shyly begins to tell his wife the story of the nun on the bridge (149).

Just as, geographically, the novel depicts Toronto as a city of gaps and abysses that need to be linked by bridges and tunnels, so Ondaatje's city becomes a kaleidoscope of multiple and mostly disconnected linguistic communities, a city of separate sites and signs, of words and stories that remain fragmented and unconnected unless they are linked by an act of personal construction, and tenuous and highly provisional patterns and structures of meaning are made visible. Not coincidentally, the novel plays countless variations on metaphors of orchestration and choreography, the weaving into patterns of complex, fluid motions of music and dance.

The character given primary responsibility for spinning separate urban sites, signs and stories into a mode of provisional order is protagonist Patrick Lewis, who in this respect metaphorically serves as stand-in for author Ondaatje. Coming to Toronto from the Canadian countryside, the Anglo-Canadian Patrick is "an immigrant into the city," the exile who experiences the city as a transformative "site of passage": standing under the vast arches of Union Station he feels "new even to himself," "the past locked away," and he steps into "the quicksands of a new world" (53-54). In the city he is divested of his old self ("He spoke out his name and it struggled up in a hollow echo and was lost in the high air of Union Station"), and he sets to work as a "searcher" for Ambrose Small, the financier of the Bloor Street Viaduct also known as the "jackal of the Toronto business world," who has mysteriously disappeared. Small's case is one of several ironic reversals played by Ondaatje in the novel: a self-made millionaire very much in the forefront of public and recorded history, Small decides to drop out of history and becomes silent and invisible by choice and preference.

Patrick's, too, is a poignant case of ironic reversal, a typical postmodern irony: possessing the dominant language, he surrenders whatever power and privileges it can bring him, and willfully chooses to place himself in the immigrant's position of anonymity, alienation and "fluidity of identity" (to borrow Mukherjee's phrase): though, as one who has English, he realizes the power of language as a means of silencing and control, yet he takes his stance on solidarity with the poor, nameless and marginalized. As one of the laborers digging the tunnels he will not reveal his knowledge of English and is "as silent as the Italians and the Greeks to the bronco foremen." Going to live in the community of Macedonians and Bulgarians, the Anglo-Canadian Patrick chooses to be "their alien," and he cherishes the linguistic boundaries that surround him:

> The southeastern section of the city where he now lived was made up
> mostly of immigrants and he walked everywhere not knowing any

language he knew, deliriously anonymous. The people on the street, the Macedonians and Bulgarians, were his only mirror.

As slowly he is taken up into the immigrant neighborhood community, he gets to know it from within, joins in its political and theatrical activities, and shares its social ceremonies as, in a colorful mixture of languages and nationalities, its members spend the city summer nights sitting out on the fire-escapes of their tenement buildings and pass around a bottle of whiskey on a string. Patrick's access to the realities of the immigrants' lives is eased and speeded up when he becomes amorously involved with Alice, a political activist who has chosen the side of the ethnic workers and is committed to breaking through their silence and powerlessness through political mime theater. Ironically, but significantly, as an Anglo-Canadian Patrick finds himself a marginalized stranger in his own culture, his own history, and his own city. Obsessed by Alice he becomes a searcher into her past and finds her history deeply involved with that of the city: Alice, he discovers, is the nun who was swept off the bridge and saved by Temelcoff, to disappear from record and from history and to reemerge in different guise as a political activist among the Macedonians: she has exchanged the religious salvation of sisterhood for the political salvation of active solidarity with the anonymous urban ethnic immigrants. Researching her personal past in the Riverdale Library, Patrick thus spins together the disparate stories of Temelcoff, Alice, commissioner Harris, the building of the bridge, and the history of Toronto, realizing that in doing so he has in effect constructed his own identity. Where before he felt he was "nothing but a prism that refracted their lives," he now experiences a magic epiphany when, for a precarious moment, things fall into place and structure, and pattern and coherence are revealed: once again, Ondaatje's metaphor is of musical orchestration:

> Leaving the library, Patrick crossed Broadview Avenue and began walking east .... He took a step forward. Now he was walking slowly, approaching a street-band, and the click of his footsteps unconsciously adapted themselves to the music that began to surround him. The cornet and saxophone and drum chased each other across solos and then suddenly, as Patrick drew alongside them, fell together and rose within a chorus.
> He saw himself gazing at so many stories .... He walked on beyond the sound of the street musicians, aware once again of the silence between his individual steps, knowing now he could add music by

simply providing the thread of a hum. He saw the interactions, saw how each one of them was carried by the strength of something more than themselves.

If Alice has been a nun ...

The street-band had depicted perfect company, with an ending full of embraces after the solos had made everyone stronger, more delineated. His own life was no longer a single story but part of a mural, which was a falling together of accomplices. Patrick saw a wondrous night web – all of these fragments of a human order, something ungoverned by the family he was born into or the headlines of the day .... the detritus and chaos of the age was realigned. (144-45)

What Ondaatje offers here, I would suggest, is a complex image of multiple applicability: a metaphor of the novel, the city, history and identity in one. Just as Patrick for a magical moment perceives his personal history and identity as a falling into place of a "mural" of separate fragmented stories and images (a decidedly urban image), so Ondaatje presents the image of the city as a momentary weaving of multiple disparate elements, images, signs and stories into a "wondrous night web" – in which each individual particle remains separate and "solo" yet in which all elements together form a musical ensemble. The musical metaphor is crucial as (unlike the image of the mural) it suggests transience rather than permanence, temporality and process rather than stasis and space: only for as long as the musical performance (or the personal construction) lasts, can there be the complex dynamics of solo and ensemble, can there be the momentary perception of coherence and order, can the city be felt as a harmonious whole. Thus the city becomes truly a kaleidoscope: with each new wrench to the lens, a new constellation of meanings and images and signs reveals itself, lasting just so long as the person administering the instrument allows. Therefore every construction of the city as whole or harmonious can only be processual, highly tenuous and personal. For Ondaatje, far from a static "mosaic" (to borrow Canada's mythical national image) the city is a fluid zone of perpetually shifting sites and signs, multiple and incompatible, not to be subjected to a fixed or dominant discourse, but always in process of dissolution and reconstitution. And precisely here, the significance of art looms large:

> *Only the best art can order the chaotic tumble of events. Only the best can realign chaos to suggest both the chaos and order it will become.*

The first sentence of every novel should be: "Trust me, this will take time, but there is order here, very faint, very human." Meander if you want to get to town. (146)

Rather than offering us the aesthetic splendors of city skylines, aerial views on urban sites, or skyscraper perspectives on urban order and design, writers of the multicultural city are inclined to subvert the comfortable aloofness (and the semblance of order) implicit in such a stance, seeking instead to take us down into the city and confront us with the chaos and tumble of life in the inner city, the under-city of streets, canyons, urban vaults and abysses. A recent novel that allows us a rare glimpse into the world of "urban Indians" is Sherman Alexie's *Indian Killer* (1996), set in the Seattle of the 1990s. Unlike Ondaatje's aestheticized and poetically sculpted prose, Alexie offers us a brutally realistic treatment of urban life in flat, no-nonsense prose which aims at confrontation and discomfort, resistance and indignation. Alexie's Seattle is a city rife with ethnic strife and racial resentment, of fierce whitist hatred of Indians and equally fierce Indian hatred of whites (racially marked by "blue eyes"). As Reggie Polatkin, a mixed-blood Indian with blue eyes, who flees Seattle at the end of the novel, puts it: no matter to what new city he would turn, "he knew that every city was a city of white men."[12] Alexie offers us a dystopian vision of the city as an apocalyptic underworld, a place of terror, darkness, and random racist violence. Seattle is stalked by a serial killer who randomly selects his white victims, and leaves them scalped and horribly mutilated, their remains marked by two owl feathers, the signature of his Indian identity – though we are never unambiguously sure that the Indian killer may not be a non-Indian in disguise. Alexie hints that the killings might be a mode of historical retribution: the gruesome revenge for over five centuries of historical pain, murder and injustice suffered by Indians at the hands of whites:

The word spread quickly. Within a few hours, nearly every Indian in Seattle knew about the scalping. Most Indians believed it was all just racist paranoia, but a few felt a strange combination of relief and fear, as if an apocalyptic prophecy was just beginning to come true. (185)

---

[12] Sherman Alexie, *Indian Killer* (New York : Atlantic Monthly Press, 1996), 409. All subsequent references will be to this edition and will be given parenthetically in the text.

The Indian Killer sets in motion a spiral of racist violence raging through downtown Seattle: groups of all-American white boys, wearing ski-masks and armed with baseball bats, brutally bash defenseless homeless Indians, while groups of Indian men retaliate by brutalizing and terrorizing randomly picked white males, and re-enacting historical massacres in the streets of downtown Seattle – making tape-recordings of their cross-examinations of their white victims before gauging out their blue eyes, an ironic travesty of the white anthropologists' recordings of oral tribal culture.

In most recent Native American literature the city is the place Indians shy away from as the site of historical exile and alienation, the place where cultural dispossession is felt most bitterly and traumatically: salvation, if any, is to be found in a return to the reservation and the rediscovery of sustaining tribal roots, beliefs and ceremonies. For Alexie's urban Indians, however, the route back to tribalism seems definitely cut off – even a long-distance phone call to the reservation ironically miscarries. Like James Welch's contemporary Indians, who mostly find themselves in a dazed state of alienation, drenched in drugs or alcoholism and incapable of breaking out of immobility, Alexie's urban Indians find little in the way of redemption or consolation. The tragic hopelessness of their condition is represented by the novel's protagonist, an Indian of unidentified tribal affiliation who, immediately on his birth, is violently snatched away from his fourteen-year-old teenage Indian mother and adopted by a white couple who – what more ironic or unlikely name for an Indian? – name him John Smith. John grows up a gentle boy, who would not even hurt a spider, and becomes a silent and withdrawn construction worker on "the last skyscraper in Seattle," but the trauma of dispossession from his Indian heritage and identity seals John's fate: as the novel goes on, he can find no outlet for the "voices" and the "music" in his head which gradually assume hallucinatory proportions and mark his behavior as increasingly erratic and suspect: John cannot shed the thought that he must kill the white man responsible for his fate. Alexie's point seems clear: John's trauma of exile from his Native roots might well have made him (as indeed many a contemporary urban Indian) into an "Indian Killer." By the end of the novel John takes his predestined leap off the last skyscraper in Seattle to merge with the city pavement.

Paramount in the novel is the question of authentic Indian identity, a question riddled with ironic and even tragic ambiguities, precisely because, in a city like Seattle, Indianness turns out to be very much in vogue and in demand: the city teems with mostly white people seeking to embrace and even claiming Indian identity, and Alexie is mercilessly ironic about wannabe Indians like Dr. Clarence Mather, instructor of Native American literature at the University of Washington, or Jack Wilson, Tony Hillerman-like author of Indian detectives, who claims to be a real Indian (but isn't) and is at work on a novel in progress called *Indian Killer*. By contrast, those who are real Indians have often been waging a lifelong battle to suppress their Indian identity: in order to gain a mode of social acceptance and cultural survival they have had to force themselves into invisibility.

Indian Killer replays a number of motifs we have encountered in Ondaatje's book, but gives them an ugly ethnic, racial twist: like Temelcoff, John Smith is a daredevil construction worker, engaged in dangerous acrobatics on the fortieth floor of the last skyscraper in Seattle. But where Ondaatje highlights the grace and artistry of Temelcoff's derring-do, John has twisted dreams of dangling his blue-eyed foreman over the edge of the fortieth floor and is convinced his safety harness, designed as it is by white men, "would only save white men. The leather, metal, and rope could tell the difference between white skin and Indian skin." (76) Urban Indians, like the workers in Ondaatje's book, mostly have been erased from public record or history; the murder of a homeless Indian woman, Beautiful Mary, found smashed to smithereens behind a dumpster, not only goes uninvestigated but remains unrecorded in the police precinct. Like Temelcoff, John mostly works in silence and invisibility, but where Ondaatje allows Temelcoff the restoration of voice, no such salvation is granted John: the victim of a racist world, his tragic fate relentlessly fulfills itself. The only way out of invisibility, the implication seems to be, is to go the way of the Indian Killer, who perpetrates his gruesome acts "silently singing an invisibility song" (152).

Perhaps the most compelling dimension of *Indian Killer* is the poignant portrait it offers of downtown Seattle's large contingent of homeless urban Indians, habitually gathered beneath the Alaskan Way Viaduct, or in the old historic Pioneer Park. Alexie takes us into their midst through the figure of Marie Polatkin, a radical Indian activist and a sharply tongued student at the University of Washington, and one of the most successful character creations in the book. Marie's acts are fueled by anger and resentment against white society, but she is also capable of compassion and grace: she knows that beneath political ideology lies the bottom line of hunger ("nothing good happens to a person on an empty stomach") and, as a volunteer worker at a shelter for the homeless, she habitually parcels out food in a battered white van: a welcome and familiar sight to the homeless, she is known to them as the Sandwich Lady, a figure of grace and consolation, who offers them "proof they were not invisible." For Marie, Indians are the archetypal homeless, and vice versa:

> she believed that homeless people were treated as Indians had always been treated. Badly. The homeless were like an Indian tribe, nomadic and powerless, just filled with more than any tribe's share of crazy people and cripples. So, a homeless Indian belonged to two tribes, and was the lowest form of life in the city. (146)

By taking us down into their world of hopelessness and hunger, of malnutrition, incurable disease and erratic mental illness, of "cardboard condominiums" and sleepless nights spent in doorways or over heating vents outside city hall, of habitual brutalization and arrest, Alexie offers us a gallery of fully humanized and individualized characters, restoring to them names and faces and personal histories, giving them voice and visibility. At most, Alexie errs on the side of benevolence: hardly any of his homeless Indians consumes alcohol or uses drugs, and some of them have the gift of articulating ironic truths that may help them to survive; as one of them, an old woman named Carlotta Lott, puts it:

> "All these white people think I'm homeless. But I ain't homeless. I'm Duwamish Indian. You see all this land around here .... All of this, the city, the water, the mountains, it's all Duwamish land. Has been for thousands of years. I belong here, cousin. I'm the landlady. And all these white people, even the rich ones living up in those penthouses, they're the real homeless ones. Those long people are a long way from home, don't you think? Long way from E-u-r-o-p-e." (251-52)

Police officer Peone, too, though not over given to tenderness, is touched by John's erratic behavior (he has found him kneeled on the streets singing Latin church songs) and ponders the plight of the homeless, so many of whom are plagued by mental problems:

> Officer Peone looked at John and wondered which mental illness he had. The Seattle streets were filled with the mostly crazy, half-crazy, nearly crazy, and soon-to-be-crazy. Indian, white, Chicano, Asian, men,

women, children. The social workers did not have anywhere near enough money, training, or time to help them. The city government hated the crazies because they were a threat to the public image of the urban core. Private citizens ignored them at all times of the year except for the few charitable days leading up to and following Christmas. In the end, the police had to do most of the work. Police did crisis counseling, transporting them howling to detox, the dangerous to jail, racing the sick to the hospitals, to a safer place. At the academy, Officer Peone figured he would be fighting bad guys. He did not imagine he would spend most of his time taking care of the refuse of the world. Peone found it easier when the refuse were all nuts or dumb-ass drunks, harder when they were just regular folks struggling to find their way off the streets. (362-63)

At the end of the novel John Smith is saved from brutalization by three white boys by Marie, the Sandwich Lady, in conjunction with six homeless Indians, men and women (again carefully individualized by Alexie), who for all they have been through somehow miraculously find the courage to go on fighting and who still find sustenance in the precarious thread of Indianness which holds them together. None such salvation, however, is granted the tragically exiled urban Indian John, who remains without language, voice or grace, "just a husk drifting into a desert wind."

SANDRA CISNEROS: CROSSING BORDERS

MARY A. McCAY

Sandra Cisneros speaks in a slight, high voice, almost like a child's. Her size and demeanor strengthen the impression of youth and naivity. In her thirties she still appears to be an adolescent playing at being an adult. Initial impressions, however, are dispelled when she reads her own work. *My Wicked Wicked Ways* (1992), a book of poems that carries the weight of Chicana experience, belies her little girl appearance. What might be taken for adolescent rebelliousness and exuberance is, instead, a Chicana way of speaking, a lilting cadence that is almost a song. When she begins to read, Cisneros turns into a fiercely independent woman whose experiences in Chicago, in the barrios of Texas, and in the not always welcoming halls of academe are transformed in her poetry and stories into rich observations about life in America. The poems peel back the layers of everyday moments, looking for a kernel of truth often encrusted by stereotypes of race, class, and gender that render the women from her community voiceless. In all her books, Cisneros charts the experience of love turned to exploitation, the ordeal of large families hiding some children so the landlord will not evict them, the hazard of being a woman used up by marriage, the history of always living in an alien land and of trying to find ways to cross borders. She is anything but silent, and she could hardly be called naive.

The preface poem to *My Wicked Wicked Ways*, with an epitaph from Mary Cassatt – "I can live alone and I love to work"[1] – signals Cisneros' gauntlet to mainstream writers that she too has a claim to authorship. She might not be Virginia Woolf's typical woman writer who will flourish with a room of her own and five hundred pounds a year, but she is laying claim to the right to write. Virginia Woolf's vision of the woman writer must, Cisneros insists, be expanded to include women of different races and classes. Until the voices from the margins are heard, women's writing will continue to be cramped

---

[1] Sandra Cisneros, *My Wicked Wicked Ways* (New York: Random House, 1992), ix. All subsequent references are to this edition and are given parenthetically in the text.

by class and race boundaries – borders that Cisneros insists people
cross. The image of the working woman living alone is extremely
important for Cisneros because in that picture is part of the struggle of
her own childhood, while in her insistence on space she does pay
some homage to Virginia Woolf. How does a girl with six brothers
find a place of her own? That question is partly answered in *The
House on Mango Street* (1989) and in several of Cisneros' poems
about her family and her neighborhood.

Cisneros is also aware, however, that simply having a room of her
own – almost a physical impossibility, while her family certainly
never had the equivalent of Woolf's five hundred pounds a year –
would not confer on her the class and ethnic privileges of
Shakespeare's family. It certainly would not make her experience
comparable to Shakespeare's precisely because money and a room of
her own could not give her the experience of Shakespeare's class and
ethnic group. While that might seem obvious to us today, for Cisneros
it is an important observation because she had to wrest it from
predominantly white writing programs at Loyola University in
Chicago and at the University of Iowa.

The expectations for women, especially for poor Latino women,
and for Cisneros herself, are very different from the self-perceived
goals and desires that run through the writing of middle-class white
women in America and Europe. Many of those women were, indeed,
the first to announce that women's experience needed to be given
voice, but it took African-American women and Latino women to
point out what Audre Lorde warns in *Sister Outsider*: we must not
claim one experience for all women, nor should we pretend to "a
homogeneity of experience covered by the word sisterhood that does
not in fact exist."[2] Sisterhood does not mean sameness, and Cisneros
very clearly highlights the difference between her experience in
America and typical Anglo experience. The differences among
women, especially those created by race and class, are the very
differences that Cisneros herself has experienced and writes about,
and her writing challenges the dominant culture in America, both male
and female, to recognize those differences.

She herself first recognized the difference while in a writing
seminar at the University of Iowa. "It wasn't," she said, "as if I didn't

---

[2] Quoted in Nancy Corson Carter, "Claiming the Bittersweet Matrix: Alice Walker,
Sandra Cisneros, and Adrienne Rich," *Critique: Studies in Contemporary Fiction*,
35/4 (Summer 1995), 195.

know who I was. I knew I was a Mexican woman."[3] What she had not known before was that she should have been writing about that experience, rather than trying to write in the same voice as her classmates. At that moment, *The House on Mango Street* began to take shape, and Cisneros found her voice.

It is the voice of women on the borders that emerges in a group of Latino writers who challenge the social and political forces which, in America, seek to suppress racial and class difference in an attempt at color and class blindness, especially among women writers who want to present a united front to the world. Indeed, that suppression, that claim to a commonality of women's experience, is a form of blindness. It is not a blindness that treats everybody as if color or class did not matter; rather, it is one that does not see a person who is not of the dominant race and class and does not understand the experiences on the margins.

Writers such as Denise Chavez, Ana Castillo, and Sandra Cisneros all look at the lives of Latino women and challenge not only the dominant culture, but the dominant form of expression privileged in that culture: the traditional modernist novel of growth, the *Bildungsroman*. In fact, so hostile are many of the Latino women writers to the male novel of adventure and growth that they not only challenge those experiences, but also write about them in forms that challenge the linear development of those types of stories.

Denise Chavez' *Last of the Menu Girls* (1986) emphasizes the importance of oral culture in the creation of fiction. Her technique forces readers to look beyond the literature of high culture to the place where creativity begins – among the women. Chavez transcribes orally transmitted stories into print form and, in doing so, privileges the voices of the streets and the barrios. In the *Last of the Menu Girls*, Chavez creates a cycle of seven highly dramatic stories dealing, much as Cisneros does in *The House on Mango Street*, with the onset of adolescence when young girls in the barrio must learn their place and prepare for their roles in the community. It is the other women in the family who teach girls how to become wives and mothers, the women their men will accept. The matrilineal power is important to the adolescent narrators of both books, but there is in that power the threat that all young girls will be confined and formed by the expectations of

---

[3]   Pilar Rodriguez-Aranda, "On the Solitary Fate of Being Mexican, Female, Wicked and Thirty-three: An Interview with Writer Sandra Cisneros," *The Americas Review*, 18/1 (Spring 1990), 65.

their culture. It is a conflict that Cisneros knows well, and Chavez sees in that struggle the tension within Latino culture. Men are privileged, and their power, instead of strengthening the community and giving it a voice outside the barrio, is turned against the women within their own community.

Ana Castillo's *The Mixquiahuala Letters* (1986) also looks at the ways women are treated in the barrio. Her book opens up other ways to create fiction, mixing imaginary and ethnographic writing. Her text negotiates the terrain between the ethnographer (usually male, usually from another culture, and usually filled with cultural prejudices) and the feminist writer who challenges all the ethnographic stereotypes of Latino culture. Castillo sees the ethnographer's study of male and female rituals in Latino culture as a way of keeping that culture weak. If the rituals that empower men disempower the women and if those rituals serve to oppress women generation after generation, it becomes difficult, if not impossible, to look at the damage being done to the group from the outside; it is being debilitated from within, and not only the women suffer from that debilitation.

Like Cisneros' writing, the cycles of stories of Chavez and Castillo are, in their marginality, places of experimentation, places where alternative visions develop, and places where political innovation and cultural creativity take place. They also happen to be places where women have a very strong voice. That voice is best expressed in Esperanza of Sandra Cisneros' *The House on Mango Street.*

The forty-five succinct stories in Cisneros' cycle range from one to five pages in length and are all narrated by Esperanza, a young girl whose name means hope, but also, as she tells her readers, "sadness" and "waiting" in Spanish.[4] Esperanza, in her desire to write and to leave Mango Street, transforms the street from "a patriarchal, ethnic minority prison into a vehicle of success within a dominant culture."[5] The girl's voice dominates and controls experience, even when that experience is painful or damaging to her. Her voice insists that women have a place on Mango Street, and she rejects the idea that they should be silent. By writing, Cisneros gives all the silent women a voice:

---

[4]   Sandra Cisneros, *The House on Mango Street* (New York: Vintage Books, 1989), 10. All subsequent references are to this edition and are given parenthetically in the text.

[5]   Carter, "Claiming the Bittersweet Matrix," 199.

My stories are dedicated to women. They are stories from my mother and from other working-class women in the barrio. They are stories I lived and stories my students lived, the stories of voiceless women.[6]

Cisneros finds in the stories of Mango Street a way to talk to Anglos and still retain her own voice; she also finds a way to escape the confining world of the barrio. Esperanza tells her friend Alicia: "No, this isn't my house I say .... I don't belong. I don't ever want to come from here" (106). Esperanza equates her dream house with her stories, her writing. It is a house "quiet as snow, a space for myself to go, clean as paper before the poem" (108). It is the writing that will take her away from the cramped, too small house that was, for her parents, a real achievement. It is also the "room of her own" that will allow her to write. Like others before her, Esperanza dreams of larger things than her parents can afford, and, by dint of the hard work she extols in the stories, she will achieve her dream. She claims for herself the American promise that hard work will bring success. More importantly, it will also bring escape.

Those promises of success and escape are tested by her own culture. The women of her world are not supposed to leave home except to marry and bear children, but Esperanza is like the great-grandmother for whom she was named. Her ancestor was born in "the Chinese year of the horse – which is supposed to be bad luck if you're born female – but I think this is a Chinese lie because the Chinese, like the Mexicans, don't like their women strong" (10). Esperanza, even as a young girl, recognizes her strength and realizes that it can cause her trouble. Her great-grandmother is more than a namesake; she is a warning:

> [She was] a wild horse of a woman, so wild she wouldn't marry. Until my great-grandfather threw a sack over her head and carried her off .... and the story goes she never forgave him. She looked out the window her whole life, the way so many women sit .... Esperanza. I have inherited her name, but I don't want to inherit her place by the window. (11)

Esperanza's grandmother is one of the *Mujeres* to whom the book is dedicated; they are women Cisneros loves, but they are women she

---

6 Bonnie Britt, "On Literature, Writer Sandra Cisneros Sees Power," *Houston Chronicle*, June 24, 1984, 5.

must also leave to their own fates in order to insure her own. In those women Cisneros says she was looking for power, but many of them have lost it. Esperanza must continue to search for her own strength.

Esperanza is much like Cisneros herself. Her childhood was also one lived in a Puerto Rican neighborhood in Chicago; she too told herself, "I've got to get out of here." Cisneros also writes of the working class women of the barrio, the women she knew when she was a child, and she gives voice to their experience:

> I knew if I wrote about the flat where we lived on top of a laundromat in Chicago, other writers couldn't touch it. They didn't know the language I grew up in.[7]

Cisneros also saw how little people of the dominant culture saw her people. Male and female, they were consigned to menial jobs, ignored until there became too many of them, and then they were chased away. Chicago did have the virtue of being large enough and far enough away from the borders so that Mexicans and other Latinos were not feared as they have become in parts of Texas and California. Chicago also created spaces for Latinos to live, hide, and work. Cisneros is aware of the very fragility of any success in the barrio, whether it be in Chicago or in Los Angeles, but she is also aware how threatened the men of the barrio are by the success of their own women. When a woman insists on her chance, there is often male resentment and anger, and that can turn to violence within the community.

That element of violence is strongly etched in *The House on Mango Street*. Cisneros gives sharply focused, clear-eyed attention to the way men treat women. Scenes of patriarchal and sexual violence are not glossed over. The adolescent Esperanza challenges the control of women through violence. She sees a woman locked in her house by her husband to insure her virtue; she sees a daughter brutally beaten by her father. Esperanza herself is raped, and all the women's lives are appropriated by the men in their families. Sally, Esperanza's friend, is an example of this appropriation. Beautiful, she is often kept home from school by her father because, as he says, "to be beautiful is trouble" (81). Esperanza speaks for Sally when she asks,

---

[7]   *Ibid.*, 5.

"Sally, do you sometimes wish you didn't have to go home? Do you wish your feet would one day keep walking and take you far away from Mango Street, far away." (82)

The sadness of that dream of walking away is seen in what happens to Sally: she "got married like we knew she would, young and not ready but married just the same." While Sally claims she is happy, Esperanza's observations show a different reality. Sally's husband, like Sally's father, imprisons her. He will not let her

talk on the telephone. And he doesn't let her look out the window. And he doesn't like her friends, so nobody goes to visit her unless he is working.

Sally moves from the brutality of her father's house to the brutality of her husband's house, and "she looks at all the things they own: the towels and the toaster, the alarm clock and the drapes" (101-102). Despite her comfortable circumstances, she is still the woman controlled by the man who buys her the domestic goods that imprison her.

Esperanza, too, is brutalized by a man who says, "I love you, Spanish girl," and then rapes her. The romantic notion of love is brutally destroyed: "his dirty fingernails against my skin, ... his sour smell. I couldn't do anything but cry" (100). The brutality that lurks beneath the relationships between men and women on Mango Street, and the ways in which women and young girls cope with that violence, signal that Cisneros is not simply drawing portraits of women as victims. Certainly Sally and Rafaela, another beautiful, dutiful daughter, are victimized by men who fear their beauty and who know well how other men behave because they behave that way themselves, but Esperanza will not be victimized. She recognizes, as she is being raped, that Sally has lied. What happens to her is not love, and she will not accept the role or be silent about the brutality. Her telling is encouraged by an invalid aunt, trapped by her infirmity on Mango Street. She warns Esperanza:

"You just remember to keep writing, Esperanza. You must keep writing. It will keep you free." (61)

Cisneros freed herself; she left Chicago, and Esperanza leaves Mango Street, but she knows that what other women tell her is true:

> When you leave you must remember to come back for the others. A circle, understand. You will always be Esperanza. You will always be Mango Street. (105)

Cisneros left Chicago to become a writer, but with each story, poem, and book, she returns to the heart of her community and gives her people voice. The voice she wants to be heard is one that she spoke of in an interview when talking about Esperanza: "We're raised with a Mexican culture that has two role models [for women]: La Malinche y la Virgen de Guadalupe. And you know that's a hard route to go, one or the other, there's no in-betweens."[8] If a Chicana woman chooses a role model other than one of the two allowed, she is betraying her culture, and that, says Cisneros, "is a horrible life to live." Of women like herself she says:

> We're always straddling two countries and we're always living in that kind of schizophrenia that I call, being a Mexican woman living in an American society, but not belonging to either culture.[9]

The machisma that she flaunts in her poetry and in some of her stories is a way of both criticizing her world and insisting on her place in it. A woman must have more options. A woman must have power.

It is not just giving voice to women trapped someplace between Mexican and American culture that makes Cisneros' fiction ethnographically interesting. She also finds a space between prose and poetry that melds English and Spanish into an almost new language. She crosses linguistic borders, and she crosses the borders of genre to capture what Latinos have brought to America. She blurs language, genre, and roles in order to find a voice for herself. In finding the way to say what her experience is – as a Latina in America, as a woman in a house and a culture full of men, and as a poet in the land of prose – she creates a new poetic self.

Her two books of poetry, collections at once funny, raucous, and deadly serious, shout several declarations of independence: from the stereotypical Chicana that white America expects her to be, from the good girl her father expects her to be, from the silent woman Latino

---

[8]   Pilar Rodriguez-Aranda, "On the Solitary Fate of Being Mexican, Female, Wicked and Thirty-three," 65.
[9]   *Ibid.*, 66.

men expect her to be, and from the woman the world expects her to be. In *My Wicked Wicked Ways* Cisneros, in a series of bad girl poems, confesses her sins, but does so largely tongue-in-cheek:

> My first felony – I took up with poetry.
> For this penalty, the rice burned.
> Mother warned I'd never wife.

There is an exuberance to the freedom the writer feels as she tests her voice and her naughtiness.

> Wife? A woman like me
> whose choice was rolling pin or factory.
> An absurd vice, this wicked wanton
> writer's life. (x)

Being a writer certainly frees the woman from the working-class world that would allow her only two roles: that of wife or that of factory worker. She escaped from the life "my father'd plucked for me." But that leaves the question: "What does a woman / willing to invent herself ... do?" (xi).

Cisneros invents herself through the poems in *My Wicked Wicked Ways* and *Loose Woman* (1994). Citing a line from Maxine Hong Kingston – "Isn't a bad girl almost like a boy?" – Cisneros opens the title section of *My Wicked Wicked Ways*. In "Six Brothers," a poem for her own siblings (she was the only girl with six brothers), she looks at Grimm's fairy tale of the six swans, enchanted brothers whose sister weaves magic shirts to turn them back into men. The girl completes the task except for the left sleeve of the youngest brother's shirt, and he returns with one swan's wing. That wing-like appendage on the youngest brother is a sign of the girl's failure. Despite her success with saving the five other brothers complete and whole, she is charged with the damage done to the sixth. That poem is a reminder of her own family because "Cisneros" means "swan," and because Chicana girls are always responsible for their brothers, no matter what the problem.

Cisneros' past, the family back in Mexico, is unknown to the writer except the story of the distant cousin who shot his wife, but she remembers her "mother's brother who shot himself. / Then there's us – seven ways to make the name or break it" (25). In her brothers her father plans a doctor, a musician, an athlete, a genius, an administrator, and finally, one son to take the business over, but for Sandra there is no job. The sons keep to the master plan,

> the lovely motion of tradition.
> Appearances are everything.
> We live for each other's expectations.

Cisneros sees her brother and muses: "I've got the bad blood in me I think, / the mad uncle, the bit of the bullet." Not only does her father have no plans for her (those plans having been written on her sex), but she finds herself trapped, earthbound as her brothers soar. Further, the youngest brother is a problem, and Cisneros sees that as the family judgment on her. As the speaker, the sister in the poem, looks at her six brothers, she says:

> My six brothers, graceful, strong.
> Except for you, little one-winged,
> finding it as difficult as me
> to keep the good name clean. (26)

Implicit in the description "little one-wing," is Cisneros' recognition of the responsibility placed on the girl. If the brother turns out badly, it will be because of the failure of the sister. While the poem contains a germ of sibling collusion, there is more responsibility and a longing to escape the female's responsibility for the men in her family.

But the poet, while understanding the things that keep her earthbound, does soar in her own way, in a way that her culture might find strange and disrespectful of the family. She writes, she takes lovers, and she insists on her independence. In "For a Southern Man," she declares:

> I've learned two things.
> To let go
> clean as kite string.
> And to never wash a man's clothes.
> These are my rules. (64)

Clearly, the poet lives by those rules, and the independence she has gained has sharpened her tongue and her pen. She does not seek absolution for the sin of being a bad girl, an independent woman; rather, she flaunts her badness, her difference.

In *Loose Woman*, her second volume of poetry, Cisneros takes the bad girl of *My Wicked Wicked Ways* one step further; she becomes the loose woman of the volume, and the title poem challenges anyone who would suppress her rebellion:

> They say I'm a beast.
> And feast on it. When all along
> I thought that's what a woman was.
>
> They say I'm a bitch.
> Or witch. I've claimed
> the same and never winced.[10]

She accepts that she is

> … a *macha*, hell on wheels,
> *viva-la-vulva*, fire and brimstone,
> man-hating, devastating,
> boogey woman lesbian.
> Not necessarily,
> but I like the compliment. (112)

She is a woman who will not be ruled or contained by labels or by social stigma, nor will she comply with custom or tradition. Let the men in her family do that. She insists:

> By all accounts I am
> a danger to society.
> I'm Pancha Villa. (113)

What Cisneros does in her poetry, and in the vignettes that slither back and forth between poetry and prose, is start a revolution for Chicana women. Like Pancho Villa, she, the Pancha Villa, calls for revolution, calls for freedom, and insists on selfhood and on womanhood. In the poem "Down There" Cisneros graphically describes what it means for her to be a woman who scratches herself where women are not supposed to scratch. Her poem "[p]icked up words that / snapped like bra straps." The poet

---

[10] Sandra Cisneros, *Loose Woman* (New York: Alfred A. Knopf, 1994), 112. All subsequent references are to this edition and are given parenthetically in the text.

Learned words that ignite
of their own gas
like a butt hole flower.
Fell in love with words
that thudded like stones and sticks.
Or stung like fists.
Or stank like shit
gorillas throw at zoos.

What Cisneros is seeking is a "poem [that] never washes / its hands after using the can" (80).

Cisneros insists on her own sexuality. She said in an interview with Pilar Rodriguez-Aranda:

> I don't see anything wrong as long as I'm in control of my sexuality. I like feeling sexy. Of course it's a kind of tongue-in-cheek pose, too.

Cisneros is able to laugh at herself as the persona of one of her poems wets toilet paper into balls so she can throw them up and have them stick on the ceiling. But there is also a deadly serious element to her work. She sees in Esperanza a girl who wants to get out of the barrio because it is dangerous for women; it is not Sesame Street, Cisneros maintained in the same interview, and it should not be romanticized as such:

> Poor neighborhoods lose their charm after dark .... if you've got to live there every day, and deal with garbage that doesn't get picked up, and kids getting shot in your backyard, and people running through your gangway at night, and rats, and poor housing .... It loses its charm real quick.

So, while the tough young persona of the poems and the struggling Esperanza are escaping through sex and through writing, they are still insisting on control. But Cisneros has also listened to the voices of the women on Mango Street. As she observed to Pilar Rodriguez-Aranda: "it's a circular thing, you leave, but you also do other work to enable other people to control their destinies as well."[11]

In a way, Cisneros, with her writing, is doing what her own mother did. Her own mother:

---

[11]   Rodriguez-Aranda, 69.

was wicked too .... She rejected her own mother as a role model and instead, adopted the cynicism, the independence and the eccentricity of her father. She had to be a woman like that in order to raise me in the wicked way that she did, because she didn't make me conform to models that were given to her. Rather than raise me in the kitchen, rather than have me take care of my little brothers like all my girlfriends did, rather than keeping me at home all the time, she had me in the library, she'd excuse me from domestic duties because I needed to read. If I had a paper to write and my brothers were making a lot of noise or if I wanted to write poetry and I didn't have a quiet space in the house, I would go crying to her and say: "Mom! the kids are in here!" And she'd say "Get out of there, kids!"[12]

So it is the mother who has freed the girl-child to be a writer, and in doing so has freed her to be a sexual being with her own desires. The writer becomes a woman who does not get raped, a woman who chooses her men, and a woman who is free to do as she chooses. In "Las girlfriends," the speaker

> kicked a cowboy in the butt
> who made a grab for [her girlfriend's] ass.
> How do I explain, it was all
> of Texas I was kicking,
> and all our asses on the line. (105)

Come the revolution, men, Cisneros insists, will have a good deal to answer for because many women will model themselves after the loose woman:

> I'm an aim-well,
> shoot-sharp,
> sharp-tongued,
> sharp-thinking,
> fast-speaking,
> foot-loose,
> loose-tongued,
> let-loose,
> woman-on-the-loose
> loose woman.
> Beware, honey.

---

[12] *Ibid.*, 79.

I'm Bitch. Beast. *Macha.*
¡*Wáchale!*
Ping! Ping! Ping!
I break things. (114-15)

Cisneros certainly breaks the tight constraints on language and voice. She also insists on breaking the genre constraints of the poem and the story, and, finally, she crashes through the most difficult border of all, the border of identity. In an interview with Feroza Jussawalla and Reed Way Dasenbrock she observed that she was aware of a cultural conflict between Chicano and Anglo groups, but that a more important conflict occurs within "Hispanic" culture – "Hispanic" being a word she hates because one day:

> the word just appeared! Just like *USA Today*. One day we were sleeping, we woke up and saw that. How'd that get there? I don't know where the word came from. It's kind of an upwardly mobile type word. The word to me came out of Washington, D.C. I use it only when I apply for a grant.

There it is, within one tiny word, the conflict between those who wish to be called Hispanic and those who find the term indicative of what Anglos want from Chicanos. However, Cisneros says, "I like the word Latino. It groups me with the other Latino groups in Chicago."[13]

Cisneros, in the comic debate over what to call herself and her people, highlights the internal tensions created by how people define themselves, and how others in the dominant culture define them. The conflict, put in terms of what people call themselves and liked to be called, is really one of position within the culture. Some wish to find their identity in the dominant culture and sink into the melting pot as so many other groups before them have done; others insist that their values and their culture enrich America, and it should not be lost or subsumed in the larger Anglo culture.

Another tension within the culture that is touched upon in Cisneros' stories and poems is her anger with Mexican men. While the imaginative literature creates beauty out of the suffering of young girls and women at the hands of their men, Cisneros is very clear:

---

[13] Feroza Jussawalla and Reed Way Dasenbrock, *Interviews with Writers of the Post-Colonial World* (Jackson: University Press of Mississippi, 1992), 294.

I'm really mad at Mexican men, because Mexican men are the men I love the most and they disappoint me the most. I think they disappoint me the most because I love them the most. I don't care about the other men so much. They don't affect my personal politics because they're not in my sphere whereas Latino men, and specifically Mexican men, are the ones that I want to be with the most, and they keep disappointing me. I see so many intelligent Mexican women in Texas and they can't find a Mexican man because our Mexican men are with white women. What does that say about Mexican men? How do they feel about themselves if they won't go out with Mexican women, especially professional Mexican women? They must not love themselves.[14]

That observation, growing out of Cisneros' experience in Texas, led her to think about Mexican men and women in her second volume of stories, *Woman Hollering Creek* (1991).

In *House on Mango Street*, Esperanza had to leave to find herself, to define herself and escape the definition that would have destroyed the poet in her. In *Woman Hollering Creek*, Cisneros has done what the aunts warned Esperanza she must do. She has gone full circle and returned to the community. Cisneros makes the journey back by examining the internal political conflicts of the community, by retelling the myths that define the community, and by challenging the archetypal Chicana female identity that so often imprisons her sisters. Finally, Cisneros examines a social system that is inherently masculine, but, because of the absence of men in the community, the solutions to the problems of definition and survival ultimately fall to the women. Clearly, *Woman Hollering Creek* is about women, strong women whose external world is defined by what Barbara Harlow calls a long history of Chicano "immigration, relocation, and political displacement in the United States."[15] Their internal, imaginative world, however, is rich, secure, free, whole, and harmonious. Finally, it is a book that brings together, at times in conflict, but often in symbiotic harmony, the two cultures – Anglo and Latina – that exist in both conflict and harmony in Cisneros herself.

The awareness of how people survive in the barrio is central to *Woman Hollering Creek*. Several stories show how the barrio protects

---

[14] Jussawalla and Dasenbrock, *Interviews with Writers of the Post-Colonial World*, 300.
[15] Quoted in Jeff Thomson, "'What Is Called Heaven': Identity in Sandra Cisneros's *Woman Hollering Creek*," *Studies in Short Fiction*, 31/3 (Summer 1994), 418.

itself from outsiders while keeping the women virtual prisoners inside, as Sally is kept prisoner on Mango Street. When women insist on freedom, males often turn violent. Nor are scenes of patriarchal and sexual violence glossed. The control of women through violence is challenged by Felice in "Woman Hollering Creek," the title story in the volume. Felice rejects the stereotypes for women, drives a pick-up truck and, like many women in *Woman Hollering Creek*, asserts, "I'll never marry."[16]

The cruelty that lurks beneath the relationships between men and women in the barrio and the ways in which women cope indicate that Cisneros is not simply portraying women as victims. Felice will not be victimized, nor will she allow Cleofilas, the young wife she rescues, to be beaten. Instead she helps her escape from her abusive husband. Felice makes a convert of Cleofilas because "Felice was like no woman she ever met" (56), and when she is driving Cleofilas across the *arroyo* named "Woman Hollering Creek," Felice "opened her mouth and let out a yell as loud as any mariachi" (55). That yell confronts the silence that has kept women trapped in the lies their fathers and husbands try to make them believe.

In *Woman Hollering Creek*, Cisneros returns to the heart of her community to show where the cultural tensions reside. The sexual relationships between men and women are paradigms of larger social tensions within the barrio and between the barrio and the larger world. "Never Marry a Mexican," a caustically funny story of love and betrayal, best illustrates how a woman in the barrio negotiates some sexual independence despite the traditional prejudices of the male. The machisma that the narrator flaunts in that story is a way of both criticizing her world and insisting on her place in it. A woman must have more options. A woman must have power, and to achieve that she must be "nobody's mother and nobody's wife" (Author's Note). That freedom also makes her as "dangerous as a terrorist" (83).

Woman Hollering Creek does not simply give voice to women suspended someplace between Mexican and American culture. In the book Cisneros crosses linguistic borders and captures what Latinas have brought to America, a history of "the awful grandmother [who] knits the names of the dead and the living into one long prayer fringed with the grandchildren born in that barbaric country with its barbarian

---

[16] Sandra Cisneros, *Woman Hollering Creek* (New York: Vintage Books, 1991), 68. All subsequent references are to this edition and are given parenthetically in the text.

ways" (19). She blurs language, genre, and finally roles in order to find a voice for herself in that "barbaric country." In learning to say what her experience is, as a Latina in America and as a woman in a house and a culture full of men, Cisneros creates a new self.

Cisneros' stories examine a social system that is inherently masculine, but that depends upon women for survival. All of her work valorizes strong women who, despite their long history of living in the houses of men, have become "Zapatistas" who challenge: "the wars begin here, in our hearts .... You have a daughter. How do you want her treated?" (105). The stories in *Woman Hollering Creek* picture the richness of life on both sides of the border between Mexico and the United States, between male and female, between Spanish and English. In this collection, Sandra Cisneros truly crosses borders.

BORDER CROSSINGS IN LATINA NARRATIVE: JULIA ALVAREZ' *HOW THE GARCÍA GIRLS LOST THEIR ACCENTS*

LOES NAS

Although the United States is usually thought of as an immigrant country, it is only in the last decades of the twentieth century that *difference* has become the central focus in the field of American Studies. This focus on difference also led to a flourishing of multi-ethnic theory and writing practice. It is within this theoretical context that I will discuss Julia Alvarez' *How the García Girls Lost Their Accents* (1991), a novel which in my view is one of the most challenging representations of a new pluralist view of American society.

Immigration – either forced (slaves, American Indians, Mexicans, Puerto Ricans, native Hawaiians, Cubans) or voluntary (white ethnic groups) – has always been a central given in the history of the United States. But until not that long ago immigration was considered to mean integration into the main stream of Anglophone society. The very fabric of society, that of an alleged shared understanding of national consensus, would have been undermined, as Gregory Jay has argued, if America's population, consisting of immigrant groups, expropriated peoples and imported slaves, would have tried to define themselves as national minorities. "Cultural and economic assimilation," writes Jay, "has historically been relatively easy for those of European descent, more difficult for those of Hispanic descent, and virtually impossible for those of African descent," and assimilation of Asian Americans still remains problematic.[1]

In 1995, according to the Census Bureau figures, Latinos[2] comprised 10.2 percent of the total U.S. population; at the present

---

[1] Gregory S. Jay, *American Literature and the Culture Wars* (Ithaca and London: Cornell University Press, 1997), 60. Exceptional in this respect are American Indians, who after the failure of attempts to wipe them out resisted becoming "just another ethnic group" and fought to protect their own status.

[2] The word "Hispanic" is resisted by many Latinos. In *The Latino Reader: An American Literary Tradition from 1542 to the Present*, eds Harold Augenbraum and

rates of growth and immigration, Latino peoples will make up one quarter of the population of the U.S. by the year 2050. Projections like this indicate that the United States is undergoing one of the most profound demographic shifts in its ethnic and racial make-up since the late nineteenth century, thereby creating a multicultural society of unparalleled diversity. By the middle of the twenty-first century the descendants of white Europeans, who have defined U.S. national culture for most of the country's existence, will be in the minority.[3]

It was only in the late 1960s and early 1970s that U.S. ethnic groups became more conscious of their status as a group; by then it had become legitimate (or no longer "un-American") for ethnic groups to express their distinctive characteristics, as opposed to an earlier Anglo-conformity model of immigration. It was only then that expressions of these diverse ethnic groups started to reflect "the tendency of the nation to see itself as a conglomerate of distinct groups rather than as a social contract among highly individual and independent persons,"[4] which had for a long time been the traditional view of American society.

Consequently the very field of American literature as a field of study was also brought into question. American literature and culture were and are no longer considered to be limited by the borders, or even powers, of the United States; symptomatic in this respect is the establishment in 2001 of the International American Studies Association, whose first conference theme – "How Far Is America from Here?" – indicated a rethinking of "American identities relationally, whether the relations under discussion operate within the borders of the United States, throughout the Americas, and/or worldwide."[5]

American Studies originally emerged at a particularly tense moment of North American nationalism, and the virtual exclusion

---

Margarite Fernández Olmos (Boston and New York: Houghton and Miflin Company, 1997), a first attempt at canonizing Hispanic American texts, the term "Latino" is preferred over that of "Hispanic American," although still considered unsatisfactory; "Hispanic" is considered politically incorrect as it is too reductive in its association with Spain, Spanish culture and white Europeans (xii), and "Chicano" and "Nuyorican," for Mexican American and Puerto Rican respectively, are considered too narrow.

[3] *The Latino Reader*, xiii.
[4] Jay, 72.
[5] IASA's first conference was held at Leiden University, The Netherlands, 22-24 May 2003.

from the canon of texts by marginalized groups – such as early Spanish and French exploration texts, or of black and Indian sermons and autobiographies – served the important ideological role of maintaining boundaries between what was truly American and what was "other," or marginal. But in the last two decades of the twentieth century texts like Gloria Anzaldúa's *Borderlands/La Frontera: The New Mestiza* (1987), and anthologies like the *Heath Anthology of American Literature*, first published in 1994, were instrumental in redrawing these boundaries, the former by problematizing and redefining Mexican-American writing as North American literature, and the latter by including, among others, American Indian myths of origin, which previously would only have found their way into anthropological or ethnographic texts.[6] Gregory Jay, however, sounds a warning against "naive pluralism or heated celebration of ethnic tradition," which in his view should be avoided: "the uncritical assertion of the value of one's personal or cultural identity is not ultimately a sufficient response to those who have, on the basis of their own identity politics, repressed and denied one's identity."[7] It is in this context that multi-ethnic writers like Julia Alvarez play an important part.

Julia Alvarez was raised in the Dominican Republic and emigrated to the United States in 1960. *How the García Girls Lost Their Accents* (1991) was her first novel. It received the PEN/Oakland Josephine Miles Award and was named by both the American Library Association and the *New York Times Book Review* as a Notable Book of 1991. Her second novel, *In the Time of the Butterflies*, was nominated for the 1995 National Book Critics Circle Award. She has since published another novel, entitled *¡Yo!*, as well as collections of poetry and essays.

Although Alvarez is often referred to as a multi-ethnic writer, her work makes it particularly clear that it cannot be assumed that the multi-ethnic writer is a spokesperson for the central experience of the writer's group. Her work clearly shows that as a so-called multi-ethnic writer one can hold one's own cultural identity and yet explore the

---

[6] Inclusion of a Zuni oral narrative from the colonial period in the anthology is in itself not unproblematic since fixing the text in print lends an unacceptable authority to the particular nuances of a particular story-teller, but its inclusion is intended to remind the reader that American society was right from the start a multicultural one.

[7] Jay, 74.

differences within the self as well as within the group, community or state one forms part of. Julia Alvarez does not, and indeed cannot, speak for, or represent her ethnic group, nor can she be considered to be representative of this ethnic group.

It was Gayatri Spivak who outlined the problematics of the double meaning of the term "representation" in her famous essay "Can the Subaltern Speak?," referring to these mechanics as "proxy" and "portrait."[8] She insisted that these two meanings should be considered separately when discussing the dynamics of "speaking for" a particular group. By charting the different family members' reactions to how an Americanized, upper-class Dominican family, forced into political exile in the United States, comes to terms with life in America, in *How the García Girls Lost Their Accents* Julia Alvarez avoids becoming a spokesperson for a generalized U.S. Latino/Latina experience and thus escapes the double bind of group identity, or "representation."

In the novel the García family moves from a position of dominance in the Dominican Republic to a racially marginalized position in the United States. Whereas the family's sense of social security in the Dominican Republic was based on class and social privilege, in the U.S. they are marked as ethnic. What makes the novel so different from other immigrant literature, apart from the fact that "it operates within the upper echelons of economic status and power in the homeland," as David Mitchell has argued,[9] is that instead of speaking for her ethnic group, Alvarez writes both inside and outside her group identity, by taking the problematics of cross-cultural and cross-class understanding, of borderlands if you will, as her subject matter.

Alvarez' characters oscillate between the promise of a life-style promulgated by middle-class consumer culture in the U.S. and a longing for a lost Dominican origin. Alvarez depicts the García family, while still in the Dominican Republic, as "consciously embracing their Dominicanized version of an exported American culture in order to maintain and bolster their economic and social

---

[8]   Gayatri Spivak, "Can the Subaltern Speak?" (1988), reprinted in *Colonial Discourse and Post-Colonial Theory*, eds Patrick Williams and Laura Chrisman (New York: Harvester Wheatsheaf, 1991), 66-111.
[9]   David T. Mitchell, "Immigration and Impossible Homeland in Julia Alvarez's *How the Garcia Girls Lost Their Accents*," in *Antipodas: Cultural Collisions and Cultural Crossings*, eds Marta Caminero-Santangelo and Roy Boland, 10 (1998), 29.

advantage."[10] After a failed CIA-backed government coup in an attempt to oust dictator Trujillo, the family has to flee from the Dominican Republic to the United States. It is ironic that the family's relocation to America means in fact an abdication of the material wealth and class privileges that symbolized their American life-style in the Dominican Republic.

In her essay "An American Childhood in the Dominican Republic" Alvarez describes the cultural appropriations and political crossings that form the backdrop of her postcolonial novel:

> What kept my father from being rounded up with the other [political dissidents of the Trujillo regime] each time there was a purge ... was his connection with my mother's powerful family. It was not just their money that gave them power, for wealth was sometimes an incentive to persecute a family and appropriate its fortune. It was their strong ties with Americans and the United States. As I mentioned, most of my aunts and uncles had graduated from American schools and colleges, and they corresponded regularly with their classmates and alumni associations .... The family subscribed to American magazines, received mail-order catalogues, and joined American clubs and honorary societies. This obsession with American things was no longer merely enchantment with the United States, but a strategy for survival.[11]

In the novel we find similar cultural appropriations and political crossings, constituting the site of borderlands, as will be referred to below. Being a Dominican American herself, rather than an American, Alvarez is aware of the difficulties involved in understanding difference. In her novel she considers the complex intersections of class, nationality and race for her Dominican American characters. In one of the sections of the novel, for instance, we find Yolanda, one of the García daughters, on returning to the island, realizing that her memories of a happy childhood on the island were at the expense of the servants which the family had employed and exploited. As David Mitchell has observed:

> Armed with a repertoire of political theories from her college classes and her own racial experiences in the U.S. which irreparably changed

---

[10] *Ibid.*, 28.
[11] Julia Alvarez, "An American Childhood in the Dominican Republic," *The American Scholar*, 57/1 (1988), 80.

her vision of home, Alvarez points to the ways in which her characters respond to the context of upper class privilege in the Dominican Republic which once went unarticulated in their day-to-day lives.[12]

Alvarez contemplates the exploitative social conditions of both cultures she has moved in and "refuses to privilege the country of origins over the newly adopted nation."[13] She is aware of the advantages offered by her insider/outsider position. In a special edition dedicated to her work, the Australian journal *Antipodes* interviewed her saying:

> Living at a distance from some of the things that truly move me deeply gives me a certain kind of freedom. I'm not controlled by forces that silence me there. Being outside the country allows me the freedom to reject the typical stance that I would have to adopt towards my history.[14]

In a similar vein Vietnamese American Trinh T. Minh-ha explicates the position of a subject who is both inside and outside as follows:

> The moment the insider steps out from the inside she's no longer a mere insider. She necessarily looks in from the outside while also looking out from the inside. Not quite the same, not quite the other, she stands in that undetermined threshold place where she constantly drifts in and out.[15]

Like Trinh, Alvarez is quite aware of the implications of this double bind of borders, borderlands and border crossings, where inside and outside change position all the time. She is also aware of the danger and impossibility of speaking for others. Thus, in her novel no attempts are made to speak with the voice of another, lower-class Dominican, one of the family servants, for instance, being aware that telling the story of the other robs that other of control over her own

---

[12] Mitchell, 31.
[13] *Ibid.*, 29.
[14] Marta Caminero-Santangelo, "'The Territory of the Storyteller': An Interview with Julia Alvarez," in *Antipodas: Cultural Collisions and Cultural Crossings*, 10 (1998), 21.
[15] Trinh T. Minh-ha, "Not Like You/Like You: Post-Colonial Women and the Interlocking Questions of Identity and Difference," in *Making Face, Making Soul/ Haciendo Caras: Creative and Critical Perspectives by Women of Color*, ed. Gloria Anzaldúa (San Francisco: Aunt Lute, 1990), 374.

story. Instead of speaking for the servant, and thus potentially violating the voice of the other, Alvarez tells the story through multiple perspectives and has the characters speak for themselves, in an unmediated way, being self-consciously aware that it is through the author that the characters are allowed to speak for themselves.

When the story offers competing versions of events for the readers to make sense of, Alvarez has deliberately created uncertainty by mixing narrative perspectives, thus invoking a site of borderlands and creating a postcolonial, that is hybrid, stance. In this sense also the author can be said to be inside and outside the text at the same time.

The chronological order of the narrative is reversed, and characters move in and out of story, identity, name. As Ellen McCracken has pointed, memory works in the same way.[16] The stories within the novel are told from various narrative perspectives with voices of different characters, and sometimes they even change within one story. Even the narratees within one story change as each of the mother's narratives about her daughters is addressed to various characters within the novel, strangers, wedding guests, the man in an adjacent seat at her daughter's poetry reading, the hospital psychiatrist, and the mother's infant father at the hospital nursery.

This notion of inside and outside, of crossing over, of borderlands, has been identified by Paul Lauter as "the historically rooted trope of the border" being "central to Mexican American writing."[17] Lauter's text in itself constitutes an exploration of the function of canons in the sense of maintaining and defining borders. Four years before, in 1987, Mexican American writer Gloria Anzaldúa was one of the first to problematize the notion of borders in North American literature in *Borderlands/La Frontera: The New Mestiza*. In her preface she writes:

> I am a border woman. I grew up between two cultures, the Mexican (with a heavily Indian influence) and the Anglo (as a member of a colonized people in our own territory). I have been straddling the *tejas*-Mexican border, and others, all my life. It's not a comfortable territory to live in, this place of contradictions. Hatred, anger and exploitation are the prominent features of this landscape.

---

[16] Ellen McCracken, *New Latina Narrative: The Feminine Space of Postmodern Ethnicity* (Tucson: University of Arizona Press, 1999), 28.
[17] Paul Lauter, *Canons and Contexts* (New York and Oxford: Oxford University Press, 1991), 78.

However, there have been compensations for this *mestiza*, and
certain joys. Living on borders and in margins, keeping intact one's
shifting and multiple identity and integrity, is like trying to swim in a
new element, an "alien" element .... No, not comfortable, but home.[18]

The concept of borderlands, of a hybridization of culture and identity,
which is troubling and liberating at the same time, comes into play in
Anzaldúa's postcolonial text. It can be read as a poetic theory about
being informed by different cultures, and in her specific case,
sexualities. Anzaldúa argues that those who inhabit borderlands
develop a new consciousness, "*la conciencia de la mestiza*," a
tolerance for contradictions leading to new ways of thinking and
being, new alliances and new strategies of resistance. For Anzaldúa
borderlands occur "wherever two or more cultures edge each other,
where people of different races occupy the same territory, where
under, lower, middle and upper classes touch, where the space
between two individuals shrinks with intimacy,"[19] as well as within
the "mixed breed," straddling two cultures.

In her book the radical alterity of contemporary ethnic and/or racial
experience is foregrounded by means of tonal and linguistic elements
in such a way that readers who are not Chicana are purposely made to
feel displaced. Carla Peterson reports in "*Borderlands* in the
Classroom" that her female, white, middle-class students at the
University of Maryland, College Park, became disgruntled with the
writer's anger, claiming that "as an American writer, she had no right
to use any language other than that of the dominant culture, English."
They also "resented her insistence that the borderland could not be
confined merely to one geographical place – the Texas/Mexican
border – or even to a place outside the self."[20] To add to the
discomfort of using an unfamiliar language Anzaldúa used eight
different varieties of Spanish alongside English in her book. Her text
thus not only forces the Anglo reader to confront the borderlands in
one's self, but also forces her to acknowledge the "significance of *who*
gets empowered to tell the story in *what* language."[21] Which brings us

---

[18] Gloria Anzaldúa, *Borderlands/La Frontera: The New Mestiza* (San Francisco:
Aunt Lute Books, 1987), i.
[19] *Ibid.*, 78.
[20] Carla L. Peterson, "*Borderlands* in the Classroom," *American Quarterly*, 45/2
(1993), 298.
[21] *Ibid.*, 299.

back full circle to Alvarez' novel, as both texts drive home the point of the centrality of storytelling within a multicultural society as "an important constitutive act of literature, literary studies and cultural work."[22]

I want to return now to *How the García Girls Lost Their Accents* to see where and how some of the borderlands operate in this particular text. Both Anzaldúa's and Alvarez' texts oscillate between different genres (albeit in very different ways), and in this way both can be said to be borderland texts. Anzaldúa's bilingual book combines several genres; it is a sort of anti-colonial literary mixture, or *mestizaje* (racial mixing), as historiography is mixed with poetry, philosophy with autobiography, English with Spanish.[23] In *How the García Girls Lost Their Accents* this takes the form of a merging of elements of the short story with those of the novel, also known as the composite novel. Composite novels are like a short story cycle; they work as a set of short stories that are interrelated to function novelistically, but can also stand on their own. Margot Anne Kelley has suggested that Alvarez' choice for this inter-genre is based on "dissatisfaction with the ideological assumptions inherent in the novel form"[24] and in general with the novel's tacit modernist assumptions of a coherent identity and a true self.

In the Alvarez novel, for instance, one of the García daughters, Yolanda, thinks, speaks and acts differently in the different parts of the text; in "Daughter of Invention" she is Yolanda, in "Joe" she is Yo and in "In the Drum" she is Yoyo. Yet as these characters are all within the body of one text, the reader presumes a coherence among the characters who all bear reference to the same. The composite form with its focus on "disparate, individual moments" suggests that, as Kelley points out, "identity is not inherent, but rather is constituted" and is "continually negotiated and renegotiated,"[25] something the traditional novelistic form with its notion of character coherence would not allow for. Through the composite novel's usage of several

---

[22] *Ibid.*, 300.
[23] Anzaldúa calls herself neither Hispanic nor Latina, but Mestiza, since all Latinos are of mixed origin: cf. her usage of eight variants of Spanish in *Borderlands*.
[24] Margot Anne Kelley, "'Daughters of Invention': Alvarez's Or(igin)ality and the Composite Novel," in *Antipodas: Cultural Collisions and Cultural Crossings*, 10 (1998), 43.
[25] *Ibid.*, 44-45.

points of view and different narrators and narratees, as referred to above, the reader gets different perspectives on various events, thus creating different epistemological positions.[26]

This uncertainty could be seen as an occurrence of borderlands. Borderlands occur in the multi-perspectives in the novel, in the oscillation between multiple first and third person narratives, breaking down the barrier between narrator and narratee, and thus creating a hybrid, or postcolonial, narrative form, mirroring the shifting and multiple nature of postcolonial identity itself. Homi Bhabha has referred to this use of multi-perspectivity as "living perplexity,"[27] when the story moves between past and present in a contestation of a controlling master narrative and the past is reverberated in the narrative present. The example of Yolanda's multiple stances comes to mind.

Borderlands also occur when a person straddles two languages. Alvarez refers to this in an interview as a process of transformation:

> It's not that I've totally lost my Spanish, but my dominant tongue is now English, and yet I'm also a person in Spanish. The process that has happened for me is that I – not just language, but *I* – have become translated, with all the richness of that word in terms of its Shakespearean meanings – being transported somewhere else – I have become translated. The minute you're in another language, you're transformed, you are another person.[28]

In the novel, as indicated by the title, the role of language in identity formation plays a major part: thus, the father progressively loses his grip on his daughters the better acquainted they get with the English language. This process culminates in the incident where he tears to shreds his daughter's speech for Teacher's Day for insubordination to his patriarchal rule, after Yolanda has finally found her voice in English after having discovered Walt Whitman's "Song of Myself."[29] Language becomes a big issue in the family when Papi wants Mami to

---

[26] *Ibid.*, 45.
[27] Homi K. Bhabha, *The Location of Culture* (London and New York: Routledge, 1994), 157.
[28] Marta Caminero-Santangelo, "'The Territory of the Storyteller': An Interview with Julia Alvarez," 16.
[29] Julia Alvarez, *How the García Girls Lost Their Accents* (New York, Plume, 1991), 142-43.

talk Spanish, but Mami refuses, speaking a mishmash of mixed-up idioms and sayings.[30]

Borderlands, as Alvarez says in the same interview, is also the space occupied between what actually happened and the memory of it.[31] It is the space occupied by Carla García's experiences of a privileged childhood when being surrounded by servants in the family compound, moving between the world of her family and that of the family's servants living in the back of the compound. Borderlands are created by multi-ethnic writers themselves, being on the move, between two countries. Migrant literature, as Elleke Boehmer has argued,[32] is characterized by the straddling of two different worlds. The immigrant is encapsulated in nostalgia, which becomes the immigrant's borderland – the space between what was left behind and what the mother country has become. In her interview with Caminero Alvarez refers to this as being frozen in time.[33] This straddling of different worlds "intensively exploits the double perspective or 'stereoscopic vision' that its in-between position allows."[34] Borrowing from Salmon Rushdie she calls the migrant novel a "translated" novel, which "creates a constant interaction of styles, voices, stories, legends, geographies"[35] reminiscent of Bhabha's "living perplexity," referred to above.

For Alvarez borderlands occur as the space where multiculturalism is located; for her multi-ethnicity is not only encapsulated in the multiplicity of each person, but also in the multiplicity of Latino culture:

> I think this multiplicity of perspectives comes from my culture. We are often members of big, bungling, tribal families in our Latino culture. You're never just one person .... I'm interested in that multiplicity, that multiculturalness, of each person. Not just the singular self, which is so much of the Western tradition; the hero on his journey, on his Odyssean voyage. I'm much more interested in the

---

[30] *Ibid.*, 135.
[31] Marta Caminero-Santangelo, "'The Territory of the Storyteller': An Interview with Julia Alvarez," 18.
[32] Elleke Boehmer, *Colonial and Postcolonial Literature: Migrant Metaphors* (Oxford and New York: Oxford University Press, 1995).
[33] Marta Caminero-Santangelo, "'The Territory of the Storyteller': An Interview with Julia Alvarez," 22.
[34] Boehmer, 241.
[35] *Ibid.*, 242.

many-mirrored reality which is very much a part of where I came from .[36]

We are all so mobile and populations are on the move and people have children formed of two or more traditions, as people get married to people that are not just in their neighborhood and in their province and in their city-state or whatever. We're creating these interesting combinations of people who hear multiple languages and see varied images and know different stories, and they pass these on to their children and the children make new combinations. To me that's what's most exciting and energizing about what's happening to literature now.[37]

Thus, although Alvarez fits perfectly in the pluralist view of American society in the last two decades, her novel is different in that it spells discursive trouble, marked as it is by transgressions, or in the words of Ellen McCracken "formal, diegetic, gender, ethnic and class trouble,"[38] thereby subtly undermining the happily pluralist view implicit in much contemporary multiculturalism.

---

[36] Marta Caminero-Santangelo, "'The Territory of the Storyteller': An Interview with Julia Alvarez," 20.
[37] *Ibid.*, 24.
[38] McCracken, 28.

STALKING MULTICULTURALISM:
HISTORICAL SLEUTHS AT THE END OF
THE TWENTIETH CENTURY

THEO D'HAEN

In its early days, American hard-boiled detective writing – like most formula stories, as John Cawelti calls them in what is still one of the best works on popular literature[1] – routinely projected the racial, ethnic, and gender stereotypes of the age. In Dashiell Hammett's *The Maltese Falcon* (1930), perhaps the best known example of the genre, Sam Spade is pitted against a fat-bellied English swindler with an upper-class accent but with a German-Jewish name, an effeminate Oriental (a Cypriot), a lower-class punk, and a promiscuous Irish hussy. Regardless of Hammett's well-known leftist sympathies, the array of opponents he has his private eye here facing neatly comprises all that America's hegemonic WASP society considered a threat to its own way of life in the interbellum.

After World War II, self-consciously ethnic practitioners of the detective genre inverted the stereotypes current in its early manifestations. This is pretty obvious in the Coffin Ed Johnson and Grave Digger Jones novels of Chester Himes, written in the 1950s and 1960s, and expressive of Harlem and New York in those decades. However, as Stephen F. Soitos has demonstrated, African-American detective writers in general modified the genre's conventions in order to both show up white America's racial prejudice and better portray African-American life.[2] The lead African-American authors provided was taken up by other ethnics. From the 1970s on we see Tony Hillerman – although not an "ethnic" himself – taking up the cause of the Navajo in his Joe Leaphorn and Jim Chee novels. Of more recent date, the Ken Tanaka novels of Dale Furutani speak for the Japanese-American constituency. Set in the gay community of Los Angeles, the

---

[1]   John G. Cawelti, *Adventure, Mystery, and Romance: Formula Stories as Art and Popular Culture* (Chicago and London: The University of Chicago Press, 1976).
[2]   Stephen F. Soitos, *The Blues Detective: A Study of African American Detective Fiction* (Amherst: University of Massachusetts Press, 1996).

Benjamin Justice mysteries of John Morgan Wilson and the Henry Rios novels of Michael Nava take up the gender issue. Nava moreover writes from a decidedly Chicano perspective.

In the range of issues they address, and in the wide social reach they demonstrate, the contemporary detectives mentioned all bear eloquent testimony to the vital role detective fiction continues to play in the cultural and even the social fabric of the United States. This fact is also brought home to the reader by the contemporary settings of these series. Remarkably, though, of late the multicultural make-up of the United States has also been the subject of much historical detective fiction. With the Easy Rawlins series of Walter Mosley, evocative of black Los Angeles in the period 1945-1972, or the Wesley Farrell novels of Robert Skinner, set in the Creole milieu of late 1930s New Orleans, the links to both contemporary multicultural issues and the detective genre are still easy to discern. With detectives set in more remote eras, it becomes less easy to do so.

The veritable explosion of historical detective fiction since 1980 has in itself been one of the more remarkable developments in crime writing. Of course, earlier decades too saw their fair share of this kind of crime fiction. On the British side, during the 1970s Peter Lovesey (1936) ran a series set in the late 1800s. On the American side, James Cain (1892-1977), of *The Postman Always Rings Twice* (1934) fame, tried his hand at historical crime fiction with *Past All Dishonor* (1946), set in mid-nineteenth-century California. From the late 1950s on throughout the 1960s Robert van Gulik (1910-1967), a Dutch diplomat writing in English, published his Judge Dee mysteries, set in seventh-century China.

The event that marked 1980 as the take-off year for historical crime fiction on a large scale was undoubtedly the publication and subsequent mega-success of Umberto Eco's *The Name of the Rose*. In 1986, Eco's novel was turned into a highly praised and hugely successful movie by Jean-Jacques Arnaud, featuring Sean Connery as the English monk William of Baskerville investigating a series of murders in a fourteenth-century North-Italian monastery. In the slipstream of Eco, the Brother Cadfael mysteries of British writer Ellis Peters (1913-1995) also became very popular in the 1980s. *A Morbid Taste for Bones: A Mediaeval Whodunit*, the first Ellis Peters volume to star the medieval Benedictine monk, had already appeared in 1977. Throughout the 1980s Peters produced new Cadfael novels at the rate of one, and sometimes two, a year, and the series was successfully adapted for television.

The result, from 1980 on, then, has been a veritable deluge of historical crime fiction. Some authors are incredibly prolific at this trade. An extreme case in point, the British writer P.C. Doherty, also writing under the names Paul Harding and C.L. Grace, as of 1990 has averaged at least two to three medieval mysteries a year, featuring various sleuths. He also writes ancient Greek mysteries under the pseudonym of Anna Apostolou, ancient Egyptian novels under his own name, Renaissance mysteries under the name Michael Clynes, and nineteenth-century mysteries as Ann Dukthas!

Regardless of whether their authors are British or American, by far the majority of series situated from the middle ages to the nineteenth century is set in England, with single novels occasionally moving to different, usually European, locales. Over the last decade, though, the number of American writers opting for an American decor to their historical crime novels has steadily grown, with a strong concentration on the nineteenth and early twentieth centuries.

For obvious reasons, I cannot deal with all – or even a representative sample – of all contemporary American writers of historical crime fiction. Instead, I have chosen to concentrate on two authors that illustrate how the evolution of the detective genre, even in this particular sub-genre that seems most remote from contemporary concerns, closely reflects developments in contemporary society. Specifically, I will discuss how the novels of Maan Meyers and of Myriam Grace Monfredo powerfully endorse multiculturalism.[3]

Multiculturalism avant-la-lettre plays a major part in *The Dutchman's Dilemma* (1995), the fourth of the "Dutchman" series by Maan Meyers, actually the husband-and-wife team Martin and Annette Meyers. *The Dutchman's Dilemma* is set in New York in 1675, some ten years after the take-over of New Amsterdam by the English. The

---

[3] Most of the novels mentioned in this article are available in mass market paperback editions, often from different publishers in the United States and the United Kingdom. Most of these novels go out of print very quickly, with only the most successful being kept available through regular reprints. For the two novels that I here look at in most detail I used the following editions: Maan Meyers, *The Dutchman's Dilemma* (1995; New York: Bantam Books, 1996) and Miriam Grace Monfredo, *Seneca Falls Inheritance* (1992; New York: Berkeley Prime Crime, 1994). References in the text are to these editions.

first novel in the series, *The Dutchman* (1992), takes place during the surrender of New Amsterdam, and recounts how Pieter Tonneman, the widowed Dutch *schout* (police constable) of New Amsterdam, who stayed on as the first sheriff of New York, falls in love with a young Jewish widow, Racqel Mendoza.

At the start of *The Dutchman's Dilemma*, Tonneman has resigned his commission, and has gone into business with his longtime friend Conraet Ten Eyck, contracting for city jobs, and serving as Post Master to New York. One reason for Tonneman resigning as sheriff is that his marriage to Racqel is not looked upon with favor by New York's Christian citizens. Especially the fact that Tonneman has stopped going to church, and that he has had his four children with Racqel accepted into the Jewish faith, sits ill with New York's authorities. Racqel herself is ostracized by the Jewish community for having married outside of her faith. What nobody knows is that after the birth of their first child, Moses, in 1665, Pieter has promised Racqel that he will convert to Judaism. Though Racqel let the issue rest for the better part of ten years, recently, after a miscarriage that has affected her badly, she has started reminding her husband of his promise.

In *The Dutchman's Dilemma*, Pieter Tonneman is pressed into service again by the First Councilor of New York, the renegade Dutchman Nicasius De Sille. Tonneman is to investigate the brutal slaughter, on a Saturday night, of a stallion, a gift from King Charles II to the English Governor of New York. At first Tonneman is reluctant to accept the commission. A different face is put upon things when during the Sunday service the stallion's penis is found in the preacher's Book of Common Prayer. Immediately, rumors start circulating about religious conspiracies. Inevitably, suspicion centers upon the Jews, Racqel's people.

Racqel herself, in the meantime, has been bidden to the house of Asser Levy, the leader of the small Jewish community of New York, and also its kosher butcher. Levy, who has studiously avoided Racqel and the Tonnemans for the past ten years, now seeks Racqel's advice. Her father was a famous physician, and she herself is very knowledgeable about natural cures and herbs. The latter skill she learned from studying the ways of the few Indians remaining in the neighborhood of New York. Levy has been ill for some time, and the regular Jewish physician, Salomon Navarro, seems unable to properly diagnose him, let alone prescribe a remedy.

Racqel eventually diagnoses Levy as having "butcher's disease," later also known as Mediterranean fever, Malta fever, undulant fever or brucellosis. When she informs Levy, he flares up in fear of losing his livelihood as a butcher, and accuses Racqel of withcraft. Terrified, she flees into the Manhattan woods north of Wall Street, then the boundary of New York. There, she runs into the schoolmaster Lester Crabtree, apparently gone mad. He had been showing symptoms similar to Levy's. Racqel realizes that he must be the horse killer, infected by the blood of the animals he has slaughtered. When Crabtree prepares to dispatch her as a witch, Racqel is saved by Foxman, the sole survivor of an Indian tribe that used to call Manhattan its home.

Tonneman in the meantime has narrowed his list of suspects to Crabtree and Navarro. Neither can account for his whereabouts on the night the Governor's horse was slaughtered, and there are other things in their testimonies that do not tally. He has also learned that comparable cases of horse-cock cutting have occurred in some New England towns. The episode in the woods with Racqel supports Tonneman's deductions about at least Crabtree, the more so as it turns out that the latter is a religious fanatic who has been preaching hell and damnation up and down New England before coming to New York.

As to Navarro? De Sille refuses to pay the agreed fee, on the pretext that the anti-English conspiracies he suspected behind the horse slaughter have not been brought to light. Tonneman announces that he will charge the amount of the fee to Navarro. To De Sille's question as to why the Jewish doctor would pay, Tonneman answers: "Elementary. I'll make it the price for not telling you he's tupping Geertruyd" (257). Geertruyd is De Sille's wife, and the woman with whom Navarro spent the night of the slaughter.

The Dutchman's Dilemma ends with a conversation between Asser Levy and Pieter Tonneman, the former preparing the latter for circumcision and conversion to Judaism. Apparently, all religious fanaticism, from both the Christian and the Jewish side, has subsided, and – although clearly there never will be much love lost between the two communities – a modicum of social harmony has been re-established. In fact, *The Dutchman's Dilemma* can easily be read as one long indictment of any kind of religious fundamentalism, and of the prejudices it fosters. There is not only the rift between Christians and Jews, but also between Protestants and Catholics, and between various Protestant sects. Of course, there is also the distrust of the native Americans, their customs and their lore. Beyond that, there is the division between the various groups, of different geographical and linguistic affiliations, inhabiting New York: English, Dutch, New England, Sephardic, native American.

If anything, then, *The Dutchman's Dilemma* is a plea for tolerance in all things, and for respect of everyone's religious, linguistic or geographical origins and affiliations. The historical backdrop against which this argument is developed is, as far as I can ascertain, accurate. Much the same message, couched in much the same terms, and with much the same attention to historical accuracy, speaks from the further novels in the Dutchman series, *The Kingsbridge Plot* (1993), *The High Constable* (1994), *The House on Mulberry Street* (1996), and *The Lucifer Contract* (1998), set, respectively, in 1775-78, 1808, 1895, and 1864. In each of them we are witness to the exploits, in detection, law enforcement, or investigative newspaper reporting, of a descendant of the original Pieter Tonneman.

The authors of *The Dutchman's Dilemma* go out of their way to establish their novel's historical credentials. Not only do they include a map of seventeenth-century New York, situating the houses of their characters as well as other relevant locations, in a footnote they also swear to the historical accuracy of some of the characters, their physical surroundings, and the medical lore employed. There are detailed descriptions of period dress, food, customs and laws, both Christian and Jewish. Still, just as the plea for tolerance this novel holds comes across as particularly apt for our own times, even if it is uttered in a historical context, so also some of the behavior of the characters strikes us as peculiarly late twentieth-century. This is particularly so when it comes to Tonneman's teetotaling, and his aversion to pipe-smoking. If the former is accounted for by the fact that Tonneman used to be somewhat of a drunk himself after his first wife's death, and that of most of his children, and before he met Racqel, the latter seems rather out of place in the mid-seventeenth century, particularly in a pioneer environment. Add to this Tonneman's exemplary behavior toward Racqel – loving, caring, never overbearing, passionate yet always full of respect – he turns into a true hero of our times, a sanitized, sensitized, and responsibilized descendant of Dashiell Hammett's Sam Spade.

Though primarily focused on Christian-Jewish relations in early New York, the unequal power relationship obtaining between men and women also forms an important subtext in *The Dutchman's Dilemma*. It is because of the skewed power relations obtaining between men and women that Hannah Trevor, in Margaret Lawrence's award-winning detective novel *Hearts and Bones* (1996), set in the wake of the American Revolution, decided not to marry again after her first husband's departure, however much her aunt was pushing her to do so. Hannah has personally experienced the fact that at the end of the eighteenth century women simply do not exist as responsible agents in the eyes of the law, and she would rather be subject to her kind and caring uncle than to an indifferent husband.

Three quarters of a century on, things had not changed very much, we learn from Miriam Grace Monfredo's *Seneca Falls Inheritance* (1992). *Seneca Falls Inheritance* is set in 1848 in the Western New York town where that same year the first Woman's Rights Convention was held. The novel is itself all about women's rights, and so are the ensuing novels in the Glynis Tryon series. In each novel the women's issue is bound up with others relevant to the nineteenth-century as an age of reform as well as to our own era of equal rights and opportunities, and of multiculturalism.

In *Seneca Falls Inheritance*, the first novel in the series, Glynis Tryon, thirty-years-old and the town librarian of Seneca Falls, chooses to stay unmarried for much the same reasons as Hannah Trevor in *Hearts and Bones*. In *North Star Conspiracy* (1993) Glynis becomes involved with the Underground Railroad, helping fugitive slaves escape to freedom. *Blackwater Spirits* (1995) sees her battling the discrimination against native Americans, and specifically the Seneca Iroquois autochthonous to America's Eastern seaboard, by white settlers. The temperance movement also plays a role in this novel. In *Through A Gold Eagle* (1996) abolitionism provides the key to the novel's plot.

In *Seneca Falls Inheritance* the plot revolves around the murder of a woman who comes to Seneca Falls to claim half of her father's inheritance. Friedrich Steicher and his wife have recently died in an accident. Their son, Karl Steicher, inherited the farm – the choicest piece of property around town. Unbeknown to the people of Seneca Falls, the older Steicher had been married early in life to a woman much his senior, Mary Clarke, in Boston. He had a daughter with her, born in 1816. Pressured by his family, who disapproved of the match,

Steicher divorced his first wife, and eventually married another woman, with whom he moved to Western New York, and with whom he had Karl. At least, this is how Rose Walker, the thirty-two year old woman who claims to be Steicher's daughter, tells the story.

Rose is murdered the night of the day she arrives in Seneca Falls. Suspicion inevitably settles upon Karl Steicher. Eventually, Rose's husband, Gordon Walker, turns up, claiming his murdered wife's inheritance for himself. Cullen, the town constable, throughout much of the book is ill with malaria – Genesee fever or swamp fever, as it used to be called in those days in the North-Eastern United States – and so is unable to do much detecting. Needless to say, Glynis does it for him. One of the townswomen gives Glynis a letter she found in a purse her husband, a drunk and a wife-beater, either found or stole. The woman is unable to say which is the case, as her husband has disappeared. Glynis recognizes the purse as Rose Walker's. The letter is addressed to Rose, but the sender's relationship to Rose remains unclear. Curious to learn anything that might help solve Rose's murder, Glynis writes to the New Haven address in the letter.

A trial is called to decide upon the truth of first Rose's, and now Gordon Walker's, claim that Rose was Steicher's daughter and is thus entitled to half of the Steicher property. The point is proven beyond doubt. Moreover, everything points to Karl Steicher as her murderer. Then, however, Karl's lawyer, Merrycoif, starts exploring whether any one else besides Karl might have had a motive to murder Rose. In particular, he starts probing into the character of Gordon Walker. In this, he is much helped by testimony from Glynis, who has received an answer to her letter to Rose's former correspondent, and who has done a lot of sleuthing on her own.

It turns out that Rose was planning to leave Walker, who is a lazy and unpleasant man, even if very good-looking. She was about to take up again with her original suitor, a junior professor at Yale. Needing money to do so, she had been prepared to settle for ten thousand dollars rather than half of the Steicher inheritance, as she told Karl when she went to see him. However, Karl sent her packing. Surprisingly, it now is Gordon who stands to gain most from Rose's death. A law then recently passed in New York – the Married Women's Property Act – stipulated that women could keep their own property even when married, at variance with earlier practice. If Rose had indeed left Gordon, the latter would have received nothing from whatever Rose inherited. With Rose dead, though, Gordon can rightfully claim his deceased wife's property. Consequently, Gordon killed Rose. He also killed Bobby Ross, the man who found or stole Rose's purse, because he was afraid that the latter had seen or heard something. At the end of the novel, and on the very first day of his trial, Gordon is shot to death by Rose's mother, Mary Clarke.

The female voice comes through very strongly in *Seneca Falls Inheritance*, and in the entire Glynis Tryon series. First and foremost, of course, there is the Woman's Rights Convention, with the presence of such historical characters as Elizabeth Cady Stanton, Lucretia Mott, and Frederick Douglass. A set of "historical notes" at the end of the novel puts these characters, the role they played in the Woman's Rights Convention, and the situation of women in the mid-nineteenth century in the United States in general, in perspective. Throughout the novel Monfredo also takes care to highlight the plight of nineteenth-century women, and particularly of married women; the eternal drudgery of household chores, the continuous childbearing and rearing, the sexual subservience to a husband, the frequent beatings they fell victim to. By choosing to stay unmarried, Glynis Tryon deliberately opts out on much of this, and Monfredo insists that Glynis was certainly not alone in this choice.

Specifically, Glynis is one of a fairly sizable portion of nineteenth-century women – at least in the United States – that preferred to develop their minds, and their artistic and aesthetic sensibilities. Here too, though, the nineteenth century raised formidable obstacles to the advancement of women. Glynis is virtually ostracized by her family for having pursued a college education, and for the same reason the Seneca Falls townspeople think her a very odd creature indeed. Monfredo makes the same point via the mention of the historical Elizabeth Blackwell. Blackwell was the first woman to become a qualified physician in the United States. She obtained her medical degree in 1849, from Geneva Medical College. The College had been opposed to her pursuing medical studies, and after her graduation the rules of admission were changed so as in future to exclude female students. One of the strongest points of *Seneca Falls Inheritance* is how the Woman's Rights Convention, and the historical conditions of women in the mid-nineteenth century, eventually all meaningfully inform the crime plot, as in the following passage:

"It was the convention," she said.

They all stared at her. Quentin Ives finally said, "The Woman's Rights Convention made you suspect Gordon Walker?"

Glynis nodded. "It was a tangled skein of connections, really." She sat down at one end of a wicker sofa, curling her feet beneath her. "I sat in the Wesleyan Chapel [the place where the Convention was held] wondering just what we women started," she explained. "What we would be leaving the next generations: my nieces, and grandnieces to come, and Elizabeth Stanton's daughters and granddaughters not even born yet. Would what they inherited be a benefit to them as we hoped – or a loss for some that we couldn't foresee? And that, in one of those twists the mind sometimes takes, made me think of the Steicher inheritance, and Rose Walker. Who, besides Karl, would lose if she lived?"

"Later, when we discovered Simon Sheridan couldn't be the guilty one, and I still had inheritance on my mind, I remembered the Married Women's Property Act. You know, it was the passage of that law just a few months ago that encouraged Elizabeth Stanton to call a convention about women's rights. I suddenly thought what a terrible irony it would be if that law, designed to protect women, had caused a woman's murder?" (276)

But however historically accurate in its depiction of mid-nineteenth-century daily life[4] and of the political and social conditions pertaining to women in that age, *Seneca Falls Inheritance* also addresses problems of all ages, and therefore also of our own age. This is most conspicuous in the sub-theme of women being bullied and beaten by their husbands that runs through the book. The maltreatment of women by their husbands formed the subject of various award-winning novels by women in the 1990s.

The undeniable success of Maan Meyers' Dutchman series and Miriam Grace Monfredo's Glynis Tryon novels proves that very contemporary, and ultimately politically extremely important concerns can be forcefully expressed in highly readable formula novels, tailored to the popular taste. Even stronger proof is the success of Steven Saylor's Gordianus the Finder, the hero-sleuth of a 1990s series set in the last decades of the Roman republic before the coming to power of Julius Caesar – but that, as they say, is another story.

---

[4] Particularly woman's life, but not only that: witness the role the railroad, which had come to Seneca Falls in 1846, plays in the solution of Rose's murder.

THE ENGLISH TRADITION IN
CONTEMPORARY AMERICAN CRIME FICTION

HANS BERTENS

When P.D. James published her first novel, *Cover Her Face*, in 1962 few readers will have suspected that James' work would give a wholly new lease of life to the at that point moribund genre – or, rather, sub-genre – of the classic English mystery novel. *Cover Her Face* is not exceptional, and neither is its police protagonist, Adam Dalgliesh. That is to say, he *is* rather exceptional – tall, dark, moody, a published poet – but not compared to most Golden Age detectives created by the women writers who in this first novel are clearly James' inspiration. Reminiscent of Ngaio Marsh's Roderick Alleyn, Dalgliesh (as far as exceptionality goes) does not particularly stand out in the company of Dorothy Sayers' Peter Wimsey, Margery Allingham's Albert Campion, or, for that matter, Alleyn himself. As we can see now, however, James' mysteries developed into complex meditations on deception, guilt, and retribution – occasionally at the expense of their mystery element – while Dalgliesh became more enigmatic and reminded us less and less of his Golden Age precursors.

That an Englishwoman who had come of age in the aftermath of the Depression (James was born in 1920), and who had worked as a Red Cross nurse during the Second World War, would set the classic mystery on a new, more serious and darker course, is, with hindsight, perhaps not so surprising. What does come as a surprise is that since the early 1980s a number of American women writers have followed James' lead in revitalizing this particular sub-genre, although not necessarily along her lines. I should emphasize that what I have in mind here is not the revitalization of the classic mystery per se such as the donnish mysteries featuring Amanda Cross' Columbia-based professor Kate Fansler, but contributions to the revitalization of the specifically English version of the mystery, complete with English characters and English settings. If successful – or at least mostly successful – as is the case with the English mystery series developed by, for instance, Martha Grimes and Elizabeth George, such contributions are genuine tours de force that derive added interest from the fact that they have been created, so to speak, from outside. Whatever else they may be, because of their non-English origin they are inevitably self-conscious constructs that built upon a deep familiarity with the conventions of the genre.

Martha Grimes, who published her first mystery in 1981, makes no attempt to hide her intimate knowledge of the classics of mystery and detective writing: references abound to both the male tradition – from Poe to Chandler – and the female one – Sayers, Christie, Josephine Tey, and the highly rated P.D. James. More in general, and in keeping with a prominent strand of the classic English mystery, Grimes' crime fiction is intensely literary. It invites us to revisit that pleasant realm of the English literary mystery created by Michael Innes, Nicholas Blake, Edmund Crispin and other highly literate writers who more than their less well-read colleagues emphasize the "comedy" part of the comedy of manners that the classic mystery so often is. Crispin's sense of comedy especially echoes in Grimes' novels. But literary history is never far away, which should perhaps not surprise us in a writer who in another life spent decades teaching English. We come across Shakespeare, Rimbaud, Marlowe, Browning, Trollope, Coleridge, *The Wind in the Willows*, and so on and so forth, in an impressive range of references, some of which are structurally functional. In Grimes' debut, *The Man with a Load of Mischief* (1981), a murder is made possible by the way a specific scene from *Othello* is staged. In *The Horse You Came In On* (1993) an early reference to Chatterton, which resurfaces at various points in the novel, introduces a story that hinges on forgery. *Horse* is more generally a good example of Grimes' literariness: the novel contains fragments from a novel in progress by one of the characters (somewhat reminiscent of Djuna Barnes' *Nightwood*), offers a fake Poe story (which cleverly announces its own fakeness), and throws in an aborted scene from a mystery two other characters are trying to cook up. As if this is not enough, for the more academically oriented connoisseur Grimes presents a deconstructionist poet who is appropriately self-serving and untalented (Elizabeth George gives a similarly dismissive treatment to a Marxist literary critic in one of her novels), next to references to such unfrequented nooks in literary history as the Algonquin Round Table. Part of the pleasure of reading Grimes, then, is the pleasure of recognition: we encounter familiar themes, familiar locales – the village of Long Piddleton which returns in all the novels is of standard postcard picturesqueness – familiar references, and familiar conventions. Clearly counting on our familiarity with the genre, Grimes conspiratorially draws us into the game she is playing: her first novel, *The Man with a Load of Mischief* (1981) comes complete with the kind of map of Long Piddleton – not wholly appropriately designed in Tolkien-like fashion – that we associate with the heyday of the classic mystery.

Grimes' two main detectives are true to the classic convention. Like P.D. James' Adam Dalgliesh, her Superintendent Richard Jury reminds us of Roderick Alleyn: good-looking, tall, formidable in an unassuming, contemplative way and yet compassionate and attentive. In many ways Jury, although a professional, resembles the highly literate and cultured amateur detective: there are books all over his apartment and as a gentleman he is essentially without ambition. His collaborator Melrose Plant, former twelfth Viscount Ardry and eighth Earl of Caverness, is a wealthy, fastidious, and somewhat diffident aristocrat who combines elements of Sayers' Peter Wimsey (the sartorial finesse and general knowledgeability), Allingham's Albert Campion (the diffident manner), and Crispin's Gervase Fen (the professorship in literature), even if Plant, unlike Wimsey, is always reluctant to leave his impressive country estate for the delights of the metropolis. But he comes complete with a gentleman's breeding and the taste in cars we expect from his kind ("Will you be requiring the Flying Spur or the Rolls, sir?"). Even some of the comedy, an aspect in which Grimes easily outdoes her female predecessors, seems familiar: Jury's relationship with his formidable, and formidably attractive, co-tenant Carole-Anne Pulatski reminds one increasingly, as the series develops, of the curious relationship between Albert Campion and the improbable Magersfontein Lugg. Like Lugg, she has a not wholly reputable background, which includes a stint as a topless dancer, goes in for a sort of possessive mothering that includes the usual attempts at emotional blackmail, and treats her charge's possessions and rooms as if they are joint property: "Carole-Anne had decided three months ago that her favorite policeman should have [his flat] redecorated and (naturally without his knowledge) had called Decors, one of the swankiest outfits in London, to come round with their swatches."[1]

---

[1] Martha Grimes, *I Am Only the Running Footman* (London: Michael O'Mara, 1986), 170.

In most of Grimes' novels the light mood that results from this sort of comedy, and gives a self-conscious twist to the tradition, is never far away. In Jury's private life we have Carole-Anne, in his professional existence there is his hypochondriac sergeant Wiggins and the feud between the cat Cyril and Jury's chief Racer, who is exactly as inferior to Jury as superiors are supposed to be, while in Melrose Plant's entourage there is the cast of Long Piddleton characters and the constant if not always convincing fuss they create. These novels are brilliantly entertaining: the comedy is woven into highly ingenious, suspenseful plots, and Grimes dances like a fencer around scenes and characters, offering a heady succession of angles and perspectives. The language sparkles, the more so since the reader is always aware that here we have an American writer reproducing impeccably British idioms and accents. The odd ones out are *The Horse You Came In On* (1993) and *Rainbow's End* (1995) in which Grimes decides to use American settings: Baltimore and New Mexico, respectively. *Rainbow's End* is an example, rare in crime fiction, of intertextuality. Like John Barth in *Letters*, Grimes brings back characters from earlier novels – the Cripps family from *The Anodyne Necklace* (1983), for instance – leading to hilarious but dense entanglements that at times obscure the fact that Jury is out there to find a killer. Curiously, with American settings Grimes is out of her element. Although she is good on American stereotypes like the awful Baltimore cabbie in *The Horse You Came In On* – as is George, by the way – she is inexplicably weak in imagining how the American cityscape must strike a fairly reclusive and utterly English upper-class character like Melrose Plant who finds it "so difficult ... to make a trip, to bestir himself, to drag himself away from hearth and home and the Jack and Hammer."[2] We never get the feeling of amazed and uneasy estrangement that we expect from Plant's confrontation with Baltimore. On the contrary, on his way from the airport to the city he reflects that "there was nothing much to see on this typical airport-to-center-city trip which could have been in London, Baltimore, New York, or anywhere except possibly Calcutta" (112). America simply does not register on Plant's consciousness. The best (and most implausible) example of this incomprehensible blindness on the part of Plant, who is otherwise fastidious enough, is his almost thoughtless

---

[2]   Martha Grimes, *The Horse You Came In On* (London: Headline, 1993), 75. Subsequent references in the text are to this edition.

putting on of the presumably not utterly clean clothes and cap of a dead bum. Perhaps we must conclude that while as an American Grimes is perfectly attuned to the strangeness of England, and can therefore create a convincing fictional representation, she is too familiar with the American scene to imagine how strange it still is in European eyes.

While in *The Five Bells and Bladebone* (1987) Grimes had already shocked her readers' expectations by withholding the true identity of the criminal – she is one of two women but we are not absolutely sure which one – in a more recent Jury and Plant novel, *The Case Has Altered* (1997), Grimes more fundamentally transcends both her own earlier novels and the limits of the classic English mystery. We have the usual comedy, although more low-keyed than usual; we have the usual problem of getting Plant convincingly into the action (at Jury's request he poses as a connoisseur of antiques); and we have the sly fun that Grimes in her more recent novels is fond of poking at her characters. Curiously, that narrative irony at times strongly reminds one of Henry James' late novels: "Plant's smile was, well, *dapper*."[3]

Although no one would describe *The Case Has Altered* as the sort of mystery the late Henry James might have produced, the novel certainly shows us what Grimes can do in the way of serious writing. Arresting and precise descriptions abound: "out in the distant pastures, the rime-caked sheep looked as if they were dressed in glass coats" (11); a house sits "behind tall, thin trees that looked more like bars than trees, straight and evenly spaced" (21); a barmaid vigorously starts "wiping down the bar. Having been left in charge, she was going to exert her limited authority and flaunt whatever sexuality she could muster" (213). Melrose Plant, in the earlier novels often not much more than an observing consciousness, is given equally convincing insights into other characters:

> ... Melrose thought this must be the source of [Parker's] magnetism .... He did not waste time in small talk; he plunged right into the way he felt about life. Unlike many who gave the impression of divided attention – whose minds, you knew, were elsewhere – Parker's attention was wholly concentrated on the person he was with; he projected a sense of immediacy. He was not afraid to reveal things about himself, which invited whoever he was with to do the same.

---

[3] Martha Grimes, *The Case Has Altered* (London: Headline, 1997), 224. Subsequent references in the text are to this edition.

This was the source of the comfort Parker unknowingly and unselfconsciously offered. One felt at home. (183)

Grimes is also quite good on the complicated and delicate relationship between Jury and the defendant, the Jenny Kennington he has first met in *The Anodyne Necklace* (1983), a relationship that here founders on a mutual lack of trust and on the woman's secretiveness. Grimes catches all the strains and the subtle emotional shifts. We find the same subtle appreciation of mood and tensions in the interrogations that Jury conducts – that of the murdered girl's family, for instance – and in the novel's dialogue. On top of this, and seemingly working with a new self-assurance, Grimes perfectly captures the desolate and wind-swept Lincolnshire Fens in winter.

In *The Case Has Altered* Grimes almost closes the gap with the serious novel. That she is well capable of this had already been illustrated by a non-series novel, *Hotel Paradise* (1996), which, although driven by a number of mysteries and a sort of investigation, is only marginally a mystery. We have the enigmatic drowning of a young girl, over forty years earlier; a murder, some twenty years before, of which the man who was found guilty is probably innocent; an unsolved murder in the present, and the unexplained appearances of a mysterious young woman, but the heart of the novel is its recreation of *temps perdu*. Central to *Hotel Paradise* is a strangely muted and innocent 1950s in an unidentifiable small town locale somewhere in the U.S. – we may be in northern Pennsylvania or upstate New York, but Grimes is careful not to give away any definite clues. Television plays no role, there are no fast food franchises, and the local sheriff on his daily rounds slots dimes into parking meters to keep his flock from breaking the law. The magical hush that plays over everything and that gives the novel its timeless quality has to do with the voice and the limited perspective of its narrator, the twelve-year-old Emma, whose discovery of who and what she is and of a wider world in which old loyalties must inevitably be redefined is the foreground for Grimes' fascinating picture of small town life in the 1950s.

Martha Grimes has done very interesting things with the classic English mystery, not to mention the mystery as a whole. Still, Elizabeth George (1949) must be considered the best of the writers who in the last two decades have revitalized the genre. Moreover,

judging by the number of reprints her books have gone through –
more than a dozen for her first novel – she is also the most successful,
so that for once critical acclaim and popular success are not at odds
with one another.

That first book, *A Great Deliverance* (1988), is a virtuoso
performance. That, however, is not what the reader expects after all
the necessary introductions have been made. In fact, George's CID
detective inspector Lynley, who will dominate the series that will
develop from *A Great Deliverance,* initially has all the earmarks of a
Lord Peter Wimsey replay and his entourage is not much more
promising. Our first glimpse of Lynley is that of a "tall man who
managed to look as if somehow he'd been born wearing morning
dress." In keeping with this, "His movements [are] graceful, fluid, like
a cat's."[4] Lynley is not only the Eighth Earl of Asherton, with an Eton
and Oxford background, he is also rich, living in posh Belgravia and
with a Bentley to take him to the ancestral estate in Cornwall if he is
so inclined. He excels, moreover, at his job. In short, as policewoman
Barbara Havers, who is assigned to work with him early in the novel –
a partnership that will turn out to be a major variation upon the
male/female partnership convention – tells herself somewhat sourly,
"He was the golden boy in more ways than one" (48). Lynley's inner
circle reflects the exceptional (and improbable) qualities of the man
himself. His close friend Simon Allcourt-St. James is a brilliant
forensic scientist and has in his early thirties "known too much pain
and sorrow at far too young an age" (36) and the women, St. James'
bride Deborah and Lynley's friend Lady Helen Clyde, are as
impossibly attractive as the girls featuring in many classic mysteries –
those of John Dickson Carr, for instance. After this, it cannot come as
a surprise that Lynley easily matches his female companions in the
looks department: he is "the handsomest man" Barbara has ever seen.
But with Barbara Havers George has already laid a potential bomb
under this paragon of looks and breeding and introduced a perspective
to which Dorothy Sayers never exposed Lord Peter Wimsey: "She
loathed him" (31).

Barbara Havers, who will become Lynley's permanent partner in
the series, in virtually every respect is his opposite. Her background
and accent are definitely working class, her education is of the

---

[4]   Elizabeth George, *A Great Deliverance* (New York: Bantam, 1989), 31.
Subsequent references in the text are to this edition.

grammar-school kind; she is plain and dumpy and is, moreover, well aware of it. In her late twenties, she still lives with her parents in the wrong kind of street in Acton, North London, and fights an utterly depressing daily battle with her mother's, at this point, still rather serene madness and her father's addiction to betting and snuff, a habit which his doctor has expressly forbidden. As if this is not enough, the father has an aversion to having a bath and has the equally unsettling, although perhaps less offensive, habit of referring to himself in the third person. Apart from the mental condition of her parents, but surely related to it, the most disturbing element in the Havers household is the shrine devoted to Barbara's long dead younger brother who died of leukemia at the age of ten, an elaborate, sick construction placed in such a way that the boy's picture can watch the "telly." Given such circumstances, we are not surprised to find that Havers has a more than average chip on her shoulder, the more so since, as we learn in a later novel, her one experience with a man has not even included the morning after. But, as Lynley realizes in *A Great Deliverance*, "There was no question of angry virginity here. It was something else" (118). It is this something else that has dogged Havers' police career so far. At one point promoted to Criminal Investigation she "has proved herself incapable of getting along with a single DI for her entire tenure in CID" (24). As a result she has been demoted, a decision that has led her "termagant personality" to explode in a memorable way. When *A Great Deliverance* opens, her superiors, aware of her undeniable ability, agree to give her one more chance, coupling her with the infallibly courteous and ever-patient Lynley, a gamble that unexpectedly pays off. This particular partnership is a brilliant innovation. While Grimes sticks to the standard combination of two males (who, in a minor deviation from tradition, are each other's equals), George makes a very uneasy male-female relationship part of her reworking of the classic format.

The Lynley-Havers relationship is a sub-theme in all of George's books, but in *A Great Deliverance*, where its foundations are laid, it plays an exceptionally important role. George brilliantly creates correspondences between the case Lynley and Havers are sent out to investigate in the imaginary Yorkshire Dales village of Keldale and Havers' personal life, sometimes even in a literal sense, as when the shrine to her deceased brother in her parents' living room is mirrored by the shrine that a murdered Yorkshire farmer has apparently devoted to his long disappeared spouse. Inexplicably, George totally implausibly arranges for Allcourt-St. James and his wife – with whom, to complicate matters, Lynley is in love – to be honeymooning in the same village. In fact, Allcourt-St. James, like Lynley presumably the product of an infatuation on the author's part with either a certain type of Golden Age detective novel or with a certain sector of English society, will never find a natural place in George's novels, his presence usually unnecessary and always forced. Only Lady Helen Clyde, who gradually replaces Deborah Allcourt-St. James in Lynley's affections and finally, after intense heart-to-heart talks in *For the Sake of Elena* (1992), consents to marry him (and actually does so in *In the Presence of the Enemy*, 1996), will become more or less integrated in the series.

But to return to Lynley and Havers: the case that takes them to Yorkshire is one in which a young woman has been found next to her father's decapitated body and has confessed to the crime only to completely shut up afterwards. The case is, however, by no means as straightforward as it seems. For one thing, the murder weapon has gone missing; for another, there seems to be no motive. Lynley and Havers succeed in unraveling an extraordinarily complicated mystery, in which one discovery leads to another. In a technique that she also used to great effect in her other novels, and that suggests a parallel with archeological excavation, George allows her detectives to strip away layer after layer of deceptions and falsehoods until finally the terrible truth stands revealed.

In *A Great Deliverance* that truth is incestuous abuse, the systematic and prolonged abuse by a religious fanatic of his two young daughters, one of whom has, years before, run away to save herself. This older sister, who is now in her mid-twenties, is in the course of the investigation tracked down by Havers and confronted with the sister she has last seen as a little girl in a harrowing scene in which she succeeds in breaking through the stupor that has overtaken the other after their father's death. Her detailed description of the father's sexual demands provokes a similar response from the younger sister who in so doing finally returns to speech, but it also has an enormous impact on Havers, who with Lynley and some others is watching the scene from behind a one-way glass panel. Havers crashes blindly from the room to find a restroom and is violently sick. The terrible form of abuse that has just been revealed to her and the overwhelming feelings of guilt experienced by the sisters – the younger turns out indeed to have murdered her father – forcibly bring home the total inadequacy of her own parents and confront her with her own feelings of guilt. We learn that Havers' parents had never visited their ten-year-old son in hospital because they couldn't cope with his illness, leaving the daily visits to his sister, the emotionally vulnerable teenager Barbara, who has never forgiven herself for not being there when he actually died and who has ever since taken a subtle, insidious and prolonged revenge: the shrine in the Havers' living-room is of her making, a way to remind her parents daily of their inadequacy and guilt, just as the shrine in the farm has probably been created by the older sister to remind her father of his failure as the husband of a runaway wife and mother. Confronting the fact that she has substantially contributed to the misery of her parents' lives and possibly even to her mother's feeble-mindedness,

> She put her head down on the porcelain and wept. She wept for the hate that had filled her life, for the guilt and the jealousy that had been her companions, for the loneliness that she had brought upon herself, for the contempt and disgust she had directed towards others. (308)

When Lynley, who has followed her, "wordlessly [takes] her in his arms," she weeps "against his chest, mourning most of all the death of the friendship that could have lived between them" (308).

As this makes clear, Havers' view of Lynley has dramatically changed. From a slick, loathsome, and impossibly aristocratic womanizer Lynley has become a potential friend, a development made possible by the mutual respect that has grown in the course of the novel by and a shared sense of humor. But Havers is also aware that an earlier and ugly personal attack, triggered by the class bias and personal unhappiness that consistently lead her to completely misconstrue his behavior and feelings, may very well have destroyed that potential friendship. This, however, is not the case. Lynley has not only in the meantime realized that Havers' unreasonable aggressiveness has more to do with her personal problems than with anything he might do or might not do, he also knows that her anger, although totally off its immediate target, is not wholly misplaced: " ... beyond Havers there was truth. For underneath her bitter, unfounded accusations, her bitterness and hurt, the words she spoke rang with veracity" (243). Lynley, who in the later novels repeatedly shows an intense self-awareness, is willing to redirect Havers' anger and to hook it up with his real shortcomings: his sexual encounter with a

Keldale witness that Havers has overheard and, more mysteriously, sins that are only hinted at when he briefly reflects on his reasons for having chosen this particular profession: *"It's a penance ... an expiation for sins committed ...."* (32). Considering that he is not in a position to cast the first stone, and usually rather a man of great compassion, Lynley is able to make allowances for Havers' personal demons and ends by giving her a chance to redeem herself and by offering the moral support that she now has come to appreciate. Fully aware of the limitations of Havers' social graces and of the fact that easy personal relationships will probably be forever beyond her, he has also come to value her honesty, her courage, her ability and her devotion to the job.

With its unexpected twists and revelations, *A Great Deliverance* is a wholly satisfying mystery in the Golden Age tradition. But it is much more than that. George gives an unprecedented depth to the conventional figure of the aristocratic detective, who in her hands, unlike earlier versions like Albert Campion and Peter Wimsey, loses every trace of P.G. Wodehouse's Bertie Wooster. Lynley is a man of great seriousness who has his own demons and who occasionally, as in an ugly scene in *In the Presence of the Enemy*, allows his anger to run away with him. This seriousness is not limited to Lynley. *A Great Deliverance* is a serious book. Havers' pain and guilt are terribly somber and so is the series of interlocking crimes that is revealed. What is perhaps worse, there is no real deliverance. A daughter is reunited with her long lost mother, but will never forget that she has been betrayed and deserted, just as she herself has deserted her younger sister. The priest who, through the confessional, was aware of the abuse, must live with the knowledge that his silence has effectively condoned the practice and has ultimately led to murder. The woman who seduces Lynley stands accused of what within the context of this novel almost constitutes a crime: a willful superficiality that must serve to protect her against responsibility. *A Great Deliverance* is about the evasion of moral responsibility, an evasion so general and so diffuse that no character fully transcends it. Only Lynley, who is atoning for earlier evasions, and Havers, in her painful recognition of what she done to her awful parents, come close.

It is this moral seriousness that marks George's distance from the classic tradition. We are of course meant to recognize her borrowings – the murder in the isolated country house in *Payment in Blood* (1989), in which, incidentally, the relationship between Lynley and

Havers is already a good deal more balanced, and the world of Cambridge colleges in *For the Sake of Elena* (1992) – but George's novels always convey a moral judgment that goes much further than anything the classics ever offered. The widespread moral irresponsibility that is inevitably revealed, and of which the actual culprit is occasionally less guilty than a good many others who will get off scot-free, reminds one of the bleak world of the classic private eye. Whereas in classic private eye fiction much of that irresponsibility is suggested, a result of metaphors and mood rather than detection, in George's fiction it is actually shown, an effect of her habit of offering a variety of characters and multiple points of view.

Apart from her complex plots, this panoramic strategy, reminiscent of mid-nineteenth-century realist fiction, is George's great strength, not in the least because it also allows her to maintain a constant level of suspense by switching perspectives (and thus cutting off the flow of information) at exactly the right cliff-hanging moment. Still, in her more recent fiction, this strength begins to develop into a weakness, paradoxically because she sets her sights even higher. Although *A Great Deliverance* is very good on its Yorkshire setting, it focuses almost exclusively on the investigation. In spite of its considerable length, the result is a taut novel that has the reader walking an emotional tightrope. With *For the Sake of Elena* we arrive at something of a turning-point. The novel is very good on the cowardly self-centeredness of the Cambridge don who is the father of the main victim; on the relationship between Lynley and Lady Helen Clyde; on the depressing sexism of a number of minor male characters; on the hatred an ex-wife feels for her former husband and his new wife. It is even better on Havers, who after the death of her father is now solely responsible for a mother who has slid into dementia and can no longer take care of herself. Especially chilling is the scene in which Havers' mother has "messed" herself because she is too scared of the hose of the vacuum cleaner, which she takes to be a snake, to leave the sofa. Livid with the woman who is supposed to look after her mother and who has deliberately left the hose on the floor to make sure that her charge would not wander off, Havers fires her and, racked by guilt, finally decides to place her mother in a home. This is what the literary George – the George giving us material that is not related to the investigation at hand – does brilliantly: relatively brief scenes of great emotional intensity and power that substantially contribute to the seriousness of her fiction.

In her most recent novels George's affinity with realism is both a liability and an asset. What works against her is her desire to provide too many minor character with a believable perspective and a matching psycho-social background. As a result *In the Presence of the Enemy*, published in 1996, runs to 630 pages while the 1997 *Deception on His Mind* in which, interestingly, Havers is given a solo performance, adds another 120 to clock in 750 pages. Keeping the reader's interest alive for such marathon runs would tax any novelist. George does not quite bring it off because not all of the perspectives she offers are equally interesting; in fact, with regard to some she would seem to be on automatic pilot, working out stereotypes along all too predictable lines, sometimes even to the point of caricature. (In *Deception* we have a German whose English is quite good, but who yet begins every other sentence with *"Ja."* In spite of what the Anglophone world may think, Germans don't have this particular addiction, not even when they speak German.)

A positive development in the recent novels is their overt interest in politics, an interest that is wholly absent from the classical tradition. Right from the start George has been a political writer in the sense that the personal in her novels always has had political overtones. Although she is obviously not a radical feminist novelist, there is always a feminist undercurrent in her fiction. Even in those cases where the criminal is a woman there is a strong suggestion that the fact that this a world in which males still call the shots has either directly or indirectly contributed to the crime. This is not to say that all of George's women are blameless victims. It is clear, however, that they must cope with both individual and social pressures of which the male characters who are the instruments of these forces are largely ignorant. Lynley is one of George's few males who at a certain point becomes aware of this. As he puts it in a conversation with his future wife:

> "All I can say right now is that I finally understand that no matter how the load is shifted between partners, or divided or shared, the woman's burden will always be greater. I do know that."[5]

In *In the Presence of the Enemy* and even more so in *Deception on His Mind* the major crimes, although as personally motivated as the

---

[5] Elizabeth George, *For the Sake of Elena* (New York: Bantam, 1992), 382. Subsequent references in the text to this edition.

murder in her first novel, are embedded in a much larger political framework. The first of these novels, published when John Major still headed a Conservative government, pits a Junior Minister who with her espousal of family values, her limitless ambition and uncompromising inflexibility (with regard to the IRA, for instance) is roughly modeled on Margaret Thatcher, against the editor of a leftist tabloid with whom she once had a brief and exclusively physical affair. This set-up enables George to bring in the hypocritical and sleazy dealings of a number of Conservative politicians and the equally unsavory practices of British tabloids. (The only indication that her sympathy lies with Labour is that her tabloid editor wakes up to his basic immorality while the Minister does not: "One couldn't walk the path he'd chosen so many years ago upon coming to London and still remain a sentient creature. If he hadn't known that before, he knew now that it was an impossibility. He'd never been so lost" [442].) Unfortunately, the novel is marred by a wholly superfluous first part in which Allcourt St. James, his wife Deborah and Helen Clyde try to trace a missing child. For whatever reason, George, for all her realism, finds it hard to cut this particular tie with the Golden Age. (Lady Helen tells Deborah, "'Darling ... just think of Miss Marple. Or Tuppence. Think of Tuppence. Or Harriet Vane'" [163].) Unfortunately, neither Deborah Allcourt nor Helen Clyde come close to Harriet Vane in terms of intrinsic interest. Lacking the anger and drive of Barbara Havers, Deborah and Helen are plucky girls in the young Tuppence mold rather than the mature and serious women that one expects a mature and serious version of Peter Wimsey to associate himself with.

It is the political factor plus the absence of the Lynley entourage – even more than the absence of Lynley himself – that makes *Deception on His Mind* so convincing, even if here, too, George errs on the side of comprehensiveness: we are simply given too many perspectives, not all of which are relevant to the story she is telling and with some of which George's imagination lets her down. But that story is gripping enough, beginning with the discovery of a dead Pakistani on the beach just north of Balford-le-Nez, an Essex seaside resort not too far from Clacton-on-Sea (the Nez in question looks suspiciously like the real-life Naze, also not too far from Clacton, in the map that George provides with a tongue-in-cheek reference to the classic tradition). To the local Pakistani community, led by a firebrand political activist, the murderer must have been motivated by racial hatred. Since this implies a white murderer the Pakistanis, whose anger explodes in a small-scale riot, suspect a cover-up. At this point Detective Chief Inspector Emily Barstow, in charge of the investigation, invites Barbara Havers, who has rather implausibly come to Balford to keep an eye on a Pakistani neighbor and his little girl, to liaise between the Pakistani community, represented by the activist and Barbara's London neighbor, and the investigating officers. Before long Barbara drifts into the investigation itself, allowed to do so by Barstow, whom she has met at a police course and for whom she has immense admiration. Emily Barstow openly defies convention with her "jet black hair, dyed punk and cut punk," is as matter of fact about sex (which is "a regular bonk with a willing bloke" [84]) as about anything else, has the figure of the "dedicated triathlete" that she is, and is in Barbara's eyes dazzlingly good at her job: "nowhere was there a woman more competent, more suited to criminal investigations, and more gifted in the politics of police work than Emily Barlow" (66).

What she is definitely not good at, however, is race relations. There is a good deal of racism in the novel, even if, as Barbara at one point tells herself, by no means all of her compatriots are racists. We have the almost intangible segregation in Barbara's hotel, for example, but also shockingly crude and mean incidents of overt racism. Gradually, Barbara's hero is exposed as a hard-line racist. For a while, Barbara is able to ignore Emily's references to "those people" and her derogatory generalizations: "'none of these yobbos can be trusted half an inch'" (609). But when Emily is fully prepared to let a "Paki brat" – the ten-year-old daughter of Barbara's neighbor – drown in order to catch a Pakistani criminal who is trying to make his way across the North Sea to Germany and has thrown the child overboard, Barbara is squarely confronted with Emily's refusal to see Pakistanis in human terms. Holding a gun on Emily, she tells her to turn the boat in which they are chasing the fleeing Pakistani and to pick up the foundering child. When Emily does not immediately respond she fires the gun but fortunately misses after which a badly shaken Emily allows her and the male detective who is also on board and who clearly sides with Barbara to save the child's life.

Race and the differences between Pakistani and English culture constitute the dominant themes of the novel. Race determines the relations between the Pakistani community and the police (ironically, and in typical George fashion, the activist turns out to be right with regard to Barstow's racism, although she is right concerning his criminal activities), while the enormous cultural differences greatly complicate the investigation and for a long time divert the suspicion from the actual murderer. A good deal more attuned to these differences than her temporary superior who is blinded by her own prejudices, it is Barbara who finally tumbles to the truth. Moreover, the issue of race is instrumental in Barbara's unprecedented pulling of a gun on a superior officer. They seem to hold each other hostage: Emily may report Barbara's insubordination leading to attempted murder while Barbara, as she is well aware, is in a position to report Emily's racism and willingness to sacrifice the life of a child to the pursuit of a personal vengeance. But there is no doubt that Emily holds all the cards: she not only outranks Barbara but she is also completely ruthless and unforgiving whereas Barbara is willing to make allowances. The fact that Barbara finally sees through Emily's "professionalism" – built to a considerable extent on self-deception and the resolute refusal of personal relationships – finally allows her to see that Emily's apparent strength is her major weakness and this realization topples Emily from her intimidating pedestal:

> Don't think [your solution of the murder] changes a thing between us, Emily was telling her. You're finished as a cop if I have my way. Do what you have to do, was Barbara's silent reply. And for the first time since meeting Emily Barlow, she actually felt free. (740)

In the course of the novels Barbara Havers gradually overcomes her crippling insecurity and pathological and often aggressive defensiveness. She frees herself first of all from Lynley. When they start working together, in *A Great Deliverance*, she tries to hang on to her instinctive loathing of him in order to protect her cut-and-dried, class-based view of everything he stands for. Eventually Lynley's competence and compassion break down her defenses and force her to revaluate her prejudices. Equally important is that Lynley, for all his easy superiority, is not infallible and occasionally allows his judgment to be affected by emotional involvement. "Stop lying to yourself," Havers tells him in *In the Presence of the Enemy*. "You're not after facts. You're after vengeance. It's written all over you" (261). And when he does not see reason, she adds for good measure: "Holy hell ... You can be a real prick"(262). Because Lynley encourages her to speak her mind, instead of pulling rank as Emily Barstow does when

Barbara sins against police hierarchy – "You're out of line, Sergeant" – Barbara can be her prickly, outspoken self.

In a parallel development, Barbara learns to cope with her suffocating feelings of guilt, which is to say that she finds a balance between her responsibilities with regard to her parents and, more in particular, her increasingly demented mother, and her responsibilities with regard to herself as an adult woman with a life of her own. Although she never overcomes her guilt – not to be confused with responsibility – she finally realizes her wish to go and live by herself. Finally, in *Deception on His Mind*, she learns to see through another false image: that of Emily Barstow, female supercop. Like Eve Bowen, the Conservative Junior Minister in *Presence*, Barstow stands for the female who has adopted the worst male traits: ruthless ambition, emotional distance, complete self-sufficiency, sexuality without affection. Realizing that Barstow's limitations far outweigh her own, she is free to be her competent and compassionate, if dumpy and rather unprepossessing self.

With Barbara Havers, we are a long way from the classic tradition. And even if Lynley is closer to some of his Golden Age predecessors, there is an awareness of human frailty and of man's self-serving stupidity that is almost wholly absent from the tradition (Dorothy Sayers' *Gaudy Night* in which, appropriately, Harriet Vane plays the leading role, comes to mind as an exception). In one of the last scenes of *Presence*, watching the murderer and "casting the observation into the light of what he'd learned about his background, Lynley fe[els] only a tremendous defeat" (620). Here the mood fuses with that of the more serious version of the private eye novel, just as it does at the end of *Deception* when Barbara feels equally "weighted down by the case" (746) – a phrase one associates with Philip Marlowe or Lew Archer rather than with an English policewoman. But, then, that policewoman has in *Presence* been badly battered by the killer she attacks to save a young boy's life and has only a couple of weeks later, still hurting from her bruises and broken ribs, fired a gun at her superior officer to save another child from drowning. Not only the mood of the private eye novel, including its inevitable defiance of authority, but also its dramatic action and the self-sacrificial interventions of the sleuth have entered George's reworking of the tradition.

NOTES ON CONTRIBUTORS

Kathleen M. Ashley is Professor of English at the University of Southern Maine, where, amongst other subjects, she teaches African-American Literature and Culture, Women Writers, and American Autobiography. She edited *Victor Turner and the Construction of Cultural Criticism* (1990) and co-edited *Autobiography and Postmodernism* (1994). She has also published essays on Zora Neale Hurston, Mary Antin, and Native American autobiography.

Hans Bak is Professor of American Literature and American Studies at the University of Nijmegen. He was a student of G.A.M. Janssens and wrote his dissertation on Malcolm Cowley under his supervision. He has edited *Multiculturalism and the Canon of American Culture* (1993), *Writing Lives: American Biography and Autobiography* (1998, with Hans Krabbendam), and *"Nature's Nation" Revisited: American Concepts of Nature from Wonder to Ecological Crisis* (2003, with Walter W. Hölbling). He is the author of *Malcolm Cowley: The Formative Years* (1993) and is currently working on an edition of *The Selected Letters of Malcolm Cowley*.

Jan Bakker taught American Literature in the English Department, University of Groningen until his retirement, and was co-editor, with G.A.M. Janssens, of *Dutch Quarterly Review of Anglo-American Letters*. His books include *Fiction as Survival Strategy: A Comparative Study of the Major Works of Ernest Hemingway and Saul Bellow* (1983), *Ernest Hemingway in Holland, 1925-1981: A Comparative Analysis of the Contemporary Dutch and American Critical Reception of His Work* (1986), and *The Role of the Mythic West in Some Representative Examples of Classic and Modern American Literature: The Shaping Force of the American Frontier* (1991).

C.C. Barfoot taught in the English Department, Leiden University, for over thirty years until his retirement in 2002, and was co-editor, with G.A.M. Janssens, of *Dutch Quarterly Review of Anglo-American Letters*. He published *The Thread of Connection: Aspects of Fate in* *the Novels of Jane Austen and Others* (1982); and has most recently edited *Victorian Keats and Romantic Carlyle: The Fusions and Confusions of Literary Periods* (1999), *Aldous Huxley between East and West* (2001), *"My Rebellious and Imperfect Eye": Observing Geoffrey Grigson* (2002, with R.M. Healey) and *"A Natural Delineation of Human Passions": The Historic Moment of* Lyrical Ballads (2004).

Gonny van Beek-van Overbeek teaches English at the Onze Lieve Vrouwe Lyceum in Breda, the Netherlands. She was a student of G.A.M. Janssens and wrote her master's thesis on Edith Wharton under his supervision. Her current research concerns the role played by Jessica Redmon Fauset in the development of African-American women's literature.

Jaap van der Bent teaches American literature at the University of Nijmegen, with an emphasis on the Beat Generation and on African-American writing. He wrote his dissertation on John Clellon Holmes under G.A.M. Janssens' supervision. He was co-editor of *Beat Culture: The 1950s and Beyond* (1999) and contributed to *The Beat Generation: Critical Essays* (2002). Currently he is working on a book about American authors in post-World War II Paris.

Hans Bertens is Professor of Comparative Literature and Dean of the Faculty of Arts and the Humanities, Utrecht University. His books include *Geschiedenis van de Amerikaanse literatuur (*1983, with Theo D'haen; revised edition scheduled for 2005), *Het Postmodernisme in de Literatuur* (1988, with Theo D'haen), *The Idea of the Postmodern: A History* (1995), *Literary Theory: The Basics* (2001), *Contemporary American Crime Fiction* (2001; with Theo D'haen) and *Postmodernism: The Key Figures* (2002; with Joseph Natoli).

Gert Buelens is an Associate Professor of English at Ghent University. His publications examine works of American literature in the context of ethnicity, gender, sexuality, rhetoric, and ethics. Recent essays have appeared in *Modern Philology, Texas Studies in Literature and Language,* and *PMLA.* He is Associate Editor of *MELUS.* He has edited *Enacting History in Henry James* (1997) and written *Henry James and the "Aliens"* (2002). He is the 2005 President of the Henry James Society.

Susan Castillo is John Nichol Professor of American Literature at Glasgow University. Her publications include *Notes from the Periphery: Marginality in North American Literature and Culture* (1995), *Engendering Identities* (1996), *Native American Women in Literature and Culture* (1997, co-edited with V. da Rosa), and *The Literatures of Colonial America: An Anthology* (2001, co-edited with Ivy Schweitzer). She has also published a book of poems, *The Candlewoman's Trade* (2003).

Theo D'haen is Professor of American Literature at Leuven University, Belgium, and Professor of English and American Literature at Leiden University, The Netherlands. He is the author of *Het Postmodernisme in de Literatuur* (1988, with Hans Bertens). His publications in American literature include *Geschiedenis van de Amerikaanse literatuur (*1983, revised edition scheduled for 2005) and *Contemporary American Crime Fiction* (2001), both with Hans Bertens.

Inez Hollander-Lake specializes in Southern letters. Her dissertation on Hamilton Basso was written under supervision of G.A.M Janssens and published as *The Road from Pompey's Head: The Life and Work of Hamilton Basso* (1999). She lives in the San Francisco Bay Area where she teaches literature and creative writing. Her new book, a memoir, *Ontwaken uit de Amerikaanse droom*, will be released in the Netherlands in 2004.

Marian Janssen is the author of *The Kenyon Review, 1939-1970: A Critical History* (1990), originally a dissertation completed under G.A.M. Janssens' supervision. She has published articles on Isabella Gardner, Grace Paley, James Wright and Karl Shapiro. In 1989-1990, she was a Fellow of the American Council of Learned Societies and a Visiting Scholar at Harvard University. In 1995 she became Director of the International Relations Office and in 2001 Director of External Relations of University of Nijmegen. She is working on a biography of poet Isabella Gardner.

Richard S. Kennedy was Professor Emeritus of English at Temple University and the author of *The Window of Memory: The Literary Career of Thomas Wolfe* (1962) and *Dreams in the Mirror: A Biography of E.E. Cummings* (1980). He was editor of *The Notebooks* *of Thomas Wolfe* (1970, with Paschal Reeves), and several editions of Cummings' poems. He edited and co-authored *Literary New Orleans: Essays and Meditations* (1992) and *Literary New Orleans in the Modern World* (1998). The author of *Robert Browning's* Asolando: *The Indian Summer of a Poet* (1993), he died on December 29, 2002, two thirds of the way through the biography of Robert Browning he was writing.

Edward Margolies, Professor Emeritus at City University New York, has written extensively on African-American literature and popular detective fiction. His publications include *Native Sons: A Critical Study of Twentieth Century Negro American Authors* (1968), *The Art of Richard Wright* (1969), *Which Way Did He Go?: The Private Eye in Dashiell Hammett, Raymond Chandler, Chester Himes and Ross MacDonald* (1982) and *The Several Lives of Chester Himes* (1997, with Michel Fabre). He is currently at work on a book on American writers and New York City.

Mary A. McCay is Chair of the English Department and Dean's Distinguished Teaching Professor at Loyola University in New Orleans, where she teaches American literature and film studies. Besides numerous articles on contemporary women writers, she has published books on *Rachel Carson* (1993) and on *Ellen Gilchrist* (1997).

Loes Nas, a former student of G.A.M. Janssens, is an Associate Professor in the English Department at the University of the Western Cape in South Africa. Her research and teaching interests are in literary theory, particularly postmodernism, narratology and deconstruction, and contemporary American literature and film. She has translated several books on contemporary South African art from English into Dutch, and on townships and gay life in Southern Africa from Dutch into English. Currently she is working on narrativist mimesis in the latest fiction of John Barth and the impact of American cultural imperialism in South Africa.

Diederik Oostdijk teaches in the English Department of the Free University in Amsterdam. Earlier, he taught American literature and American Studies at the University of Nijmegen where he also completed his dissertation on Karl Shapiro's editorship of *Poetry* magazine in 2000, under G.A.M. Janssens' supervision. He has published articles on the poetry of James Dickey, Randall Jarrell, Robert Lowell, and Karl Shapiro.

Peter Rietbergen is Professor of Cultural History at the University of Nijmegen. His publications include *Pausen, prelaten, bureaucraten* (1983, on seventeenth-century papacy), *De eerste landvoogd: Pieter Both* (1987, a biography of the first governor-general of the Dutch East Indies), *Geschiedenis van Nederland in Vogelvlucht* (1993, published in English as *A Short History of the Netherlands*, 2000), *Dromen van Europa* (1994, a collection of essays), *Europe: A Cultural History* (1998), *De retoriek van de Eeuwige stad: Rome gelezen* (2003) and *Japan verwoord: Nihon door Nederlandse ogen, 1600-1800* (2003). As Nicolaas Berg he has written a historical novel, *Dood op Deshima* (2001), set in mid-seventeenth-century Japan.

Mathilde Roza teaches American literature at the University of Nijmegen. She is presently finishing her PhD-thesis on the American novelist, short-story writer and art critic Robert Myron Coates (1897-1973), on whom she has also published several articles.

Derek Rubin teaches in the American Studies program at Utrecht University. His dissertation was on *Marginality in Saul Bellow's Early Novels: From* Dangling Man *to* Herzog (1995). He has published essays on, among others, Philip Roth and Paul Auster, and is co-editor, with Hans Krabbendam, of *Religion in America: European and American Perspectives* (2004). He is currently editing a volume of essays by fiction writers on being Jewish and a writer in America.

René Verwaaijen, a junior lecturer in American Literature at Nijmegen from 1980 to 1987, was a teacher of English at Maastricht College of Professional Education, School of Translation and Interpreting. In 1997, he finished his PhD-thesis *Alfred Kazin: Selfhood in America*, under G.A.M. Janssens' supervision. He is currently employed as legal editor at Balance Texts and Translations, a translation agency with offices in Amsterdam and Maastricht.